Believers Church
Bible Commentary

Elmer A. Martens and Willard M. Swartley, Editors

BELIEVERS CHURCH BIBLE COMMENTARY

Old Testament
Genesis, by Eugene F. Roop
Exodus, by Waldemar Janzen
Judges, by Terry Brensinger
Jeremiah, by Elmer A. Martens
Ezekiel, by Millard C. Lind
Daniel, by Paul M. Lederach
Hosea, Amos, by Allen R. Guenther

New Testament
Matthew, by Richard B. Gardner
Mark, by Timothy J. Geddert
Acts, by Chalmer E. Faw
2 Corinthians,
  by V. George Shillington
Colossians, Philemon,
  by Ernest D. Martin
1 and 2 Thessalonians,
  by Jacob W. Elias
1–2 Peter, Jude, by Erland Waltner and J. Daryl Charles

Editorial Council
David Baker, Brethren Church
Lydia Harder, General Conference Mennonite Church
Estella B. Horning, Church of the Brethren
Robert B. Ives, Brethren in Christ Church
Gordon H. Matties, Mennonite Brethren Church
Paul M. Zehr (chair), Mennonite Church

Old Testament Editors
Elmer A. Martens and Allen R. Guenther (for Jeremiah), Mennonite
  Brethren Biblical Seminary, Fresno, California (for both)

New Testament Editors
Willard M. Swartley and Howard H. Charles (for Matthew),
  Associated Mennonite Biblical Seminary, Elkhart, Indiana (for
  both)

Believers Church
Bible Commentary

1-2 Peter, Jude

1 Peter
Erland Waltner

2 Peter, Jude
J. Daryl Charles

HERALD PRESS
Scottdale, Pennsylvania
Waterloo, Ontario

Library of Congress Cataloging-in-Publication Data
Waltner, Erland, 1914-
[1 Peter]
1-2 Peter, Jude.
    p.   cm. — (Believers church Bible commentary)
Includes bibliographical references and index.
Contents: 1 Peter / Erland Waltner — 2 Peter, Jude / J. Daryl Charles.
ISBN 0-8361-9118-8
    1. Bible. N.T. Peter, 1st—Commentaries. 2. Bible. N.T. Peter, 2nd—
Commentaries. 3. Bible. N.T. Jude—Commentaries. I. Charles, J. Daryl,
1950-   2 Peter, Jude. II. Title. III. Title: First, Second Peter, Jude.
IV. Series.
BS2795.3.W35 1999
227'.9207—dc21   99-13143

The map "The Circulation of 1 Peter" is adapted from *1 Peter*, by Wayne Grudem, Tyndale NT Commentaries, Grand Rapids: Eerdmans, 1988, page 19.

Bible translations are by the authors or used by permission with all rights reserved from *New Revised Standard Version Bible,* copyright 1989 by the Division of Christian Education of the National Council of the Churches of Christ in the USA; NIV, from *The Holy Bible, New International Version* ®, copyright © 1973, 1978, 1984 by International Bible Society, Zondervan Publishing House; GNB, from the *Good News Bible;* KJV, from *The King James Version of the Holy Bible.*

BELIEVERS CHURCH BIBLE COMMENTARY: 1-2 PETER, JUDE
Copyright © 1999 by Herald Press, Scottdale, Pa. 15683
    Released simultaneously in Canada
by Herald Press, Waterloo, Ont. N2L 6H7. All rights reserved
Library of Congress Catalog Card Number: 99-13143
International Standard Book Number: 0-8361-9118-8
Printed in the United States of America
Cover and charts by Merrill R. Miller
08 07 06 05 04 03 02 01 00 99 10 9 8 7 6 5 4 3 2 1

To order or request information, please call
1-800-759-4447 (individuals); 1-800-245-7894 (trade).
Website: www.mph.org

To my life partner, Mary Winifred,
for patience and encouragement
during the writing process,
and to our daughters, Mary, Irene, Kathy, and Rose,
each a special gift of God
—*Erland Waltner*

To Ted Dorman,
a pastor-teacher, colleague, and friend
—*J. Daryl Charles*

Abbreviations

*	The Text in Biblical Context
+	The Text in the Life of the Church
//	parallel (to)
=	parallel to
x	times
[Authorship]	typical reference to essays that precede the Bibliography
ca.	about
cf.	compare
e.g.	for example
esp.	especially
LXX	Septuagint, Greek translation of OT
notes	Explanatory Notes, in canonical sequence for each book
NT	New Testament
par.	parallel to; parallel(s)
OT	Old Testament
TBC	The Text in Biblical Context
TLC	The Text in the Life of the Church

Contents

Series Foreword 11

1 Peter, by Erland Waltner

Preface to 1 Peter 15
Introduction: A Letter Encouraging Christian Hope 17

The Opening Greeting, 1:1-2 . . . . **23**
The Celebration of Christian Hope and Its
  Life Impact, 1:3-12 . . . . **30**
*Biblical Hope and Grace 43
*The Practice of Blessing 45
*The Experience of New Birth 45
*The Significance of the Resurrection 46
*Hope as Inheritance 46
*Rejoicing in Suffering 47
*Prophets Who Were Seers 47
*What's That About Angels? 48
+The Ambiguity of Hope 49
+Hope in Anabaptist Perspective 50
+The New Birth Yielding New Hope 51
+Theology of Hope 52
+Personal Pastoral Experience 54

*The Text in Biblical Context
+The Text in the Life of the Church

The Changed Lifestyle of Hope, 1:13—2:3 . . . . **56**
*The Linkage of Hope and Holiness 67
*The Concern for Human Conduct 67
*Mutual Love in the Faith Community 68
*Putting Off Unfit Garments 69
*Milk as Spiritual Nourishment 69
+Holiness and Discipleship 69
+The Way to the City of Peace 70
+Nourishment for Maturity 71
The Community of Hope, 2:4-10 . . . . **73**
*Bridge Between the Testaments 79
*Images of Building Stones 79
+Christ Is Our Cornerstone 80
+Anabaptist Stones 80
+The Church of the Savior 81
Christian Witness in Hostile Society, 2:11—3:12 . . . . . **82**
*Christian Witness in All Circumstances 103
*The Love Response to Household Codes 104
*Nonretaliation, Love of Enemy, and Blessing 105
+Anabaptist Self-Definition 107
+Nonviolent Resistance in Martin Luther King Jr. 109
+I Love Idi Amin 111
+Hostages Who Rejected Hating Their Captors 112
+Wrestling with Abuse and Violence Today 114
+Anticipatory Forgiveness 115
+Embodying Forgiveness 116
Christian Response to Suffering for
 Righteous Living, 3:13—4:19 . . . . **119**
Chart: Three Major Interpretations of 3:19-20 127
*Witness Under Stress 142
*The Vicarious Death and Exaltation of Christ 143
*Baptism in the New Testament 144
*The Relationship of Suffering and Sin 145
*The Church as Stewardship of Gifts 146
*The Suffering of Christ's People 147
+Blandina, Perpetua, and Felicitas—Martyrs 148
+Witnessing While Suffering 149
+Noah, the Flood, and Anabaptist Baptism 150
+The Church as a Stewardship of Gifts 152
+Suffering for the Name of Jesus 152
+Christian Martyrdom in the Twentieth Century 153

Leadership and Loyalty in the Suffering
    Church, 5:1-11 . . . . **155**
Conclusion, 5:12-14 . . . . **163**
    *Church Leadership as Shepherding 166
    *The Theology of Humility 167
    *Resisting the Evil One 168
    +Early Anabaptist Views of Church Leadership 169
    +The Ambiguity of Humility 171
    +The Call to Resistance Today 172

Outline of 1 Peter 174
Essays for 1 Peter 176
    Authorship 176
    Christology 178
    Eschatology 179
    The Household Codes 180
    Chart: Household Honor Codes in the New Testament . 181
    Images of the Church and Church Leadership 183
    A Theology of Suffering 184
Map: The Circulation of 1 Peter 188
Bibliography for 1 Peter 189
Selected Resources for 1 Peter 197
Erland Waltner, Author of the Commentary on 1 Peter . . . 199

2 Peter, by J. Daryl Charles

Preface to 2 Peter, Jude 203
Overview of 2 Peter 206

The Author, His Audience, Purpose for
    Writing, Authority, 1:1-21 209
Profile of Apostasy, 2:1-22 229
Exhortation to the Faithful, 3:1-18 245

Outline of 2 Peter 259
Essays for 2 Peter 260
    Authorship of 2 Peter 260
    The Ethical List as a Teaching Device 263
    Virtue as a Theme of 2 Peter 265
Bibliography for 2 Peter 268
Selected Resources for 2 Peter 272

Jude, by J. Daryl Charles

Overview of Jude 274

The Author, His Audience and Purpose for Writing, 1-4 281
Profile of the Unfaithful, 5-19 291
Profile of the Faithful, 20-23 312
Tribute to the One Who Keeps, 24-25 322

Outline of Jude 329
Essay for Jude 330
  Apocalyptic Literature 330
Bibliography for Jude 334
Selected Resources for Jude 340

J. Daryl Charles, Author of the Commentary on
  2 Peter, Jude 341
Index of Ancient Sources for 1-2 Peter, Jude 342

Series Foreword

The Believers Church Bible Commentary Series makes available a new tool for basic Bible study. It is published for all who seek more fully to understand the original message of Scripture and its meaning for today—Sunday school teachers, members of Bible study groups, students, pastors, and other seekers. The series is based on the conviction that God is still speaking to all who will listen, and that the Holy Spirit makes the Word a living and authoritative guide for all who want to know and do God's will.

The desire to help as wide a range of readers as possible has determined the approach of the writers. Since no blocks of biblical text are provided, readers may continue to use the translation with which they are most familiar. The writers of the series use the *New Revised Standard Version*, the *Revised Standard Version*, the *New International Version*, and the *New American Standard Bible* on a comparative basis. They indicate which text they follow most closely, as well as where they make their own translations. The writers have not worked alone, but in consultation with select counselors, the series' editors, and the Editorial Council.

Every volume illuminates the Scriptures; provides necessary theological, sociological, and ethical meanings; and in general, makes "the rough places plain." Critical issues are not avoided, but neither are they moved into the foreground as debates among scholars. Each section offers explanatory notes, followed by focused articles, "The Text in Biblical Context" and "The Text in the Life of the Church."

The writers have done the basic work for each commentary, but not operating alone, since "no . . . Scripture is a matter of one's own

11

interpretation" (2 Pet. 1:20; cf. 1 Cor. 14:29). They have consulted with select counselors during the writing process, worked with the editors for the series, and received feedback from another biblical scholar. In addition, the Editorial Council, representing six believers church denominations, reads the manuscripts carefully, gives churchly responses, and makes suggestions for changes. The writer considers all this counsel and processes it into the manuscript, which the Editorial Council finally approves for publication. Thus these commentaries combine the individual writers' own good work and the church's voice. As such, they represent a hermeneutical community's efforts in interpreting the biblical text, as led by the Spirit.

The term *believers church* has often been used in the history of the church. Since the sixteenth century, it has frequently been applied to the Anabaptists and later the Mennonites, as well as to the Church of the Brethren and similar groups. As a descriptive term, it includes more than Mennonites and Brethren. *Believers church* now represents specific theological understandings, such as believers baptism, commitment to the Rule of Christ in Matthew 18:15-20 as crucial for church membership, belief in the power of love in all relationships, and willingness to follow Christ in the way of the cross. The writers chosen for the series stand in this tradition.

Believers church people have always been known for their emphasis on obedience to the simple meaning of Scripture. Because of this, they do not have a long history of deep historical-critical biblical scholarship. This series attempts to be faithful to the Scriptures while also taking archaeology and current biblical studies seriously. Doing this means that at many points the writers will not differ greatly from interpretations which can be found in many other good commentaries. Yet these writers share basic convictions about Christ, the church and its mission, God and history, human nature, the Christian life, and other doctrines. These presuppositions do shape a writer's interpretation of Scripture. Thus this series, like all other commentaries, stands within a specific historical church tradition.

Many in this stream of the church have expressed a need for help in Bible study. This is justification enough to produce the Believers Church Bible Commentary. Nevertheless, the Holy Spirit is not bound to any tradition. May this series be an instrument in breaking down walls between Christians in North America and around the world, bringing new joy in obedience through a fuller understanding of the Word.

—*The Editorial Council*

1 Peter

Erland Waltner

Preface to 1 Peter

First Peter became personally important to me while I was still a seminary student. I was yearning to be both a nonresisting Christian (my Mennonite ethical heritage) and an evangelical believer, taking with full seriousness the whole Bible and especially Christ's saving work on the cross. For me, these strands come together in 1 Peter 2:21-25. There I saw Jesus Christ both as the Supreme Pattern of nonretaliating love and as the Redeemer, dying on the cross for human sin and thus making our salvation possible.

First Peter was also one of the first books I taught in seminary, in 1954 during a joint summer school session of Goshen College Biblical Seminary (Goshen, Ind.) and Mennonite Biblical Seminary (Chicago). This joint summer school helped lead to the establishment of the Associated Mennonite Biblical Seminary in Elkhart, in which I have given most of my ministering years as teacher and administrator. Among my students in that first seminary class on 1 Peter was David Schroeder, who now many years later has served as a critical reader and scholarly adviser in the preparation of this commentary. Since then I have taught 1 Peter and preached from it many times.

When identifying *kērugma* (the preached Word) and *didachē* (the taught Word) in the New Testament (NT) was in vogue, I assigned students to distinguish between these two elements in 1 Peter. The results led to the verdict that the two cannot be separated in this epistle. This deepened my own sense of wholeness in Scripture, between faith and life, between ethics and theology, between proclamation and *paraenesis* (moral instruction). In reading and interpreting Scripture, I have moved away from an either-or analytic approach

15

(the truth must be either this or that), and toward more of a both-and approach (truth, paradoxically, may have more than one dimension). While open to deal with historical critical issues, I have followed a hermeneutic of trust more frequently than a hermeneutic of suspicion. In short, I have tried to let the texts speak for themselves.

During four decades of teaching 1 Peter, I have not tired of listening to the texts. I continue to be fascinated, intrigued, inspired, challenged, and confronted by the word of the living God which meets me there. That word is amazingly inclusive and relevant, both theologically and ethically. It puts accents on—

• hope, transformed lifestyle, and Christian community;
• witness through appropriate subordination and word;
• constructive nonretaliating response to suffering injustice; and
• a strong concern about leading and following in the church.

This letter touches some of the most controversial and most promising and challenging items in contemporary Christian discourse.

I have also taught this letter transculturally—in Taiwan, in Japan, in Saskatoon to a mixed Chinese and Canadian student group, and in Anglo and Latin-based cultures. I have found that 1 Peter communicates effectively in both a transcultural and a monocultural situation.

In work on this commentary, I have moved beyond my own intense encounters with the biblical text and have surveyed numerous other commentaries and resources, for which I am indebted and deeply grateful. I have given particular attention to the use made of 1 Peter in early Anabaptist writings and thus discovered its remarkable influence on the faith heritage I call my own.

To the many colleagues, former students, and manuscript readers who have helped, I express deepest gratitude for their painstaking and helpful counsel, especially to David Schroeder (Winnipeg) and Willard M. Swartley (Elkhart, Ind.), the NT editor of this commentary series. I give special thanks to Rosalie Grove, who helped with computer work and copyediting. For errors that may be found, however, I carry responsibility.

As shown in the dedication, I express deep gratitude to my life partner, Mary Winifred, and to our four daughters, the women in my life.

May God be pleased to use this commentary for kingdom purposes of enhancing righteousness, peace, and hope. To God be all glory!

—*Erland Waltner*
Associated Mennonite Biblical Seminary
Elkhart, Indiana

Introduction

A Letter Encouraging Christian Hope

Encountering First Peter

The significance of 1 Peter is out of proportion to its size. It consists of 105 verses (NRSV), easily placed in two columns of modern newsprint. Its importance for biblical studies, its impact on the Reformers and the early Anabaptists, and its potential significance for contemporary church life and ethics—all these are larger than the brevity of the letter suggests.

The history of the letter's acceptance and influence, however, is uneven. Apparently it was widely and readily accepted as apostolic from the time of Eusebius (A.D. 260-340). In 1905 biblical scholar Charles Bigg could write, "There is no book in the NT which has earlier, better, or stronger attestation" (Bigg: 7). Luther praised 1 Peter as "one of the grandest books of the NT, and it is true gospel" (Luther, 1982:2). Calvin, likewise, considered it apostolic and gave it full-length treatment in his commentaries.

In more recent times, rigorous biblical criticism diverted attention from 1 Peter's central message, probing its authorship, setting, purpose, and literary form. By 1964, Bishop Stephen Neill called it "the storm center of NT studies" (Neill: 343). In 1992, John H. Elliott spoke of it as an "exegetical stepchild" of biblical studies (in *ABD*, 5:270).

Currently, something of a restoration and rehabilitation may be underway and well-deserved. Already in 1978, Leonhard Goppelt listed 326 scholarly items in his bibliography on 1 Peter, 148 of them commentaries. Since then a host of new commentaries have appeared on these same 105 verses of holy Scripture. However, new challenges have also surfaced, especially from liberation scholars who consider this epistle deficient in making a clear case for the liberation of slaves and of women (Balch, 1981; Corley: 349-360). A significantly different and positive perspective is represented by Mary H. Schertz in her scholarly analysis of "Nonretaliation and the Haustafeln in 1 Peter" (258-286).

Why 1 Peter Was Written

Read at face value, 1 Peter was written to scattered Christians residing in Asia Minor (present-day Turkey)—to the Roman provinces of Pontus, Galatia, Cappadocia, Asia, and Bithynia. Described as "strangers and pilgrims" (KJV) or as "resident aliens" (Elliott, 1981), these Christian believers lived in a hostile environment. They were experiencing trials and were sometimes falsely accused. Some of them were mistreated by their employers or slave masters; some of their women were married to non-Christian husbands; and all of them were subject to some forms of abuse and suffering.

The letter reminds them that they have experienced the hope-giving grace of God in the coming, life, death, and resurrection of Jesus Christ. They are called to shape their lives accordingly, especially in how they respond to their experiences of suffering. The basic exhortation is for them to stand fast in the grace of God (5:12), which they experience even in their painful encounters, and follow in the pattern of Jesus (2:21), doing what is good and right.

First Peter as a Letter

During most of the centuries since 1 Peter appeared, readers have considered it to be a letter because of its opening and closing sections. Letter writing of the time commonly began with a simple formula of giving first the name and some descriptive title of the writer, next the designation of the intended reader(s), and then a formal greeting. Likewise, generally a letter would include closing greetings, as well illustrated in Pauline and other NT letters.

In the case of 1 Peter, however, some views emerged out of critical studies about earlier sources, including the proposal by Richard Perdelwitz in 1911 that 1:3—4:11 was a baptismal exhortation or sermon, while 4:12—5:14 was epistolary. He suggested that these two parts were later put together.

This view was elaborated by later scholars, Windisch and Preisker, who read the document as a baptismal liturgy. In 1954 Frank L. Cross suggested that 1 Peter is a baptismal eucharistic liturgy for a Paschal vigil on Easter evening. John H. Elliott appropriately observes that such theories "must be judged more imaginative than cogent" (in *ABD*, 5:270).

In this commentary, 1 Peter is viewed as a unified letter. This does not exclude the possibility of the writer including a variety of source materials.

First Peter differs from some Pauline letters, however, in that it is written to an audience much wider than a single congregation. It thus may have been a circular letter, intended to be carried and read to scattered congregations in various provinces of Asia Minor. It is possible that the order of the provinces named was to be the order in which the letter-bearer was to bring the epistle to these scattered congregations of the people of God.

This Letter as Truly Apostolic

While there has been much more scholarly controversy over the authenticity of 2 Peter, the authorship of 1 Peter has also been vigorously debated. This commentary affirms this letter as Petrine, but acknowledges a need for understanding different perspectives held by competent biblical scholars. Three different views are possible: (1) Peter the apostle wrote it, as the letter itself claims. (2) It is pseudonymous, written in the name of Peter but by a later hand. (3) It is essentially Petrine but an amanuensis (secretary), possibly Silvanus (5:12), collaborated with Peter in drafting it [Authorship].

The Date and Place of Writing

Going with apostolic authorship, we may assume a date of circa A.D. 62-64 as the time of writing, and the place as Rome, assuming that *Babylon* (5:13) is a pseudonym for Rome (cf. Rev. 17–18). Calvin argued for a literal Babylon, assuming that Peter had traveled widely, but Luther read Babylon as figurative for Rome. Luther's interpretation continues to prevail.

The suggested date assumes that Peter was alive and that Nero was emperor (54-68). The traditional date for Peter's death is around

64, and his arrival in Rome not earlier than 62. However, certain scholars, including William Ramsay and J. Ramsey Michaels, have argued that Peter lived much longer. Earlier some associated this letter with the persecution under Domitian in 96 or under Trajan in 117. Their arguments are partly based on the view that the persecutions described in 1 Peter, especially in 4:16, are official and state-ordered, a position that biblical scholars no longer consider necessary.

The Circumstances of the Readers

The text of 1 Peter gives many clues about the circumstances of those addressed. They live as scattered faith communities spread across what came to be called northern Asia Minor. Peter is a Jewish Christian, and some of his addressees may have shared his ethnic background. Yet it is probable that most of them were Gentile Christians, relatively recent converts to Christianity. Ethnically, then, they were mainly Greeks, but legally they were under Roman law.

The letter itself indicates that the social status of these believers was difficult. Living in scattered communities, they represented a minority status. Peter calls them "resident aliens" who were not truly at home in the social communities in which they resided. In various ways they lived on the borderline between Christian faith and non-Christian peoples. Their neighbors not only misunderstood them but also made false interpretations and leveled unfounded accusations against the followers of Jesus Christ.

Interpreters who have studied 1 Peter through sociological lenses have helped us understand that the Christians' status and condition in society was even more difficult than earlier thought. Elliott speaks of them as "homeless strangers," sharpening the contrast between the meanings of *oikos* (house, household) and *paroikos* (sojourner, resident alien, refugee). Thus the title of his book on 1 Peter, *A Home for the Homeless*. While Peter uses the concept of "resident aliens" in a metaphorical sense, their legal and cultural status was complicated and socially marginal. They lived in a truly oppressive and hostile environment.

Beyond that, however, their status boundaries were much more limited, much more sharply defined, and more hierarchical than those of so-called democratic societies. Likely many of them were slaves. The understanding of citizenship was complex, and lack of clarity in one's status could be oppressive. As John Crook observes, "The origins of the complexities of citizenship and non-citizenship lie in the history of ancient Greece, where the Greeks (for reasons, indeed, only dimly understood today) organized themselves politically not into a nation but into a large number of tiny nations, city-states, whose members had rights and duties within their own state but were without duties or rights—were foreigners—in the state on the other side of the mountain" (37).

Their life was burdened also by the household codes (German: *Haustafeln*), prevalent in the Greco-Roman culture, that sought to define rights and duties, not in terms of equality but on the basis of a hierarchical system of authority and submission *[Household Codes]*.

The believers' relationship to government was further complicated by the spread of the emperor cult, which deified the emperor and insisted that this should be ritually acknowledged by all in the empire. Early Christianity insisted that Jesus is Lord, not Caesar (cf. 1 Cor. 12:3). Any deviation from the pagan household codes could be interpreted as an attempt to undermine the prevailing culture and loyalty to the emperor. Hence, the status of Christians became precarious and led to persecutions at both local and empire levels. Not only did these readers need a true home. They also needed the courage we call hope.

Under the household codes, the status of slaves and women became particularly difficult and sometimes oppressive. In the prevailing hierarchical system, they felt powerless. They needed not only hope but also real encouragement and empowerment.

The Central Message of 1 Peter

The writer of 1 Peter seeks to apply the teaching of Jesus on loving the enemy to the life situation of the scattered Christians of Asia Minor, coping with a hostile environment. The letter encourages and empowers them to live and bear witness as Christians. They are under suspicion, falsely accused, and sometimes abused both psychologically and physically. Discouragement and hopelessness tempts them. The believers themselves and others tend to regard them as powerless and helpless in the Greco-Roman society of which they are a part.

The word of Peter is that these Christian believers, though aliens and strangers, are indeed the people of God, chosen by God, graced by God, given dignity, strength, and destiny, and born anew to a living hope. They are, therefore, called to live in holy obedience toward God and in love toward one another. They are to be a worshiping and serving people who face their experiences of suffering (1) in the light of how Christ has faced and triumphed in suffering, and (2) in the light of the coming judgment of God, which will be impartial, just, and vindicating.

Peter instructs them to accept and respect all persons and human social structures, even though sin has corrupted them. This, however, does not mean simply settling for the status quo. They are to live redemptively, following Christ and doing what is good and right in the situations and relationships that arise in a fallen and hostile world. With dignity and trust in God, they are to endure the variety of sufferings they are facing. They are to break the cycle of violence by not striking back or cursing their enemies, thus following the example of Jesus.

They are, in short, embracing the grace and enabling of God to pursue peace and keep on doing good and right. As they do so, they may possibly win some nonbelievers to Christian faith. But in any and every case they are to remain faithful to the teaching and example of their Lord Jesus Christ, through whose life, death, and resurrection they are finally saved.

As living stones, they are to be active participants in God's household, which is a stewardship of God's gifts. They are all, as pastors and people, women and men, slaves and free, to remain strong and firm in the grace of God and in their pilgrimage of faith, hope, and love. This includes resisting Satan and all forms of evil that threaten their lives and witness.

1 Peter 1:1-2

The Opening Greeting

PREVIEW

The opening lines of this text identify its present form as a letter. Thus the writer includes the name and title of the writer, a description of the intended first readers, and a formal greeting. An unusual element here is the way the readers are identified, both spiritually and geographically. Scattered in five provinces of Asia Minor (Pontus, Galatia, Cappadocia, Asia, Bithynia), they are designated as *sojourners* who have been *chosen* by God as a people of dignity and purpose.

Their relationship to God rests on divine foreknowledge, involves a process of being made holy, and yields a life cleansed for obedience to Jesus Christ. Three parallel phrases, embodying an implicit trinitarian experience of God, speak of God as the foreknowing Father, of the life-transforming Spirit, and of Jesus Christ, in whom is cleansing and forgiveness and to whom the believer yields in obedience. They speak of the basis, the process, and the purpose of Christian experience.

The greeting itself, *Grace to you and peace be multiplied*, is terse and formal. But since the same words recur in the closing greeting (5:12-14) with strong emphasis, their meaning here also speaks in more than formal tones. Grace and peace, in one perspective, are what this letter is all about. Grace and peace, too, is what the gospel of Jesus Christ is about.

OUTLINE

Name and Title of the Writer, 1:1a

Designation of the Readers, 1:1b

Their Spiritual Status, 1:2a

Grace and Peace Be Yours, 1:2b

EXPLANATORY NOTES

Name and Title of the Writer 1:1a

The writer of this letter identifies himself as *Peter, an apostle of Jesus Christ.* The writer here uses his nickname Peter, "Rock," which Jesus has conferred on him (John 1:42). He identifies himself as an apostle, meaning "one sent." Classically, the term was used for an envoy "who has full powers and is the personal representative of the one sending him" (Müller, in C. Brown, 1:127). Paul uses this self-designation freely and often, but Peter modestly uses it only here. In 5:1 he speaks of himself as a fellow *elder*, thus claiming some official authority.

Throughout most of Christian history, this letter has been accepted as authentic and apostolic, linked to the well-known Peter of the Gospels and the book of Acts. Many readers find this linkage confirmed in other traces of self-identification in subsequent parts of the letter.

In addition to calling himself an apostle (1:1), he also calls himself an elder (5:1), a witness (5:1) and, implicitly, an exhorter (2:11; 5:12), and a proclaimer (5:12). He identifies relationships with other leaders, with Silvanus (5:12) as faithful *brother*, with Mark (5:13) as a *son*, and with other elders by calling himself a *fellow-elder* (5:1). Some have claimed to hear in the letter echoes of apostolic experience of the resurrection event (1:3, 8) and of the crucifixion (2:21-25). Some have heard echoes of Peter's personal experience of temptation and denial (1:7), of being renamed (2:4), of disloyalty to Jesus (3:15), and of commissioning (5:2), recalling the narrative in John 21:15-19.

Despite the long and strong tradition of Petrine authorship, it has been challenged by eminent Christian scholars who consider the letter pseudonymous (Beare, Best, Elliott, and Goppelt). Others affirm it as authentic and apostolic (Marshall, Grudem, Davids, Michaels [with reservations], and earlier scholars Bigg and Selwyn). Kelly appears undecided, remaining open to Selwyn's suggestion that Silvanus may indeed have assisted in the drafting of the epistle.

Those who object to Petrine authorship present several arguments: (1) The quality of the Greek used in this letter, "some of the best Greek in the whole NT" (Beare), is beyond that which Peter the fisherman would have used. (2) The OT (Old Testament) quotations coming from the Septuagint would not have been used by Peter, who was partial to the Hebrew. (3) There is no mention of Paul although the letter is addressed to people in Paul's area of mission activity. (4) Many concepts are "Pauline" and thus must come from a later time. (5) The references to persecutions suggest a later date. They also consider it likely that if Peter had written it, there would have been more references to the earthly life of Jesus.

To this writer, the arguments for authenticity and against pseudonymity seem stronger. The posture taken here is that the Peter who is well-known elsewhere in the NT is the author, with the possibility that the help *by Silvanus* (5:12) may indicate his assistance in drafting the letter, not acting just as a letter carrier (Grudem: 199-200). This may help account for the quality of the language and the style *[Authorship]*.

Designation of the Readers 1:1b

Much scholarly attention has been given to the intriguing description of the intended readers: *the exiles of the Dispersion in Pontus, Galatia, Cappadocia, Asia, and Bithynia.* Most versions of the NT render this phrase somewhat differently, especially in translating *exiles (parepidēmois)* and *Dispersion (diasporas).* Precisely who are these exiles, sojourners, refugees, or aliens? Are the terms *strangers (paroikoi) and exiles (parepidēmoi)*—both appearing in 2:11—to be taken literally, as Elliott argues in *A Home for the Homeless?* Or is Elliott overstating his case and thus losing the power of an inspiring metaphor? Were these readers all literally "resident aliens" in an ethnically or politically hostile environment? Or is this Peter's way of describing the Christian believers' pilgrimage in the same kind of world that rejected Jesus? Both alternatives are possible and were likely intended.

Why are they scattered or dispersed? Is *Diaspora* here meant literally, in a historical and geographical sense, or is this also primarily metaphorical. As metaphor, it reminds us that Christians are often scattered in the sense that they reside among neighbors who are resistant and hostile to Christian faith and witness.

At one level, this letter seems to be addressed to Jews who have become Christians in the scattered provinces named. This view is supported by the use of *Diaspora*, the numerous uses of OT images, concepts, and actual quotations, and the early assessment of Eusebius that this letter was addressed "to those of the Hebrews in the Dispersion."

Other clues, however, suggest that Gentiles are present and probably predominant in these congregations. Thus a major metaphor denotes that those who had formerly not been a people of God have now become such (2:9-10). Michaels (xlvi) notes that "there is near consensus that 1 Peter was in fact directed to a predominantly Gentile audience," based on the implications of 1:14, 18, 21, and 4:3-5. By taking the entire epistle seriously, instead of only reading selected passages, we may recognize that these scattered Christian communities included mixtures of Jewish and Gentile Christians, with the proportion varying from one locale to another. Believers of both backgrounds are fully respected and valued, and their unity in Christ is blending them into a true new peoplehood.

The provinces named include what came to be known as Asia Minor. Pontus lay on the south coast of the Black Sea. Galatia made up the central part of Asia Minor. Cappadocia was southeast of Galatia. Asia lay on the east coast of the Aegean Sea and included "the seven churches in Asia" (Rev. 1:4). Bithynia touched the south shore of the Black Sea, west of Pontus. Under Rome, Pontus and Bithynia became one province. Naming them in this order may have suggested that this was to be a circular letter and was to be carried by a messenger (Silvanus, 5:12) from one community to the next in this sequence (see map on page 188).

Their Spiritual Status 1:2a

More significant than their ethnic background, social status, or place of residence is their relationship to God. Employing the OT language of election, or choseness, Peter from the outset calls his readers, both Jewish and Gentile, the *elect* of God, the *chosen* people of God (2:9), now involved in a transforming process empowered by God's Spirit, to become a community of obedience to Jesus Christ, redeemed, forgiven, and cleansed by his blood.

Three parallel prepositional phrases in 1:2 outline this "trinity of experience" (Hunter: 90). First, God is perceived and named as the *Father* who knows and destines beforehand, who is the Father of Jesus Christ (1:3), and who is the trustworthy and impartial judge

(1:17; 2:23). In this, Peter follows the usual way of speaking of God that Jesus had modeled in addressing God as "Abba" (Mark 14:36). God as Father is recognized as the initiator of salvation and acknowledged as the true author of grace and peace.

The second phrase, *sanctified by the Spirit,* involves an activity of the Spirit called sanctification or consecration. This anticipates the emphasis on the holiness of God. The author calls the people of God to be holy, set apart (1:14-16; 2:9). This has implications for morality as well as status. The operative agent is the Spirit of God, working in responsive persons. It is a process and not only an act.

The third phrase is more complex, with Jesus Christ as the unifying element. Introducing a high Christology, Peter declares the purpose of God through the work of the Spirit to be obedience to Jesus. This involves being *sprinkled with his blood,* cleansed from sin (cf. Lev. 5). This blood, described as *precious* (1:19), denotes the costliness of redemption and is by implication the resource for our healing (2:24).

This appeal to Father, Spirit, and Jesus Christ lays the foundation for Peter's message to believers enduring oppression. While on earth, struggling with false accusations, oppressive masters, imperfect spouses, and taunting neighbors, Peter's readers are to understand their special place of dignity and destiny in the purposes of God. Their experiences of suffering, affirmed to be temporary, are to be understood in the perspective of a divine presence, a purpose for which they have been chosen, and a purpose to which they are called.

Grace and Peace Be Yours 1:2b

While this formal greeting itself is brief, consisting of five simple Greek words, the implication is tremendous. *Grace* is one of the key words of the letter (1:2, 10, 13; 2:19-20; 3:7; 4:10; 5:5, 10), culminating in the manifesto: *this is the true grace of God; stand fast in it* (5:12). *Peace,* and how to find it and live it, likewise becomes a major concern (2:21-25; 3:8-12). One may indeed recognize in *grace* and *peace* the inseparable elements of the gospel of Jesus Christ which the writer to the Ephesians also recognized and emphasized (Eph. 2). The prayer of greeting not only desires that the readers may experience grace and peace, but that these may be multiplied for and in them, in abundance.

THE TEXT IN BIBLICAL CONTEXT

In contrast with Paul, whose apostolicity was often challenged, Peter asserts his apostolic commissioning and authority briefly and unapologetically. In several greetings, Paul elaborates his apostolic appointment and call (Rom. 1:1-6; Gal. 1:1-2a; 1 Cor. 1:1). One might take as special pleading Peter's appeal to being a witness of the sufferings of Christ and a partaker of the glory to be revealed. Otherwise, Peter's claim to be a "sent one" of Jesus Christ, commissioned by the Lord, is simple and direct.

The early readers of this letter seem not to have thought of the writer being someone other than the Peter of the Gospel narratives. That Peter is the fisherman called and renamed by Jesus, the sometimes aggressive and impulsive spokesperson among the twelve, the one who boasts of his loyalty to Jesus and yet denies knowing him just before the crucifixion.

In addition to self-consciousness of apostolic call, Peter shares with Paul a concept of belonging to an elect or chosen people of God. The concept and language of election go back to Jesus, according to the Gospels (Matt. 20:14-16; 22:14; 24:22, 24, 31 // Mark 13:20, 22, 27; Luke 18:7), and is also used by Paul (Rom. 8:33; 16:13; Col. 3:12). Peter uses the concept of election not only in his opening greetings but also in 2:4, 6, 9, always of the communities of believers in Jesus Christ. The concept is one way of accentuating the initiating grace of God in the experience and destiny of God's people.

In addressing churches composed of both Gentiles and Jews, 1 Peter gives special significance to the truth that not only Jews as a nation but also the Judeo-Gentile-Christian congregations are the chosen of God. Together they become the elect nation (2:9), the people of God whose very existence—and message as well—challenges existing beliefs and prevailing pagan ethics.

The NT does not develop a full doctrine of God as triune. Yet this passage, along with several texts from Paul (1 Cor. 12:4-6; 2 Cor. 13:13; Eph. 4:4-6) and the baptismal formula (Matt. 28:19-20; Eph. 4:4-6; Jude 20-21), are foundational to a trinitarian understanding of God.

Intriguingly, Hunter (90) speaks of this passage as a "trinity of experience." He suggests that careful understanding of the ways Christian believers together were experiencing God led them eventually to speak of God as "Father, Son, and Holy Spirit."

The linkage of obedience and sprinkling in 1:2 may reflect Exodus 24:7-8. After the people accepted the terms of the covenant, blood was sprinkled on them to seal the covenant. The issue of sequence may not be central here, but since sprinkling also has a connotation of cleansing related to forgiveness (1 John 1:9; Heb. 10:22), we may understand that Jesus Christ becomes the central point of relationship. We are to become obedient to Jesus Christ, and through Christ to God. We are also forgiven and cleansed through what Christ did for us in giving his blood (1:19; 2:24).

THE TEXT IN THE LIFE OF THE CHURCH

Those who read the writings of early Anabaptists readily become aware that they were not only steeped in Scripture but also that 1 Peter was among their most commonly mentioned biblical writings.

Dirk Philips, for example, read 1 Peter as describing the church of God as it was meant to be, "born of God" and as a "pilgrim in the world." The image of the church as a community of pilgrims in this world was based on the stories of Abraham, Isaac, and Jacob, especially as interpreted in Hebrews 11, but also in the expressions of "strangers" and "exiles" used in 1 Peter 1:1, 17; 2:11. This basic image of the Christian life was also shared and popularized by John Bunyan in *Pilgrim's Progress*. Bunyan, however, focused more on individual experience, while Philips and other Anabaptists were more aware of their corporate pilgrimage in the world.

According to the *Martyrs Mirror* (*MM*: 529-530), Adrian Corneliss was imprisoned at Leyden and put to death for the testimony of Jesus in 1552. He identified himself with those who were serving and suffering "among the scattered flock of Israel." In his admonitions to friends, he quoted from 1 Peter 2:1-5, 9, as well as various other passages.

Another Anabaptist martyr, Jacob Chandler, in what is called his fourth letter, wrote to his children in a confession of faith and linked the sprinkling of the blood in 1 Peter 1:2 with the atoning death of Christ. This, he says, is to be remembered in the communion service by one who is truly "a child of the NT" (*MM*: 806).

Similarly, a letter of Tijs Jeuriaenss, written from prison to a friend in Edam in 1569, uses precisely the language of 1 Peter 1:2 (*MM*: 827).

Clearly these early Anabaptist believers and martyrs had been profoundly shaped by the context and language of 1 Peter. They found in this and other NT writings strength for their commitment to Christ and facing the consequences of that faith.

1:3-12

The Celebration of Christian Hope and Its Life Impact

PREVIEW

Writing to scattered Christian believers experiencing various kinds of human suffering, Peter begins this letter with praise. Paul also commonly opens his letters with a passage of praise and thanksgiving (Rom. 1:8-10; 1 Cor. 1:4-9; 2 Cor. 1:3-7; Col. 1:3-8). This opening section encourages a spiritual understanding and attitude that Peter is especially seeking to build in the hearers of the letter. We call them *hearers* because we assume that the letter was likely read in the scattered congregations to the listening people.

Peter begins with blessing God, inviting the same in his hearers, and bidding them to view their life experiences from the perspective of the Christian hope. This hope is both their gift from God and their message to proclaim in word and life. They have been born anew into a life characterized and transformed by Christian hope. This hope in turn changes both their inner experience and their outer relationships and conduct.

The goal of their life of hope is salvation, which Peter perceives as yet to be completed in the future. Already, however, they may experience joy, even while they are being tested in their faith in Christ. Theirs is an inheritance that cannot be destroyed nor corrupted. This is being kept securely for them in heaven. They, as heirs, are being kept to receive it. While in this world, they are resident aliens, sometimes misunderstood, misinterpreted, mistreated, and maligned. Some of them are abused physically, socially, or spiritually. Their status with God, as people of God, however, is one of high privilege. Their situation has been foretold by prophets and has even become the unattained object of angelic desires (1:12).

OUTLINE
The Ground and Assurance of Christian Hope, 1:3-5
    1:3   The Ground of Hope
                  Praise to a Merciful God
                  The Common Ground of Christian Hope
                  A New Birthing of Hope
                  Internalizing the Resurrection of Jesus Christ
    1:4-5   The Assurance of Hope
                  An Inheritance in God's Safe Deposit
                  Heirs Protected to Receive What God Gives
                  Salvation, the Goal of Hope

The Joyful Benefits of Christian Hope, 1:6-9
1:6-7   In Experiences of Trials
1:8-9   In Anticipating the Completion of Salvation

The High Privilege of Christian Hope, 1:10-12
1:10-12a   Hope Fulfills the Prophetic Search
1:12b   Hope Attracts the Attention of Angels

EXPLANATORY NOTES
The Ground and Assurance of Christian Hope 1:3-5
1:3 The Ground of Hope
Praise to a Merciful God
    Blessed be the God and Father of our Lord Jesus Christ. Blessing God as the Lord (Yahweh) was a common OT worship pattern. It is especially common in Psalms (18:46; 28:6; 31:21; et al.) and specifically in doxologies (Ps. 41:13; 72:18-19; 89:52; 106:48). The root meaning of the word used here for *bless* is "to speak good of" or "to praise." The blessings of God on the people were often pronounced at the close of a service as the worshipers were about to return to their homes. The community, in turn, responded to the

blessings of God with words of adoration, such as "Bless the Lord" or "Praise be to Yahweh."

Peter uses the language of blessing again in 3:9, where he enjoins the hearers to *bless,* rather than *revile* persons who have reviled them. He assures them that they are called to *receive blessing* themselves.

For Peter, God is not only to be recognized but is to be praised. This is implicit in his description of the people of God, who are to bring spiritual sacrifices acceptable to God (2:5, 9) and to glorify God (4:11, 16). Peter in this letter occasionally bursts forth into expressions of praise (4:11b; 5:11). He yearns that as an outcome of Christian life and witness, neighbors who are not yet believers may also come eventually to *glorify God* (2:12).

Here Peter uses precisely the same words as Paul in 2 Corinthians 1:3 and in Ephesians 1:3 when he speaks of God as *the Father of our Lord Jesus Christ.* He has already spoken of God as the One who with foreknowledge has chosen the hearers to be a special people (1:2). He uses the word *God* thirty-nine times in this brief letter, indicating his pervasive God-consciousness. God's presence and grace are central in his experience. He links the designations *God* and *Father* only in these opening verses, but does speak of God as Father again in 1:17.

Peter does not limit his image of God to being a Father, but neither does he avoid this language which Jesus, according to the Gospels, had also frequently used (Matt. 6:9; Mark 14:36; Luke 12:32; John 14:10). God is for Peter the Sovereign One (1:2), the Holy One (1:15-16), the Impartial and Just One (1:17; 2:23), the altogether Trustworthy One (2:23; 4:19), the Faithful Creator (4:19), and especially the Merciful One (1:3; 2:9-10).

Since for Peter *the Spirit of Christ* has already been present in the OT prophets (1:11), it is clearly the metaphorical significance of the word *Father* which prevails in describing the relationship of God to Jesus. God is the Father of both Jesus and of the followers of Jesus in the sense of a "spiritual family relationship." This metaphor is further enhanced by the image of believers being *born anew* (1:3) by the seed of the living and enduring word of God (1:23), and by calling the believers newborn babes desiring spiritual milk (2:2).

The Common Ground of Christian Hope

The ultimate ground of Christian hope is the nature and action of God rather than human potential or ingenuity. Peter speaks of God having *great mercy,* even as Paul speaks of God being "rich in mercy" (Eph. 2:4). Moreover, like Paul, Peter associates the inclusion of the Gentiles with Jews in the people of God as a demonstration of God's mercy. Whether of Jewish or Gentile background, they who once had not been a people, are now a people of God. They who once had not known mercy, now have received mercy (2:10; cf. Hos. 2:23).

On this common ground of divine grace, Jew and Gentile can come together. In the OT, Jews celebrate that God is "merciful and gracious, slow to anger, abounding in steadfast love" (Exod. 34:6; Ps. 103:8). Gentiles, as Paul also argues in Romans, likewise come into the divine favor and family on the same basis of grace (Rom. 3:23-24; Eph. 2:8-9). For Peter, this grace is revealed and embodied in Jesus Christ.

For Peter, the mercy of God appears as one dimension of God's grace. Peter uses the word *grace* essentially as Paul uses it, to denote "the essence of God's decisive saving act in Jesus Christ which took place in his sacrificial death" (H. H. Esser, in *DNTT*, 2:119, 122). In restating the purpose of his writing, Peter in 5:12 declares, "I have written this short letter to encourage you and to testify that this is the true grace of God."

The word *mercy*, used less frequently both in the NT and also by Peter, has the connotation of "the emotion roused by contact with an affliction which comes undeservedly on someone else" (Esser quoting R. Bultmann, in *DNTT*, 2:594). Mercy is often linked with compassion, language that fits 1 Peter in dealing with undeserved suffering.

Peter, as well as Paul, is emphatic that Christian hope and salvation rest ultimately on the gracious action of God in Christ rather than on human deserving or moral achievement (Eph. 2:8-9).

A New Birthing of Hope

Prominent in this passage is a particular experience of divine grace, a *new birth*, being born anew, mentioned here and also in 1:23. Though this is not a technical term for conversion, it evokes an image that appears also in John 3:5, 7, in the conversation of Jesus with Nicodemus. Jesus emphasized that without a new birth, a birth "from above," Nicodemus could not see the kingdom of God even though he was regarded as a teacher in Israel.

The concept of a *new birth* appears also in Titus 3:5, where Paul links the mercy of God with an experience of "rebirth and renewal by the Holy Spirit." In each instance, with slightly different vocabulary, the image speaks of the significant change which faith in Jesus brings about in the life of the believer.

The essence of this change in 1 Peter is that the believer in Christ experiences a *living hope* that had not been there before. *Hope* now becomes an important term for Peter, and he speaks of the implications of this hope again in 1:13, 21, and 3:15. He also points to the exemplary pioneer women who hoped in God (3:5). Peter's use of the word *hope* is infrequent. Yet the idea of hope is pervasive in this letter to those who, under the pressure of a hostile environment, may be tempted to lose hope and respond to abuse with some form of retaliation.

It is unlikely that Peter here intends to contrast Christian with Jewish faith. More likely, he is contrasting the believers' present attitude toward the future with their former perception when they were not yet Christian believers (2:13; 4:3; cf. Eph. 2:11). To speak of a *living hope* follows naturally from the image of being *born anew* and anticipates the images of being newborn *babes* (2:2) and *children* (1:14; 3:6).

This newly experienced living hope is precisely what will now make the difference in how the hearers will be able to face their own immediate and ultimate futures, including suffering in a variety of forms. It will enable them to follow in the steps of Jesus (2:21) when encountering reviling and abuse in a hostile world. Without hope, they may be tempted not only to renounce their faith in God but also to respond to their enemies in ways which would compromise their witness in a world of injustice and violence.

Internalizing the Resurrection of Jesus Christ
One particular event in the incarnation has become for Peter the historical ground for this hope: *the resurrection of Jesus Christ.* This event is crucial in the experience of Peter, as shown in the Petrine tradition of the Gospels and Acts (Luke 24:12; John 21:2-23; Acts 2:14ff.; et al.). In this letter the resurrection of Jesus Christ is not only the historical basis for the living hope (1:20); it is also basic in the experience of Christian baptism (3:21). For Peter, the resurrection of Jesus Christ is not only a doctrine to be believed, but a reality to be experienced and internalized as living hope.

The merciful action of God was demonstrated in the resurrection of Jesus Christ. Likewise, the resurrection of Jesus Christ is linked to the action of the new birth that takes place in the experience of the Christian believer. Living hope, for the recipients of this letter, is not viewed as an ideal or an imperative, but as present internal experience with external consequences. They are a new people of God because they have been given a new life through the merciful action of God. In mercy, God has raised Jesus Christ from the grave and is raising believers out of their former deadness into a new life of faith, hope, and love.

1:4-5 The Assurance of Hope

An Inheritance in God's Safe Deposit

Peter describes the content of this living hope with the image of an indestructible *inheritance*. The promise of inheritance occurs again in 3:9: *It is for this that you were called—that you might* inherit *a blessing*. It is also implicit in 5:3, where he speaks of the people of God being a *heritage*, or *those in your charge*. The negative reference to *futile ways inherited from your ancestors* (1:18) uses a different concept and vocabulary.

In this passage, the terms *hope, inheritance*, and *salvation* become a "virtual identity" (Achtemeier: 95, quoting Grosheide). The image of inheritance here is intended to emphasize its divine origin and also its eschatological expression. In the OT, inheritance was often associated with the possession of land. Peter, writing mainly to Gentile Christians, uses the term metaphorically to speak of the Christian's possession of the hope of eternal life and of the coming kingdom of God. Clearly, this heavenly inheritance is not only for the individual but "points to the restoration of the community of the righteous and the destruction of evil" (Perkins: 31). It is an "expected possession" (Hiebert: 48), as also in Colossians 3:24 and Hebrews 7. This is the heavenly kingdom that will be fully manifested when Christ is fully revealed (1:7b). Peter echoes the promise of Jesus, "It is your Father's good pleasure to give you the kingdom" (Luke 12:32).

Three emphatic adjectives describe the Christian's inheritance as (1) *imperishable*, free from death or decay; (2) *undefiled*, free from uncleanness or moral impurity; and (3) *unfading*, free from the natural ravages of time, as in the fading of flowers (Michaels: 21). Neither corruption from within nor corrosive forces from without can destroy this inheritance that is fully guaranteed to believers. These adjectives, perhaps chosen because in Greek each begins with the letter α, emphasize the assured permanence of what God has given them, and also that this heavenly inheritance transcends any earthly wealth. Similarly, Jesus emphasized "laying up treasure in heaven where neither moth nor rust corrupt and where thieves do not break in and steal" (Matt. 6:19-20).

This incorruptible inheritance is being *kept in heaven*, literally "in the heavens." In the NT this expression at times becomes another way of speaking about God's presence and realm. "The kingdom of heaven," as in Matthew, means the same as "the kingdom of God" does elsewhere. The focus here is not on a safe space or place but on the total competence and trustworthiness of God, who makes promises of inheritance and who can be counted on to be entirely faithful in making good on these promises.

Heirs Protected to Receive What God Gives

Not only is the *inheritance* in the trustworthy hands of God; so are Christian believers being *protected* or *guarded*, a military term. Peter invokes another image of a powerful God who protects his own people against enemies, making it unnecessary for them to fear, hate, or destroy enemies. He describes the ongoing response of this people to their God as *faith*. This response of faith in God is now being put to a test in their encounter with suffering (1:7). The outcome of their faith is their salvation (1:9). Through Jesus Christ they have come to this faith. Both their faith and their hope are set on God (1:21). They are now to remain steadfast in their faith, resisting the devil, until God restores them fully in the end (5:10).

Faith as a companion of hope is essentially an ongoing trust. In anticipating the future, faith becomes hope. Faith and hope in turn become active in love. Their faith is to be more than professed belief. Faith is to be an internalized, permeating confidence. In facing what is ahead, as hope, it responds appropriately to the complete trustworthiness of God. Paul likewise says we are saved "by faith" (Eph. 2:8) and "by hope" (Rom. 8:24). Thus Peter links faith and hope and recognizes that these become the enablers of a genuine love for Jesus Christ (1:8), for fellow believers (1:22; 4:8), and also for enemies (3:8-9).

In this passage, we see a grammatical shift in persons, from first to second. Peter has been dealing with Christian truth generally and inclusively when speaking of the mercy of God, the resurrection of Christ, and even the new birth of hope. Now he addresses his readers directly and personally: all this is *for you* (1:4).

Salvation, the Goal of Hope

The basic meaning of salvation is deliverance. Salvation, for Peter, is a controlling theme (1:5, 9, 10; 2:2). He speaks of the *salvation of their souls* as being *the outcome of their faith* (1:9). When Peter mentions *souls*, however (as also in 1:22; 2:11, 25; 3:20; 4:19), this does not indicate a dualistic view of human beings. Instead, he is speaking of the whole self, especially but not exclusively of its inward dimensions. Also, he does not emphasize the individual over against the community, but rather addresses the whole self in the context of Christian community, which has both present and eschatological dimensions. Of this salvation (1:10), the prophets of old have spoken and researched.

According to 2:2, salvation involves spiritual growth (*into salvation;* see notes on 2:2). This is implied in the image of newborn babes craving spiritual milk as well as in the image of building up (2:5). The phrase *for a salvation* (1:5) is best understood as entering into the full dimensions of salvation, rather than initial entry into the experience of deliverance. The notion of *tasting* in 2:3, drawn from Psalm 34:8a, is adapted by Peter to indicate his assumption that they have already entered a saving relationship with God and are among the newborn (1:23). Regeneration is thus perceived as initiation into salvation; the spiritual growth that follows moves them toward its fullness. According to 3:21, the water of baptism becomes a sign of salvation. In 4:18, the verb *save* is used in an OT quotation concerning the righteous and sinners.

For Peter, salvation is both process and possession, something already present and experienced (3:21), and something yet to be revealed in the last time (1:5). In Peter's perspective, it is a goal toward which the believer and the community of faith are moving (1:9).

The expression *the last time* introduces the eschatological dimension of Peter's understanding of salvation. This *last time* seems broadly equivalent to the expression *at the revelation of Jesus Christ* (1:7) or *the day of visitation* (2:12). It is related to *the end of all things* (4:7) and to the revealing of Christ's *glory* (4:13; 5:1).

As Michaels (23) puts it, "Salvation . . . is the final display of the 'power of God,' no longer simply to protect his people, but to vindicate them once and for all against their enemies, and usher them into their inheritance." In this perspective, salvation has both personal and corporate dimensions, setting people free from multiple bondages, for the service which such freedom makes possible in this life (2:16) as well as for eternity (4:19; 5:10).

The Joyful Benefits of Christian Hope 1:6-9

1:6-7 In Experiences of Trials

Verse 6 can be read either as indicative, *In this you rejoice,* or as imperative, *Rejoice in this.* While commentators debate this issue, the first is preferred, implying that the living hope into which they have been born makes it possible for them to rejoice even in the presence of suffering. Similarly, Acts 5:41 reports that the apostles "rejoiced that they were considered worthy to suffer dishonor for the sake of the name." *In this* (1:6) refers back to all that God has done for them through Christ. It continues the description of their transformed experience, their birth into living hope. This is consistent also with the reference to rejoicing in 1:8-9, which describes present rejoicing in anticipation of the full salvation yet to be realized. Such rejoicing is understood as a dimension of the transforming hope which has come to them through God's grace in the resurrection of Jesus Christ.

Peter does not identify the antecedent of *this* (1:6) with "the last times" or with some other detail in preceding verses. Instead, he seems to be referring to all that he has said in 1:3-5 about the mercies of God, the living hope, the security of the inheritance, and the full deliverance that the Christian anticipates. All of these together make it possible for the Christians of Asia Minor to respond to their various experiences of suffering in a grace-empowered way, with joy.

Peter uses two words for *joy* in this epistle. *Rejoice (agalliaō)* means to be extremely joyful or glad, especially in outward expression such as worship (1:6, 8; 4:13). *Joy* (chara) or *rejoice (chairete)* is closely related to grace (*charis*) and commonly expresses a marked sense of well-being or wholeness (1:8; 4:13). Peter's use of the two words together probably indicates emphasis rather than a concern with special nuances of meaning.

This passage also gives the first explicit reference to suffering experienced by the hearers. Peter considers this theme repeatedly, with much attention and instruction. Suffering is indicated as already present and not simply a future possibility. Moreover, it is perceived as necessary in some sense, or at least inevitable, given the circumstances. This does not imply that God designs or sends human suffering. Yet Peter does acknowledge that God's will allows for and even embraces some suffering (4:14). As Davids (56) notes, "Suffering may not be God's desire, but it is not outside his sovereignty."

Their suffering comes in various forms and is limited; otherwise, its precise nature is not described here. This passage mentions *various trials* (1:6). It is not likely that Peter here is referring to state-initiated persecution of Christians on a large scale, as has sometimes been inferred from the expression "suffer as a Christian" (4:16). Their suffering includes a variety of problems identified later as being falsely accused (2:12; 3:16; 4:14), in some cases also physically beaten unjustly (2:18-20), being married to a husband or possibly a wife who is not a believer (3:1, 7), or being reviled (3:9).

One perspective that Peter introduces here is that suffering may even become beneficial as a process that proves the genuineness of Christian faith. Those of Jewish background were familiar with the OT stories of how the faith of Abraham, Isaac, and Jacob had been tested. Israel as a people often failed the test of their faith in troubling times. Jesus, on the other hand, is presented as one who met the test of faith and suffered in an exemplary way (2:21-25; 3:18; 4:1). Here Peter affirms the faithfulness of those to whom he is writing.

Moreover, the recipients are also familiar with the analogy that Peter introduces comparing their precious faith to gold, a precious metal. Gold is indeed subjected to testing by fire, burning away any impurities and leaving only the pure metal (cf. 1 Cor. 3:12-14; Mal. 3:2-3). Peter is not focusing on the purification of their faith but rather on proving its genuineness. This will come to be fully recognized at the revelation of Jesus Christ, commonly spoken of as Christ's second coming. Peter uses the word *revelation* rather than the more common term "coming" (*parousia*), literally "presence," in speaking of this event. Peter indicates that in this finally and fully revealed presence of Jesus, the genuine faith of these Christians of Asia Minor will bring them praise and glory and honor. In short, their full vindication will come when Jesus comes.

This then is one major benefit of a *living hope:* it makes possible a patient response to temporary suffering, bearing witness to the genuineness of Christian faith, and bringing honor to God. By implication, it is possible for Christians to fail the test. One can respond to suffering despondently, and then bring dishonor and disgrace to the One professed as Lord. How Christians respond to suffering is a special concern for Peter.

1:8-9 In Anticipating the Completion of Salvation

By speaking of the revelation of Jesus Christ as an event to come, Peter implies that Jesus is invisible to his present readers. This fact Peter now recognizes and emphasizes. These Christians, in contrast to those who had been eyewitnesses of the incarnation (cf. 5:1), have never seen Jesus with human eyes, nor do they now see him as a visible presence. Nevertheless, having heard the gospel proclaimed (1:12, 25), they have come to love and believe in Jesus. The linkage of loving and trusting, both verbs in the present tense, makes this a remarkable couplet. Loving Christ and trusting Christ may not be identical. Yet to separate love and trust diminishes both words in describing the believer's relationship to Jesus Christ.

The object of love and faith is Jesus Christ rather than simply God, as is common in the OT and in the Gospels (cf. Mark 12:28-29; Deut. 6:4-5). This introduces us to Peter's high Christology (2:4-8). Peter does not only claim that his apostleship comes from Jesus Christ (1:1), and that his and their hope derives from the resurrection of Jesus Christ (1:3). In addition, the crucified Christ (1:19) is the power of redemption, the pattern for Christian ethics (2:21), and the assurance of the final triumph of Christ. In that triumph, human hope is consummated (1:7; 4:11; 5:10).

As they remain firm in their faith (5:9, 12b), the outcome is the *salvation* of their *souls.* Peter uses the word *soul* somewhat differently than does Paul. Paul tends to use the term *soul* as denoting either the fallen human self or mortal nature in contrast to the spiritual, life-giving person (cf. 1 Cor. 2:14-15; 15:45). On the other hand, Peter is more like Luke in tending to use *soul* in the Hebraic sense, for the total person, the whole self (1:9, 22; 2:11, 23; 3:20; 4:19). Salvation of souls then has to do not with some invisible part of persons which departs at death, but with their whole beings as those whose hope is in God as known in Christ. This fits Peter's emphasis on the importance of Christ's resurrection as ground of our Christian hope for time and eternity.

The High Privilege of Christian Hope 1:10-12

1:10-12a Hope Fulfills the Prophetic Search

In this passage Peter explains a special point concerning the salvation he has mentioned in 1:9. The explanation follows this *a b b' a'* type of structure (chiasmus, from the Greek letter χ):

    a Inquiries of prophets in the past
        b Divine revelation to prophets in the past
        b' Divine announcement to Christians in the present
    a' Inquiries of angels in the present (Michaels: 39)

Peter's basic purpose is to help his readers understand that their situation, in spite of temporary suffering, is one of high privilege. In some ways that privilege even exceeds that of the OT people and their prophets, who anticipated and foretold the coming of Christ. It is even better than angels who, with curiosity and possible envy, notice God's redemptive grace operating among the Christians of

Asia Minor (1:12).

While some scholars (e.g., Selwyn: 134) have argued that these prophets include NT Christian prophets, most agree that Peter is thinking of OT prophets. This consensus is strongly supported by the contrast between past and present, between the prophets who searched (1:10-11) and preachers who proclaimed the gospel (1:12). Their OT prophetic ministry has included both the searching and the inquiring. The point of their search has had to do with a *person* and a *time* or "circumstance" when the grace of God for salvation would be made manifest. They were seeking to know when and where the Messiah would come, and how he would be recognized.

Peter notes the *Spirit of Christ* was operating in these prophets, even as the *Holy Spirit* is operating in the proclaimers of the Christian gospel. Some early Christians argued that *Spirit of Christ* means the preexisting Christ. While the concept of a preexistence of Christ was present in the early church (John 1:1-4; Phil. 2:5-11; Col.1:15-17), it need not be Peter's point here. *Spirit of Christ* may simply be understood as the Holy Spirit in the OT prophets bearing witness to the coming of Christ (Hiebert: 67).

The essential content of what was revealed to and then predicted by the OT prophets has to do with the sufferings destined for Christ and the subsequent glory. Peter himself so understands the writing of Isaiah 53, as illustrated in this letter (2:22-24). As Grudem (70) observes, the Messiah's subsequent glory is likewise profusely documented in the OT (Pss. 2; 16:10; 45:7; Isa. 9:6; 40:3-5, 9-11; 42:1-4; 61:1-3). This basic perspective in reading aspects of OT prophecy is strongly shared by Matthew and Luke, who frequently note how Scripture is fulfilled in the coming, death, and resurrection of Christ (cf. Luke 24:25ff.).

This letter, however, stresses the OT prophets being able to recognize that the more complete fulfillment of God's promises would come in a later day, beyond their own time and experience. This understanding of OT prophecy is also shared by Paul (Rom. 4:23-24; 15:4; 1 Cor. 9:9-10; 10:11). Moreover, Peter in Acts 2:25-36 makes precisely this same point in applying the word of David in Psalm 16:8-11 directly to Jesus and the events which were then being experienced.

1:12b Hope Attracts the Attention of Angels

This almost cryptic remark, *things into which angels long to look*, concludes this section celebrating the Christian hope. It is quickly dismissed by some commentators, but arouses the curiosity of others. Peter speaks of angels not only here but also in 3:22. Both these references are casual, however, rather than a point of emphasis.

The *things* in view here likely include all that Peter has been talking about in the preceding verses, not only that which the prophets were seeking but all that God has done in bringing believers into a living hope.

Angels, literally "messengers," here used without an article, are named alongside the prophets as those who have desires. The prophets wanted to know about the coming Christ and thus searched and inquired. The wishes of the angels are less explicit but also have to do with that which has happened to Christian believers through Christ. The vocabulary reminds us of the word of Jesus to his disciples: "Many prophets and saints . . . desired to see what you now see, yet never saw; to hear what you hear, yet never heard it" (Matt. 13:17).

Further, the verb *to look,* used to describe the intensity of the interest of the angels, means "to bend over," "to be looking or peering into something." It suggests curiosity about something hidden or interest in seeing something spectacular. The concept that angels take interest in human affairs is also reflected in the words of Jesus in Luke 15:7, 10: the angels rejoice over a sinner who repents (Hiebert: 71). Peter's concern is not to emphasize either the activity or the authority of angels. The focus is rather "on their intense interest in what has taken place and on the limitations of their power and knowledge" (Michaels: 49).

This implies that the significance of Christian redemption indeed goes beyond the realm of human beings. This may also be implicit in 3:19, and is explicit in 3:22, where Peter further speaks of angels, authorities, and powers. The Christian hope made possible through Jesus Christ touches the realm of heaven, the trans-human world as well as human history. This invests the experience of Christians in Asia Minor with extraordinary significance and helps give their suffering transcendent meaning. Peter wants them to know that they have certain advantages beyond those of the OT prophets and even beyond those of angels.

THE TEXT IN BIBLICAL CONTEXT

Biblical Hope and Grace

The English word *hope* translates the Greek *elpis* (noun), and *elpizō* (verb). In contrast to the usual positive connotation of the English word *hope*, the Greek originally could indicate not only positive expectation but also the negative, fear. E. Hoffman says that "living hope as a fundamental religious attitude was unknown in Greek culture" (in *DNTT,* 2:239). Seneca called hope "an uncertain good." In contrast, biblical *hope* is strong, confident, and ground for transformation of life.

The Greek words for *hope* translate several different Hebrew words which embody the notion of "stretching out toward," "waiting for," or "longing for." While much OT language for hope has a secular meaning, the basic religious message is that Israel is to *hope* in Yahweh (e.g., Ps. 71:5; Jer. 14:8; 17:13). The OT also warns against false hope, sometimes spread by false prophets, but true hope is a gift from God (Isa. 40:31; Ps. 42:5). Waiting on God allows believers to be at peace, inwardly, but it does not mean inactivity. Such hope in God is lived out in daily faithfulness.

In the NT the noun *hope* occurs 53 times and the verb 31. Somewhat surprisingly, the vocabulary of hope is not common in the four Gospels but appears frequently in Acts and in the NT epistles, especially in Pauline writings. Hoffman (in *DNTT,* 2:241) observes that in the NT, *hope* is never an indication of "a vague or fearful anticipation, but always the expectation of something good." Hope comes to be a part of the familiar triad, "faith, hope, and love," as in 1 Thessalonians 1:3 and 1 Corinthians 13:13. None of the three thereafter stands entirely without the others. There can be no hope without faith in Christ; hope and faith without love would be unfruitful.

Hoffman (in *DNTT*, 2:242-243) identifies three major factors that give hope its importance in the NT: (1) Its content: it is never focused on self but is always centered on Christ and on God. (2) Its basis: it does not rest on human achievement but always on the gracious work of God in Jesus Christ. (3) Its nature: it is a gift of God's grace.

Alan Richardson (109) notes that the NT understanding of hope is best expressed in 1 Peter 1:3 and 13. Peter grounds hope in the resurrection of Jesus Christ and also sets it into an eschatological context of anticipating "the revelation of Jesus Christ, i.e., the Parousia."

In summary, biblical hope means expectation, confidence, and waiting on what God is doing and will yet do through Jesus Christ and the Holy Spirit. The response is essentially trust and peace, inwardly and in relationships.

Charis, the Greek word for *grace,* has a rich cluster of meanings, including "grace, gracefulness, graciousness, favor, thanks, and gratitude." Closely related terms are *charisma,* "gift given out of goodwill"; *charisomai,* "to show favor or kindness, give a favor, to be gracious to someone, to pardon"; and *charitoō,* "to endue with grace." Taken from the classical Greek, the root includes "things that produce well-being." Used as a noun, it means "grace, favor, beauty, thankfulness, gratefulness, delight, kindness, expression of favor, good turn, benefit" (Esser, in *DNTT,* 2:115).

In the OT, the word *charis* appears 190 times in the Septuagint, translating a variety of Hebrew words but particularly *hen* (61 times). H. H. Esser says that in this usage, "it denotes the stronger coming to the help of the weaker who stands in need of help by reason of his circumstances or natural weakness. He acts by a voluntary decision, though he is moved by the dependence or the request of the weaker party" (in *DNTT,* 2:116).

The NT employs *charis* 155 times, of which 100 are in letters of Paul, and ten in 1 Peter. Paul is the champion of the doctrine of justification by faith through grace. For Paul, *grace* is the essence of God's decisive saving act in Jesus Christ, which has taken place in his sacrificial death, and also the essence of all its consequences in the present and future (Rom. 3:24ff.; Esser, in *DNTT,* 2:118-119).

Peter's understanding and use of *grace* in this epistle is congruent with that of Paul, though Peter does not link it directly with justification. Peter speaks of God's *grace* being given through Jesus Christ (1:10), after being announced by the prophets. It is to be revealed in the future, and it should determine conduct and hope (1:13). Further, believers are called upon to be good stewards of the diverse and multiform *grace of God* that creates and sustains their life in community (4:10). *Grace* is also what makes it possible for believers to endure undeserved suffering (2:19). Moreover, this letter is written to testify to the *true grace* of God (5:12), in which believers are enjoined to stand fast, even though, as the letter makes clear, they face suffering and abuse.

According to the NT understanding, our salvation comes as a gift by grace through faith. So also our life of faithful forgiving and non-retaliating discipleship is empowered by grace.

The Practice of Blessing

The biblical practice of blessing either persons or God, as well as being blessed, involves two different terms. Blessing or *praise* (*eulogia*) means essentially something good or laudable said about something or someone. On the other hand, *blessed, fortunate, happy* (*makarios*) is often used to introduce a wisdom saying, to make a wise observation, or to offer congratulations to those in view. Peter uses both terms in this letter. Both are translated "blessed."

The term that literally means "to speak good of" is used in some form 640 times in the LXX (the Septuagint). Most commonly it translates the Hebrew word for *bless* (*barak*) and is often used in contrast to *curse* (*qalal*). The temptation to speak ill of others and even of God is never distant when persons are subjected to experiences of suffering, as is the case in 1 Peter. Peter recognizes the temptation to revile those who revile (2:23; 3:9) and calls on his readers explicitly to bless, to speak good of those who may speak ill of them.

We are told that Job, in his experience of severe trial, was tempted by his wife to speak against God, yet Job continues to bless God (Job 2:9-10; 1:21). In various psalms also, the writer is aware of losses and hurts in life, yet affirms praise for God (Ps. 42:5-6, 11).

The second term for *blessed, fortunate, or happy* (*makarios*) is commonly used in what we call beatitudes (cf. Matt. 5:3-12). The root of this term means "free from daily cares and worries" or "happy," and in the NT it comes to mean "religious joy which accrues [from one's] share in the salvation of the kingdom of God" (F. Hauck in *TDNT*, 4:367). These beatitudes commonly are a form of a wisdom saying, declaring an observation, and expressing congratulations rather than making an exhortation. Peter uses this language in 3:14, echoing one of the beatitudes of Jesus (Matt. 5:10).

The Experience of New Birth

Peter's language in speaking of the new birth is similar to John 3:3 but not identical with it. There Jesus tells Nicodemus that to enter the kingdom of God, he must be "born from above," which Nicodemus takes in the physical sense of being physically reborn (3:4). Peter uses the term *born anew* in 1:3, 23, and a related adjective in 2:2, where he speaks of *newborn infants*. The new birth for Peter is an action of God by which Christian believers have come into a new life, transformed by hope (1:3) and love (1:22-23).

The image of a divine begetting (Kelly: 48) also appears in 1 John 2:29; 3:9; 4:7; 5:1. The Christian is one "born of God." James 1:18

likewise states that God "gave us birth by the word of truth," and Titus
3:5 speaks of "the water of rebirth and renewal by the Holy Spirit."
Paul also builds on the imagery of birth from the Spirit (Gal. 4:29-31)
or through the gospel (1 Cor. 4:15). Yet in speaking of the same reality, Paul tends to prefer another set of images: dying and rising again
(Rom. 6:4-9) through the Spirit (Rom. 8:11), being created anew
(2 Cor. 5:17; Gal. 6:15), and progressive inner transformation and
renewal (2 Cor. 3:18; 4:16).

Debates have flourished over the origin of the image of the new
birth or regeneration. Pagan mystery cults do speak of their followers
as having been "reborn" through a sacramental initiation. However,
Peter's use of this image has its origins in primitive Christian tradition,
including the teachings of Jesus on becoming like little children (Matt.
18:3; Mark 10:15; Luke 18:17), and in the story of Nicodemus (John
3:3-8; cf. Kelly: 50).

The Significance of the Resurrection

The crucifixion of Jesus and his resurrection figure prominently in this
letter. Yet Peter emphasizes the resurrection as involved in the new
birth of hope. The resurrection of Jesus Christ has a climactic place
in the structure of the Gospels as well as in the experience of the early
church recorded in Acts. This provides a background for understanding why the resurrection of Jesus has become so significant for Peter
personally. Paul in 1 Corinthians 15:5 speaks of the risen Christ
appearing first to Cephas (Peter), next to the Twelve, and then to five
hundred brethren at one time. Acts portrays Peter as the great
preacher of the resurrected Christ (Acts 2:24; 3:14).

The doctrine of the resurrection of Jesus is significantly linked with
the experience of Christian hope. Paul develops this linkage in
1 Corinthians 15:17, 19: "If Christ has not been raised, your faith is
futile and you are still in your sins. . . . If for this life only we have
hoped in Christ, we are of all people most to be pitied." The linkage
is pervasively implicit in the NT. Without a risen Lord, the early
church would not even have come into existence. Without a living
Lord, there would be no living hope in Christian terms. Without the
risen Lord, the NT as we have it would not have been written.

Hope as Inheritance

To Jewish members of the community the image of an *inheritance*
was familiar from OT practices. The promises given to Abraham,
Isaac, and Jacob involved not only progeny but also land. They saw

Canaan as the Promised Land, as their inheritance. Inheritance, then, had to do with that portion of the land or of family wealth that might be apportioned to descendants, generally effective on the death of the parent. The word *inheritance* occurs almost 200 times in the Greek version of the OT (the LXX), indicating how prominent this concept was for the Jewish people.

Jesus also used this image and vocabulary to speak of "inheriting the kingdom" (Matt. 25:34) or of "inheriting eternal life" (Matt. 19:29; Mark 10:17; Luke 10:25; 18:18). For the apostle Peter, this would have been familiar and powerful language, both because of his Jewish background and because of his familiarity with the teachings of Jesus.

Rejoicing in Suffering

Suffering is a special concern of Peter in this letter. Early in his writing, he mentions the paradoxical response of Christians to their adverse circumstances and experiences. To speak of rejoicing in suffering seems almost glib, if not offensive. Yet this linkage too needs to be seen in the context of the NT story. Christians do rejoice even in their suffering.

The portrayal of the early church in Acts describes believers as rejoicing even when they suffered dishonor while witnessing obediently to their faith (Acts 5:41). Paul, in writing to the Philippians from prison, with outcomes uncertain, speaks repeatedly of joy (1:4, 18; 2:17) and exhorts his readers to rejoice with him (2:18; 4:4). Karl Barth called this Paul's "defiant Nevertheless" (120). To the Thessalonians, Paul also speaks of troubled conditions coming, yet he exhorts, "Rejoice always" (1 Thess. 5:16). Similarly, the writer to the Hebrews reminds readers that they once accepted joyfully the plundering of property (Heb. 10:34).

Prophets Who Were Seers

While prophetic ministry has a large and significant place in the biblical story, Peter introduces only one limited dimension of it. Instead of focusing on prophetic social concern and the call for justice, which is indeed a large part of biblical prophecy, Peter highlights one special aspect. He affirms that the OT prophets who spoke concerning the coming sufferings and glory of Christ did so with an awareness that they were speaking of future realities. These events would happen later than their own day.

The Gospel writers Matthew and Luke share with Peter an interest in presenting Jesus Christ as the fulfillment of OT predictive prophecy. This interest is profusely illustrated in Matthew and in the sermons in Acts. Luke (24:25-27, 45-48) likewise illustrates this perspective clearly. Hebrews also regards the OT as God's oracles that often speak of Jesus.

Peter claims for these OT prophets the inspiration and guidance of the Holy Spirit, a belief that fits the second letter that bears his name (2 Pet. 1:21). These letters implicitly perceive God as revealing, through the Holy Spirit, truth and perspectives beyond the prophets' own natural powers of observation. Thus prophets, on occasion, speak more truth than they personally understand clearly.

Peter's frequent use of the OT writings, including Leviticus, Psalms, Proverbs, Isaiah, and Hosea, reflects a similar theological perspective. Peter reads the OT as authoritative Scripture, as indicated by 1:16a, *for it is written*, and 2:6a, *for it stands in scripture*. He uses such passages to support what he has been saying. However, he applies such Scripture to new situations. Thus in 1:25 he takes Isaiah's *the word of the Lord which endures forever* and identifies it with *the good news that was announced to you*. For Peter, the prophetic word in the OT is not limited to the prophet's immediate situation but has significance also for the Christian believers to whom he is writing.

What's That About Angels?

Peter's somewhat provocative reference to the curious angels also must be read in biblical context. Most people in the biblical world believed in the reality of spiritual beings transcending humans. They also distinguished between Gabriel and other good archangels (Luke 1:19; cf. 1 Thess. 4:16). Angels appear from time to time in the Bible story (Gen. 16:7-11; et al.). Daniel names Gabriel, who gives wisdom to the prophet, and Michael, the Jew's patron angel (Dan. 9:21; 10:13, 21; 12:1). The pseudepigraphical book of 1 Enoch (9:1) names four archangels (Michael, Uriel, Raphael, Gabriel) looking down from heaven on the violence taking place on earth.

The word *angel* basically means "messenger or an ambassador in human affairs who acts on behalf of God or a god." It is found 175 times in the NT and is common in the synoptic Gospels, Acts, and especially Revelation. Peter speaks of angels not only in 1:12 but also in 3:22, where angels are linked with authorities and powers, all being subjected to Christ.

The Sadducees did not believe in the existence of angels, but the

Pharisees and many other Hebrews did (Matt. 22:23; Acts 23:8). Peter shares in this belief. Nevertheless, like Paul, he is clear that Jesus Christ is always superior to the angels. Peter would agree with Paul's warning to the Colossians not to become involved in false humility and the worship of angels (2:18). This may be a warning against some gnostic preoccupation with beings intermediary between God and people.

Both here and elsewhere in the NT, angels have their place in the scheme of spiritual reality, as positive messengers of God or as beings who need to be brought or kept under the lordship of Christ. Here, however, the concern of Peter is not some true doctrine of angels, but to assure the Christians of Asia Minor that their own status with God is one of high privilege. Even the spiritual world represented by angels has noticed and is curious about what happens to persons who have become participants in the living hope arising out of the resurrection of Jesus Christ.

THE TEXT IN THE LIFE OF THE CHURCH

The Ambiguity of Hope

The need for renewal of human hope persists through the generations. Ephesians describes those outside of Christian faith as being "without hope" (Eph. 2:12). The philosopher Sophocles wrote, "Not to be born at all—that is by far the best fortune; the second best is as soon as one is born with all speed to return thither to whence one has come" (quoted in Barclay: 203). A more contemporary sense of hopelessness is eloquently expressed by Jean-Paul Sartre in his play, *No Exit* (Clowney: 43).

The context may involve the survival of humanity threatened by spreading violence and nuclear war, ecological pollution, and dangerous depletion of nonrenewable resources through waste or overpopulation. The outcome of the contest between human hope and despair often seems to be in question. The church, like Peter, perceives Christ as a hope-giver and has often recognized its role as a community of hope in the world.

Erich Fromm, in his massive study on *The Anatomy of Human Destructiveness*, concludes with an epilogue: "On the Ambiguity of Hope." As a Jewish psychoanalyst, in the wake of the Holocaust, he wrestled with the thorny problem of the causes of human destructiveness in war and otherwise. Fromm observes that neither optimism nor pessimism will do as an appropriate response to this kind of evil in our world. For different reasons, neither the optimist nor the pessimist is very helpful in confronting and combating destructive evil. The optimist tends to say, "Nothing needs be done." The pessimist tends to say, "Nothing can be done." Thus neither helps.

Within the framework of his own Jewish background, Fromm calls for faith and hope. He says, "To have faith means to dare, to think the unthinkable, yet to act within the limits of the realistically possible; it is the paradoxical hope to expect the Messiah every day, yet not to lose heart when he has not come at the appointed hour. To hope is not passive and it is not patient; on the contrary, it is impatient and active, looking for every possibility of action within the realm of real possibilities" (438).

For Christian believers, who affirm that the Messiah has indeed come in Jesus of Nazareth, the call to trust and hope remains at the heart of life. This becomes particularly important for those who experience adversity, abuse, or persecution in any form. Therefore, 1 Peter was quite significant to early Anabaptists.

Hope in Anabaptist Perspective

Few resources illustrate the impact of Peter's letter more dramatically than Thieleman J. van Braght's *Martyrs Mirror* (*MM*) which is replete with biblical references linked to the faith and martyrdom stories.

Well before the rise of the Anabaptist movement, there was severe persecution in Flanders, Artois, and Hainault, where "Peronne of Aubeton, a pious woman, [was] publicly burnt for her faith, about A.D. 1373." "Condemned as a heretic to be publicly burned, . . . she testified that the 'trial of her faith was more precious than of gold that perisheth, though it be tried with fire'" (*MM*: 332-333). She was quoting 1 Peter 1:7.

Included also is "A Testament written by Jelis Bernaerts to his wife, when he lay in prison at Antwerp, where he was put to death for the Word of the Lord, A.D. 1559." Bernaerts quotes virtually verbatim from 2 Peter 1:2-3, Titus 3:5, and 1 Peter 1:3-7. Then he tells his wife, "Hence be of good cheer, my most beloved, even though still much more tribulation should come upon you; for we know that we must through much tribulation and suffering enter into the kingdom of God" (*MM*: 624).

An epistle from Hendrick Alewijns "sent to the beloved children of God in Zealand, was written in prison at Middleburgh. There he steadfastly testified to the truth of God with his death, on the 9th of February, A.D. 1569." He likewise referred repeatedly to the message of 1 Peter: "Yea, we confess and declare with all saints rich in hope, that this present time is short, and that the sufferings of this time, for righteousness, are small, and hence not worthy to be compared with the glory that shall be revealed in us (Rom. 8:18), as we here follow. Believers, rightly esteem the sufferings of the present time, because of the hope, promise, and reward" (*MM*: 745).

Klaus von Graveneck, a Protestant Swabian nobleman wrote of the suffering and execution of Michael Sattler, the South German Anabaptist leader burned at the stake in Rottenburg in 1527:

> So it seemed good to us to make known in print this authentic and wonderful story and report the trustworthy persons herein named, so that many might see how God so marvelously deals with His saints here, and tests them as gold through fire, that is, with manifold temptation and testing, as it stands in 1 Peter 1 [1:7], so that everyone might use and strengthen his faith, might not let himself be turned away from the bright and clear Word of God. (Sattler: 68-69)

Echoes of 1 Peter are also readily heard in the hymn of Felix Manz, Anabaptist martyr by drowning in January 1527. It is still used in congregations of the Anabaptist tradition (*Hymnal*: 438).

> I sing with exultation, all my heart's delight
> is God who brings salvation, frees from death's dark might.
> I praise thee, Christ of heaven, who ever shall endure,
> who takes away my sorrow, keeps me safe and secure.
>
> God sends him as example, light and living guide.
> Before my end he bids me in his realm abide,
> that I may love and cherish his righteousness divine,
> that I with him forever bliss eternal may find.
>
> Sing praise to Christ our Savior, who, in grace inclined
> to us reveals his nature: patient, loving, kind.
> His love divine outpouring, displayed to ev'ryone.
> is fashioned like his Father's as no other has done.
>
> Christ bids us, none compelling, to his glorious throne.
> They only who are willing, Christ as Lord to own,
> they are assured of heaven, who will right faith pursue,
> with hearts made pure do penance, sealed in baptism true.

The New Birth Yielding New Hope

Menno Simons, early Anabaptist leader in the Netherlands, considered the new birth (1 Pet 1:3, 23) of such importance that he wrote one of his most vigorous treatises on the subject (ca. 1537). The full title of his writing is: *The New Creature: A Fair and Fundamental Instruction from the Word of the Lord, Urgently Admonishing All Men Who Call Themselves Christians to Seek the Heavenly Birth and the New Creature, Without Which No Man Who Has Come to Years of Understanding Is or Can Be a True Christian.*

This ponderous title summarizes an emphasis pivotal in Menno's theology and ethics. He writes, "This regeneration of which we write, from which comes the penitent, pious life which has the promise, can only originate in the Word of the Lord, rightly taught and rightly understood and received in the heart by faith through the Holy Ghost." Of those who have experienced this truly, he claims,

> Hatred and vengeance they do not know, for they love those who hate them; they do good to those who despitefully use them and pray for those who persecute them. . . . They feed the hungry, give drink to the thirsty. They entertain the needy, release prisoners, visit the sick, comfort the fainthearted, admonish the erring, are ready after their Master's example to give their lives for their brethren. . . . They are the children of peace who have beaten their swords into plowshares and their spears into pruning hooks, and know war no more. (Menno: 93-94)

Much of this treatise is polemical and goes into considerable detail concerning the moral implications of Christian faith and hope. Like Peter, Menno Simons sees the new birth as an action of God in the heart of those who respond with obedient faith to the Word of God. This is for him the experiential ground of authentic human hope.

Theology of Hope

Theologians through the ages have inquired into the meaning of faith, hope, and love. The "theology of hope" has been given special attention in recent decades. Many have participated in this process, and one of the most prominent is Jürgen Moltmann, a Reformed theologian, whose first decisive book, *Theology of Hope*, was published in German in 1964 and translated into English in 1967. Later, on October 11, 1982, as guest theological lecturer at the Associated Mennonite Biblical Seminaries in Elkhart, Indiana, he shared his spiritual pilgrimage.

Moltmann told of his involvement as a German youth in World War II, witnessing the death of several of his army comrades, and experiencing personal despair:

At that point there were a few of my comrades who—later on I found out they were devoted Christians—helped me to build up a new strength of life, a new power of survival. I called this hope. So the first experience of a rebirth to life and to the will to survive came to me—thanks to a hope for which there was no visible evidence in this camp at all. Only a few other persons witnessed to me that there is a God in whom I can trust and whose promise is trustworthy. (Moltmann, 1983:11)

He tells even more of his story in prison camp in "Wrestling with God," an address given at Norton Camp fifty years later (Moltmann, 1997:1-9). After obtaining a copy of a Bible, he first began to read the Psalms, especially Psalm 39. Step by step, his faith and his hope grew. From this turning point in the life of Jürgen Moltmann came a highly productive ministry as a theologian, teacher, and author whose "theology of hope" has had worldwide impact. For Moltmann, as for Peter, the resurrection of Jesus Christ remains a central point of departure. He writes, "The Christian hope for the future comes of [from] observing a specific unique event—that of the resurrection and appearing of Jesus Christ" (Moltmann, 1967:194).

In *The Source of Life*, Moltmann retells his story of the awakening of hope in his life as "Wrestling with God." He recalls how while beginning to read the Bible,

I came to the story of the passion, and when I read Jesus' death cry, "My God, why have you forsaken me?" I knew with certainty: this is someone who understands you. I began to understand the assailed Christ because I felt he understood me: this was the dying brother in distress, who takes the prisoners with him on the way to the resurrection. I began to summon up the courage to live again, seized by a great hope. . . . This early fellowship with Jesus, the brother in suffering and the redeemer from guilt, has never left me since. (1997:5)

A later chapter is entitled "Born Again to a Living Hope," drawing directly on the language of 1 Peter. In this he notes that the birth imagery employed by Peter "suggests an image of the Holy Spirit which was quite familiar in the early years of Christianity, especially in Syria, but got lost in the empire of Rome: the image of the mother. If believers are born of the Holy Spirit, then we have to think of the Spirit as the 'mother' of believers and in this sense as a feminine Spirit" (1997:35). This perspective helps to give balance to the more common use Peter makes of God as "Father."

Henri J. M. Nouwen, widely read Roman Catholic writer, confirms the imperative of Christian hope for persons engaged in ministry:

While personal concern is sustained by a continuously growing faith in the value and meaning of life, the deepest motivation for leading our fellow man to the future is hope. For hope makes it possible to look beyond the fulfillment of urgent wishes and pressing desires and offers a vision beyond human suffering and even death. Hope prevents us from clinging to what we have and frees us to move away from the safe place and enter unknown and fearful territory.... It is an act of discipleship in which we follow the Lord, who entered death with nothing but bare hope. (76-77)

Walter Wink, in his three-volume study of the NT meaning of "The Powers," also struggles vigorously with the question of hope in the presence of human evil, especially as systemic domination. He seeks to unmask the evil power of domination and violence. In *Engaging the Powers*, he reaffirms the thesis that in Christ the destructive powers of oppressive human systems have been broken. Christians may and ought now to live as those who love their enemies and respond to evil with good, thus breaking the cycle of human abuse. History, he proclaims, belongs to the intercessors. "Intercession is spiritual defiance of what is, in the name of what God has promised" (Wink, 1992:292). This too is a contemporary expression of the living hope that Peter talks about.

Personal Pastoral Experience

The first Easter after the bombing of Pearl Harbor (1941) and the entry of the USA into World War II, a young pacifist pastor was serving the Bethel Mennonite Church in Mountain Lake, Minnesota. Struggling with the implications of the dark clouds of war both in Europe and in the Pacific, he sought words from God to interpret the meaning of the resurrection of Christ for that situation. Over fifty years later one of the persons present on that April 5, 1942, sent this former pastor, now retired, a summary of what she heard that day. That message served to sustain her in Christian hope not only through the war years but later as well:

There Will Be Another Dawn

The day in which we live seems to be another "Good Friday" in the world. All that is good and true and pure, it seems, is being nailed to the cross. A sinister darkness has enveloped the earth, and the lights of hope are going out one after another. Men's hearts are full of fear and pessimism. And while the world is on the brink of ruin, we stand by, helpless and confused.

How good it is to remember in this Easter Season that "on the third day Jesus rose from the dead." On the first "Good Friday" the truly Good, and True, and Pure, yes, the Son of God, was nailed to an old rugged cross. Then, too, there was darkness upon the earth while sinners scoffed and believers stood by in helpless confusion.

On that third day there came a new Dawn to end that starless night. Death could not hold its prey. The angel's message rang out with new hope—"He lives." Tear-stained faces glowed with new hope, downcast eyes were lifted up to behold a risen Savior, brokenhearted men stood up with new courage. New life had come out of Death.

Before there could be an Easter, however, there had to be a "Good Friday." Before there can be New Life, there must be Death. Darkness precedes the dawn. But here is the glorious Easter message: THERE WILL BE ANOTHER DAWN when the dark night is ended and the King of Righteousness shall put His enemies under His feet and shall reign forever. (E. Waltner in Pankratz)

1:13—2:3

The Changed Lifestyle of Hope

PREVIEW

In 1:1-12 Peter has greeted his readers and reminded them of God's renewing action in their lives, giving them a living hope. Now he begins to spell out some basic implications of this life of hope. From describing how things are, theologically, he now focuses on how things should be behaviorally.

The author exhorts his readers to have their minds firmly established in this hope. He calls them to holiness in their conduct (1:15), and to reverent fear in their walk (1:17). He asks them to show fervent love (1:22) and spiritual growth (2:1-3).

Christian hope, indeed, expresses itself in worship and praise. It also involves an inner transformation which, as a new birth, changes the outward life. Holiness, reverence, and love are the three major ethical qualities that Peter here uses to lay a solid groundwork for the further lofty patterns of faithful discipleship that he develops later in this letter.

OUTLINE

Hope Changes the Lifestyle, 1:13-21

1:13	The Alignment of the Mind
1:14-16	Obedient Children of a Holy God
1:17-21	Reverent Fear in Redeemed People

56

The Call to Holy Love, 1:22—2:3
    1:22-25   Heart with Loving Heart United,
                   Purified and Newborn
    2:1-3   Putting Off Malice; Craving Nourishment as Babes

EXPLANATORY NOTES

Hope Changes the Lifestyle 1:13-21

1:13 The Alignment of the Mind

An emphatic *therefore* introduces this major transition in the letter. The writer is referring back to all that he has said up to this point rather than just to the word on prophets and angels (1:10-12), or on the outcome of their faith as salvation (1:9). The word *therefore* leads into three imperatives, which appear as participles in the Greek: (1) *prepare your minds for action,* (2) *discipline yourselves, and* (3) *set all your hope on the grace that Jesus Christ will bring you when he is revealed.*

The first segment, also translated *Gird up the loins of your minds* (KJV), invokes a familiar metaphor. This recalls the experience of Israel in Exodus 12:11. The people were instructed to eat the Passover with "your loins girded." In Luke 12:35, Jesus calls for watchful alertness: "Be dressed for action and have your lamps lit." As a metaphor, it refers to arranging one's clothing so that action is not impeded, as in tucking in a flowing part of an outer garment. We might say, "Roll up your sleeves and get to work." Christian hope does impact the mind and frees it of impediments to Christian action.

The second segment uses language associated with avoiding drunkenness and is sometimes rendered, *Remain sober.* It has the force of calling into use the power of the mind, to give full attention to the reality at hand. The believers are to be awake and alert, keeping full control of their ability both to think and to act. Peter knows that various pressures bearing on the faith and life of the hearers can distract and confuse them. Only a disciplined mind, properly focused, can give them the stability and stamina they need. Peter uses the same expression also in 4:7 in speaking of the prayer life, and in 5:8 where he warns against the assaults of the devil. Disciplined awareness is another dimension of Christian hope.

The third segment expresses the essential point toward which the previous imperatives have moved. *Set all your hope on the grace that Jesus Christ will bring you when he is revealed.* Grammatically, this has the force of a directive or command, a call to complete trust. Here hope virtually takes the place of faith (Goppelt:

108). Peter calls for total confidence, not only in what God has already done but specifically in what God will yet do through Jesus Christ. The orientation is not only historical but also eschatological. Hope remembers the Exodus and the risen Jesus, but also anticipates Jesus Christ yet to be revealed. Hope has its basis in history, but its goal is in the future.

The central object of this hope is grace, the active love gift of God which pervades the whole letter (1:2, 10; 2:19-20; 3:7; 4:10; 5:5, 10, 12). The future of grace is even more glorious than its past. Peter wants his readers to be confident of this grace. On this grace, they are to build their ethical behavior.

1:14-16 Obedient Children of a Holy God

In marking out more specifically what Christian hope implies for the lifestyle of the believer, Peter uses the image of children. This is congruent with the concept of God as Father (1:2-3, 17) and the image of a new birth (1:3, 23). Speaking of groups of people metaphorically as *children* is common usage, as in references to "children of light" or "children of darkness" and similar expressions in the Qumran writings (Vermes: 126ff.).

What is striking here, however, is that Peter speaks of his hearers as *obedient* children, appealing to a positive self-image. Peter does not enjoin them to become obedient or to become holy. He speaks of them as already obedient and already holy because of their relationship to God.

Obedience is important in Peter's perspective. He has indicated that God's purpose for the hearers includes *obedience to Jesus Christ* (1:2). Moreover, he speaks of how their souls have already been purified by their *obedience to the truth* (1:22). He also refers to Sarah's *obedience* as a model of the holy women of old (3:6). Such obedience is now explained as involving both negative and positive dimensions. On one hand, it calls for a nonconformity to former desires which they had once followed in ignorance. On the other, it calls for a holy style of living.

A direct clue to the nature of these former desires and resulting lifestyles, which they are no longer to pursue, is given in 4:3. Peter speaks of *former licentiousness, passions, drunkenness, revels, and lawless idolatry,* in which they once engaged. Similarly, in 2:11 he enjoins them *to abstain from the desires of the flesh that war against the soul.* These are only examples of Peter's concern but reveal the kind of nonconformity to which Peter calls them. One implication of Peter's concept of human desires is that holiness has behavioral dimensions.

The content of the positive call to holy living, however, is more difficult to define. This call certainly does apply to the whole of life, not only selected segments. Peter's understanding of holy living is rooted in the very nature of God, who calls them to holiness. The Scripture from Leviticus (11:44-45; 19:2) is invoked as motivation. Peter is calling his readers to become Godlike in resisting evil desires, and Christlike in following the pattern of Jesus Christ (2:21), particularly in response to suffering.

Peter is clearly concerned about human conduct in history and not only about a hope that involves destiny beyond the earthly life. His word *conduct* recurs again and again in this letter (1:15, 17-18; 2:12; 3:1-2, 16). Some conduct may be futile in its yield (1:17) or good (2:12; 3:1) or even chaste (3:2), giving a witness to nonbelievers (2:12; 3:1), perchance winning them to Christian faith. This is not to be confused with salvation through good works, but rather as the expression of the newborn faith, hope, and love which transforms the believer.

To support and motivate response, the author invokes a basic OT principle from Leviticus (11:45; 19:2): *for it is written, "You shall be holy, for I am holy."* In appealing to this passage, Peter is using "one of the favorite passages in early Christian ethical teaching," possibly because Jesus alludes to it in Matthew 5:48. "In citing it, Peter sets his argument on firm ground" (Marshall: 69).

Coming from what is sometimes called the Holiness Code (Lev. 17–26), the passage quoted is directed to "Aaron and his sons, and to all the people of Israel" (17:2). While this may have had special significance for the OT priesthood, Peter here and elsewhere in this letter is using "priestly terms." He applies these to the whole people of the congregations to whom he is writing, not only to its leadership (Michaels: 60). The call to holy conduct applies to the whole people of God. David Schroeder notes, "Even those who are aliens, slaves, and women are called to be moral agents" (1997 comment on ms.).

1:17-21 Reverent Fear in Redeemed People

The call to a lifestyle of reverent fear is prefaced with the observation that the readers think and speak of God as *Father.* That practice reaches back into the OT but was given new emphasis and meaning by Jesus, including his instruction to pray, "Our Father . . ." (Matt. 6:9). This fits the preceding image of being children (1:14) and having been born anew (1:3) and anticipates being *born of imperishable seed* (1:23).

The conditional clause introducing 1:17 can be rendered with *if,* for contingency, or with *since,* indicating an ongoing practice. As in the NIV, the second option is preferred because the issue here is not raising a question about their practice, but describing a practice which has implications for their lifestyle (Achtemeier: 124).

Since they call God *Father,* however, they are to be aware that God is also *judge* and, indeed, an impartial one. A judge discerns right from wrong, truth from falsehood, integrity from deception. Their confessions of faith and also the shape of their conduct are open to this *Father-judge.* Hence, it is appropriate for Peter to call them to a life of reverent fear.

The word *fear* (*phobos*) is easily misunderstood. Its range of meanings include both negative nuances, such as being frightened or terrified, as well as positive, such as being reverent and filled with awe and wonder. Assuming that the writer is Peter, who had learned from Jesus the meaning of the word "Fear not" (Luke 5:10; 12:5), the positive meaning here is best understood in the sense of reverent fear.

As Goppelt (113) observes, this passage links together what belongs together, "hope for grace" (1:13) and fear (1:17). He notes, "The address 'Father' in prayer is the most direct expression of certainty about God that was transmitted from Jesus to the disciples according to the gospel tradition. . . . According to Paul (Rom. 8:15; Gal. 4:6), . . . the most important witness of the Spirit for one's relationship to God [is] the witness that summons one to freedom from fear." Since Jewish children were taught to respect their fathers, it is possible, as Michaels (61) suggests, that Peter is here extending this perspective to those who call God "Abba" or "Father."

The deeper motivation for a lifestyle characterized by reverent fear, however, is awareness of the high cost of their new freedom in Christ (2:16). Here Peter introduces the image of redemption by way of a *ransom* to indicate how they have come into this new freedom which is theirs. This image also comes from Jesus. In Mark 10:45 he speaks of the Son of Man giving his life a *ransom* for many.

The concern here is not to develop a particular theory of the atonement but rather to emphasize *from what* they have been redeemed and *at what cost.* They have been set free from a former way of life that is (1) inherited from their fathers, and (2) is empty or futile. Already in 1:14, Peter has spoken of the passions of their former ignorance. In 4:3-4 he goes into some detail about their former way of life. The focus here may well be on the past of those who have been Gentiles. Yet Jewish Christians are also aware of the emptiness and futility of a life not yet been made free through Christ. A lifestyle not redeemed by Christ needs transformation both in orientation and in substance, a change of inward and outward dimensions.

This has happened for the readers, but now Peter reminds them at what cost this has become possible. He does this by dramatically contrasting Christ's redeeming death on the cross with material valuables (1:18-20):

> You were ransomed, . . .
> not with perishable things like silver or gold,
> but with the precious blood of Christ,
> like that of a lamb without defect or blemish.

The concept of redemption through costly action is pervasive in the OT (I. H. Marshall: 71). Here Peter applies it directly to what happened to Jesus in the crucifixion. This fits with an early and extensive tradition in the early church, as reflected in the NT (Mark 10:45; Rom. 3:24; 1 Cor. 1:30; Eph. 1:7; Col. 1:14; 1 Tim. 2:6; Titus 2:14; Heb. 9:12, 15). The particular imagery Peter uses appeals to regulations concerning the Passover lamb in Exodus 12:5 and to language from Isaiah 52–53 (also used in 1 Pet. 2:22-25). The central concern of Peter is not to construct a full doctrine of the atonement, but to signal the great cost of redemption so as to evoke reverent fear.

Peter elaborates further elements of his Christology in 1:20-21. Two foundational elements are identified as follows:

> He was destined before the foundation of the world,
> but was revealed at the end of time for your sake.

To speak of Jesus Christ as destined or predestined reflects the perspective of 1:2, where Peter speaks of Christian believers as *chosen and destined*. It anticipates what he says in 2:8 about unbelievers being *destined* to stumble in their disobedience. But in this passage, the focus is on Jesus Christ as having been destined, not simply as the preexistent One to come into the world, but to take a particular redeeming role at great cost. *The foundation of the world* (cf. Matt. 23:35b; Luke 11:50; John 17:5, 24) is essentially "from all eternity" (Michaels: 62) or "from the beginning of time." This perspective concerning an eternal design of God is widely represented in the NT (Rom. 16:25f.; 1 Cor. 2:7; Eph. 3:9; Col. 1:26; Titus 1:2; cf. Best: 91).

Moreover, the "revealing" or "appearing" of Jesus Christ in history in the fulfillment of his destiny has particular significance for hearers of this letter. The incarnation in human history has come within the framework of God's eternal purpose. Peter particularizes this by declaring that it is *for your sake.*

This is further elaborated in 1:21, where Peter reminds the hearers that their own experience of Christian faith and hope has indeed come as a response to God's action in raising Jesus from the dead and giving him glory. This may well reflect early Christian liturgy in which the resurrection and triumph of Christ are joined together as a single action of God (Best: 91). Peter's purpose here, however, is not to develop a full-orbed Christology but to provide a profound and comprehensive grounding in God's eternal purpose for the holy lifestyle to which he is calling them.

Peter speaks of both *faith* and *hope.* While the two are closely related in tradition and experience, for Peter they are not identical. Faith generally means a trust relationship that binds the believer to the one or One in whom this trust is placed. Hope generally implies trust in relation to one's future. However, as Michaels (70) notes, "In 1 Peter, faith no less than hope is pointed toward the future, and hope no less than faith is a response to God's work of redemption through Christ (v. 3) and governs the conduct of Christians in the present (3:15-16)."

The Call to Holy Love 1:22—2:3

With Goppelt and others, we may observe continuity from 1:22 to 2:3, across the chapter division after 1:25. Peter has called his hearers to activate Christian hope with conduct that is both obedient (1:14) and reverent (1:17). Now he calls his readers to holy love in human relationships, especially within their community of faith. Those who see baptism as a central focus in 1 Peter, identify 1:22 with the moment of baptism. Yet 1:22 is better understood as a turning point that introduces the all-important theme of Christian love. This passage speaks both of "brother-love" or "family-love" (*philadelphia*) and of *agapē* love, but not as a contrast.

In a profound sense, Peter is here calling them to the fundamental ethic which begins with love within the community. He moves on to neighbor love and finally to love of enemy, a distinctive marker of the community of hope and love. Piper, in "Hope as the Motivation of Love," has demonstrated how this theme and its structure in the subsequent passages move to a grand climax in 3:8-12 (1980: 212-231).

1:22-25 Heart with Loving Heart United,
Purified and Newborn

Peter now recognizes that God's work in the lives of his hearers has not only given them a new hope (1:3) but has also purified their souls. Peter uses this term to denote the whole person, in the sense of "your lives," not simply some part of it (Michaels; as also in 2:25; 4:19). This purification has come through their obedience to the truth, meaning the gospel. It is designed to bring them into a right relationship with each other, here spoken of as family or sibling love (*philadelphia*), literally "brotherly love."

This family love is characterized as *genuine mutual love*. It is *genuine*, without hypocrisy or pretense, as he also emphasizes in 2:1, where he urges that any remaining polluting traces of insincerity be put away. It is also mutual, for one another or reciprocal. This is what distinguishes "family love" from neighbor love (Goppelt: 123) and thus belongs to the family image which Peter is using.

The central imperative, however, is that they are to love each other *deeply from the heart*. This imperative is framed by two perfect participles, *purified* (1:22) and *born anew* (1:23). The two images represent two sides of the same experience. Goppelt observes, "As purification, this event saves them from all that has gone before; and as new birth, it opens a person to that which is new" (Goppelt: 126).

This purification is not ceremonial cleansing, as inferred by those who see 1 Peter as a baptismal sermon or a baptismal liturgy (Cross). Instead, it means cleansing lives of attitudes and practices that destroy right relationships (Michaels).

Obedience to the truth (1:22) is essentially an active faith response to the gospel, which Peter calls *the living and abiding word of God* (1:23). This is the word that has been preached to them (1:25).

Their response is to be not only attitudinal but also behavioral. The purification of their souls that this brought about has involved both an initial action, sometimes called justification, as well as a continuing process, sometimes called sanctification. *Souls* denotes whole persons rather than only the spiritual dimension of personhood. The perfect participles used show that something decisive has happened, with continuing impact. Nothing in life remains quite the same when this faith response to the gospel takes place.

What has been transformed is their relationship to each other as "family love" (*philadelphia*). Peter uses similar language in 2:17 and

5:9, applying it to the whole community of believers. In 3:8 he uses "family love" as an adjective to describe the attitude that members of this community should have to each other. The Greek root literally means persons coming out of the same womb, siblings, those who call one another brothers and sisters. This love is described as "sincere" and "unhypocritical," genuine and without pretense.

The emphasis on mutual love within the community, however, is not in 1 Peter contrasted with love for neighbor or even enemy, as was the case among the Essenes (Goppelt). Instead, "sibling love" is represented as extending "beyond the family" to neighbors and even to those who may abuse or hurt us, in line with the call of Jesus, "Love your enemies" (Matt. 5:45 = Luke 6:27).

While a decisive event has taken place, something more is needed. Peter shifts his language now to *agape*-love and calls for this to be *earnest* and *from the heart*. Earnestness has to do with fervency and depth. *From the heart,* "from the core of reflection and will" (Goppelt: 124-125), expresses essentially the notion of sincerity or genuineness. The Greek word, however, also includes the meaning of loving each other "unremittingly." Their affection for each other is to be "constant and enduring, unshaken by adversity or shifting circumstances" (Michaels: 76). Herein lies the greater challenge of Peter's call to holy love in the Christian community.

The exhortation to unremitting love in the community is reinforced and enabled by the image of the new birth through the living and abiding word of God. Peter supports this by an adapted quotation from Isaiah 40:4-6 that also contrasts the perishable and the imperishable. He has already used that kind of analogy in 1:18, where he spoke of how their redemption was grounded not on perishable gold or silver, but on the precious blood of Christ.

Here Peter speaks of *seed* (*spora*), using this term rather than the more common Greek word *sperm* (*sperma*), likely because he has the process of sowing in mind, as in the Isaiah passage. The seed is the word of God, characterized as living, creatively active, and abiding or enduring. This brings to mind the word of Isaiah, on transitory human history and beauty contrasted with the enduring Word of God. It also reminds us of the word of Jesus, "Heaven and earth will pass away, but my words will not pass away" (Mark 13:31; and *//*).

Thus Peter brings together the concept of constant "family love" and the notion of regeneration through the seed of the word of God. This new birth makes possible a community of hope. It also makes possible a community of mutual love, not based on a natural congeniality but on a life-giving process that enables people to keep on loving one another. As Goppelt (127) puts it, "The new 'I' is capable of demonstrating love since it is no longer [living] in a selfish direction but [living] for the One who called it forth." Michaels (80) comments, "[Peter] knows that brotherly affection among those who are not literally brothers and sisters is impossible without purification of the soul, and that mutual love even in a community of shared belief is impossible without the new birth of which Jesus had spoken in the Gospel tradition."

2:1-3 Putting Off Malice; Craving Nourishment as Babes

Moving from a general exhortation to practice constant community love, Peter now identifies several specific implications. Negatively, this calls for *putting off* attitudes and characteristics that destroy love in the community. Positively, this calls for continuing spiritual growth that comes through craving and receiving proper spiritual nourishment, *pure spiritual milk.*

When speaking of that which interferes with love in the community, Peter uses the image of *putting off* as one might put off an unfit garment. James (1:21) and Paul (Eph. 4:31) likewise use the same image. Peter's list of what is to be discarded includes the following:

- *all malice,*
- *all guile,*
- *insincerity,*
- *envy,* and
- *all slander.*

Malice includes all ill will, a general attitude contrary to the atmosphere and ethic of love. *Guile* means deceitful practices. (Peter, quoting Isaiah, later says that Jesus was entirely without *guile:* 2:22.) *Insincerity* is the practice of hypocrisies, pretense. James Denny once called *envy* "the last sin to die in the Christian community" (cf. Barclay: 225). More recently René Girard, speaking of "mimetic desire" and "mimetic rivalry," has identified envy as a root cause of human conflict and violence. One wants what another has, either in material or spiritual gifts (cf. Wink, 1992:145). *Slander* has to do with the practice of "putting one another down," as through put-downs in human interaction and conversation. Barclay (225) calls this "gossiping disparagement." None of the above attitudes or actions belongs in the loving Christian community. All are to be eliminated.

Such a high goal for loving community, however, is not achieved by either command or aspiration. Such movement comes only through grace and spiritual growth. This in turn can happen only with unadulterated spiritual nourishment. Peter next introduces the image of *pure spiritual milk*. They are to *long* or *crave* for such milk continually and intensely. Then he uses images of growing (2:2b) and tasting (2:3). These images are not uncommon in the language of early Christians (Goppelt: 129).

Pure spiritual milk in 2:2 refers to *the living and enduring word of God* (1:23), which Peter identifies with the *good news* that has been preached to them (1:25b). The Greek word for *spiritual* (2:2) is from the root *logos,* "word," and leads to three possible meanings: (1) milk of the word of God (Kelly: 85), (2) rational milk (as common with Greek philosophers), or (3) *spiritual milk*, as in NRSV. This living and enduring word of God, identified as "the gospel," is further defined in 2:3 as Christ. Peter draws on Psalm 34:8, "O taste and see that the Lord is good," and applies it to Jesus Christ. In the following passage, he continues to speak of Christ as central to the purposes of God in human history. Michaels (88-89) discerningly observes that not only milk but also blood, water, and wine are all used as images of the life God has given us in Jesus Christ. "The medium by which the milk is received is the proclaimed message of the gospel, but the milk itself is more appropriately interpreted as the sustaining life of God given in mercy to his children."

That you may grow into salvation refers to the purpose of this nourishment. The phrase *into salvation* (2:2), not in the later Greek text on which the KJV is based, is in current English versions using earlier manuscripts. At this point Peter drops the metaphorical and returns to eschatological language. He speaks here of *salvation* or "deliverance" in the perspective of its completion. Here, as also in 1:9, *salvation* is future rather than present.

In the movement from regeneration to the completion of salvation, growth is not only hoped for but is an essential process. As process, salvation is possession and promise. It has a past, a present, and a future dimension. We have been saved, are being saved, and will be saved. Therefore, salvation is not to be understood in only one time dimension. One may speak of its beginning for the believer, a continuing journey on which the believer travels, and a completion yet to be realized.

According to Michaels, Goppelt, and others, *if you have tasted that the Lord is good* should be treated as a first-class conditional sentence, which assumes a positive situation: indeed they have tasted the goodness of God, and of Jesus Christ. The word for *goodness* (*chrestos*) may be used here as a pun, linked with Christ (*christos*) (Best: 99). Instead of inviting the readers to *taste* the Lord, Peter is actually reminding them of the goodness of the Lord that they have already experienced. This goodness should keep on stimulating their spiritual appetite and prompt them to keep on coming to Christ, as he exhorts in 2:4. Peter is remembering rather than quoting Psalm 34:8. In 3:10-12, Peter comes back to the same psalm.

THE TEXT IN BIBLICAL CONTEXT

The Linkage of Hope and Holiness

Biblically, hope and holiness are linked, and not only in 1 Peter. The linkage identified in Leviticus is invoked in the Petrine text itself. Israel as the people of God is not only called to obedience but was to understand itself as a people of promise. The covenant promise to Abraham, Isaac, and Jacob was to become a paradigm for Israel. The model of father and child means that the child is to manifest characteristics of the parent. So also Israel, as a people of hope because of the covenant, was to reflect moral qualities of their forebears and ultimately of God.

Likewise, the Pauline tradition links hope and holiness in Romans 12:1-2. Readers are warned not to be conformed to the world, but to be transformed by the renewing of their minds. This inward transformation has outward expression. Hence, Paul enjoins them to present their bodies as a living sacrifice. The chapter continues to call the Romans to a life of nonretaliating love and peace. That indeed does not conform to this world.

The Johannine tradition reflects a similar perspective. First John 3:2-3 says, "Beloved, we are God's children now; what we will be has not yet been revealed. What we do know is this: when he is revealed, we will be like him, for we will see him as he is. And all who have this *hope* in him purify themselves, just as he is pure."

The Concern for Human Conduct

While the concern for human conduct is common in 1 Peter, it is also broadly characteristic of NT Christianity and beyond. It finds expression in what is commonly called *paraenesis,* "counsel." The word refers to a literary genre of moral instructions aimed at changing the audience's behavior. Such paraenesis appeared throughout the Near East and was commonly used as a device for social formation and control (Thuren: 17). Some scholars try to identify subcategories of paraenesis. However, a broader definition is preferred, including "exhortation and admonition, aimed at affecting the audience's attitudes and behaviour" (Thuren: 18).

Such exhortation is common in the NT epistolary writing, especially Pauline. It is also prevalent in the Gospels and in apocalyptic writing. Grammatically, paraenesis is often expressed by the use of the imperative mode or the use of conjunctions such as "so then" or "therefore." Martin Dibelius considered virtually the whole of the book of James as paraenesis (Thuren: 17), with its emphasis, "Be doers of the word, and not merely hearers who deceive themselves" (1:22).

Of the many Pauline illustrations, note Romans 12:1: "I appeal to you therefore, brothers and sisters, by the mercies of God, to present your bodies as a living sacrifice, holy and acceptable to God, which is your spiritual worship." Or 1 Corinthians 15:58: "Therefore, my beloved, be steadfast, immovable, always excelling in the work of the Lord."

Likewise, Hebrews 12:1 exhorts, "Therefore, since we are surrounded by so great a cloud of witnesses, let us also lay aside every weight and the sin that clings so closely, and let us run with perseverance the race that is set before us." An example from the Johannine writings would be 1 John 4:11, "Beloved, since God loved us so much, we also ought to love one another."

Thuren analyzes the whole of 1 Peter as a significant example of early Christian *paraenesis.* The letter is so deeply concerned about the attitudes and behaviors of believers in response to the hostility and suffering they are experiencing.

Mutual Love in the Faith Community

The call to mutual family love within the faith community is deeply rooted in the Bible and especially in the NT. The expressions "brotherly love" and "love one another" are virtually synonymous. Paul speaks of *philadelphia* to the Thessalonians as something they do not need to have explained since God has taught them to do this (1 Thess. 4:9). In Hebrews, the writer urges simply that this continue among his readers (13:1). First John insists that loving one another (3:11, 23; 4:7, 11-12) and loving the brother or sister (2:10; 3:10, 14; 4:20-21) are essential relational qualities of those who participate in God's love.

Like Peter, other NT writers insist that such mutual love be genuine and not an imitation (Rom. 12:9; 2 Cor. 6:6). This profoundly echoes the teaching of Jesus in the Gospel of John that *agape*-love, a self-giving love that values another as much as or more than oneself, is to be the distinguishing mark of the community of disciples

(13:34-35). This strong active mutual love within the community of faith is to move out beyond the immediate community, to reach neighbors and even enemies, as Jesus also taught (Matt. 5:43-48; Luke 6:27-36).

Putting Off Unfit Garments

When Peter seeks to motivate mutual love in the community, he speaks of putting off unfit garments. This imagery occurs elsewhere in the NT. James 1:21, Ephesians 4:25, and Hebrews 12:1 use the same basic metaphor. Sometimes the positive form of this image is used, as in Ephesians 4:25, where readers are enjoined to "put off" or "get rid of" the old and to "put on Christ." For the positive dimension, see also James 1:21, Colossians 3:8, and Ephesians 4:31 (cf. Zech. 3:1-5; Isa. 61:10).

In 1 Peter 2:1-3 the positive dimension, "put on Christ," comes in another form, in the call to *crave spiritual milk so that by it you may grow into salvation.* This comes in a context where the focus moves from the word of the living God to an invitation to keep coming to Jesus Christ, the living stone. Hence, Peter's call fits Paul's plea to "put on Christ."

Milk as Spiritual Nourishment

In 1 Corinthians 3:1-2, Paul uses the image of milk to speak of the basic elements of the gospel needed before the new believer is ready for "solid food." A similar usage appears in Hebrews 5:13. Such a distinction is not made in 1 Peter 2:2. Yet in all these passages, the concern for growth through proper nourishment finds expression. Goppelt notes that the image in 1 Peter recalls some passages in the *Odes of Solomon* as well as some Essene texts in the Dead Sea Scrolls. Thus the language was not confined to the Christian community. This, however, does not prove direct borrowing of this image from Hellenism or from mystery religions, as some have inferred.

Broadly, the image of infants craving pure milk is in harmony with the image of new birth and the anticipated continuation of new life through nourishment, anticipating growth as maturation. It is a multidimensional metaphor with a powerful spiritual application.

THE TEXT IN THE LIFE OF THE CHURCH

Holiness and Discipleship

Alan Kreider, in *Journey Towards Holiness: A Way of Living for God's Nation,* explores the relationship between a Wesleyan understanding of holiness and an Anabaptist understanding of discipleship. He also seeks to bring together the personal and the social dimensions of the biblical call to holiness. In the foreword, Howard S. Snyder, a representative of the Wesleyan tradition, notes that John Wesley stressed personal holiness and "social holiness." Wesley taught "that one can experience true Christianity only in fellowship with other believers. The ideal of holiness is not solitary saints, Wesley argued, but holy community" (in Kreider: 9). This perspective Kreider shares, and he applies it further to the responsibility of Christian communities living in a secular and pagan world.

While 1 Peter 2:9, echoing Exodus 19:6, speaks of believers as "a holy nation," 1 Peter 1:14-15 is the decisive text. "This is where the action is," says Kreider (36). "Mysteriously but potently, God is using this puny but transnational nation to bless the entire creation. Other nations including the mighty Roman empire could be his tools for a time. But he has entrusted his project to the 'holy nation' that he has chosen. Through it he will prepare the way for the holy city."

At the level of transforming personal encounter with Holy Scripture, Katie Funk Wiebe writes of her experience with a devotional reading based on 1 Peter 1:16, *Ye shall be holy, for I am holy* (Revised Version, 1881). "Continually restate to yourself what the purpose of life is. The destined end of [humankind] is not happiness nor health, but holiness." For her, these were the right words coming at the right time. She bears witness, "That day my weak faltering faith received strength. My aimless feet were put on course. My ambitionless life was given a goal. A lost sheep was found. A rebellious spirit yielded to the Master. Godliness, not getting blessings from God, was God's goal for my life" (Wiebe in Koontz: 186).

The Way to the City of Peace

C. J. Dyck in *Spiritual Life in Anabaptism* includes "The Way to the City of Peace," a conversation between Jan and Pieter Pietersz, representing two pilgrims in dialogue. Pietersz, a Waterlander Dutch Mennonite, was reacting against the frequent use of excommunication and banning by other Dutch Mennonites. In his appeal for high ethical living and especially for generous giving to those in need, he uses 1 Peter 1:19. "Particularly since they know the love and faithfulness of their Lord, who has bought them with his own blood in love, that drives these citizens to share this love with others" (Dyck: 246). Later he uses this same verse as a basis for encouraging the pilgrim on the way of trust. Jan says, "Yes, my friend, let us have courage and believe in the promises, acknowledging the true offering of the innocent Lamb and his blood, which is shed for the forgiveness of our sins" (Dyck: 260).

In early Dutch Anabaptism, Dirk Philips and Menno Simons tried so hard to establish a pure church, leading to many instances of excommunication. Another movement developed, the "Waterlanders," emphasizing unity and peace. "Love, clear teaching, and compassion replaced the ban. An emphasis on spiritual guidance replaced a legalistic reading of the Scriptures" (Dyck: 231). In the "City of Peace" dialogue of the pilgrims, Jan and Pieter, Jan appeals to 1 Peter 1:22—2:3 to underscore the necessity of the new birth. He describes the newborn as those who

> are not selfish in the smallest things, or concerned for their own wealth as merchants, but for the general welfare. Therefore, in the City of Peace their works benefit the entire body; they have one heart and one soul among each other (Acts 2:45; 4:32). Their buying and selling is simple, without deception, or scheming, where, at the least, no one seeks to undermine or gain advantage over another, treating others as they would want to be treated themselves (1 Pet. 2:1; Matt. 7:12). (Dyck: 254)

Nourishment for Maturity

It is common to bemoan a growing biblical illiteracy in the church. The Bible is disregarded and not even known. When people yearn for love to prevail in the church and in the world, the effective source of such love seems to be absent. Spiritual lives are anemic and ineffective, in part because the sources of mutual love have been forgotten. The serious reading of Scripture has too often been left to biblical scholars and theologians.

In the later Middle Ages, Geert Groote (1340-1384) came to be called the Fountain of Modern Devotion. He was an intellectual who sensed the limitations of academic theology. Groote began an "unwavering emphasis upon the use of the Bible in Christian formation," including the laity. In contrast to others, "Groote applied a simple devotional use of the Bible, approaching once again that of Augustine, in which the biblical text as the Word of God (*verbum Dei*) became the source of meditation or, in the technical language of monasticism, 'rumination' for Christian living." He held that "the inherent texture of Scripture was meant to stimulate the twofold love of God and neighbor. In short, the Bible itself stood as the vehicle of growth in the Christian life." Later this developed into such movements as the Deventer Brethren of the Common Life (Maas and O'Donnell: 112-113).

This emphasis on the devotional use of Scripture, combined with the influence of Thomas à Kempis in his book *Of the Imitation of Christ,* thus blended the vertical quest to love God with the horizontal practice of serving the neighbor. Both streams drew heavily on concepts in 1 Peter. Integrated together, they became a new emphasis in the history of spirituality (Maas and O'Donnell: 120-128).

2:4-10

The Community of Hope

PREVIEW

Peter has just testified how through the resurrection of Jesus Christ, believers have been born anew into a living hope, expressing holy obedience, reverent fear, and mutual love. From exhortations with both individual and social implications, Peter now speaks more directly of the believers' corporate life as a community of hope. He does not use the language of church (*ekklēsia*), as common in Ephesians. Yet he uses the images of growth and building, which Paul also uses. Peter interweaves images of house (*oikos*) or household with images of priesthood and peoplehood. Fluidity rather than precision mark his use of images. Central, however, is the place of Jesus Christ, Christology explicated by use of the central image of "the stone" that draws on numerous OT Scriptures.

Translators and commentators differ on whether this passage is to be read as indicative (descriptive) or imperative (command). Yet there is no significant conflict over the theological or ethical interpretation. This commentary, following the NRSV, assumes the imperative.

Here Peter seeks to help his readers understand who they are as a new house or household of God, made up of "living stones" built on Jesus Christ, the Living Stone. They are to be a people of God with a royal priestly function in the world. Michaels suggests, plausibly, that the original intention is to give mostly Gentile converts to Christianity a sense of continuity with "a Jewish identity." As Paul pleads in Ephesians, Gentile believers are indeed also "the people of God." This is one of the seminal passages from which the church in history, especially the Anabaptist-Mennonite tradition, has drawn significant strands of self-understanding.

OUTLINE

Come to the Living Stone, 2:4-5

As Understood in Scripture, 2:6-8

You Are God's Own People, 2:9-10

EXPLANATORY NOTES

Come to the Living Stone 2:4-5

The text begins with a strong and warm invitation to *come* (an imperative participle) and to keep on coming to Jesus Christ, here called *a living stone*, echoing OT Scriptures. Striking in this passage are OT quotations and allusions, used in midrashic style, with freedom of interpretation. The image of the stone is a significant linkage in the passages used from Isaiah 28:16; Psalm 118:22; and Isaiah 8:14. Later, the image shifts to peoplehood and employs references to Exodus 23:22; 19:5-6; Isaiah 43:20-21; and finally Hosea 1:6, 9; 2:1, 23.

The metaphor *living stone*, which Peter applies first to Jesus Christ and then also to Christian believers, is truly daring in the sense that a stone is not naturally associated with life. The Greek word *lithos* here does not mean natural rock, but rather a stone that has been hewn and dressed, readied for use in construction. The metaphor is also characteristically Petrine, who speaks of *living* hope (1:3), and of the *living* word of God (1:23). The use of *living* in this metaphor suggests the life-giving and life-nurturing quality of Jesus Christ, as in 1 Corinthians 10:4, where Paul calls Christ "the spiritual rock."

Peter immediately introduces a contrast that provides a framework for his later affirmations. Christ as *living stone* is the One *rejected by mortals yet chosen and precious in God's sight*. The *living stone*, then, is a *rejected* stone but becomes the *chosen* stone, the *precious* stone. In this passage it is not a Jewish rejection of Jesus Christ that is in view so much as the Greco-Roman rejection of Jesus, the neighbors of the Christian believers to whom Peter is writing (Achtemeier: 161).

Then Peter applies the same image to the Christian believers themselves. He enjoins them, *Like living stones, let yourselves be built into a spiritual house.* This is the horizontal dimension of *coming to him.* Coming to Jesus Christ is for Peter not only an individual conversion. It also includes becoming part of a household and of a people. Metaphorically, it is a process of being incorporated into a structure, a household, a community. Here speaking of becoming a house or home stands in contrast to their experience as *aliens and exiles* (2:11) in the world. In a world in which they are "not at home," they not only have a true spiritual home but are themselves, as a community, to be "a home for the homeless" (Elliott: 1981).

A somewhat similar approach to corporate life is discernible in *The Manual of Discipline* from Qumran, which speaks of its community as "a House of Holiness for Israel." Yet there is no warrant to assume direct dependence (Gaster: 39-60; Goppelt: 96). Much more likely in Peter's awareness were the words of Jesus, "On this rock I will build my church" (Matt. 16:18), as well as rebuilding the temple in Mark 14:58 (= Matt. 26:61), and the building image used at the close of the Sermon on the Mount (Matt. 7:24-27).

The Christian community as a *spiritual house* is then further described as a *priesthood,* assigned to offer up *spiritual sacrifices.* In this context, the word *spiritual* means "nonmaterial" in both occurrences. Peter is speaking metaphorically. But it is also likely that he embraces the notion of Paul to mean "the house where the Spirit of God dwells" (Eph. 2:21-22) and where "sacrifices" have moved beyond OT practices. In this passage, the mixture of the images of household and temple shows Peter's freedom in using both images and biblical passages or allusions.

Peter calls them *to be a holy priesthood* and *offer spiritual sacrifices acceptable to God through Jesus Christ.* This calling defines further who they are and what they are to be doing. Later he speaks of them as *a royal priesthood, a holy nation* (2:9). The designation of the community of faith as a *priesthood* touches a major debate of the Reformation concerning the meaning of "the priesthood of all believers." While this expression is often used to indicate the right of direct access to God, Peter's purpose here, instead, is to denote a function, a ministry, or a service. As understood in the NT, the *spiritual sacrifices* include both the function of worship and prayer, as well as the function of ministry and service (Rom. 12:1; Heb. 13:15-16). The whole of the Christian community is to be involved in this worship and in service, prayer, and ministry.

As Understood in Scripture 2:6-8

Peter wants to undergird and support the call to keep coming to Jesus Christ and to be built up into a spiritual temple. Hence, he now invokes Scripture drawn from the Psalms and Isaiah. In verse 6 he draws in Isaiah 28:16, also used by Paul in Romans 9:33. He uses the passage freely, drawing some elements now found in the Septuagint (Greek) and some in the Masoretic Text (Hebrew), but quoting neither exactly.

Peter retains the image of *cornerstone* to indicate that the church is built on Christ, as foundation, which Paul also emphasizes in 1 Corinthians 3:11: "For no one can lay any foundation other than the one that has been laid; that foundation is Jesus Christ." In this image, Jesus Christ is both foundation stone and cornerstone, the stone from which the building derives its proper angles. An alternate reading of "capstone" or "keystone" in place of *cornerstone* is unlikely, since in Peter's imagery Christ as *stone* is also one over whom unbelievers *stumble.*

Again Peter is stressing the chosenness and the preciousness of Christ, in contrast with the devaluation heaped on Jesus by those who rejected him. However, Peter's special concern may well be to emphasize the final phrase: *Whoever believes in him will not be put to shame,* following the Septuagint rendering. This is a way of assuring vindication for believers who are currently suffering and experiencing demeaning treatment from others, possibly recalling Psalm 34:5b, since the same psalm is again quoted in 3:10-12.

To you who believe he is precious renders the original in a traditional way, applying the preceding verse to Jesus. However, as Michaels proposes, it could also be translated, "The honor belongs to you who believe." The experience of believers is being identified with the experience of Jesus Christ. Even as Christ experienced both rejection and reclamation, so it is with those who trust in Jesus. This interpretation is strengthened by the contrast in the second part of the verse: *But for those who do not believe . . .* The experience of believers is being contrasted with that of unbelievers, and not only their view of Jesus Christ. The emphasis on *believe* has to do not only with mental assent, but with trusting to the point of building a lifestyle in congruence with Jesus Christ.

To elaborate on the contrast between believers and unbelievers, Peter adapts Psalm 118:22 (also used in Matt. 21:42) and Isaiah 8:14 (also used in Rom. 9:33). Psalm 118:22, probably an early proverb, was applied first to Israel, then to Jesus, and now also, by implication, to Christian believers. What was once scorned has been given a place of decisive importance.

God has given to Jesus Christ universal significance. Hence, those who reject Christ by not building their lives on him, experience offense in Christ. "Either one sees and becomes 'a living stone,' or one stumbles as a blind person over Christ and comes to ruin, falling short, i.e., of one's Creator and Redeemer and thereby of one's destiny" (Goppelt: 146). In 2:8b Peter explains theologically that unbelief becomes *disobedience,* its destiny. "Rejection of the gospel message is, therefore, a responsible act of the will, disobedience, and blindness from God" (Goppelt: 147).

You Are God's Own People 2:9-10

Peter has invited his readers to keep coming to Jesus and to allow themselves to be built up into a living, worshiping, and serving household of God. He has supported and motivated his hearers through Scripture. Now Peter reminds them once more, in a grand summary, who they really are and what they are to be doing.

In contrast to the stumbling and disobedient in society, Peter describes his readers with at least four basic images:

- *a chosen race,*
- *a royal priesthood,*
- *a holy nation,* and
- *God's own people.*

These images come directly from Exodus 23:22 (cf. 19:5-6) and Isaiah 43:20-21. Goppelt helpfully observes how the terms *race* (*genos*), *nation* (*ethnos*), and *people* (*laos*) are used side by side, suggesting three perspectives: Peter "characterizes a people having a common origin, describes a people with the same customs, and represents a people pursuing a common goal" (148).

Essentially, Peter is using terms traditionally applied to Israel. Now he extends the application to include the believers in Asia Minor who are mostly of Gentile background. Peter's emphasis is not on contrasting the Old Israel and the New Israel, but rather on declaring the inclusiveness of the true Israel of faith.

They are *a chosen race* even as Christ had been chosen by God to be the foundation and cornerstone of God's house. The word *race* as used here differs significantly from modern usage in which differentiation of skin color rather than common origin is noticed. *Royal priesthood* follows Exodus 19:6 (*LXX*) and probably means the priesthood which belongs to God, the King (Michaels: 109). The term *nations*, used in 2:12 and 4:3 as a plural, generally means *Gentiles*, but here in the singular as *holy nation* it is a common NT term for true Israel.

Achtemeier suggests helpfully that Peter calls the church "a body of priests in the service of God their 'King,' to whom they owe their allegiance as his people" (165). This anticipates Peter's later concern about a proper relationship to a human emperor (2:13-17). *God's own people* recalls Isaiah 43:21 and likely includes not only the notion of special belonging, but also of special destiny. Michaels thus prefers to render it "people destined for vindication" (109). Taken together, this cluster of descriptive images constitutes a climax and provides a transition to his next declaration concerning mission.

The mission of this people of God is to *proclaim the mighty acts of God*, not only with their lips but also with the patterns of their lives. This becomes the thrust of his message in 2:11—3:12. Balch reads this mission primarily as "worship." Elliott reads it primarily as proclamation. But Michaels suggests it echoes Isaiah 43:21-22 and translates, "sound the praises," insisting that worship and proclamation, whether within or beyond the congregation, whether in word or in deed, all go together (Michaels: 110). This more comprehensive understanding is preferred.

Praises is explicated as the action of God calling people out of darkness into light. This is the worthy thing that God has done. Again this includes both God's call to salvation (5:10) and the call to holiness, including a life-sustaining pattern of behavior (1:15; 2:21; 3:9). *Darkness* here refers to their former ignorance (1:14) and futile traditions (1:17). Coming into *light* employs another common NT image for conversion (Acts 26:18; 2 Cor. 4:6; Col. 1:12). After conversion, believers are exhorted to "walk in the light" (Eph. 5:8-14; 1 Thess. 5:4-5; 1 John 1:5-7; 2:9-11).

The marvel and glory of this transformation in identity and morality is now underlined with a further interpretive use of imagery from Hosea 1:9 and 2:1. Peter rearranges the material for his own purposes, to draw a contrast between what was once and what is now. With a touch of irony, he emphasizes the great mercy of God in incorporating the Gentiles into "the people of God." Wayward Israel had been restored, and Hosea's unfaithful spouse had become the bearer of children and given a place of dignity and honor in the family. Likewise, they also as Gentiles are a reclaimed and restored people. Once indeed they were *not a people*, but now they are *God's people*. Once they had experienced being outside of *mercy,* but now they have experienced the restoring, life-giving, and transforming *mercy* of God in Jesus Christ, *the living stone*, on whom they are being built into a community of hope.

THE TEXT IN BIBLICAL CONTEXT
Bridge Between the Testaments

As much as any passage in 1 Peter, this text of 2:4-10 interweaves OT and NT. Peter does not emphasize the theme of fulfillment as much as points of continuity. Peter draws on Exodus, Psalms, Isaiah, and Hosea, on the Torah, the Prophets, and the Writings, to help his readers understand their continuity, not only with Jesus Christ, but with Israel as the people of God in history. His generous, free—and even audacious—use of biblical imagery portrays powerfully the flow of God's redemptive and reconstructive purposes.

Of eighteen clear allusions to the OT in 1 Peter, five of these are found in 1 Peter 2:4-10. These references include words and images, ideas and practices, history and prophecy. In this way Peter participates with other NT writers in helping readers recognize the basic unity of the biblical documents, in which the OT story not only provides a background for but also significantly helps shape the NT story (Swartley: 1994).

Images of Building Stones

Peter's use of the image of stones applied both to Jesus Christ and Christian believers is a dramatic characteristic of this passage. Yet this image is also found elsewhere in Scripture. Note, however, that the word used here is *lithos* and not *petros*. It may be homiletically tempting to try to connect this passage in 1 Peter with the Matthean record of Jesus saying to Peter, "You are Peter (*Petros*), and on this rock (*petra*) I will build my church" (Matt. 16:18). Linguistically, this is not appropriate, though the notion of "building" on a solid foundation is common to both passages.

The image of the building stone, however, does link the passages from Isaiah 28:16; Psalm 118:22; and Isaiah 8:14 with Matthew 21:42, 44; Mark 12:10; Luke 20:17-18. It also links Acts 4:11 with Romans 9:33 and 1 Peter 2:4-8. In each case, the writer exercises discernible freedom. John E. Toews has carefully traced the fluidity of the stone image in OT and rabbinic traditions, arguing that in Isaiah 28:16 it referred to "the law" rather than serving as a messianic passage. It was Jesus who began to apply this image to himself (Toews, 1977:184-200).

The synoptic Gospels use Isaiah 28:16 to conclude the Parable of the Wicked Tenants, forecasting the crucifixion of Jesus. Luke elaborates the image of the stone to include the notion of stumbling as well as of being crushed by a falling stone. In Acts 4:11, where Peter is defending himself before the Sanhedrin, he uses this same Scripture image to explain the preaching of the crucified and raised Christ in Jerusalem.

THE TEXT IN THE LIFE OF THE CHURCH
Christ Is Our Cornerstone

Since the fifth and sixth century, Christians have sung an anonymous lyric known as "Christ Is Our Cornerstone" (*Hymnal,* 43). This is based directly on 1 Peter 2:6. A contemporary hymn written by Marilyn Houser Hamm (1974) celebrates the use of the "stone image" applied to the community of faith:

> Behold the Lord has called His children His own,
> and with our risen Lord, we are living stones,
> [refrain begins] Living stones, living stones,
> to build up the kingdom, living stones, [refrain ends]
> Behold the Lord has called His children His own,
> to build up the kingdom, living stones.
>
> Behold what a pleasant and beautiful sight
> Are those who have come from darkness to light as [refrain]
> How happy are those come from darkness to light,
> to build up the kingdom, living stones.
>
> Weak and yet strong with the Spirit to lead,
> We are molded to oneness, a growing seed, [refrain]
> Molded to oneness, a growing seed,
> to build up the kingdom, living stones. (Schmidt: 60)

Anabaptist Stones

David Joris (1501-56), Dutch Anabaptist prophet from Delft, challenged some of the biblical literalism of Menno Simons. He uses the imagery of our text with dramatic force:

> The construction of the house of God, built on Mt. Zion, does not happen quickly. . . . So prepare your stones, namely, make your hearts level and straight. Become square and leveled, without flaws, without crack or blemish. Pay attention to this first. For when one builds a house from expensive, hewn stone, one does not first build the stone walls or the framework. But they are prepared, cut straight, planed level, prepared so they will fit. Whatever does not fit must be removed before one can bring together the pieces so that they can be butted together. Pay attention.

Now, therefore, O you stones, you believing hearts, allow yourselves to be well hewn, cleansed, leveled, and made fitting and square by the masons. Behold, if you do not do this, then you will not be able to have or maintain a place in the house of the Lord. . . . If you do not arrange yourselves next to the foundation stone, cornerstone, proofstone, and valuable elect cornerstone (1 Pet. 2:4-8), then you will have no place in the valuable work of God. (Dyck: 176-177)

The Church of the Savior

Elizabeth O'Connor in *Letters to Scattered Pilgrims* reveals that 1 Peter 2:9 played a significant role in the emergence and development of The Church of the Savior in Washington, D.C. She reports,

Since its beginning in 1947, the Church of the Savior in Washington, D.C., has been committed to the revolutionary concept of the priesthood of all believers. The church that takes that thought seriously must think of itself as a seminary to train laity for ministry in the world. A School of Christian Living has been basic to our implementation of the biblical teaching: You *are a chosen race, a royal priesthood, a consecrated nation, a people set apart . . .* (1 Pet. 2:9) The School's primary goal has been to help participants to exercise their gifts and to discover the work which each has been born to do. (xiii)

Five decades later, that expression of discipling Christianity still continues to live and bless many.

2:11—3:12

Christian Witness in Hostile Society

PREVIEW

Peter has proclaimed Christian hope and called believers to holy love lived out in Christian community. Now he shifts attention to the situation and calling of the church living in the midst of a pagan society. This society is not only without Christian faith but in various ways exhibits hostility toward believers, and sometimes is oppressive and abusive. In this larger section, 2:11—3:12, the writer gives both general guidelines and even specific counsel on how to respond as a missionary community in Christian witness.

First he addresses the whole community in general in 2:11-17, and then focuses on mistreated slaves (2:18-25) and vulnerable married persons (3:1-7). He concludes this section with another appeal to the entire community (3:8-12) before moving on to more direct teaching concerning the Christians' experience of suffering and their appropriate response (3:13—4:19).

This section is characterized by realistic awareness of the misunderstandings and hostility that the Christians of Asia Minor faced. They are victims of false accusations (2:12), and resident aliens of provinces and an empire in which their status is vulnerable (2:13-17). Slaves experience brutality and abuse (2:18-25), and wives are married to non-Christians (3:1-6). Husbands need to learn to live with consideration toward their wives, something they do not observe in pagan neighbors (3:7). Even in the church, they need to find ways of returning good for evil (3:8-12). Here then Peter moves the application of holy love beyond the Christian community, to include the love of neighbor, and the love of enemy.

At the strategic center of this challenging passage comes an exalted portrayal of the cross (2:21-25) and the call to follow Jesus in responding to unjust suffering (2:21; 3:9). This is the high calling of Christian believers. This passage, sometimes called Household Codes, is also punctuated with the repeated call to a voluntary subordination or deference to "fallen" orders. Hence, it also becomes one of the most controversial and challenging parts of 1 Peter. Some liberationist interpreters are inclined to dismiss the call of this larger passage as being oppressive to slaves and women. They ask us to recognize interpretations that have impeded and prevented or postponed the liberation of slaves and of women (Corley: 1994). These challenges need to be taken seriously. They also call for a rereading of the texts from a missionary perspective.

Another perspective is to see 1 Peter, including this section, as a letter intended to encourage and empower people to be and act Christian in their particular world. Peter has reminded believers of their new birth (1:3) and implications of this for their lifestyle (1:13). He has called them to be *holy* (1:15) even as God is holy. In this section, then, Peter addresses them as morally responsible persons, though in that social context, slaves and sometimes women were not perceived as morally responsible. Others, such as masters or husbands, were expected to make significant moral choices for them.

Peter, however, here addresses even slaves and women as *free people* (2:16), implying moral responsibility in various contexts (civil, workplace, and marriage). Persons considered morally powerless are encouraged and empowered to exercise their new being as followers of Jesus Christ, even when their behavior may be different from society's expectations.

OUTLINE

True Witness of Maligned Believers, 2:11-12

Witness as "Citizens" Under a Hostile State, 2:13-17

Witness as Mistreated Servants Following Jesus, 2:18-25
    2:18-20   The Situation of Mistreated Servants
    2:21-25   The Pattern of Responding: The Cross

Christian Witness in Marriage, 3:1-7
  3:1-6   Christian Wives of Unbelieving Husbands
  3:7   Christian Husbands Who Show Consideration

Witness of the Unified and Forgiving Community, 3:8-12

EXPLANATORY NOTES
True Witness of Maligned Believers 2:11-12

This passage is best understood as a general introduction to the section that continues to 3:12. Some see the section extending all the way to 4:11 (Michaels: 115). As basic exhortation, it includes dimensions both negative (*abstain*) and positive (*conduct yourselves honorably*). These are two sides of the same call, elaborated as "good or right conduct" (2:11, 15, 20, 24; 3:11; 4:19).

Becoming warmly pastoral, Peter now calls them *Beloved*, giving expression to his own exercise of mutual love, to which the family of God is called. He recognizes their status in relation to the world. They are *aliens*, "those who live alongside others," and *exiles*, "those who are temporary sojourners." He likely does not intend a major contrast of meaning in the two terms. By using both, he emphasizes that Christian believers are on a pilgrimage through this world, where they are truly not "at home." In *A Home for the Homeless*, Elliott (21ff.) emphasizes the literal and sociological meaning of these terms, that these believers were disenfranchised and "second-class citizens." Hence, he calls them "resident aliens and visiting strangers." This interpretation is helpful though not totally convincing. Peter may be remembering Psalm 39:12, which also uses both terms to describe the status of Israel in the world.

Abstain from the desires of the flesh that war against the soul is the negative imperative. The call to *abstain* is terse and emphatic, brooking no compromise. In form this follows familiar Greek ethical instruction warning that "natural impulses" need to be kept under control to achieve greater good. The *desires of the flesh*, not necessarily evil in themselves, surely include more than destructive sexual lusts. In light of the calling to holy love in this context, these include all those impulses that violate love (2:1).

In anticipation of what is to follow, *desires of the flesh* also include temptations to violence that arise in responding to false accusations (2:12), mistreatment by unjust masters (2:18), or the experience of any kind of *evil* (3:9) at the hands of another. Furthermore, Michaels suggests that such *desires* include natural impulses toward comfort, self-protection, and self-gratification that get in the way of God's intention (117). *War against the soul* has to do with that which mars or destroys human personality, human relationships, or true community. *Soul* is used not to denote some part of personality but rather the totality of human life as God intended (as in Mark 8:35-37).

Conduct yourselves honorably among the Gentiles is the positive imperative. The word for *honorably* (*kalēn*) modifies *conduct* and may be translated "good," virtually synonymous with the word *good* (*agathon*) in 2:14 and elsewhere in 1 Peter. The content of "good" needs to be discerned from the succeeding context. Here *Gentiles* refers to non-Christians generally rather than simply to non-Jews, which is the more common meaning. The concern of Peter is that if non-Christians perceive the conduct of believers to be "good," they may themselves also become believers.

Though they malign you as evildoers indicates either theoretically or actually that they do not yet understand Christian faith and action. Hence, they bring false accusations against believers. Indeed, early Christians were accused of secrecy, conspiracy, and sedition (cf. 2:15-16). These accusations may simply have taken the form of malicious gossip by neighbors, but may also have become a legal accusation (4:16).

In any case, Peter has a missionary interest: *that they may see your honorable deeds and glorify God when he comes to judge.* Peter cannot assure his readers that their good deeds will lead to the conversion of nonbelievers, but he clearly is hoping for this to happen. Peter's purpose here echoes the words of Jesus in Matthew 5:16. Beyond their conversion, Peter yearns that the lives of the converts will in turn *glorify God*, that they themselves will live in ways that will bring yet others to the same God.

Some translations speak of "the day of visitation" as *when God comes to judge.* The Greek word for this, *episkopēs,* literally means exercising oversight. It reflects the belief in a divine intervention in human affairs as God comes to judge and to bless. The Qumran writings also reflect this eschatological expectation, surely present also in Jesus and in the early church. It is not adequate to understand the expression as meaning "anytime that Gentiles repent" (Michaels: 120). The motivation for good conduct in a hostile world includes the hope for the conversion of nonbelievers, a hope based on an eschatological understanding of God's relationship to human history.

Witness as "Citizens" Under a Hostile State 2:13-17

Citizenship under Roman law in areas where the readers lived was a complex matter. John Crook makes us aware that under Roman law, people (male or female) are either slaves or free. Free people are either free by birth or free by grant of freedom from slavery (freedmen). Free people are also either Roman citizens or "Latins" or peregrines (migrants or travelers). Moreover, among the city states of Greece, one could be a "citizen" of one local state but not of another. In short, the whole issue of rights and privileges as citizens was both confused and oppressive (Crook: 36ff.). It is understandable that people would not think kindly of their rulers.

We also need to be aware of the cult of the emperor, which had been developing in these areas. This cult ascribed to the emperor more than human status and began to require rituals of emperor worship. In some areas the populace was even more eager than government officials to demonstrate devotion and allegiance to their rulers as being gods.

Peter recognizes that, as a community of believers, they must live out their Christian life in the context of a secular state. In Asia Minor, the state has to do with *governors* and an *emperor*. Government represents one of the existing orders in which certain roles and responsibilities prevail, sometimes called Household Codes. In the NT, these rules include husbands and wives, parents and children, the older and the younger, masters and slaves, and rulers and citizens *[Household Codes]*.

In this passage the broad framework is introduced in 2:13 and concluded in 2:17. Each part must be read carefully to be understood. A finely crafted literary structure is employed, as outlined here:

2:13   The General Imperative: Defer to or recognize the authority of every human creation, creature, or institution.
2:14   The Elaboration on Human Government
  • ruling persons: the king as supreme
                governors as those sent by him
  • ruling functions: to punish those who do wrong
                to praise those who do right
2:15   The Divine Intention
    • by you doing right
    • to silence the ignorant and foolish
2:16   The Christian Calling
    • live as free, not misusing freedom for evil

• but live as servants of God
2:17   The Recapitulation
         a Honor everyone
           b Love fellow believers
           b' Fear God
         a' Honor the king (cf. Michaels: 123)

*For the Lord's sake accept the authority of every human insti-
tution* (2:13, NRSV). However, Michaels makes a strong case for
another translation: "Defer to every human creature for the sake of
the Lord," taking the Greek word *ktisis* as "creature" instead of "institution" (121). He thus moves a step beyond Goppelt's translation:
"Subject yourselves for the Lord's sake to every human creature"
(179). These translations open the way to read this text in a liberating rather than an oppressing way. Achtemeier renders it, "Be subordinate to every human creature because of the Lord" (179).

One hinge in the interpretation of this text has to do with whether
hupotassō always means "obey, submit to, subject yourself to," or
"be subordinate to," "accept the authority of," or "defer to." We must
consider the wider range of meaning of the Greek word, and the context of this passage, where believers' first loyalty is God's authority in
Christ. In that light, we agree with Achtemeier that Peter here "advocates finding one's proper place and acting accordingly. . . . It is not
a command unquestioningly to obey everything anyone says" (182;
cf. Acts 5:29; Yoder, 1972:212).

Achtemeier also argues that there is no support in other Greek literature or in this text for rendering *anthropinē ktisei* as "human institution." The passage speaks of the emperor and of governors; later,
applications are made to masters (2:18) and husbands (3:1). All these
are human beings, not institutions (182), though as human beings
they live and function within a complex of relationships that we have
come to call "orders" or "institutions." These institutions include government, households, and marriage, which 1 Peter presents as examples of a larger principle.

The translation of this phrase is the other hinge in a reinterpreta-
tion of this passage. This view renders *anthropinē ktisis* as "human
creation or creature" rather than "human institution," shifting the
central focus from the social structure to the creature or person, and
from sociological roles to personhood. This direction of interpretation
was already advocated by Cranfield in 1950: "We can render *ktisis*
by 'creature,' its proper meaning, and the adjective *anthropinos* will

then indicate that of creatures, it is human beings that are intended" (57).

Thus 2:13 can be read as a principle that is to govern all human relationships, whether personal or institutional. It can be understood as a further extension of the call of Jesus to love one another, not only within the community of faith, but also beyond it, even loving the enemy, because the "enemy" is also a human creature or a human creation. However, to shift the focus from social structure to the person by no means implies Christian indifference toward the social structure.

The particular form of the *ktisis* in Peter's first example is civil government. Peter speaks specifically of *the emperor*, literally *the supreme king*, and of *governors* as those commissioned by the emperor. He identifies the proper function of such civil rulers, at least in part: *to punish those who do wrong and to praise those who do right.* In principle, this recognizes both a negative or restraining function of civil government, as well as an encouraging or positive one.

In the context of emperor worship present in that culture, Peter is desacralizing government, including the emperor, and putting it into a properly human perspective. Achtemeier suggests that this is "designed to give Christians a reason for civil disobedience (loyalty will overcome false accusations)" (180). In this sense the imperative, rather than being oppressive, is an encouragement and empowerment to keep on "doing right" in whatever situation or relationship one finds oneself.

The counsel Peter gives may, however, also have strategic intentions, especially for missionary purposes, as an application of 2:11-12. A theological dimension is explicitly included: it is *God's will* that by *doing right*, the false accusations against Christians, arising out of *ignorance*, might be stopped, as projected in 2:12.

Enhancing further the portrayal of their relationship to God, Peter now describes them as *servants* or *slaves* of God, an expression Paul also applies to himself. He introduces the great paradox that the Christian is truly free (in Christ) even while being a servant of God. He cautions that this freedom is not to be abused *as a pretext for evil.* In the divine pattern for the Christian life, freedom in Christ is not simply for self-expression or enjoyment but for the service of God. To silence *the foolish* who bring false accusations, freedom acts in the service of divine love.

Sharpening his imperatives, Peter concludes and sums up this passage with four interrelated exhortations: (1) *Honor everyone;* show respect for all people—a restatement of 2:13. (2) *Love the family of believers*—a restatement of 1:22. (3) *Fear God*—echoing 1:17. (4) *Honor the emperor*—applying the principle of love, including love of enemy, even to the person who occupies the highest position in the government of the time. It is important, however, that only God and not the emperor be feared and recognized as God.

If the traditional view is correct that Nero was then the emperor, Peter's call to practice love for the enemy is dramatically underscored. Nero's reign in the sixties was oppressive. To *honor the emperor*, rather than to fear him, would be a suitable application of the explicit teaching of Jesus on response to enemies: "Love your enemies, do good to those who hate you, bless those who curse you, pray for those who abuse you" (Luke 6:27).

Witness as Mistreated Servants Following Jesus 2:18-25

2:18-20 The Situation of Mistreated Servants

A second illustration for the practice of loving the enemy involves servants abused by their masters. To designate these servants, Peter deviates from the usual language of "slaves" (*douloi*) and "masters" (*kurioi*) (Col. 3:22; Eph. 6:5), and uses *servants* (*oiketai*) and *masters* (*despotai*). While *douloi* and *oiketai* are not essentially different in meaning, the latter focuses on the household slave. Peter is likely seeking to avoid confusion since he has already spoken of all believers as being *douloi,* servants of God (2:16), and speaks of God or Jesus as *kurios,* Lord (2:13; cf. 3:12, 15).

The *masters* served by Christian slaves, however, include both those who are *kind and gentle*, probably meaning "fair and just" (Michaels: 138), and some who are *harsh*. These harsh masters, either actually or hypothetically, can also act cruelly and entirely unjustly (2:19). The contrast here is not between slave masters who are believers and those who are unbelievers; instead, the focus is on how they treat their slaves. In this situation, Peter is addressing slaves rather than slave masters, and telling them how to relate to unjust treatment at the hands of *harsh* (literally "twisted" or "perverted") masters.

Peter counsels slaves to "defer" (Michaels: 137) or "be subordinate with all godly reverence" to their masters (Achtemeier: 189). The participle here simply carries forward an application of the principle already set forth in 2:13: *Be subordinate to every human creature.* Hence, *Slaves, accept the authority of your masters with all deference.* This applies both to good and to harsh masters. Peter does not say explicitly that such *authority* comes directly from God; he may mean that the social order in which they all live gives such authority to these masters. Peter here implies that the arrangement between slave and master is a human reality with which they need to learn to live *as free people* (2:16).

The call to do this *with all deference* is linked directly with 2:17, which calls on them to *fear God* rather than people. This is also consistent with 1:17, where Peter has reminded them that they are to *live in reverent fear* (notes for 1:17). This, however, does not mean that in Peter's view, slavery is divinely ordained; nor does it mean that Christians are simply to give in to systemic evil. In 2:20 Peter speaks explicitly of the situation in which the Christian slave has been doing *good* or *right* and is mistreated for it. In that case, Peter says the slave has been acting with moral responsibility, as a true moral agent. This implies that the slave can choose how to respond to the injustice or the abuse a cruel master may inflict. Peter is encouraging and empowering such slaves to keep on acting as Christian moral agents. This is a direct challenge to the evil system of slavery, in which moral responsibility is denied to the slave.

The motivation for such a surprising response to unjust treatment comes first in some reminders of words of Jesus, particularly his teaching about loving your enemies. Then Peter moves on, more generally, to a portrayal and interpretation of the example of Jesus in his response to suffering on the cross. What was already implicit in 2:18-20 becomes explicit in 3:9, *Do not repay evil for evil or abuse for abuse; but, on the contrary, repay with a blessing.* This teaching explains how to break the cycle of violence and echoes Jesus' teaching in Matthew 5:38-48 and Luke 6:27-35 on nonretaliation and love for enemies.

Peter, using essentially the same motivational appeal as Jesus did, affirms, *It is a credit (or grace, charis) to you if, being aware of God, you endure pain while suffering unjustly* (2:19). This "awareness of God" reflects the *reverent fear* of 1:17. The Greek word used is sometimes translated "conscience" but is here better understood as "awareness" or "God-consciousness." The notion of *credit* (literally *grace*) in this passage refers "not to that which God gave freely . . . but to that which counts with God or that with which God is pleased" (Michaels: 139).

Rhetorically, Peter asks whether being patient while experiencing "deserved suffering" is particularly worthy; he implies the answer no. But enduring undeserved suffering, according to Peter, does receive *God's approval.* Here, then, Peter is applying the teaching of both nonretaliation and love of enemy to the experience of Christian slaves suffering unjustly at the hands of their "twisted" masters.

God's approval in the Greek text is literally "grace before God." Some understand this to mean that such response to abuse is empowered by and participating in the grace that comes from God. Others think it means that God recognizes and affirms or approves this kind of participation in the grace-filled way of Jesus Christ (Goppelt: 199). These two perspectives are not mutually exclusive and may be included in a larger understanding of God's grace.

Schroeder has noted that "Christian slaves are opposed as wrongdoers precisely because the world feels threatened when the 'powerless' begin to act as responsible persons. Their actions upset the system! But Christians may have no other choice but to suffer if they are to be Christian in the world" (1990:53). In such a response to abuse, these slaves would be exercising their freedom as Christian persons. They choose to resist retaliation on the basis of their relationship with God.

2:21-25 The Pattern of Responding: The Cross

The larger motivation for nonretaliatory loving response to unjust treatment, however, is couched in terms of the Christian calling to follow the pattern of Jesus: *For to this you have been called, because Christ also suffered for you, leaving you an example, so that you should follow in his steps.* This in turn is followed by portraying the nonretaliating Jesus suffering death on the cross, in the light of Isaiah 53:4-6, 9.

The image of "calling" appears repeatedly in 1 Peter. God is clearly the One who calls. The hearers are the ones being called to holiness (1:15), to live in the light (2:9), to follow Jesus in responding to unjust suffering (2:21), to inherit a blessing through nonretaliating love (3:9), and to eternal glory in Christ (5:10). God's call thus has both present and eschatological dimensions. The calling is another aspect of the living hope into which they have been born (1:3).

The appeal to the suffering of Jesus Christ, mentioned in 1:19 as a precious and adequate redemption offering, is in 2:21 invoked as vicarious, being *for you*, as also in 2:24 and 3:18. What Christ did on the cross is not only something to be contemplated and appreciated but also to be claimed and appropriated by the believing follower of Jesus.

Such an appropriation of the meaning of the cross includes the recognition of nonretaliating suffering, as Jesus suffered on the cross, becoming an *example* for believers, who *should follow in his steps.* The word for *example* (*hupogrammon*) is used only here in the NT but commonly in patristic writings. Clement of Alexandria uses it of "letters of the alphabet for children to copy" (Michaels: 144). More commonly it is used as example or model. Goppelt suggests "guiding image" as a good rendering, preferring this to "model," which may give rise to an inappropriate view of the imitation of Christ (204); not all aspects of Christ's life and work can be literally copied. However, as Yoder has persuasively argued, the way of the cross is said repeatedly in the NT to be an example for us (1972:97).

To speak of Jesus as *example* and of following *in his steps* blends two different but related images. The concept of "following Jesus" emerges from the experience of disciples who joined those traveling with Jesus during his earthly ministry. They were listening to his teachings, walking the Palestinian roads with him, and even making their way with him to Jerusalem, where he was put to death on a cross. Following Jesus came to be a standard way of speaking of a commitment to trust Jesus, to learn from him, and when persecuted, to suffer for faith in him.

The image of *following in his steps,* literally "footprints," comes more from Greek usage than from Hebrew. The only exact parallel is in Philo (Goppelt: 205). Connecting this image with the story of Jesus, who called disciples to *follow* him (as in Mark 1:17), makes this passage crucial in defining the Christian understanding of discipleship. After the death and resurrection of Jesus, this language can only be understood metaphorically. It comes to mean "going behind someone, becoming that person's student, and thereby participating in his destiny" (Goppelt: 205). Here Peter uses the image in its third sense of participating in the destiny of Jesus, but with lifestyle implications for discipleship.

In this context, the ethical implications of discipleship are also present, especially in light of Peter's implicit appeal to the teaching of Jesus in 2:19-20 and to Isaiah 53 in later verses. Hays comments, "The appeal to Jesus' conduct in his passion, not to any specific teaching of Jesus, but to the familiar picture which emerges here is thoroughly consonant with the texts . . . in the Sermon on the Mount" (332). This is a decisive element in Peter's moral vision.

The words of 2:23 are not found in Isaiah 53 but are likely Peter's own commentary on how Isaiah 53:9 applied to the behavior of Jesus as he was being abused. This use of Isaiah 53 is one of the most striking features of this passage. The reference is free rather than verbatim, following the Septuagint more closely than the Hebrew text.

Scholars continue to debate on whether Peter's use was based on an early Christian hymn rather than on the OT texts themselves. Applied to Jesus, it clearly echoes the Gospel reports on the conduct of Jesus during his trial. It interprets the meaning of his suffering and death as being in innocence and resulting in an atonement for human sin.

"He committed no sin, and no deceit was found in his mouth" applies Isaiah 53:9 directly to Jesus. Linking this verse with 2:24, Peter is declaring that Jesus suffered and died for the sins of others rather than for his own. He was an innocent sufferer. Hence, the example applies to the situation of Christian slaves who, while not "sinless," were still suffering unjustly.

Peter has already indicated that Jesus Christ, dying on the cross, was like "a lamb without defect or blemish" (1:19). His point in using the Isaiah reference here is to emphasize that Jesus did not suffer for wrongs he had done but rather as one who had done good or right (2:15, 20b) and yet suffered for it. The reference to *deceit* not only refers to speech but to his character and lifestyle. He was "free of every kind of evil speaking" (Michaels: 145). Peter notes the similarity of Jesus' experience to experiences the Christians in Asia Minor are having. He underscores the manner in which Jesus responded to the unjust treatment he suffered.

Peter gives special attention to speech, possibly because much of the abuse suffered by the Christians in Asia Minor came in the form of verbal abuse (2:12, 15; 3:16; 4:4, 14). He is concerned that they do not respond in kind (3:9; Michaels: 145). Peter is probably remembering both the teaching of Jesus (Luke 6:28) and the behavior of Jesus during his trials and crucifixion. Jesus indeed did not *return abuse*, nor did he *threaten*.

Instead of retaliating, either verbally or otherwise, Jesus *entrusted himself to the one who judges justly*. The original text leaves open the question of whether Jesus entrusted *himself* to God, as in the NRSV, or whether he entrusted his accusers and the administration of justice to God. The former is the more common reading. But it is also possible to read it as Michaels (147) prefers, that Jesus entrusted his abusers into God's hands. This is suggested in the prayer "Father, forgive them; for they do not know what they are doing" (Luke 23:34). *The one who judges justly* corresponds to the introduction of God's impartial judgment in 1:17, and to the recognition of God's judgment in 4:5, 17.

In 2:24-25, Peter moves on to elaborate the redeeming benefits of the suffering and death of Christ on the cross, without further developing the image of the cross as example. The intertwining of the exemplary and the redemptive strands in Peter's theology of the cross is complementary and wholistic. The cross is not only example; it is also redemptive. It is not only redemptive; it is also exemplary.

He himself bore our sins in his body on the cross again returns to Isaiah 53:4-6 and uses excerpts intermittently. Peter adapts the text to apply the meaning of the suffering and death of Jesus. *In his body* interprets the expression "his own self" (Isa. 53:4a, LXX). *On the cross*, literally "on the wood," was used in ancient literature to refer to a stake or gallows. In the NT the phrase becomes a designation of the cross of Jesus (Acts 5:30; 10:39; Gal. 3:13). It is likely based on the LXX of Deuteronomy 21:23 (Michaels: 148). Peter interprets the cross as vicarious, physical, and politically humiliating.

So that, free from sins, we might live for righteousness sets forth the divine purpose and intention of the cross. Peter first notes the redemptive intention (1:18-19), to emancipate us from the blight and power of sins. Then he gives the creative intention, to motivate and enable a life of righteousness, "doing good." *Free from sins* translates what literally reads "having parted from sins." This is similar to Paul's common expression "dead to sin" (Rom. 6:11). *Live for righteousness* likewise parallels Paul's language and is used by Peter as *honorable* conduct (2:12), *doing right* (2:15), or *doing good* (3:13, 17; 4:19b).

By his wounds you have been healed is drawn from Isaiah 53:5b. The reference to bruises or wounds reminds us of the mistreatment slaves receive at the hands of cruel masters (2:20). Yet the reference is more directly to the wounds experienced by Jesus before and during his crucifixion (2:23-24). Peter is not speaking only to mistreated slaves. The meaning of *heal*, in Peter's use of it here, is primarily a reference to the conversion of readers to Christian faith and life, as indicated in 2:25. Metaphorically, life lived in sin, without Jesus Christ, is represented as "sickness"; life brought into an obedient faith and love relationship to Christ is considered "healing" from "the illness of sinning" (Goppelt: 215).

For you were going astray like sheep is a way of describing their former life in sin. They were participating in the "sickness" from which they needed to be healed. *But now you have returned to the shepherd and guardian of your souls.* Peter indicates both the nature of their healing and the process by which it has occurred.

The linkage of "turning" and "healing" may have been suggested by Isaiah 6:10b. However, it is more likely an echo of how Jesus spoke of the purpose of his coming, to seek and to save the lost (Luke 19:10), the lost sheep (Luke 15:3-7). "Returning" is a common biblical way of indicating conversion. Believers have "turned" from a self-centered life, engaging in various kinds of sins, to a God-centered life, seeking to overcome the power of sin and self-centeredness and to live in the service of God and others (2:16).

Peter here introduces the image of Jesus as *shepherd*, combining it with a related and supporting image of *guardian*. He returns to these significant images in 5:2-4. The shepherd image appears in the OT (Ezek. 34), in the synoptic Gospels (Matt 9:36 = Mark 6:34; Matt. 26:31 = Mark 14:27), and in the Gospel of John (10:2ff.). The more functional term *guardian*, literally "overseer or overlord," "combines the ideas of God's close and tireless scrutiny of the human heart, on one hand, with the protecting care of his people, on the other" (Michaels: 151).

Christian Witness in Marriage 3:1-7

3:1-6 Christian Wives of Unbelieving Husbands

This passage has often been misunderstood and misused, thus giving offense to many present-day readers. Therefore, we must read it with special care. It immediately follows the counsel given to slaves, with its call to nonretaliation, and is followed shortly by the general call not to return evil for evil or abuse for abuse, but to repay with blessing (3:9). John Piper has argued convincingly that returning good for evil is a central thrust of this whole passage (1980:212-231).

In the Greco-Roman world, it was expected that the wife would worship the gods worshiped by her husband, and that the entire household would be unified in its religious loyalties (Goppelt: 219). However, Peter does not encourage Christian wives to accept the faith position of their unbelieving husbands. They are to remain Christian. On the other hand, Peter may be aware of cults that renounce marriage and even encourage women to leave their husbands. For Peter, this is also not the appropriate option for believing women married to pagan husbands.

Wives, in the same way, accept the authority of your husbands. Here is another application of a basic ethical principle that Peter offers as an appropriate pattern of witness for abused persons, whether they be male or female. The phrase *in the same way* links the exhortation directly to Peter's word to slaves in 2:18 and anticipates the word to husbands in 3:7.

The particular missionary situation Peter envisages is that of a wife who has become a Christian believer but whose husband does *not obey the word*, is not yet a Christian. In short, it addresses the issue of how to be a Christian wife in a religiously mixed marriage. Peter expects the wife to keep her faith in Christ and thus encourages and empowers her to act as a moral agent in a situation where pagan society expects her to give up her faith. She is to remain strong and firm in Christ even while finding her appropriate place in the marriage relationship.

The pattern of this passage is essentially parallel to 2:18-25 in that it begins with a basic imperative (3:1), then moves on to an elaboration of the attitude or action involved (3:2-4), and finally gives an example (3:5-6). Since this is addressed primarily to women, Sarah becomes the example.

The basic imperative, a participle that parallels 2:18, is here also translated as *accept the authority* (NRSV) rather than earlier renderings of "submit yourselves" or "be subject to." This is Peter's way of recognizing the authority of the social order as represented in the "station codes" (Goppelt) or *Haustafeln [Household Codes]*. Peter calls for *purity and reverence* (3:2b) in their lives. This is not only a "missionary strategy." It is also an expression of basic Christian discipleship such as he has already set before slaves of sometimes unjust and abusive masters. Such a lifestyle represents "conduct which does justice to marriage" (Goppelt: 220).

Pagan husbands are described as those who *obey not the word*, meaning *the living and abiding word of God* (1:23b). Peter indicates that the behavior of Christian wives, a form of *honorable deeds* (2:12), is a life expression of that living word. Such behavior may result in the conversion of pagan husbands to Christian faith. This is the implication of being *won over without a word by their wives' conduct. Without a word* may be countering a temptation to use argument or nagging or a manipulative method of persuasion to bring about a change in their husbands. Peter gives no guarantees of missionary success but indicates that such an outcome is possible.

Schroeder notes that Peter is addressing the social situation in which the faith and morality of the wife is assumed to be determined by the husband. Peter, however, envisions the possibility of a "new order" within the context of the "old order." The wife is free to be a Christian, even if the husband is pagan, and may even anticipate the possibility of his conversion. This message begins to change the whole social system (1990:42).

The wives' honorable conduct becomes a Christian witness in a religiously mixed marriage and includes issues of physical adornment. Peter is voicing Christian concerns of the time, echoing Hellenistic warnings against ostentatious outward adornment. He moves to his central point that true *adornment* is *the inward self with the lasting beauty of a gentle and quiet spirit.* Essentially the same perspective is presented in 1 Timothy 2:9-10. Even Plutarch comments, "[What] adorns or decorates a woman . . . makes her more decorous. It is not the gold or precious stones or scarlet that makes her such, but whatever invests her with something which betokens dignity, good behavior, and modesty" (quoted in Michaels: 159).

Extravagant adornment was sometimes disapproved because it flaunted wealth or was intended to be sexually provocative, suggesting involvement with current cults (Michaels: 160). This is not, as it has sometimes been interpreted, so much a prohibition of jewelry or of particular hairstyles. Instead, it is a call to appropriate stewardship and modesty in attire, with clear priority given to inward spirituality.

When speaking to abused slaves, Peter previously has invoked the example of a nonretaliating Jesus. Now when speaking to wives of non-Christian husbands, he invokes the example of OT *holy women who hoped in God and used to adorn themselves by accepting the authority of their husbands.* The particular case he names is that of *Sarah,* who *obeyed* (literally "listened to") *Abraham and called him lord.* Here Peter weaves together the call to holiness (1:15), the call to hope (1:3), the call to subordinate themselves to other persons and social structures (2:13; 3:1), and the call to appropriate adornment (3:3-4). He is applying these to the special circumstances of women whose husbands are not believers.

The mention of *Sarah* refers to Genesis 18:12. She had been told about having a son and responded with laughter, saying, "This has never happened to me, and my lord [meaning Abraham] is too old." It is easy to quibble with Peter that his example does not fit his point. For one thing, Abraham was a "believer," not a pagan. Abraham then is not parallel to the nonbelieving husband of 3:1. For another, Sarah in the Genesis text was quite amused and skeptical. Instead of focusing on the larger theology of the Genesis passage, Peter seizes on one detail, the use of the word *lord,* which, notably, was not common usage when women spoke of their husbands.

Peter's point is that Sarah showed respect for Abraham, her husband, and that this is a pattern also appropriate for a Christian wife to emulate. In showing such respect in their marriages, these women in Asia Minor will be daughters of Sarah (Achtemeier: 216). Michaels similarly observes that Peter's argument here is "from the greater to the lesser: if Sarah 'obeyed' Abraham and called him 'Lord,' the Christian wives in Asia should at least treat their husbands with deference and respect" (165).

The deepest motivation for such honorable conduct, including modest cosmetics, is invoked by declaring that *the gentle and quiet spirit . . . is very precious in God's sight* (3:4). This is parallel to the motivation given slaves not to retaliate (2:19-20).

Peter has a closing word for wives: *You have become her [Sarah's] daughters as you do what is good and never let fears alarm you.* "Doing what is good" is the positive and creative response to the painful situation of these wives, in their religiously mixed marriages. Peter clearly calls not to simple resignation or passivity but to constructive attitudes and activity. By living creatively and courageously, they will not allow fears to control their hearts or behavior. In short, like the holy women of old, they will continue to be active in service and in witness (3:15) as faithful followers of Jesus Christ, even as they learn what it means to be "daughters of Sarah."

In summary, this passage, sometimes misunderstood and misinterpreted as oppressive, is a call to women to exercise their new freedom in Christ in a way that will challenge wider societal norms. Schroeder notes that this is a situation in which "the head of the house determined to what extent religious liberty would be permitted and which deities would be allowed to be worshiped." Thus open verbal or public proclamation of their faith is not what Peter recommends. Instead, in that circumstance, with hope for transformation, they bear witness with few or no words, but with being who they truly are, women free in Christ, living chastely and faithfully, doing what is right, without fear (Schroeder, 1990:55-56).

3:7 Christian Husbands Who Show Consideration

While Peter's word to Christian husbands is shorter verbally than that to wives, it is no less demanding. In appealing to traditional household codes, Peter in 3:1-7 for the first time addresses both parties, husbands as well as wives. There has been no explicit word to slave masters nor to civil rulers. Achtemeier helpfully notes, however, that Peter's shift in language here may indicate that he is speaking more broadly than simply to a husband-wife relationship. This can include "the way males in the household deal with female members" (217).

In the same way parallels the opening words to wives in 3:1, but now it is husbands who are addressed. The Greek word in this case has the general implication of a reciprocal relationship: as "for your part" (Michaels: 167). But obviously Peter is addressing Christian husbands rather than pagans. Thus he also speaks more generally than when he addresses the particular problem of wives in religiously mixed marriages. Not only similarities but also differences are involved.

The basic imperative (translating a participle) is *show consideration for your wives in your life together.* Michaels strikingly translates this, "You husbands in turn must know how to live with a woman" (167). *Show consideration* translates an expression that literally means to "live together according to knowledge." This includes far more than knowledge about sex and gender differences and dignity. Such "knowledge" is formed not only by information, but also by the difference Christ makes in human relationships and human love (1:22—2:3). In the larger context of the continuing call to deference and reverence, it includes a call to respect the full personhood of the woman in a marriage relationship.

Whether the woman is a believer in this case is not clearly stated. Schroeder assumes that she is not Christian, thus making the situation an exact counterpart to wives with nonbelieving spouses (3:1). If the wife is not a Christian, she will indeed be challenging the prevailing societal norms of the wife conforming to the husband's worship. But then, facing this situation, the Christian husband is to deal with her considerately, exercising essentially the same kind of gracious love that Peter has just recommended to Christian wives with spouses who are not believers. The husband then also is to deal with her as an individual whose personhood is to be respected, even though in pagan society he may well suffer "possible loss of face" or even more.

In short, "In these specific exhortations it is clear that every person who has been born anew to a living hope in Christ is a free and responsible person. All are equally responsible. No one can say that circumstances do not permit him or her to be Christian. They belong to the people of God; all are to live as God's people in the world" (Schroeder, 1990:56-57).

The way Peter speaks of a woman is sometimes misunderstood and misrepresented: *paying honor to the woman as the weaker sex.* The Greek word used means "vessel" rather than "sex" and does not necessarily imply a generic judgment about women being weaker than men, either physically or psychologically, as is commonly understood. "The author intends, rather, to make the point that the wife belongs to those who, even according to the Jesus-tradition, are to receive the special attention and care of *agapē.* This was the case especially in the light of their social and legal standing in marriage in the ancient world and in an economic structure which was heavily dependent on physical labor" (Goppelt: 227).

Michaels likewise says, "The notion that women are 'weak,' or 'weaker' than men, was commonplace in the ancient world. . . . But Peter uses it not to denigrate women but to foster respect (*timē*), the core of his advice to Christian husbands" (169). In any case, these married women in their social and cultural setting are less powerful than their husbands and, at least in that sense, "weaker." The Christian husband is to understand that acting considerately gives honor to one less powerful, for whatever reason.

Instead of denigrating women, Peter affirms that they are *also heirs of the gracious gift of life.* The Greek text speaks of being "joint heirs" or "co-heirs" of this gracious gift. This approaches the decisive insight given by Paul in Galatians 3:28: in the community of Christ "there is no longer male and female; for all of you are one in Christ Jesus." Far from ignoring or denying gender differences, this honors each equally.

In the final clause, Peter gives further motivation for husbands taking appropriate responsibility for a mutually supportive spousal relationship: *so that nothing may hinder your prayers.* He clearly assumes that these husbands seek to practice an active and effective life of prayer as part of the spousal relationship. Peter recognizes that the prayer life of both husband and wife can be blocked, interrupted, or utterly cut off by wrong or destructive domestic or community relationships. Jesus taught likewise (Matt. 5:23; 6:12, 14-15; cf. 1 Cor. 11:33f.; James 4:3).

Achtemeier summarizes correctly: "The point is clear: men who transfer cultural notions about the superiority of men over women in the Christian community lose their ability to communicate with God" (218).

Witness of the Unified and Forgiving Community 3:8-12

Peter has begun this section of his letter by addressing the entire community, first as pilgrims and sojourners in the world, and then as "citizens" who must learn to show deference and respect to every human creature. He has addressed more specifically the abused domestic slaves, the wives of non-Christian husbands, and finally Christian husbands. Now Peter again addresses the entire Christian community consisting of scattered clusters of believers in Asia Minor. He sees them as communities of believers living out the virtue and witness of Christian love (1:22ff.). They are a people of God proclaiming the excellencies of the One who has called them into light (2:9-10).

The spotlight now falls again on their mutual relationships as sisters and brothers in the household of faith and hope. *Finally* introduces a closing series of exhortations and a supporting Scripture from Psalm 34:12-16. The passage has striking parallels in Romans 12:14-17, though the sequence is different. It also seems to reflect various elements from the Sermon on the Mount, particularly how Christians are to respond to abuse and evil, especially within the Christian community. Note the parallels between the texts in the chart.

Psalm 34:12-16 (LXX: 33:13-17)	Romans 12:14-17	1 Peter 3:9-12
Which of you desires life, and covets many days to enjoy good? Keep your tongue from evil, and your lips from speaking deceit. Depart from evil, and do good; seek peace, and pursue it. The eyes of the Lord are on the righteous, and his ears are open to their cry. The face of the Lord is against evildoers, to cut off the remembrance of them from the earth.	Bless those who persecute you; bless and do not curse them. Rejoice with those who rejoice, weep with those who weep. Live in harmony with one another; do not be haughty, but associate with the lowly; do not claim to be wiser than you are. Do not repay anyone evil for evil, but take thought for what is noble in the sight of all.	Do not repay evil for evil or abuse for abuse; but, on the contrary, repay with a blessing. It is for this that you were called—that you might inherit a blessing. For "Those who desire life and desire to see good days, let them keep their tongues from evil and their lips from speaking deceit; let them turn away from evil and do good; let them seek peace and pursue it. For the eyes of the Lord are on the righteous, and his ears are open to their prayer. But the face of the Lord is against those who do evil."

Five adjectives are used to describe the quality of the believers' relationship to each other. The first of these is *have unity of spirit,* literally "be of one mind." As Paul exhorted the Philippians (2:2-6), so Peter admonishes his readers to keep their minds moving in the same direction. Then they may have, as Paul put it, "the same mind . . . that was in Christ Jesus" (Phil. 2:5). Their thinking and striving is to reach the same ultimate goal, the mind of Christ, rather than for self-actualization (Rom. 12:16).

Moreover, they are to have *sympathy* or "compassion." This, as

Romans 12:15 indicates, includes the capacity to rejoice with those who rejoice, and to weep with those who weep. While sympathy and empathy are not identical, both qualities may well be included in Peter's thought.

The central quality, however, is *love for one another* (*philadelphia*), the term for mutual love in the Christian community, properly embracing both sisters and brothers.

A fourth quality is *a tender heart*, or "good-hearted" (Selwyn: 189), "that inner turning of one's attention to one's neighbor in which one not only gives something, but also gives one's self" (Goppelt: 253).

The fifth characteristic is *a humble mind*. The Greek word used only here in the NT directly reflects the model of Jesus Christ (Matt. 11:29), which became a vital element in ideal Christian relationships (Eph. 4:2; Phil. 2:3; Kelly: 136). It denotes appropriate rather than inflated assessment of oneself in relation to others and to God. Peter will emphasize this virtue again in 5:5-6, where humility is commended with a supporting text from Proverbs 3:34.

From this list of positive virtues, Peter now turns to the focal issue of loving one's enemies. As a clear echo of the teaching of Jesus in Matthew 5:44 and Luke 6:27ff., Peter now exhorts, *Do not repay evil for evil or abuse for abuse.* This again picks up the strand of ethical response given to the abused domestic slaves (2:18-20). Yet it also broadens and generalizes that counsel to include also other than slave-master conflicts and abuses. Peter thus parallels the word of Paul in Romans 12:17a, "Do not repay anyone evil for evil."

Peter emphasizes the positive expression of Christian love in community conflicts: *But, on the contrary, repay with a blessing.* This is the principle of "returning good for evil" taught by Jesus (as above) and by Paul (Rom. 12:14, 17b, 19-21). Peter reinforces this further with another statement of the Christian's calling: *For it is to this that you were called—that you might inherit a blessing.* Does this mean that by blessing our abusers we inherit the blessing of God? Or does it mean that because we have inherited the blessing of God, we are now to bless others, even the abuser? Both readings have been advanced. Piper (1980) argues well that here, as elsewhere in 1 Peter, hope is offered as motivation for the practice of love, including loving the enemy.

The blessing inherited by the believer has already been identified in 1:4 and stands in contrast with "the futile ways inherited" from ancestors (1:18). Through their new birth to hope (1:3, 23), the readers have entered into that fellowship in which both women and men are co-inheritors of "the grace of life" (3:7). This is the hope of eternal salvation (1:9) in which they grow, as nourished in the word (2:2-3), and out of which they live the life of mutual love and nonretaliation toward abusers, responding instead with blessing. To bless means literally "to speak well of" but includes active yearning and praying for the salvation of one's abuser. It means to respond to opponents "with the active consolation of salvation that rests on intercession oriented toward salvation (*heilswünschende Fürbitte*)" (Goppelt: 235).

This exhortation is further enforced and clarified in the adapted use of Psalm 34:12-16. Using the style of proverbial wisdom, the Psalmist says that those who long for *life* will refrain from any speech (1 Pet. 3:10b) or action (3:11a) which would harm others (3:9a). Instead, such a person will "do good" (3:11a) and seek and pursue peace (3:11b). The desired life includes not only the future but also the present peace already experienced through the new birth. The exhortation in 3:9 calls for restraint and transformation of speech in the context of human conflict. James urges the same (1:26; 3:11-12). The call to "do good" is frequent in 1 Peter. The exhortation to pursue peace with all people, rooted in Matthew 5:9, is also articulated in Hebrews 12:14 and by Paul in Romans 12:18.

THE TEXT IN BIBLICAL CONTEXT

Christian Witness in All Circumstances

The unit 1 Peter 2:11—3:12 discloses a broad missionary motif shared with other NT writings. Peter assumes that when Christians conduct themselves in honorable and right ways, especially in their response to abuse and evil, others may be won into the circle of Christian faith and fellowship. He particularly expresses this in 2:11-12, in the hope that those who now bring false accusations against Christians may *glorify God when he comes to judge*. It is even more explicit in the appeal to Christian wives. By their *pure and reverent* conduct, they may "win over" husbands who are still nonbelievers (3:1). Later, Peter will speak of making a *defense* for their faith before *anyone who demands from you an accounting for the hope that is in you* (3:15). This broadly fits with the portrayal of Peter in Acts 4:20: "We cannot keep from speaking about what we have seen and heard."

In the NT the gospel of Jesus Christ comes as a message of hope to the hopeless (Eph. 2:11-13), encouragement to the discouraged (1 Thess. 4:18; 5:11; Rom. 5:3-5), and empowerment to those who are considered or who consider themselves as powerless (Eph.

6:10ff.; 2 Tim. 2:1). The Holy Spirit's ministry is to comfort, strengthen, guide, and empower (Acts 1:8). This is available also to those who in society are seen as morally limited or even powerless, such as aliens, strangers, slaves, and women. The Spirit empowers people to live as Christians in adverse situations and to bear faithful witness to Christ in hostile and unjust circumstances.

It is particularly the resurrection of the crucified Jesus that initiates and energizes early Christian witness, testified to by Peter (1:3, 21; 2:4; 3:21b). This carries forward the mission motif in the Gospels, both synoptic and Johannine, and in Acts (Matt. 28:18-20; Mark 16:7, 20; Luke 24:44-49; John 20:21, 30-31; Acts 1:8ff.). In this perspective, one purpose of 1 Peter is to give encouragement to suffering Christians to maintain faith and hope. It also provides perspectives of missionary strategy in situations where Christian faith is not only new and misunderstood, but actually facing some forms of abuse and persecution.

The Love Response to Household Codes

Peter has already made clear that the Christians in Asia have started with a new birth, based on the resurrection of the crucified Christ from death (1:3, 23). They have become part of a community marked by a lifestyle of holy love (1:14-15, 22; 2:1-3). Peter must also help them know how to respond to the hostility they encounter in society. This includes their daily work space (as domestic slaves, for example) and their marriages (3:1-7). They are in the particular circumstances of Greco-Roman households, with oppressive societal expectations. Yet they are to live out their Christian faith and life in the light of Christ's embodiment of forgiving and nonretaliating love, without simply acquiescing to systemic evil.

In this Peter draws on a common Christian tradition, ultimately rooted in the teaching of Jesus, but using what have been called "Station-Codes" (Goppelt) or "Codes of Subordination" (Selwyn) or more commonly "Household Codes."

The comparative study by Selwyn [Household Codes] indicates that 1 Peter reflects these codes more extensively than other NT writings, including Romans, Colossians, Ephesians, 1 Timothy, Titus, and James. Peter's references have their own characteristics. Only in 1 Peter 3:1-7 do we find reciprocal address, more common in Colossians and Ephesians where both wives and husbands, children and parents, and slaves and masters are addressed.

Intensive study of these station codes over the decades reflects a movement in understanding away from an emphasis on "obedience" on the part of the weaker to the stronger party. Instead, interpreters see an emphasis on respect and deference, which however is to characterize the attitude of each believer toward other believers and also to nonbelievers and even enemies. From the study of these passages in their larger context, we hear a pervasive and compelling call for humility and mutual respect for persons. This newer understanding was already sounded clearly by Cranfield and Kelly and has been amplified by Goppelt, Michaels, and Achtemeier. It is a marked development over the "institutionalization" of the social orders, as emphasized by Charles Bigg in 1901.

An additional contribution to our understanding of a Christian use of the Household Codes comes through Schroeder (1990) and Yoder, (1972, ch. 9). They introduce the concept of "revolutionary subordination" as a way of reading the Petrine and other such texts. Central to this approach is anchoring Christian ethical response in the life and teaching of Jesus, observing that Christian faithfulness is exercised in the context of "fallen" societal structures, and affirming our new freedom in Christ. We seek a "new way" or a "third way" to live out who we are as "followers of Christ" and "people of God." Under divine grace and the work of the Holy Spirit, this becomes a way of personal and societal transformation that transcends the otherwise predictable and continuing cycle of abuse and violence.

Nonretaliation, Love of Enemy, and Blessing

Peter grounds his emphatic teaching on loving the enemy in an early Christian tradition going back to the teaching and example of Jesus. He reaches even further back to Isaiah 53, from which he quotes, and Psalm 34, which he uses at the close of this passage.

As noted, Peter adapts verses from Isaiah 53 in appealing to abused domestic slaves to "endure" even when suffering for having chosen to do "right." Instead of retaliating, they are to respond with active but forgiving love, not returning evil for evil and abuse for abuse, but instead "blessing." They are to invoke the gracious favor of God in impartial judgment (2:23b) and merciful salvation (3:9).

Beyond the particular phrases Peter draws from Isaiah 53, however, the larger mood and spirit of the passage speaks powerfully of the posture of "the Suffering Servant." This figure responds to hostility and enmity with restoring love and thus is in continuity with what Peter is saying to the Christians of Asia Minor. In short, as Piper has written, the hope that believers have not only makes possible but also energizes and guides the kind of response they are to make in their situations of suffering evil and abuse (Piper: 1980). For some people today, this theme of love for the enemy is clearly offensive to what is considered the natural and rational response to abusive treatment. Thus the very concept of loving the enemy continues to be rejected by a society in which attitudes and practices of mutual destruction prevail.

Wink, in his probing studies on the Christian's relation to "the powers," holds that the teaching of nonretaliating love belongs to the earliest levels of NT ethics. He identifies the way of Jesus as a "Third Way," an alternative to "fight" or "flight" patterns. Wink observes numerous elements of Jesus' teachings in Romans 12:14-17 and 1 Thessalonians 5:15, as well as in 1 Peter 3:9. He concludes, "We appear to have here an extremely early fixed catechetical tradition, preceding even the earliest preserved epistle" (1992:186). The gospel calls us, "Do not mirror evil" but follow a "third way." This "is neither submission nor assault, neither flight nor fight, a way that can secure your human dignity and begin to change the power equation" (1992:185).

The issue of how this applies to the Christian's relationship to the state remains a large and complicated one and moves beyond the boundaries of this commentary. Neither the NT as a whole nor Peter in particular develops a clear theology of the nature and function of the state and of Christians' relation to it. What becomes particularly problematic for Christians is the state's use of violence to enforce justice, both in national and international life. The state often violates the protection of the innocent, the marginalized, and the disenfranchised, as well as the welfare of the whole society as it squanders the resources of earth.

Miroslav Volf, a Croatian theologian, responds to the phenomenon of "ethnic cleansing" in the former Yugoslavia. He affirms Peter's theology of nonretaliation in his book *Exclusion and Embrace:*

> The NT radicalized this process of the theologization of divine anger and boldly proclaimed God's monopoly on violence, at least as far as Christians are concerned. Whatever relation may exist between God's and the state's monopoly on violence—Romans 13 and Revelation 13 give radically different answers to the question—Christians are not to take up their swords and gather under the banner of the Rider on the white horse, but are to take up their crosses and follow the crucified Messiah. In 1 Peter we read: "Christ also suffered for you, leaving you an example, so that you should follow in his steps. . . . When he was abused, he did not abuse in return; when he suffered, he did not threaten, but he

entrusted himself to the one who judges justly" (1 Peter 2:21, 23; cf. Romans 12:18-21).

The close association between human nonviolence and the affirmation of God's vengeance in the NT is telling. The suffering Messiah and the Rider on the white horse do indeed belong together. . . . They are not accomplices in spilling blood, but partners in promoting nonviolence. Without entrusting oneself to the God who judges justly, it will hardly be possible to follow the crucified Messiah and refuse to retaliate when abused. The certainty of God's judgment at the end of history is the presupposition for the renunciation of violence in the middle of it. (Volf, 1996:302)

THE TEXT IN THE LIFE OF THE CHURCH

Anabaptist Self-Definition

Even a cursory survey of early Anabaptist materials reveals that 1 Peter 2:11—3:12 was particularly important in Anabaptist formation. Dirk Philips, an early Dutch Anabaptist leader, makes no less than forty references to this section; *Martyrs Mirror* is laced with references to and quotations from the same section. The most frequently mentioned verses are 2:13-17; 2:19-25; and particularly 2:21, which strongly shaped Anabaptist understanding of what it means to be a Christian disciple. From the following citations, we see that these texts in 1 Peter filled out the basis for the Anabaptist refusal of the sword and also empowered them in their experiences of suffering. They show that the suffering Christ was their defense, comfort, and hope.

In his *Enchiridion* or *Handbook*, Dirk Philips appeals repeatedly to 1 Peter 2:21 when he speaks of the Christian life as "following in the steps of Jesus" (64, 71, 82, etc.). Likewise, Menno Simons, in responding to "The Blasphemy of John of Leiden," referred to how Christ fights his enemies with "the sword of his mouth" (Rev. 2:16; 19:15):

> If Christ fights His enemies with the sword of His mouth, . . . and if we are to be conformed unto His image, how then can we oppose our enemies with any other sword? Does not the Apostle Peter say, For even hereto were ye called, because Christ also suffered for us, leaving us an example, that we should follow in his steps? (Menno: 44)

Michael Sattler, of the South German Anabaptists, also appeals to 1 Peter 2:21 in the Schleitheim Confession. Concerning the magistracy, he says believers are to "follow Jesus" in declining to serve as an earthly ruler: "Peter also says, Christ suffered for us (not ruled), that you should follow after his steps" (Sattler: 40). In Sattler's letter to the congregation at Horb, he admonishes, "Persevere in prayer, that you might stand worthily before the Son of Man. Be mindful of your predecessor, Jesus Christ, and follow after Him in faith and obedience, love and long-suffering" (61-62).

Pilgram Marpeck's undated letter "Concerning the Love of God in Christ" testifies to Peter's teaching. His editors say, "The whole letter is as powerful a statement on the power of love and nonviolence as one can find in Anabaptist literature." Marpeck appeals to 1 Peter 3:9:

> You will be in need of patience (that is, patience in time of evil tribulation). And do not resist evil with evil, but overcome evil with good. Thus and in no other way has Christ overcome the world that we may be joyful in hope and so to overcome and await our Savior, according to His promise, who will be our victory and our overcoming (Marpeck: 539).

Balthasar Hubmaier, less radical in his renunciation of the sword than other Anabaptists, in his Article on "Government" uses 1 Peter 2:13-17:

> St. Peter also has something to say about it. Thus, "Be subject for the Lord's sake to every human creature, to the king as supreme, to princes as sent by him to punish those who do wrong and to praise those who do right." Then Peter adds a brief word which comprehends the entire matter: "Fear God. Honor the emperor."

Among the great number of references to this section of 1 Peter in the *Martyrs Mirror* is a series of prison letters from Jerome Segers to his wife, Lijsken Dirks. He repeatedly draws on 1 Peter to encourage her to faithfulness, declaring, "Christ also suffered for us, leaving us an example, that we should follow His steps; forasmuch then as Christ hath suffered, arm yourself with the same mind (1 Pet. 2:21—4:1; *MM:* 512).

On the night of his execution, September 12, 1551, Jerome wrote a similar letter (*MM:* 520-521). This is followed by a report of Lijsken's valiant resistance against all attempts to persuade her to recant, including the pleas of two monks. It tells how she continued to witness to her faith in word and song even while she was in prison. Finally, she was drowned in the Scheldt River. This report makes two further references to 1 Peter 1:20-21 (*MM:* 522).

Peter Riedemann, in his tract, "Let Us Love One Another," 1529-32, elaborates, "But brotherly love implies that we lay our lives down for each other, just as Christ did for all of us, and gave us an example to follow his steps, 1 Peter 2:21. So we should not live for ourselves alone, but serve our brothers—not seek our prosperity or betterment, but theirs" (Dyck: 101).

Pieter Pieterzoon's treatise *The Way to the City of Peace,* about 1625, makes frequent appeal to this section of 1 Peter. Pieter represents the Waterlanders, Dutch Mennonites less legalistic than the direct followers of Menno Simons. In the dialogue of this book, Jan says,

> Their Lord himself gave his blood, thereby setting them an example to follow him, to suffer with him, 1 Pet. 2:21; 2 Tim. 2:12. That is the surest way and gives their spirit the greatest comfort when they follow in suffering. . . .
>
> It is this teaching which the citizens of the City of Peace obey, showing themselves gentle toward all people, giving shelter to them as commanded. They are obedient to the authorities in all things that are not contrary to the holy laws of their spiritual king, who has taught them not to resist the evildoer; even as an innocent lamb cannot bite a piece of flesh out of a wolf, so also they do not resist in such situations. . . . What is more, they love their enemies, pray for their persecutors, and do good to those who cause them suffering, Matt. 5:39; Rom. 12:20; 1 Pet. 3:9. They repay evil with good and bless those who curse them, and if they faithfully keep their Lord's commands, it is as sweet to them as honey and more precious than many pieces of gold. They carry these burdens so lightly that they lead them right to the heavenly Jerusalem. . . .
>
> Above all, they pray diligently for the authorities, even though they may be somewhat opposed to them, 1 Pet. 2:13, for they conduct themselves well toward all people, even though some hate them and resent their freedom; but this all happens because the poor blind people know neither God nor his Son, who wishes to forgive them and open their eyes, 2 Tim. 2:2. (Dyck: 270-271)

These selected illustrations show that early Anabaptists were reading 1 Peter as Scripture. It inspired them and was a trustworthy guide for their faith and practice. Their minds and hearts were nourished by these and other NT Scriptures. Their theology and ethics were shaped by these texts. Their arguments with their adversaries were buttressed by an appeal to these texts. When they suffered imprisonment and martyrdom, these passages emboldened and sustained them.

Nonviolent Resistance in Martin Luther King Jr. (1929-68)

Few Christian peacemakers in the modern era have wrestled more vigorously with the Petrine teaching of nonviolent love toward abusing enemies than Martin Luther King Jr. His extensive preaching and writing on this theme is brought together by James Melvin Washington in *A Testament of Hope: The Essential Writings of Martin Luther King, Jr.* In his theological development, King had moved from an optimistic view of humanity to the "realism" of Reinhold Niebuhr, recognizing the sinfulness of humanity. He began to seek for a Christian way of dealing with entrenched human evil in the structures of society. His concern was especially for civil rights, but also for the preservation of the human race from nuclear war and destruction.

In his "Stride Toward Freedom," he looks for another way to move toward justice and freedom. He refuses to settle for simple acquiescence to the status quo, rampant with injustice particularly toward persons of his own race. He pleads, "To accept passively an unjust system is to cooperate with that system; thereby the oppressed become as evil as the oppressor. . . . It is a way of allowing the conscience to fall asleep. At this moment the oppressed fails to be his brother's keeper. So acquiescence—which is often the easier way—is not the moral way" (482).

However, King does not accept the alternative of responding to oppression and abuse with violence and corroding hatred. He says, "Violence is immoral because it thrives on hatred rather than love. It destroys community and makes brotherhood impossible. It leaves society in monologue rather than dialogue. Violence ends by defeating itself. It creates bitterness in the survivors and brutality in the destroyers. A voice echoes through time, saying to every potential Peter, 'Put up your sword' " (482-483).

From the rejection of the alternatives of acquiescence and violence, King poses a third way which he calls "the way of nonviolent resistance." This way seeks to avoid the immoralities of acquiescence and violence. He says, "With nonviolent resistance, no individual or group need submit to any wrong, nor need anyone resort to violence in order to right a wrong" (483). Prophetic of his own violent death, he declares, "The way of nonviolence means a willingness to suffer and sacrifice. It may mean going to jail. . . . It may even mean physical death. But if physical death is the price a man must pay to free his children and his white brethren from a permanent death of spirit, then nothing could be more redemptive" (485).

Martin Luther King Jr. described this as the way of following Jesus, even unto possible death. For King, this became reality. While not all agreed with King's interpretations of the way of nonviolent resistance—and Peter did not foresee the circumstances of King's crusade—it is hard to fault King's courage and commitment. In recognition of his work against injustice in nonviolent ways, the Nobel Peace Prize was awarded him before his death.

I Love Idi Amin

I Love Idi Amin, by Bishop Festo Kivengere (1977), was written with the assistance of Mennonite missionary Dorothy Smoker. It is a remarkable testimony of receiving grace to love a persecuting head of state. It recounts in a personal way the story of the martyrdom of Archbishop Janani Luwum of Uganda at the hands of Idi Amin. Kivengere was outraged at this atrocity and the subsequent danger to his own life, since he had also publicly deplored Idi Amin's actions. He was forced to leave the country. As he left, he assessed his own attitude toward his political ruler:

> Peace is not automatic. It is the gift of the grace of God. It always comes when hearts are exposed to the love of Christ. But this always costs something. For the love of Christ was demonstrated through suffering, and those who experience that love can never put it into practice without some cost.
> I had to face my own attitude towards President Amin and his agents. The Holy Spirit showed me that I was getting hard in my spirit, and that my hardness and bitterness toward those who were persecuting us could only bring spiritual loss. This would take away my ability to communicate the love of God, which is the essence of my ministry and testimony.
> So I had to ask forgiveness from the Lord, and for grace to love President Amin more, because these events had shaken my loving relationship with all those people. He gave assurance of forgiveness on Good Friday, when I was one of the congregation that sat for three hours in All Saints' Church in London, meditating on the redeeming love of Jesus Christ. Right there the Lord healed me. . . . I knew I had seen the Lord and been renewed: love filled my heart. (62)

At the 1978 gathering of the Mennonite World Conference in Wichita, Kansas, a year later, Bishop Festo Kivengere spoke in the same spirit of reconciling love toward enemies that Peter encouraged in his epistle. Kivengere had himself participated actively in protesting the killing of about three hundred thousand political opponents by Idi Amin (Bergman, 1996b: 82).

In "Janani Leads Me to the Cross," Nancy Mairs writes how she personally has been led into a deeper awareness of the meaning of the death of Jesus. She recalls events that led to the execution of Janani Luwum and the "exile" of Festo Kivengere. Mairs notes how Janani had anticipated that his open witness might lead to his death. Janani had requested a personal audience with Idi Amin and was summarily put to death.

Mairs writes of the execution: "Having refused to sign a confession, he prayed for his captors as he was undressed and thrown to the floor, whipped, perhaps sodomized, and then at 6:00, shot twice in the chest. Prison vehicles were driven over his body to suggest the automobile accident the government announced the next morning (showing one wrecked car in the newspaper and quite another on television), and then it was sent to the home village for hasty burial" (Bergman, 1996b: 84).

Mairs reflects,

> Here and there redemption flickers, as in the case of Uganda's Janani Luwum, whose murder twenty years ago by military dictator Idi Amin haunts me. I sense that unless I can make some sense out of Jesus' death, I can't possibly understand Janani Luwum's. Or perhaps it's the other way around. At any rate, I need to plumb an experience that's quite beyond me, and probably will remain so my whole life: the willingness to turn one's life over to people who are wicked rather than to repudiate what one believes to be good. (Bergman, 1996b: 80)

This is contemporary wrestling with what Peter believed and wrote in his epistle.

Hostages Who Rejected Hating Their Captors

Out of the last two decades of the twentieth century have come testimonies of a number of persons who were taken hostage in the conflicts in the Near East. They were held hostage for several years, between 1984 and 1991, and on release showed a remarkable reluctance to speak ill of their enemies or captors. These include Father Lawrence Martin Jenco, Presbyterian missionary Ben Weir, and journalist Terry Anderson, as well as hostage negotiator Terry Waite. Several of these survivors have published their experiences in book form.

In *Bound to Forgive: The Pilgrimage of Reconciliation of a Beirut Hostage,* Jenco shares his pilgrimage from capture, due to mistaken identity, to release and forgiveness. Terry Anderson, a fellow hostage during most of Jenco's imprisonment, writes in the Foreword:

> This book is a true account of my friend and brother, Lawrence Martin Jenco. He is not a saint, not quite. . . . But mainly his account is filled with gentleness, as he is. The love for others that spills from him flows from these pages. Most of all, his faith in a kind and loving God shines

brilliantly. . . . Father Jenco has taught me many things about myself, about forgiveness and humility, about how love for God demands that we love our brothers, even those who believe themselves our enemy. (9)

Jenco deals with his personal struggle with anger over the unjust and prolonged imprisonment he suffered, then concludes by saying,

Some people advise me to forgive and forget. They do not realize that this is almost impossible. Jesus the wounded healer, asks us to forgive, but does not ask us to forget. That would be amnesia. He does demand that we heal our memories.

I don't believe that forgetting is one of the signs of forgiveness. I forgive, but I remember. I do not forget the pain, the loneliness, the ache, the terrible injustice. But I do not remember to inflict guilt or some future retribution. Having forgiven, I am liberated. I need no longer be determined by the past. I move into the future to imagine new possibilities. (Jenco: 135)

In *Hostage Bound, Hostage Free,* Ben and Carol Weir report the experience of Ben, a Presbyterian minister who was a hostage from May 1984 to September 1985. While his incarceration as a hostage was shorter than that of some others, he also endured trauma. He responds to his experience of mistreatment and abuse as follows:

Life is divinely given. Each person is to be respected and deserves to be heard. The captors themselves need to be set free. We are all recipients of God's mercy and forgiveness. On that basis we can begin to trust each other and find the constructive things we can do together as Muslims and Christians.

What a time to engage in Christian mission! While we become advocates for the homeless, the unemployed, the disenfranchised, and the discouraged within our own borders, we are called to look beyond our own society to the world and its needs. Faith lets you know that you can't just stand back and say, "I'm not here," hoping the trouble will go away. We must learn to live together. (Weir: 182)

The witness of these surviving hostages is remarkable. They refused to revile their captors in Lebanon and thus reflect in some measure an earnest following of Jesus in a situation of great injustice. They were taking seriously the teaching of Jesus to love the enemy and not to retaliate, as expressed in 1 Peter.

Wrestling with Abuse and Violence Today

Scarcely any theme is more urgent for church or society today than the question of how to respond to the prevalence of abuse and violence in the modern world. Scarcely any teaching of Jesus speaks more directly to this than learning "to love our enemies," which is the backdrop of the concerns of 1 Peter.

The theme clearly is being discussed in the thought life of the church today, including believers church denominations, but also beyond these circles (see bibliography). On a scholarly level, Willard M. Swartley has edited twelve exegetical essays treating these themes throughout the NT. This book, *The Love of Enemy and Nonretaliation in the New Testament,* includes contributions from several faith traditions and national settings. Notable also is *Love Your Enemies: Discipleship, Pacifism, and Just War Theory,* by Lisa Sowle Cahill, professor of Christian ethics at Boston College.

John Piper has wrestled exegetically with the most pertinent passages in 1 Peter, as shown by his 1980 article in *New Testament Studies:* "Hope as the Motivation for Love: 1 Peter 3:9-12." A challenge to some aspects of traditional enemy-love interpretations has come in *Peace Theology and Violence Against Women,* edited by Elizabeth G. Yoder. In his book *Non-Retaliation in Early Jewish and New Testament Texts,* Gordon M. Zerbe devotes chapter 7 to "Non-Retaliation in 1 Peter." Richard B. Hays in *The Moral Vision of the New Testament* discusses the same theme helpfully in chapter 14, "Violence in the Defense of Justice," drawing also from 1 Peter (Hays: 317-346).

The ethical application of Jesus' teaching on loving an enemy remains a controversial subject in debates on Christian ethics. Yet it is surprising how scantily it is represented in the current liturgical prayers and hymns of denominations who include themselves among "Peace Churches." One exception is the "Prayer for Enemies" appearing in *Hymnal* (727):

> Merciful and loving Father,
>   we ask you with all our hearts
>   to bountifully pour out on our enemies
>   whatever will be for their good.
> Above all, give them a sound and uncorrupt mind
>   with which they might honor and love you
>   and also love us.
> Do not let their hating us turn to their harm.
> Lord, we desire their amendment and our own.
> Do not separate them from us by punishing them;

deal gently with them and join them to us.
Help us to see that we have all been called to be citizens
of the everlasting city;
let us begin to love each other now
because love is the end we seek. AMEN.
(Barbara Greene and Victor Gollancz, in *God of a Hundred Names*)

It is important in preaching or teaching from 1 Peter 2:11—3:12 that the redeeming and liberating motifs in the section be recognized, identified, and emphasized. Some traditional preaching and teaching of this section has tended to enforce societal patterns of oppression and even abuse. We need to understand the call to follow Jesus in situations of suffering and abuse and to love rather than destroy the enemy by violence. Yet we must not simply acquiesce to existing evil, whether occasional or systemic. Jesus and Peter call for a new kind of response. This new response is possible only by divine grace and empowerment.

Anticipatory Forgiveness

The subject of forgiveness has become difficult in our time, when the focus is often on peace and order. It is particularly hard for persons belonging to an oppressed group, whether racial minorities or women, to hear the call to forgive. In any case, it is argued that "forgiveness is impossible without genuine repentance." Nevertheless, Jesus on the cross prayed hopefully, "Father, forgive them; for they do not know what they are doing" (Luke 23:34).

A rare expression of such anticipatory forgiveness comes from the witness of a French Trappist, Father Christian de Chergé, who along with six other monks on May 24, 1996, was murdered by Islamic terrorists in Algeria. Before his martyrdom, he had left with his family a testament, "to be opened in the event of my death" (Chergé: 21):

If it should happen one day—and it could be today—that I become a victim of the terrorism which now seems ready to encompass all foreigners living in Algeria, I would like my community, my Church, my family, to remember that my life was given to God and to this country. I ask them to accept that the One Master of all was not a stranger to brutal departure. I ask them to pray for me: for how could I be found worthy of such an offering? I ask them to be able to associate such a death with the many other deaths that are just as violent, but forgotten through indifference and anonymity.

My life has no more value than any other. Nor any less value. In any case, it has not the innocence of childhood. I have lived long enough to know that I share in the evil which seems, alas, to prevail in the world, even in that which would strike me blindly. I should like, when the time comes, to have a clear space which would allow me to beg forgiveness of God and of all my fellow human beings, and at the same time to forgive with all my heart the one who would strike me down.

I could not desire such a death. It seems to me important to state this. I do not see, in fact, how I could rejoice if this people I love were to be accused indiscriminately of my murder. It would be to pay too dearly for what will, perhaps, be called "the grace of martyrdom," to owe it to an Algerian, whoever he may be, especially if he says he is acting in fidelity to what he believes to be Islam. . . .

My death, clearly, will appear to justify those who have judged me naive or idealistic: "Let him tell us now what he thinks of it!" But these people must realize that my most avid curiosity will then be satisfied. This is what I shall be able to do, if God wills: immerse my gaze in that of the Father, to contemplate with him his children of Islam just as he sees them all shining with the glory of Christ, the fruit of his passion, filled with the Gift of the Spirit, whose secret joy will always be to establish communion and to refashion the likeness, delighting in the differences.

For this life given up, totally mine and totally theirs, I thank God who seems to have wished it entirely for the sake of the joy in everything and in spite of everything. In this "thank you," which is said for everything in my life from now on, I certainly include you, friends of yesterday and today, and you my friends of this place, along with my mother and father, my brothers and sisters and their families—the hundredfold granted as was promised.

And you also, the friend of my final moment, who would not be aware of what you were doing, Yes, for you also I wish this "thank you"—and the *adieu*—to commend you to the God whose face I see in yours.

And may we find each other, happy "good thieves," in Paradise, if it pleases God, the Father of us both. Amen.

(trans. Monks of Mount Saint Bernard Abbey, Leicester, England)

Embodying Forgiveness

L. Gregory Jones, in *Embodying Forgiveness,* includes a chapter on "Loving Enemies." From this chapter and its larger context, I have developed theses about the place of forgiveness in peacemaking:

1. Loving and forgiving enemies lies at the heart of following Jesus in the way of God's peace.

2. To love and forgive does not mean surrendering to or ignoring abuse and injustice.

3. To love and forgive does mean desisting from all vengeance in thought, word, or deed. Vengeance belongs to God, not humans, but humans are to seek to overcome evil with good (Rom. 12:19-20).

4. Anger and confrontation may be a normal and essential element or step in loving and forgiving enemies, but this step is not a place to park.

5. The "unforgivable sin" is the sin we refuse to recognize or acknowledge, thus blocking Holy Spirit healing.

6. The image of God as holy and just, as well as loving, including the concept of judgment with differing eternal destinies, is essential in a biblical understanding of loving and forgiving enemies. Human history alone cannot bear the total burden of perfect justice.

7. Personal and political forgiveness are intertwined and interactive. A peace church which loses the practice of personal forgiveness eventually loses its corporate witness for peace.

8. Both repentance for sinful abuse and forgiveness of the enemy happen only as an operation of divine grace.

Bill Bosler was pastor of the Miami (Florida) Church of the Brethren until December 22, 1986, when he was murdered in the church parsonage by an intruder. The murderer also attacked the pastor's daughter, SueZann, stabbing her six times and leaving her for dead. The perpetrator, Bernard Campbell, was soon found, arrested, tried, and sentenced to death. He was twenty at the time of the crime.

Ever since the tragedy, SueZann Bosler and other members of the congregation have acted in the spirit of Christian forgiveness and nonretaliation. They "have determined to overcome evil with good, rather than being overcome with it themselves" (Fields: 12). SueZann, who was twenty-four years old when her father was murdered, had affirmed her faith in the way of peace and forgiveness and had opposed the death penalty. Even at Campbell's first trial, SueZann declared to the judge, "I believe in the value of all human life, and that includes James Bernard Campbell's" (13).

Since the first trial in 1988, numerous appeals have been made to change the verdict of death. The court attempted to keep SueZann from giving testimony. When she was finally asked in court whether she hated the murderer, she replied quickly with a firm "No." She was not allowed to speak to the jury in court, and so she said privately,

> All I wanted to say was a very simple thing: I forgive James Bernard Campbell for what he's done. I respect his life and value it here on this earth. . . . I have tried for ten and a half years to bring some good out of this. I'm doing it the best way I know how. I am at peace with myself. That is all I wanted to say. (15)

Partly as a result of her witness, the death penalty was commuted to life imprisonment. Then SueZann was allowed to say to the jurors, "Thank you for giving life and not death to James Bernard Campbell. . . . I'm so overwhelmed. . . . This is the happiest moment of the past ten and a half years. I can't thank you enough. . . . I have worked hard for this life to be spared. Now I can go on with my own life" (16).

The teaching of Jesus to love enemies and to refrain from revenge and retaliation is clear, including the call to suffer injustice patiently and in the spirit of forgiveness. Likewise, it should also be clear that such texts are never to be used to justify domestic violence or to suppress the gifts of women in the ministry of the church or in society.

3:13—4:19

Christian Response to Suffering for Righteous Living

PREVIEW

In this section Peter deals with the Christian response to suffering head-on. He does not elaborate a theology of suffering by addressing the persistent question of why so much suffering happens in a world created and sustained by a God who is merciful and good. Instead, he seeks to guide and motivate a Christian response that arises out of hope, faith, and love, rather than out of human frustration and anger.

Essentially, two angles of vision emerge in this segment, to view suffering at the hands of others (1) in the light of Christ's sufferings (3:13-4:6), and (2) in view of coming judgment (4:7-19). Interwoven are counsels on the life of the people of God as witnesses in the world (3:13-17) and as a community of love (4:7-11). These two themes, witnessing community and suffering love, are skillfully and powerfully interwoven.

OUTLINE

Christian Suffering in Light of Christ's Suffering, 3:13—4:6
3:13-17   Christian Witness While Suffering
3:18-22   The Vicarious Suffering and Exaltation of Christ
4:1-6   The Value of Suffering Like Christ

119

Christian Suffering in View of Coming Judgment, 4:7-19

    4:7-11   The Loving and Serving Community Facing the End

    4:12-19   Facing Suffering for the Sake of Christ

EXPLANATORY NOTES

Christian Suffering in Light of Christ's Suffering 3:13—4:6

3:13-17 Christian Witness While Suffering

The structure of the passage may be outlined as follows:

3:13	A Rhetorical Question: Who will harm you?
14a	A Beatitude: Even if you suffer, you are blessed.
14b	A Double Exhortation: Do not fear or be intimidated.
15a	An Alternative to Fear: Sanctify Christ as Lord.
15b	A Further Exhortation: Always be ready—
	to make a defense
	to anyone who asks/demands
	of the hope in you
16	A Caution Concerning Attitude and Conduct: But do it—
	in gentleness and reverence.
	Keep conscience clear
	so abusers are put to shame
	by your good conduct.
17	A General Proverb: It is better to suffer for good, than to suffer for evil.

The opening question (3:13) marks a thematic turning point: *Now who will harm you if you are eager to do good?* The believers' experience of suffering in the midst of a hostile environment has already been noted in 1:6f.; 2:12, 15, 19ff.; and 3:9. Now it becomes a central focus. Peter envisions a situation in which they are *eager*, literally "zealous," to *do good* (3:11). This expression means the same as *doing what is right* (2:20) or being *righteous* (3:12). In Hellenistic and Jewish as well as in Christian usage, it denotes "persistent and total, even passionate, giving of oneself for good," as Peter has been urging his readers to do throughout his writing (Goppelt: 249).

    Is this question *Who will harm you?* simply rhetorical, as a wisdom saying, implying that when one zealously does good, no one will hurt you? Some read it that way. Yet the preceding context makes it clear that Peter is not naive (2:19-20). Ideally, the practice of good in society deflects evil consequences. However, Peter is realistic about human experience. People who practice doing good may also experience evil at the hands of others, and sometimes precisely because of the *good* they are doing.

The experience of *harm* in this passage is not based on ordinary human observation but rather on a word of Jesus, as in Matthew 5:9-16, that it is possible to overcome evil and experience good outcomes. While good people may be hurt while doing good, God can and does transform that hurt so it does no ultimate harm to the one who lives in hope. To read human experience in the perspective of hope means taking the eschatological realities seriously.

The question in 3:13 marks a thematic shift in the sense of focus. The entire section of 3:13-17 is directly shaped by the adapted quotation from Psalm 34:12-16 in the preceding verses. The contrast, both in the psalm and in Peter's commentary, is between doing good and doing evil as these relate to suffering. This moves on eventually to a generalized conclusion in 3:17: *For it is better to suffer for doing good, if suffering should be God's will, than to suffer for doing evil.*

In this passage, Peter is pressing another notch in his rejection of retaliation and his call to end the cycle of returning evil for evil. This is another strand in the call to love one's enemies and to seek to overcome the evil practiced by them with good practiced by Christian believers.

The beatitude in 3:14, following immediately the question of 3:13, appears as a direct application of Matthew 5:10: "Blessed are those who are persecuted for righteousness' sake." This same reassurance is also given in 1 Peter 4:14. The word *blessed* denotes "the concept of good fortune mediated by the gospel." The "person who participates in God's salvation . . . is safe in God's blessing (4:14; cf. 3:9)." In short, "while being prepared to suffer, [they are to] accomplish good in society" (Goppelt: 242).

Peter now moves on to the double exhortation for those in whom hope has come alive through the resurrection of Jesus Christ: *Do not fear what they fear, and do not be intimidated.* They are not to fear other humans in the way human fear tends to operate, fearing the harm others can do to the believer. He echoes Isaiah 8:12 with a slight change in the translation from the Hebrew, literally saying, "Do not fear the fear of them." He means, "Do not fear what people fear." The Septuagint rendering identifies this fear as fear of the king of Assyria. Peter's use may thus include both the notion of fearing the way people fear and the specific instance of fearing humans, accusers and abusers, who may exercise hurtful power against believers (3:16).

In any case, their alternative to fear and intimidation is to recognize in their hearts that Jesus Christ alone is Lord: *But in your hearts sanctify Christ as Lord.* Peter has already identified Jesus Christ as Lord (1:3; 2:3, 13). Now he emphasizes that what they confess, that Jesus is Lord, must be experienced inwardly, *in your hearts.* This confession is the counterpart and antidote to intimidating fear in the heart. To *sanctify* Christ as Lord is to recognize Christ as holy, as the complete embodiment of what we are called to be by a holy God (1:15).

"It is this 'holy fear' or respectful awe, focused on Christ, that drives out other fears, and makes possible an honest and effective response to interrogation" (Michaels: 187). J. B. Phillips' translation of 3:15 expresses it well: "You need neither fear their threats nor worry about them; simply concentrate on being completely devoted to Christ in your hearts."

Peter has introduced the notion of readiness in 1:5, and he now anticipates 4:5. In 3:15 he exhorts believers, as followers of the risen Lord, always to be *ready to make your defense to anyone who demands from you an accounting of the hope that is in you. Defense,* sometimes used to denote a formal response to charges in a court of law, is here used likely in the sense of Philippians 1:7, 16, when Paul speaks of the "defense of the gospel." It applies to informal response to questioning that occurs in missionary situations when nonbelievers raise questions, sympathetically or suspiciously, about the nature and implications of Christian hope. In this context, challenge rather than support is assumed.

Here Peter uses the word *hope* consistently with his earlier repeated references to hope (1:3, 13, 21; 3:5). *Hope* is what marks the clear difference between Christian believers and their non-Christian neighbors (Eph. 2:12). To this hope, they have been born anew through the resurrection of Jesus Christ and their faith in him. Through this hope, they have been set free from their ancestral ways and now may live in the fear and love of God (1:21). This hope has formed them into a new people of God (2:9-10). Hope now enables them to face false accusations, injustices, and even persecution.

The emphasis on *being ready always,* and *responding to anyone,* indicates a generalized posture rather than a particular crisis being faced. This counsel is broadly consistent with the experience of Peter as reported in Acts when called on to explain early apostolic experience and behavior (Acts 2:14; 3:12; 4:8ff.; 5:29). The same Peter who here emphasizes maintaining a loving and nonretaliating attitude toward enemies, however, also urges readiness to engage in verbal witness on behalf of Christian faith.

Given the prevailing circumstances of dialogue with pagans, Peter, however, cites several cautions. Such verbal witness is to be given with *gentleness and reverence*. Peter has already urged Christian women to practice *gentleness* in relating to non-Christian husbands (3:4), but here this attitude is called for among males as well. The *reverence* he enjoins appears to carry further the notion of holy awe toward Christ as Lord, commended in 3:15. Goppelt notes that "they do not condemn others but seek to win them over to the grace in which they themselves have become participants" (244). In this, they are aware of responsibility before God and of God's judgment, not only of human response.

A second condition is that their conduct is to be consistent with their verbal witness. Peter says, *Keep your conscience clear.* Peter uses the word "conscience" in 2:19 and now here in 3:16, 21 in the sense of "a moral or spiritual awareness of God, and of oneself before God" (Michaels: 189). Living in good conscience does not, according to the NT, imply moral perfection. The pastoral epistles can speak of "good conscience" (1 Tim. 1:5, 19) by one who called himself also "the foremost of sinners" (1:15). This is possible for one who presently lives by faith in Christ (Phil. 3:12; Rom. 12:3). However, the phrase does also denote a personal integrity before God (Michaels: 190).

Peter relates "keeping conscience clear" directly to an experience of being maligned and being abused for good conduct. As one responds to experiences of false accusation and possible abuse, the awareness of God is to function with approval of the action contemplated or taken. This is the *conscience;* the word literally means "knowing with."

Keeping conscience clear, in this passage, is associated with *good conduct in Christ.* The use of *in Christ* is likely not meant in the theologically developed sense in which Paul speaks of the believer being "in Christ," but rather in the sense of a moral life shaped by the believer's relationship to Christ.

The result of both living in good conscience and making our defense of our hope may eventually *put to shame* those who set themselves against believers. Verse 16 here, in part, follows the pattern of 2:12 in structure, referring to a case in which accusers "abuse" the good conduct of believers, either verbally or by action. The outcome anticipated, however, is different. In 2:12 the conversion of pagan accusers is considered a possibility. Here in 3:16, however, such a positive outcome is not mentioned. Instead of *glorifying God on the day of visitation,* the false accusers will be *put to shame.*

" 'Shame' in the OT and Jewish literature often connotes utter defeat and disgrace in battle, or before God. To be 'put to shame' is to be overthrown and left at the mercy of one's enemies" (Michaels: 190-191). In the NT, it means being humiliated (Luke 13:17; 2 Cor. 7:14; 9:4). The passages in 1 Peter, taken together, indicate that faithful discipleship and faithful witness cannot guarantee the hoped-for historical outcomes. But in any case, eschatological vindication is assured.

Extending the instruction of 3:13-16, a generalization is now cast into proverbial form: *It is better to suffer for doing good, if suffering should be God's will, than to suffer for doing evil* (3:17). This is what Peter had already said to the abused household servants (2:19-20), but here the application is more general. It is *better*, "more helpful, more useful for the Christian . . . since in such suffering they may . . . be confident that God is for them" (Goppelt: 246) and that the beatitude in 3:14 truly applies to them. Suffering for doing good is contrasted with suffering for doing evil.

Michaels (191-192) challenges identifying *doing good* in this passage as simply a reference to "social or civic righteousness, the performance of good deeds in conformity to the laws of the state." He also resists identifying *doing evil* with civic criminality, as some commentators have done. In 4:15, Peter warns his hearers to examine themselves as to why they suffer. Yet even there the category of evil is not simply legal criminality, nor is suffering "as a Christian" equated with "doing good."

3:18-22 The Vicarious Suffering and Exaltation of Christ

In this section, Peter, for the third time in his letter, discloses his theology of the cross in an emphatic way. The first is in 1:14-21, where he has sought to motivate holy conduct by calling attention to the cost of redemption and the place Jesus Christ has in the scheme of the history of hope now open to believers. The second comes in 2:21-25, to clarify and support his counsel to abused slaves, to respond to evil treatment even as Jesus had responded when facing the cross. Now, in 3:18-22, Peter appeals a third time to the significance of the cross. But this time he moves on to include the resurrection and exaltation of the risen Lord.

The appeal to Christ in 3:18 parallels the similar appeal in 2:21. In each case, after counseling Christian response to abusive behavior, Peter portrays and interprets the death of Jesus on the cross.

Verse 18a becomes a key statement of Peter's implicit theology of the cross, declaring the vicarious character of the death of Christ and its benefits. Even as Peter expresses the apostolic teaching concerning the atoning significance of Christ's death, he does not lose sight of or abandon the exemplary significance of the cross declared explicitly in 2:21. What happened in the suffering and death of Jesus guides believers in their response to what happens in a hostile world.

Peter affirms at least four aspects of Christ's death in the first part of the verse: (1) Christ suffered for sins. (2) This suffering was "once for all." (3) Christ was innocent, suffering on behalf of the guilty. (4) The purpose of Christ's death was to bring us to God. The last part of 3:18 affirms (1) the death of Jesus *in the flesh* and (2) the raising of Christ to life *in the spirit*.

The language of "suffering for sins" in this passage may reflect the Greek translation of the OT in Leviticus 5:6-7 and Ezekiel 43:21 (Achtemeier: 247). However, the emphasis here is to contrast, differentiate, and identify the suffering of Christ as being unique. Peter has already spoken of the suffering of Christ in 1:18-19, where he stresses the costliness of redemption from sin. In 2:24, he underscores its glorious purpose and consequences. In the first reference, Peter draws on the imagery of the sacrificial lamb, without defect or blemish. In the second reference, he draws on the imagery of Isaiah 53, which also includes the lamb imagery but applies it to "the suffering servant." For Peter, Jesus Christ is not only the innocent victim; he is also the volunteer who gave himself in life, suffering, and death for the sins of the world (2:23-24).

Peter also emphasizes the uniqueness of the atoning suffering of Jesus in his use of *once, hapax,* 3:18 (Achtemeier: 251). The suffering and death of Jesus are spoken of as *example* to be followed (2:21). Now here Peter asserts a "once-for-all-time" character of the suffering and death of Jesus Christ, not to be repeated (Best: 138). A significant element in early Christology was that this sacrifice of Christ marked the end of repeated sacrifices for sin (Heb. 9:25-28).

In one perspective, the death of Christ is totally unique, never to be repeated. In another, it is an *example* or illustration of a righteous person suffering for the unrighteous. The early church called Jesus Christ the Righteous One (Acts 7:52; 3:14; 1 John 2:1, 29; 3:7). The suffering of the righteous or innocent in the place of or for the sake of the unrighteous, as suggested in Isaiah 53, is also common in the NT (Matt. 27:19; Luke 23:22, 47; Acts 3:14; 2 Cor. 5:21). Peter has been addressing Christian slaves who have suffered at the hands of unrighteous masters, even while the slaves were doing right (2:20). This is one instance of how, in Peter's view, *it is better to suffer for doing good, . . . than to suffer for doing evil* (3:17).

The purpose of Christ's vicarious suffering was *to bring you to God*. We note the unexpected shift from first to second person, though many manuscripts use first person. Readers interested in the Greek variants behind this verse and the reasons for the present English rendering may consult Metzger (692-693). The belief that Christ's death provided a new access to God is also expressed in Romans 5:2 and Ephesians 2:18; 3:12. This is an aspect of the uniqueness of Christ's death (Best: 130).

The last part of 3:18 employs a double contrast between dead and alive, flesh and spirit. The verse refers to the death of Jesus Christ by crucifixion and then to the resurrection, which is a major emphasis in 1 Peter (1:3). Peter employs the common NT language of flesh and spirit to identify two different modes of being or two ways of conducting lives (Achtemeier: 249).

The larger structure of thought in 3:18-22 has striking resemblances to 1 Timothy 3:16. It includes not only the death and resurrection of Christ but also the ministry to the spirits in prison (3:19-20) and his ascension and exaltation (3:22). The larger movement must be kept in view in seeking to understand this highly complex passage. The message is that Christ not only suffered and was raised, but also that he ministered and was exalted.

Intertwined in this motif, however, are a number of intriguing and controversial elements that have given rise to voluminous research and writing by many scholars. These include the attempt to interpret what Christ did between his resurrection and his ascension. What was this journey during which he *made a proclamation to the spirits in prison*? What was their connection with Noah and with the Flood? What was preached and for what purpose? What does all this have to do with baptism and its significance for the Christian believer?

It is not the purpose of this commentary to discuss in detail the various interpretations proposed. We offer here, however, three basic directions taken by scholars. These different interpretations deal with several basic questions: (1) What is the meaning of *in which*, opening 3:19? (2) Who are *the spirits in prison*? (3) What was this *prison*? (4) What is the meaning of *he went*? (5) What was the message that Christ preached?

McKnight (216-217), broadly elaborating on Kelly (151-156), has offered a helpful summary of three basic views, from which the following chart has been developed, with adaptations:

Three Major Interpretations of 1 Peter 3:19-20

Elements	Descent into Hades	Preexisting Christ	Triumphant vindication
in which	Christ in the Spirit	Christ preexisting in Noah	spiritual existence of Christ between resurrection & exaltation
spirits	fallen angels of Gen. 6:1-4	contemporaries of Noah	fallen angels of Gen. 6:1-4
prison	underworld/Hades	metaphor for ignorance/sin	place of binding/pits of darkness, as in 2 Peter 2:4
he went	descent to underworld/Hades	metaphor for Jesus present	ascent of Jesus to spiritual world
preached	genuine offer of salvation	offer of salvation to the contemporaries of Noah	proclamation of victory over the spirit world

In this commentary the third line of interpretation is preferred, with respect for the other views. The first interpretation emphasizes a line in the Apostles' Creed, "he descended into Hades" or "the abode of the dead." However, it leaves ambiguous the purpose of such a visit and of its meaning for the Christians of Asia Minor. The second view focuses on the fallen generation of Noah and empha- sizes, by use of metaphor, the working of the spirit of Christ in the person of Noah himself. This interpretation raises questions about why that particular segment of the dead should be singled out for such a ministry. Also, as Kelly notes (153), both the first and the second approach raise the issue of "a second chance" for those who died without faith, a point not elsewhere taught in the NT.

The third view, emphasizing the vindication of Christ, speaks more clearly to the needs of those addressed in 1 Peter. These believ- ers suffer for their faith and seek to respond to their situation in the light of Christ's sufferings. This third approach takes seriously the influence of 1 Enoch (10–16; 67–69; etc.; see Charlesworth). This is an apocalyptic and pseudepigraphical writing that speaks of Enoch visiting the evil spirits and fallen angels. He announces to them, not a gospel of salvation, but the reality of their doom, to be imprisoned in the earth in darkness, awaiting final fiery judgment (1 En. 10:4-6; 14:5; 16:1-3; 21; cf. Jude 6). The fallen angels are punished in the Flood as a warning to evil kings and rulers who control the world (1 En. 67:12).

Even as the suffering Jesus was vindicated, so the suffering believ- ers will be vindicated. Even as Jesus continued to minister through proclamation, the suffering followers of Jesus are to continue to bear witness to the triumph of Christ, even before pagan rulers. This encourages them to continue to bear witness to the hope which lies in them (1 Pet. 3:15) since Christ also, their example (2:21), contin- ued his ministry of proclamation even after he died in the flesh.

Moreover, this proclamation bears witness to the universal signifi- cance of the suffering, death, resurrection, and exaltation of Christ (3:22). What happened to and through Jesus manifestly transcends local space and time and realm. Such an understanding of Jesus' vin- dication gives profound meaning to the experiences of suffering believers as followers of Jesus Christ.

This third line of interpretation also does better in answering a key question: What would this reference about *proclamation to the spir- its in prison* mean to the Christians of Asia Minor? It brings them encouragement, which they deeply need, to remain strong in their commitment to Jesus Christ in the face of present and future suffering. It tells them that even as Christ suffered on the cross, innocently and unjustly, and was finally vindicated in his resurrection and exaltation, so they as Christ's followers may also be assured of final vindication. Meanwhile, they continue in trusting God and doing right.

The other major strand in this section involves the place of baptism. This is the only passage in the epistle in which baptism is clearly mentioned, though some scholars have viewed the entire writing as a "baptismal liturgy," but this is unlikely (see p. 19, above).

Peter's reference to the days of Noah reminds him of the Flood. The Flood calls to mind the water from which and by which Noah and his family were saved. This then reminds him of baptism, which involves the use of water. *Water* here is used symbolically; he deliberately sets aside the notion of cleansing the body by the literal use of water.

The precise sequence of Peter's thought remains somewhat puzzling to us, but the direction is clear. As water was important in Noah's experience of being saved, so also baptism becomes important in the believer's experience of salvation.

Peter speaks of baptism positively as *an appeal to God for a good conscience*. An alternative is to render the Greek as *a pledge of a good conscience to God*. In this commentary, the latter reading is preferred, following Beasley-Murray (262). He summarizes his vigorous discussion of this passage:

> The chief point of this passage is its emphatic denial that the external elements of baptism constitute either its essence or its power. The cleansing in baptism is gained not through the application of water to the flesh but through the pledge of faith and obedience therein given to God, upon which the resurrection of Jesus Christ becomes the saving power to the individual concerned.
>
> Observe carefully: it is not said that the giving to God of an answer saves; the risen Christ does that, "baptism saves . . . through the resurrection of Jesus Christ." But the response is at the heart of the baptism wherein the Lord makes the resurrection effective. (265)

This view of baptism expresses well our understanding of believers baptism.

Schertz, wrestling with the meaning of 3:19-22, has offered a creative and intriguing interpretation that explains the moral argument of this text. Thereby she shows how it functions in relation to Peter's larger emphasis on nonretaliation. She identifies a structural chiasmus as follows:

A =19-20a. In the spirit in which he was resurrected (an understanding drawn from the preceding hymn by means of a relative pronoun), Christ went and preached to the captive spirits. These spirits are identified with the ones who were disobedient in the days of Noah. . . .

   B = 20b. Noah persevered against these spirits, built the ark in obedience to God, and few (eight) were saved.

   B¹ = 21. The believers have their own salvific "ark," the communal bonds of baptism which, as the author explains, is not a cleansing but an appeal in good conscience to that greater reality concretized in the resurrection of Jesus Christ.

A¹ = 22. Finally, the image is emphatically concluded with the author's statement that Jesus is at the right hand of God with all these (formerly disobedient) angels, authorities, and powers subject to him.

Schertz admits that the complex imagery of this section "may never be completely available to the reader with a modern worldview." Yet the chiastic correspondences suggest that "the author is adding another cosmic level to the point he has made previously from a social or moral standpoint (good behavior will shame your opponents) and from a personal standpoint (you were brought to God by the nonretaliatory Christ)." In other words, believers resist evil "by bonding in baptism and not repaying in kind. That resistance is grounded in a hope that is, in turn, grounded in cosmic reality" (277-278). Christ is at God's *right hand,* reigning in honor and power. *Angels, authorities, and powers* are already *made subject to him* (3:22).

The nonretaliatory and suffering Christ, vindicated by God, announced victory over the imprisoned spirits. Therefore, the nonretaliatory readers, even though suffering injustice and abuse, will also be vindicated by God and triumph over their opponents. If those who malign believers really listen to them giving account of their hope in Christ (3:15, 22), perhaps some will be converted. However, the emphasis here is on the abusers being put to shame before God (3:16).

4:1-6 The Value of Suffering Like Christ

Peter has encouraged the believers to be faithful in following the pattern of Jesus Christ in their response to suffering. He has assured them of ultimate vindication in their identification with the suffering of Christ (3:13-22). Now he explains the positive values of suffering.

Continuing to speak of Christ's suffering *in the flesh* (4:1; 3:18), Peter now enjoins hearers, *Arm yourself with the same intention.* He gives his motivating reason: *For whoever has suffered in the flesh has finished with sin.*

The first part of this verse seems clear enough, asking hearers to allow Jesus Christ to be their pattern in their suffering. They are to be prepared or *armed* for such experiences by having the same mind (attitude, intention) as Jesus had.

The last part of the verse is less clear. Who is this one who has suffered and has finished with sin? Is this Jesus Christ, considered by Peter as the sinless one (2:22)? Is this the Christian believer? Or is this a universal observation? And in what sense does it then mean to be *finished with sin?*

There are three common interpretations: (1) Peter is speaking generically of suffering. People who suffer learn eventually to turn away from sins which cause suffering. Suffering in this sense has a general cleansing effect. (2) Peter is referring to those who, having chosen Christ in conversion, have also chosen to turn away from lives of sin. (3) Peter has in mind only Jesus Christ as the one who is finished with sin, in his once-for-all atoning death for sin (3:18).

The second view or possibly a combination of the second and third is preferred, in my judgment. The emphasis falls on the sinless Christ as the one who makes it possible for sinners to convert from sin to righteousness.

Peter fills out the meaning of *finished with sin:* Christians intend *to live for the rest of their earthly lives no longer by human desires but by the will of God.* This is equivalent to the divine purpose of the atonement: so that *free from sins, we might live for righteousness* (2:24). To clarify further, Peter introduces another "catalogue" of sins by describing the lives they formerly lived but have now left behind: *living in licentiousness, passions, drunkenness, revels, carousing, and lawless idolatry.* These are sinful activities in which they were formerly involved. Now, to the surprise and annoyance of their former friends, they no longer participate in these deviations from God's will.

Licentiousness and *passions* both have to do with acts of sexual immorality. These words make more specific what Peter spoke of in 1:14 and 2:11: destructive aspects of human desire. Two other passages that catalogue such sins are 2 Peter 2:18 and Romans 13:13. Destructive sexual indulgence and deviations were part of the social climate of Asia Minor, where these Christians lived.

A second cluster of sinful activities included *drunkenness, revels, and carousing.* These abuses of human appetites are labeled in ways that even non-Christian moral standards rejected. The expression *lawless idolatry* most clearly reflects Peter's Jewishness. He denounces idolatry, in which God is being replaced by some other object of devotion and worship that is forbidden in the Ten Commandments. The Greek word used here is plural, suggesting a variety of acts. By implication, Peter says that pagan morality is characterized by seeking life's fulfillment in other ways than in God, and that these other ways not only disappoint but *wage war against the soul* (2:11). This is the lifestyle that Christian believers have abandoned. They have *finished with sin* (4:1b).

Peter elaborates on the reaction of pagan neighbors to the conversion in lifestyle they observe in Christians. They are *surprised*, "with implications of disappointment and anger" (Michaels: 233), because Christians no longer join with the pagans in these activities, implying that formerly they did so. The practice of sinful living is not simply a fantasy for these Christians but a memory. These Christians have formerly run with the pagans in *the same excesses of dissipation*. In their expressed response to Christian conversion, the pagan Gentiles *blaspheme,* uttering false verbal accusations against the Christians. Peter says they *malign you as evildoers* (2:12; 3:16), speaking from ignorance (2:15).

In 3:15 Peter posits the experience of being asked to give an account of the hope that believers profess. Here in 4:5, Peter now assures the believers that their hostile adversaries will need to give account before the same One already identified in 1:17, the One *who judges all impartially*. In 2:22, Peter had spoken of how the abused Jesus had committed himself *to the one who judges justly*. It is possible that Peter is remembering the word of Jesus, "I tell you, on the day of judgment you will have to give an account" (Matt. 12:36; cf. 2 Cor. 5:10).

The expression *the living and the dead* is used by Peter (4:5) and Paul (Rom. 14:9) to include all persons now living as well as people who have already died. Those who may bring the Christian before human courts will ultimately also face divine judgment. For this they will themselves be judged since *they will have to give an accounting to him who stands ready to judge the living and the dead* (1 Pet. 4:5; cf. 3:16, *put to shame*). Here Peter begins to make a transition to focus on the coming judgment.

Considerable controversy surrounds 4:6. It is added to verse 5, which completes the basic affirmation that ultimately those who suffer for righteousness will be vindicated, and those who abuse the faithful will face God in judgment. Peter, however, adds, *For this is the reason the gospel was proclaimed even to the dead, so that, though they had been judged in the flesh as humans judge, they might live in the spirit as God lives.*

Who are these dead to whom the gospel has been preached? Three views have emerged: (1) They are the same dead to whom Jesus preached as indicated in 3:19. (2) They are the spiritually dead of any age who need the life-giving gospel of salvation through Jesus Christ. (3) They are the believers in the Christian communities of Asia Minor who have already died, some through martyrdom. To them the gospel has been proclaimed before their death and has been received in faith by them. Thus they will be raised to life in the Spirit that is eternal (cf. 2 Macc. 7:14).

We join those who affirm the third position. In this interpretation, the preached gospel offers the gift of salvation through Christ. The dead are early Christians who have already died by the time 1 Peter was written. Their death reminds us of the reality of judgment and that the purpose and outcome of the gospel is eternal life *in spirit.*

This third interpretation fits best with Peter's concern to encourage his readers. It connects with Peter's view that believers have an eternal hope (1:5) because of their response to the gospel that has been preached to them (1:22). It responds to the human concern for those who have once lived and been loved among them, but now have died (cf. Matt. 27:52-53). Similarly, Paul told the Thessalonians not to "grieve as others do who have no hope" (1 Thess. 4:13).

Michaels helpfully observes, "To make his case, it was not essential for Peter to demonstrate that all the 'dead' had heard the gospel of Jesus Christ, only that some had. If he could show this, it meant that the Christian gospel belonged to the past as well as to the present, so that the crisis faced by the readers of the epistle had significant antecedents" (236).

Some view the judgment in 4:6 as human judgment. Human authorities persecuted Christians, who thus were *judged in the flesh,* according to human judgment (4:6), in contrast to divine judgment (4:5). This is somewhat like the contrast between the human and divine assessment of Christ in 2:4: *rejected by mortals yet chosen and precious in God's sight.*

In any case, 4:6 gives us an indication of the purpose of preaching the gospel, whatever may happen to us in life, including the possibility of martyrdom. The purpose of gospel preaching is that we may live for God in spirit, both in this life and the life beyond. This third position is preferred over the long tradition of interpretation that associates 4:6 with a descent of Christ into Hades, thereby linking the verse to 3:19.

Christian Suffering in View of Coming Judgment 4:7-19

4:7-11 The Loving and Serving Community Facing the End

While the theme of judgment has been present in 1 Peter before (1:17; 2:7-8, 12; 4:5-6), this focus now is sharpened even further. Christ coming to be revealed in the last time (1:5, 7) is a dimension of the living hope to which we are born anew (1:3).

Peter declares, *The end of all things is near* (4:7). Later he declares, *The time has come for judgment to begin with the household of God* (4:17). It is this eschatological expectation which provides a framework for the imperatives contained in these passages. In the tradition of Jewish and early Christian prophecy, Peter sees history as movement toward a consummation. That consummation involves both the vindication of righteousness and the judgment of unrighteousness *[Eschatology]*.

Far from being an incidental parenthesis in the theme of suffering and hope in 1 Peter, this passage interweaves the eschatological basis for Christian ethics (1:3-5, 7, 9, 13; 2:12; 3:16; 4:5-6, 13, 17-19; 5:1, 4, 6) with the place of the people of God, the church, in the ongoing purposes of God (1:1-2, 10-12, 22; 2:1-10; 3:8-12; 5:1-4). Here these two dominant themes come together with power and beauty (McKnight: 235-236), leading into a ringing doxology.

Peter has previously focused more on the role and responsibilities of Christians in facing a hostile world. Now he focuses on the relationship of believers toward one another within the community of hope. Earlier he told them to love the neighbor, including the enemy. Now he underscores the mutuality of Christian love in the congregation itself.

The first imperatives have to do with the life and ministry of the Christian communities and are introduced by *therefore*:

4:7b   *Be serious and discipline yourselves for prayers.*

4:8   *Above all, maintain constant love for one another.*

4:9   *Practice hospitality* (RSV).

4:10   *As good stewards, . . . serve one another.*

One mark of the church facing challenge and hostility in the light of *the end of all things* is its life of prayer. What Peter has assumed concerning the practice of regular prayer in the Christian home (3:7), he now also assumes in the life of the Christian community. He uses a general term for praying or entreating, which we see well modeled in the Lord's prayer; it includes petition. The use of the plural in 3:7b, *so that nothing may hinder your prayers,* and in 4:7b, *Discipline yourselves for the sake of your prayers*, indicates that a regular pattern of praying is envisioned, not a single act. The church is seen as a praying community (cf. Acts 2:42; 4:23-31).

To maintain such a life of prayer, two special qualities are enjoined: *Be serious,* and *Discipline yourselves.* The first word means literally "to think clearly" or "to keep one's head," an appropriate admonition when facing the consummation of history. For Peter, prayer includes and does not exclude an appropriate involvement of the rational mind. The second verb, translated *discipline,* means "to give full attention." This is a call for attentiveness, focus, and deliberate mental concentration in the practice of prayer. Believers are tempted to let eschatology become a temptation for speculation, and to let the prayer life lose its focus. Hence, this exhortation has a remarkably timeless message for today's church at prayer.

A second characteristic of the suffering church living in the end-times is the practice of mutual love. Peter had already introduced this and emphasized in 1:22–2:3 and reemphasized it in 3:8. He now underscores it once more in this context of contemplating suffering yet to come. The emphasis here is sounded with *above all.* As in 1:22, this *love* is to be *constant,* fervent, or unremitting. McKnight comments, "They are to work at loving one another because doing so in the midst of stress is difficult" (237). It is characterized by mutuality; they are to *love one another,* not only their neighbor or their enemy.

Motivation for such love is expressed in *for love covers a multitude of sins.* What can this mean? Proverbs 10:12b says that "love covers all offenses" in the sense of minimizing or overlooking them. This is in the spirit of 1 Corinthians 13:5-7, not keeping record of grievances but "bearing all things" (I. H. Marshall: 144). But Peter, who tends to use the Septuagint when he quotes from the OT, is not quoting Proverbs here. It is more likely that he is using a contemporary saying loosely based on Proverbs 10:12b, which also finds expression in James 5:20 (Michaels: 247).

Michaels suggests that Peter may be linking this expression with being *finished with sin* (4:1), and that this happens in the experience of the loving Christian community, in mutual giving and forgiving. In this sense, it is an expression of the "binding and loosing" of which Jesus spoke in Matthew 18:18. McKnight comments helpfully that whatever meaning is intended in this ambiguous proverb, "the community that loves one another is able to forgive one another more rapidly when minor issues arise" (238).

The practice of being *hospitable to one another* is a further expression of mutual Christian love. The word itself literally means "love of the stranger." Even within the community of faith, because of the diversities of personhood represented, each is in some sense yet a "stranger" to the other. Since hospitality has to do with offering the stranger welcoming space, attention, and love, this becomes one of the highest forms of mutual love in the social expression of Christian faith. This had a particular meaning in terms of welcoming visitors or newcomers, especially itinerant messengers, into the home or into the fellowship. It also has timeless and transforming meaning for the practice of mutual love.

Note the qualifier that such hospitality is to be *without complaining,* which may be linked with the notion that *love covers a multitude of sins.* Without such ungrudging, uncomplaining mutual love, expressed in hospitality, the suffering community of hope is unprepared for what lies ahead.

Gifts of Grace. The final expression of mutual love in this section is the employment of the manifold gifts of grace in the service of one another. *Like good stewards of the manifold grace of God, serve one another with whatever gift each of you has received.* Peter's reference to gifts bears some similarities to Paul's in Romans 12:6-8 (cf. 1 Cor. 12:8-10, 28-30; Eph. 4:11). In this setting the emphasis is on their employment for mutual benefit and to express mutual love. Note the sequence: Love one another (4:8), be hospitable to one another (4:9), and serve one another (4:10).

The gifts themselves are expressions of *the manifold grace of God.* They are diverse, though Peter does not elaborate on their variety as Paul does. Each gift (*charisma*) comes as God's *grace,* which is a pervading theme in this epistle (1:2, 13; 2:20; 3:7; 5:10). In receiving and using these gifts, the believers become *stewards.*

The stewardship image is a striking extension of the portrayal of the readers as aliens and exiles (1:1; 2:11). They are pilgrims in the world, but now are themselves a *house* since they have become the people of God (2:4-10) and thus are servants of a household (*stewards*). Not only do they have pastors or church leaders (5:1-4), but they themselves have a stewardship, a household management to exercise. Behind this imagery of the spiritual household lies their experience of the Greco-Roman household including not only the biological family but servants as well. The concept of administration or management is not foreign or negative in Peter's view of God's church. In the spirit of mutual love and service, when all is for the *glory of God* (4:11), the image of management is integral to the functioning of God's household.

Two broad kinds of gifts are identified: the gift to speak, and the gift to serve (4:11). The word for speak (*lalei*), is a general term, but in this context it is not simply "conversation" but "authoritative speech in worship assemblies" (Michaels: 250). It could include not only "preaching and teaching" (Kelly: 180), but also words of prophecy or of wisdom and of knowledge, as shown in Paul's list of gifts (Rom. 12:6; 1 Cor. 12:8). In exercising this gift, however, one should have the attitude of *speaking the very word of God*. In Romans 3:2, Paul applies the same expression, literally "the oracles of God," to the Jewish Scriptures. Here Peter is both broadening and deepening the understanding of oral discourse in the life of the Christian community, moving beyond formal prophecy.

The word for serve (*diakonei*, 4:11) is likewise broad in its connotation and was introduced in 4:10. It includes "the conduct of worship services, healing, administrative and judicial leadership, and helping or giving to the poor" (Acts 6:1-6; Michaels: 251). Ministries of speaking are sometimes identified as "ministries of the lips," while those of serving are "ministries of the hand." Obviously, the imagery is fluid.

Such serving, however, is to be done *with the strength that God supplies*. The promise of the Holy Spirit is associated with power (*dunamis*). So when Peter speaks of *strength* (*ischuos*, 4:11), he has the power of the Spirit in mind, though using different words (Goppelt: 305). In short, God-inspired utterance and Spirit-empowered service are to characterize the ministry of God's suffering people living in hope. This is a dimension of the encouragement and empowerment given to believers who are resident aliens, slaves, or partners of unbelieving spouses. Peter urges them to keep on doing right.

The purpose and outcome of such church ministry is *that God may be glorified in all things through Jesus Christ*. In 2:12 Peter has spoken of the hope that pagan Gentiles one day might glorify God. Here the focus is on the mutual sharing and ministry of those within the circle of faith. All that Christian believers say and do ought to glorify God, to bring honor and praise to God, a concept deeply imbedded in the Psalms and throughout the OT. The NT addition is that such honor and glory to God come *through Jesus Christ*. This again indicates the central role Jesus Christ has in Peter's theology. Christians speak and serve "in the name of Jesus Christ" to glorify God.

Peter has just declared glorifying God to be the function of the church. He adds his own word of praise-benediction: *To him belong the glory and the power, forever and ever. Amen*. Whether "him" refers to God or to Jesus Christ is argued by commentators (Michaels:

255). One may have a good theological debate over whether Peter intends to be theocentric or Christocentric. Personal or ecclesiastical self-glorification is certainly ruled out. In a trinitarian understanding, when we glorify God in the name of Jesus, Jesus Christ is glorified as well. For Peter, Jesus Christ remains central in Christian proclamation and Christian service (1:2, 3, 21; 3:15, 21-22; 4:13).

4:12-19 Facing Suffering for the Sake of Christ

In this section Peter responds to the question of how Christians should face their experiences of suffering. In effect, he says,

4:12	Expect suffering.
4:13-14	Rejoice in suffering.
4:15	Examine yourself in suffering.
4:16-18	Glorify God in suffering.
4:19	Trust God and keep on doing good.

The idea of suffering as a faithful believer was already introduced in 1:6. What is new in this section is the possibility of suffering persecution precisely for being a Christian (4:16).

The focus here has returned to the experience of Christians in the midst of hostile society, after the focus on life and ministry within the believing community itself (4:7-11). We reject the notion that 4:12-19 is a separate letter, as some have suggested. Yet we recognize that the letter now takes a somewhat different form, instructing believers directly on how to respond to persecution.

Expect Suffering. Again the believers are addressed as *Beloved* (cf. 2:11). The counsel is direct: *Do not be surprised at the fiery ordeal that is taking place among you to test you.* The metaphor of suffering being like a purging fire to identify and purify precious metals (1:7) is again employed to indicate experiences of suffering ahead. The central and first exhortation is that Christians must learn to expect suffering. Suffering is not to be considered *strange* or unexpected. Some Christians still find it hard to internalize acceptance of suffering. The metaphor embodies the notion of suffering as a time-bound experience and one that has some positive values.

Rejoice in Suffering. Instead of surprise and bitter complaint about what is happening, Peter says, rejoice insofar as you are sharing Christ's sufferings, so that you may also be glad and shout for joy when his glory is revealed. Here Peter indicates that some suffering of believers is indeed a participation (koinoneite) in the sufferings of

Christ, which Peter has been describing in 1:19; 2:21-24; and 3:18. Peter earlier used the language of participation in 4:4, about no longer taking part in the sinful patterns of the pagan world.

The call to rejoice in suffering, so strange to many modern Christians, has precedents in Jewish apocalyptic literature. The writer of 2 Baruch, a pseudepigraphal book, speaks to the righteous: "For surely as you endured much labor in the short time in which you live in the passing world, so you will receive great light in the world that has no end" (48:50). In 52:6-7 he writes, "Enjoy yourselves in the suffering which you suffer now. . . . Prepare yourselves for that which is kept for you, and make ready your souls for the reward that is preserved for you" (Charlesworth, 1:637, 639).

Peter, however, echoes more directly the words of Jesus in Matthew 5:12 (Michaels: 262). Peter's assumption is that such rejoicing happens only through Christian faithfulness, as in suffering unjustly (2:19) for *doing what is right* (3:14), *for the name of Christ* (4:14), or *as a Christian* (4:16). The use of *insofar* (4:13) implies that not all experiences of suffering call for rejoicing. This contrasts with an earlier rendering of "inasmuch" (KJV). According to Acts 5:41, Peter was speaking out of experience.

What enables Christians to rejoice in such circumstances is the anticipation of the final revealing of Christ as vindication. This will occasion further gladness and shouts of joy, as we also see in the Pauline tradition (Rom. 5:2-5; 8:17, 18; 2 Cor. 4:16-17).

Peter's counsel is motivated further and reinforced by a beatitude in 4:14: *If you are reviled for the name of Christ, you are blessed.* This recalls the beatitude of 3:14, also pronouncing a blessing on those who suffer for righteousness' sake. New here is the specific mention of suffering verbal abuse for the name of Christ. Peter's language is close to Matthew 5:11, "for my sake," and Luke 6:22, "for the sake of the Son of Man." Now the believers' confession of Jesus Christ and their ministry in the name of Christ have become the occasion of ridicule, whether by officials or simply by neighbors.

The promise embedded in this beatitude is that *the spirit of glory, which is the Spirit of God, is resting on you.* Peter may be reflecting the promise of Jesus that the Holy Spirit would stand by his followers when they would be questioned by authorities (Mark 13:11; Luke 12:12). But more likely he is adapting language from Isaiah 11:2a, understood in the early church as applying to Jesus. Now Peter applies it to faithful believers who are persecuted for the name of Jesus. The presence of the Holy Spirit resting on the persecuted believing community is indeed *the spirit of glory.*

Examine Yourself in Suffering. Since not all suffering is *for the name of Christ,* Peter urges them to examine themselves and ascertain that none of them suffers as *a murderer, a thief, a criminal, or even as a mischief maker.* Peter is here warning against presumption and is commending self-examination. Peter's list of wrong reasons for suffering is intriguing. Beginning with murder and theft, obviously wrong (Exod. 20:13, 15), he moves to crime, a general term for various misdemeanors. *Mischief maker,* a "busybody" or "meddler," literally means one who acts like a bishop in the affairs of another without having jurisdiction. Even this, while not a misdemeanor or a crime, occasions suffering that is not included in suffering for Christ's sake.

Glorify God in Suffering. After the warning against suffering for wrong reasons, Peter says, *Yet if any of you suffers as a Christian, do not consider it a disgrace, but glorify God because you bear this name.* Many have tried to find in this verse a clue for the time of writing. Some think it refers to one of the official persecutions of Christians, whether under Nero, or Domitian, or Trajan. With more careful reflection, however, we know that Christians have suffered for that name at many other times as well. So this is no clear indicator of the time of composition.

To suffer *as a Christian* is about the same as suffering *for the name of Christ* (4:14). The name *Christian* is used for "the disciples" of Christ also in Acts (11:26; 26:28). It means Christ's adherents, those who belong to him. This name was attached to them by their Jewish and pagan neighbors rather than chosen by the followers of Jesus, and perhaps began as a term of ridicule rather than respect. The reference to *suffering as a Christian* here does not necessarily mean that Christian faith has been declared illegal or criminal. It simply indicates that their adversaries, including sometimes the police and the courts, even in Nero's reign, were persecuting believers not so much for certain behaviors but because of their faith and character (Goppelt: 322).

David Schroeder suggests, "It could well be that Christians were being persecuted because they were bringing a new ethic into the Greco-Roman household. Since the household is the microcosm of the macrocosm, the larger society feared the new ethic and saw it as treason" (letter of 1997).

In this situation, Peter declares, *Do not consider it as a disgrace; do not be ashamed.* One common human response to abuse, including undeserved abuse, is feeling shame and disgrace. But Peter declares that shame is not appropriate in this situation. Instead, he calls for an alternative response: *Glorify God because you bear this name.* Here the *name* is not simply *the name of Christ,* as in 4:14, but rather the name *Christian,* which indeed incorporates the name of Christ (Goppelt: 328).

The same two alternatives, shame and glorifying God are also identified in 2:12 and 3:16, which applies them to pagan neighbors. In 4:16, the terms apply to the believers themselves. The reminder to glorify God was sounded in 4:11 in the exercise of Christian community. Here it has to do with the way Christians continue "to acknowledge their faith in Christ openly and without fear, regardless of the consequences. As in the case of their ministry to one another, glorification of God depends on attitudes and behavior toward other people" (Michaels: 269). If they live as Christians, they will not be put to shame in God's judgment. So meanwhile, there is no need to count it a disgrace to suffer as a Christian.

Suffering as a Christian either is already or about to become reality (4:16). Now Peter adds a further explanation (4:17a), a rhetorical question (4:17b), an OT quotation (4:18), and a concluding exhortation (4:19). He sees this suffering itself as a beginning of judgment for the household of God.

The *time of judgment* here is perceived as ongoing, beginning with the experience of persecuted Christians and continuing until the "imminent, universal, final judgment" (Goppelt: 329), of which Peter has spoken repeatedly (1:17; 2:23; 4:5). The suffering of the righteous is itself an indication that God's judgment is beginning for all peoples. This belief has numerous precedents in the OT and other Jewish literature (listed in Goppelt: 330-331).

Suffering among Christians is mentioned in 1 Corinthians 11:22, in relation to abuses of the Lord's Supper. In 1 Peter 4:1-6, suffering is associated with the experience of Christians who, upon conversion, distance themselves from their former sinful practices and associations. However, 4:18 appears to contrast Jesus' faithful followers' experience in judgment with the experience of those who persecute them. Peter intends to encourage believers who remain faithful under the stress of abuse and persecution.

The image of the church as house or household, first introduced in 2:5, is again evoked to sharpen the distinction between the faithful and the unfaithful. They are distinguished both in attitude and in destiny, between those who are at home in God and those who disbelieve and abuse the faithful. This contrast is further sharpened in the quotation of Proverbs 11:31 (LXX), shaped as a rhetorical question. In this passage, the righteous are saved, but with hardship or difficulty.

The destiny of the ungodly and the sinners is not made explicit. But by implication it is manifestly worse than anything followers of Jesus would ever experience. Intriguingly, Peter leaves this to the reader to consider.

Trust God and Keep On Doing Good. In this situation, Peter exhorts, *Let those suffering in accordance with God's will entrust themselves to a faithful Creator, while continuing to do good* (4:19). Peter stops short of declaring that suffering is imposed on Christians. Yet he does indicate that such suffering even for righteousness is permitted by God (3:17) and is better than suffering for doing evil. Peter urges Christians to entrust themselves to God. The Greek text speaks of "souls" being yielded to the care of God even as Jesus yielded himself on the cross, invoking Psalm 31:5 (cf. Luke 23:46).

Only here in the NT is God spoken of as *a faithful Creator.* Both designations of God speak powerfully to one suffering abuse. God who is *Creator* is surely able to provide present care and ultimate justice for those created. Experience and history have already proved that this God can be trusted fully. Peter has given a truly powerful image for casting oneself and one's destiny into the hands of God, even as Jesus did (Luke 23:46), and as Peter calls us likewise to do (5:7, 10).

THE TEXT IN BIBLICAL CONTEXT

Witness Under Stress

Much of the NT reflects situations in which Christians face their call to be witnesses to Christ under conditions of opposition and adversity. Jesus recognizes that his disciples would face such reality and sought to prepare them. He tells them, "Take heed to yourselves, for they will deliver you up to councils, and you will be beaten in synagogues, and you will stand before governors and kings for my sake, to bear testimony before them" (Mark 13:9-10; Matt. 10:17ff.; Luke 21:12ff.).

In the Farewell Discourses of the Fourth Gospel (John 14–16), Jesus speaks repeatedly of coming hostility and persecution, as in 15:20-21: "Remember the word that I said to you, 'Servants are not greater than their master.' If they persecuted me, they will persecute you. . . . But they will do all these things to you on account of my name, because they do not know him who sent me." Peter would remember these and many other warnings of Jesus.

Acts reports the experiences of the early church, including the time after Pentecost when Peter faces opposition from the Sanhedrin (Acts 4–5). Before that council, Peter declares, "We must obey God rather than any human authority. The God of our ancestors raised up Jesus. . . . And we are witnesses to these things" (Acts 5:29-32). "As they left the council, they rejoiced that they were considered worthy to suffer dishonor for the sake of the name" of Christ (5:41). According to Acts, Peter was among those considered worthy to suffer for Christ.

The writings of Paul also are full of references to witnessing to the truth of the gospel under stress (2 Cor. 6:7-12; 11:23-33; cf. Acts 16–19; 27–28). Peter, in writing to the Christians of Asia Minor, describes some particular circumstances under which they may be called on to give the reason for their hope. His word in this letter reinforces the larger NT tradition of Christians bearing witness boldly and yet humbly under conditions of hostility and stress.

The Vicarious Death and Exaltation of Christ

Human suffering is real and prevalent in the world created and sustained by a loving God. It continues to be a serious intellectual problem to many in contemporary society. Yet Peter does not shrink from this engaging theme. He declares the suffering of Christ, leading to his death, to be an essential step in Christ's path to vindication and exaltation, and necessary for human salvation (3:18-22). This fits with the NT understanding that the suffering and death of Christ was more than a noble example to be emulated; it also had redemptive and atoning significance.

The vicarious suffering of the Servant is described in Isaiah 53:4-6. Peter applies this portrayal to Jesus in 2:22-25 and carries this forward in 3:18. Both Peter and Paul speak of the vicarious suffering of Christ and of his later exaltation by God. Paul's use of the so-called Christ-hymn in Philippians 2:5-11 links in a confessional sequence the self-emptying of Jesus in the incarnation, his death on the cross, and his exaltation. In Romans 5–6, Paul elaborates the meaning of Christ's death for our sins, and in 1 Corinthians 15:3 he declares this to be at the heart of the gospel he proclaims.

Peter's theology of the cross and its dominance in the epistle has been noted (1:2b, 18-19; 2:4-8, 21-25; 3:18; 4:1, 13; 5:1). It falls within the broader early Christian understandings of this historical-theological event of the NT, especially in Pauline theology. For Paul, the preaching of the cross is basic (1 Cor. 1:18, 21; 15:3; Rom. 1:16; Gal. 3:1; Phil. 2:5-11). In these passages, the death of Jesus is understood as gospel, as "good news" for sinful humanity. God's love in Christ is thus not only made manifest but also made effective and redemptive for those who trust in the power of forgiving love supremely demonstrated in that death.

However, neither Paul's nor Peter's theology of the cross stops with suffering and death. It moves on to the resurrection and exaltation of the crucified Jesus. The resurrection becomes the ground of Christians' living hope (1:3). The exaltation of the suffering, risen Jesus (3:22) becomes an ultimate encouragement for the suffering believer to follow the example of Jesus in facing suffering (2:21). However, for both Paul and Peter, it is a participation, by faith, in the sufferings and exaltation of Christ, which through the Spirit enable Christians to keep on trusting God and doing good (4:13, 19).

Paul speaks of being crucified with Christ, yet living (Gal. 2:20), of being united with Christ in death and resurrection (Rom. 6:5ff.). Second Timothy 2:11 expresses the same image. The theme of being united with Christ in death and resurrection functions both as encouragement in suffering and as call to live in newness of life. This includes both pastoral and ethical elements.

Peter declares that the exaltation of Jesus Christ involves also the dethronement of powers (3:22). This declaration also has a broader NT context (Paul on "powers" in Rom. 8:38f.; 1 Cor. 2:8; 15:24-25; Eph. 1:20f.; 2:1f.; 3:10; 6:12; Col. 1:16; 2:15). Several significant discussions relate the exaltation of Christ to the dethroning of these powers: Berkhof, *Christ and the Powers;* Yoder, *The Politics of Jesus* (135-214); and Wink, *Unmasking the Powers.*

Baptism in the New Testament

One of the better works on this theme is still that of Beasley-Murray. He deals not only with the origins of baptism but also with baptism in the synoptic Gospels and Acts, Pauline literature, Johannine literature, Hebrews, and 1 Peter (242-262).

Beasley-Murray's perspective is one that affirms the baptism of believers rather than infants. In developing his doctrine of baptism, he relates the practice to grace, to faith, to the Spirit, to the church, to ethics, and to hope. Finally he speaks of its necessity in the life of an obedient community composed by faithful followers of Jesus. After his extensive study of each NT reference to baptism, he develops a

"Doctrine of Christian Baptism" involving, in summary, the following theses:

1. Christian baptism involves the operation of divine grace. The language of "sacrament" applied to baptism may or may not be appropriate. Yet 1 Peter 3:21 makes it clear that its power lies not in the water of baptism but in *the resurrection of Jesus Christ* (265).

2. Faith, which is also by grace, "is needful *before* baptism, that Christ and the Gospel may truly be confessed in it, *in* baptism, to receive what God bestows, and *after* baptism, in order to abide in the grace so freely given and to work out that grace which God has wrought within" (274).

3. Baptism "in the name of Christ, which is 'putting on' Christ, . . . cannot be other than baptism in the Spirit (1 Cor. 6:11; 12:14)." Because the NT associates baptism with the work of the Holy Spirit, baptism is always the true context of regeneration (277).

4. "Baptism into Christ is baptism (in)to the Church; it cannot be otherwise, for the Church is . . . the body of Christ" (279). In the NT the church is perceived primarily as visible. Hence, the believers church emphasizes that baptism involves initiation into a visible congregation of believers.

5. In the apostolic church, "baptism is a moral-religious act" (284). It assumes a conversion of moral lifestyle as emphasized particularly in 1 Peter. For this reason, it is commonly associated with catechetical instruction so that the new believer may have guidance for the new faith and life coming from his new allegiance to Jesus Christ. Some have argued that 1 Peter 1:3—4:11 was precisely such a set of instructions, yet this has been challenged. In this commentary, we have assumed that 1 Peter is a letter rather than a catechism.

6. Baptism participates in the eschatological hope for the vindication of the crucified Christ, and this embraces vindication for his followers (290-296). This ultimate victory of Christ and the redeemed is also clearly taught in 1 Peter, which stresses participation in the coming glory of Christ.

7. All of the above indicates the great importance of Christian baptism for the believer. Yet we must still conclude that it is not the water or the rite of baptism that saves. The Savior is Jesus Christ, in whom the believer has redemption and eternal hope (290-305).

The Relationship of Suffering and Sin

The relationship between suffering and sin, in its broader framework, is a recurring theme in biblical theology. Virtually every book of the

Bible touches it in some way. The problem of suffering is addressed particularly in the book of Job. Job rejects the conventional wisdom that suffering is directly the consequence of sin. The innocent and the righteous also suffer. This understanding finds its highest expression in Jesus, the sinless one, who took it upon himself to suffer and die for others.

Peter does not address in any theological depth the question of suffering in its relation to human sin. In 2:20 he uses the word for sins when he speaks of the occasions when servants may be buffeted for their sins, in contrast to the times when they are innocent. In 2:22 he speaks of Jesus Christ having done no sin. According to 2:24, Christ is the one who took on himself our sins on the cross, so that hereafter we should be dead to sin. This perspective is repeated in 3:18 and touched on again in 4:1. The other use is found in 4:8, declaring that love covers a multitude of sins.

In short, Peter has recognized that humans, including Christians, may on occasion suffer for their own sins. However, Jesus Christ himself died for human sin, so that we might become "dead to sin" and thus stop sinning. The letter also expresses this in other ways.

On suffering and sin, Peter is expressing essentially Pauline perspectives. However, he does not elaborate themes of forgiveness of sin as Jesus and Paul did. The theme of sin is especially dominant in Romans 5–6, in Ephesians 2, and in Hebrews.

The Church as Stewardship of Gifts

Peter's description of the church functioning as a community of forgiving love and welcoming hospitality (4:9) merges into a household of shared gifts (4:10). This also participates in some aspects of the Pauline doctrine of charismatic gifts introduced in Romans 12:6-8; 1 Corinthians 12:4-10; and Ephesians 4:11-12. The gifts identified in each case are as follows:

Romans 12	1 Corinthians 12	Ephesians 4	1 Peter 4
prophecy	wisdom	apostles	speaking
ministry	knowledge	prophets	serving
teaching	faith	evangelists	
exhortation	healing	pastors	
generosity	miracles	teachers	
leading	prophecy		
compassion	tongues		
	interpretation of tongues		

Obviously the lists are quite different, keeping us from attempting to establish one comprehensive biblical list. Neither are they ranked, as we may be tempted to do. Each gift is significant, to be recognized where present, and not to become an occasion for rivalry or dissension. Together these gifts represent resources of the Holy Spirit for the life and ministry of the community of faith and hope.

The Suffering of Christ's People

Peter places special emphasis on how Christ's people share with Christ in suffering. Bertil Gärtner observes that in the NT, the idea of suffering is inseparable from the concept of Christian koinonia (*DNTT*, 3:724). To suffer as a Christian (4:16) is to "participate or fellowship" in the sufferings of Christ (4:13). Paul called it "sharing" in the "sufferings" of Christ (Phil. 3:10), suffering "with" Christ, and anticipating being "glorified with him" (Rom. 8:17).

The experience of suffering for the sake of Christ is also a fellowship of the followers of Christ with each other, as well as with their crucified Lord. Peter speaks in 5:9b of the sufferings of brothers and sisters throughout the world, as does Paul in 1 Thessalonians 2:14. In the local congregation the followers of Christ are to experience compassion by absorbing with forgiveness the hurts that occur among them (1 Pet. 3:8-9), even as Paul in Romans 12:14-21 calls for mutual forgiving love, overcoming evil with good, and rejecting vengeful response.

Such practice involves suffering for Christ's people. When done in Christ's name, it is part of "the fellowship of his sufferings" (Phil. 3:10, KJV) in our experience of living with one another. In Colossians 1:24, Paul speaks of his own suffering on behalf of the believers at Colossae. He says he is able to rejoice in this, knowing that it is "completing what is lacking in Christ's afflictions for the sake of his body, that is, the church." Thus Paul closely identifies both with Christ and with Christ's people, not as a redeemer, but as a missionary.

Of the 42 times that the Greek word *paschō* ("suffer") is used in the NT, 12 of these appear in 1 Peter. Four refer explicitly to the suffering of Christ (2:21, 23; 3:18; 4:1), and seven speak of the suffering of Christians (2:19-20; 3:14, 17; 4:15, 19; 5:10), while the second use in 4:1 remains ambiguous, depending on the interpretation given. Of all the NT uses, 20 refer to the suffering of Christ and 19 to the suffering of Christians; the rest are used in other ways. This concentration in 1 Peter marks it as an epistle of suffering as well as an epistle of hope [Suffering].

Peter's theology of the cross is a significant witness in the larger NT understanding of the meaning and challenge of the suffering and death of Jesus Christ. For the apostle Paul, "The cross of Christ is seen as the saving event which radically transforms the world, providing a completely new motivation for action and thought (E. Brandenburger, *DNTT,* 1:397). Paul understands the gospel as the good news of the cross and resurrection of Jesus Christ (1 Cor. 15:4), which may be foolishness to those who perish. But for believers, the gospel is "the power of God and the wisdom of God," bringing salvation and peace (1 Cor. 1:18-25; Eph. 2:13-14; Col. 1:19-20). Paul says that in Christ, "God was reconciling the world to himself" (2 Cor. 5:19-21). Understood in trinitarian terms, God was giving himself in Christ so that humankind might be redeemed from sin and brought into fellowship with God. In the power of the Spirit, they might live for God and the kingdom of love, peace, and justice.

Peter's theology of the cross places special emphasis on following Jesus in the way of the cross (2:21-25). This corresponds to Paul's language of participating in the sufferings of Christ (Gal. 2:20; Col. 1:24; Phil. 3:10-11). Peter shares with Paul the concern that the mind of Christ, as demonstrated in his humility and death (Phil. 2:5-11), find embodiment in the faith, conduct, and lifestyle of the believer (1 Pet. 2:21; 4:1-2).

In the NT the cross remains always in some dimensions as a divine mystery. It has come to be understood as God's action to redeem humanity from sin and its consequences, personally and corporately. The cross opens the way to forgiveness, reconciliation, love, peace, and righteousness.

THE TEXT IN THE LIFE OF THE CHURCH
Blandina, Perpetua, and Felicitas—Martyrs

We have general awareness that in the early church many died as martyrs for the Christian faith. However, we have not always given attention to the noble women among them. The stories of Blandina, Perpetua, and Felicitas may include a mixture of history and embellishment, yet they bear witness to the significant role of women as carriers of Christian faith in the early centuries. Blandina was martyred at Lyon, and Perpetua twenty-five years later at Carthage, probably on March 7, 203.

Of Blandina, it is reported that, after the death of bishop Pothinus, she emerged "as the leader and inspirer of the confessors" (Frend: 3-5). She had been a slave whose mistress was a Christian, though her master was not. After the authorities were aware that Blandina was, in fact, a Christian leader, "she was kept back until the final day of the games, and with a youth named Ponticus, faced the full fury of the crowd. On this occasion she inspired others 'like a noble mother encouraging her children' and finally went triumphantly to her death. Even those who wished her end concluded 'that no woman had suffered so much in their experience.' "

Perpetua, on the other hand, was a member of the urban upper-middle class in Carthage. She also was "the acknowledged leader of the group of Christians arrested probably early in 203." From her diary, we learn of her concern about her infant child as well as her conflict with her father. He tried to persuade her to yield to her persecutors for his own sake and the sake of the child, yet she remained firm. Perpetua had a slave Felicitas, also a believer, who was to be turned over to the beasts shortly after giving birth to her child. Perpetua remained steadfast in her faith, bearing witness to her executioners. As a Christian mistress, she encouraged and gave help to her Christian slave, Felicitas, even as both of them died for their faith in Christ (Musurillo: 100-131).

Anne Jensen, in her scholarly work on *God's Self-Confident Daughters: Early Christianity and the Liberation of Women*, gives further details and helpful historical and theological interpretations of these martyrdoms. Blandina was "a slave as Mother of the Church" (90-93), and Perpetua and Felicity were "Mothers and Martyrs" (93-100). Jensen sees the significance of these women martyrs as substantial, inspiring, and influential. They gave strong personal and public confessions of faith in Jesus Christ quite independent of the faith posture of male members of their respective households or families.

Witnessing While Suffering

A survey of sixteenth-century Anabaptist writings reveals that the concept of suffering and missionary witnessing are often linked. This is particularly true in *Martyrs Mirror,* where extensive use is made of 1 Peter, including this section.

Jacques Mesdagh, was one of four martyrs burned at the stake at Kortrijck in Flanders on November 8, 1567, "in the market place, before the city hall." He had been imprisoned "with iron fetters on his feet, for more than twenty months," and on September 9, 1567, wrote a letter of faith and witness to his sister, abounding with biblical language and references. At least eight passages of 1 Peter are quoted or mentioned, including 1 Peter 3:13-14 (*MM:* 715-721).

Mesdagh's farewell immediately follows a similar letter written by
"Cornelis the Shoemaker" to his wife, who likewise was "burned with
three others" in the great marketplace at Antwerp on September 13,
1567. He encourages her, "Hence, fear not them that kill the body;
for they cannot harm the soul. Let us therefore not grieve because of
the work of the Lord, . . . but as Christ says, Rejoice, and be glad
therein, for it shall be rewarded you in heaven: and as Peter says,
Praise and glorify the Lord in this matter (Matt. 5:12; 1 Pet. 3:15;
4:16)" (*MM*: 713-715).

Similar witness is given by Walter of Stoelwijk, martyred in 1541
(*MM*: 455ff.), and Bartholomeus Panten writing to his brother Karel
in Haarlem in 1592. Panten tells of his own imprisonment and tor-
ture at Ghent, and quotes 1 Peter 3:14-15 to provide biblical understanding of his experience (*MM*: 1082-1083). These are but samples
of eloquent witness by early Anabaptists who were inspired and
undergirded by the message of 1 Peter to persecuted believers. They
endured their suffering until they were put to death. They also witnessed to family members and others concerning "the hope" that was
in them as they faced execution.

Balthasar Hubmaier, Anabaptist pastor in Waldshut, considered
himself a friend of Ulrich Zwingli and wrote his "Theses Against Eck,"
Hubmaier's earlier university teacher and later a leading Catholic
polemicist against the Zwinglian Reformation. Hubmaier began with
the words, "Every Christian is obligated to give account for his hope
and thereby of the faith that is in him to whoever desires it (1 Pet.
3:15)." In the heat of theological controversy, 1 Peter provided for
him ground and motivation in debate with the opponents of early
Anabaptist faith and teaching (Hubmaier: 51).

Peter Riedemann, a leading Anabaptist and Hutterite, quoted
1 Peter 3:15 on the title page of his major *Confession of Faith*.
During 1540-42, in prison for his faith, he gave this account for his
hope, writing for the Lutheran ruler, Philip of Hesse. This *Confession*
remains the basic charter for the Hutterites even today.

Noah, the Flood, and Anabaptist Baptism

Suffering Anabaptists found much in 1 Peter to sustain them in their
experience of persecution. Yet their appeal to 1 Peter 3:20-22 on the
subject of baptism receives even more attention. The theologians,
such as Balthasar Hubmaier, Dirk Philips, and Pilgram Marpeck,
appealed to 1 Peter 3 in defending their view of baptism, and many
Anabaptist martyrs followed their lead.

Hubmaier writes substantially on 1 Peter 3:20ff. (1) He sees Noah's ark as a "figure" of baptism. (2) Eight persons believed the Word of God before they entered the ark, hence supporting the idea of believers baptism rather than infant baptism. (3) Water baptism does not wash away our sins nor save us, but "only the certain knowledge of a good conscience toward God through the resurrection of Jesus Christ." (4) It is the baptismal candidate personally, not a parent or "godparent," who is to make "the answer of a good conscience toward God" (Hubmaier: 134-135).

Pilgram Marpeck similarly comments on 1 Peter 3:21:

> Now listen to what Peter says. He says that baptism saves us. Why? Is it because we are dunked into water or because *it is poured over us?* Oh no, for he differentiates between true baptism and the mere shedding of the pollution of the flesh. This last act alone cannot do it; only the covenant of a good conscience with God has the power to save. . . . Such a conscience, however, can be created and achieved only by the Spirit of God, who cleanses the heart and unites us through faith. . . . Otherwise, baptism is of no use and is only a mockery in the presence of God. (Marpeck: 187)

Later Marpeck affirms the value of baptism:

> In the ark there were eight people who were preserved through water and, in the same way, baptism saves us (1 Pet. 3:20f.). We enter into the holy church by baptism, obedient to God and fulfilling his will. In the same way as it happened to those who entered the ark, *so too, through baptism with water, the world is condemned and the children of God preserved; through baptism, a man enters into the body of Christ, yes, into Christ Himself, as the true ark wherein, through the word of obedience, one can be preserved from the flood.* (Marpeck: 200-201)

Dirk Philips likewise repeatedly appeals to the same passage and the same image (79, 81-2, 101, 272, 322, 418, 420, 422). Thus it is clear that early Anabaptist leaders drew heavily on 1 Peter 3:20-21 in their argumentation over believers baptism. The impact of these verses is similarly reflected in the confessions and letters written by Anabaptist martyrs, as recorded in *Martyrs Mirror* (806, 65, 369, 683, 824, 30, 66, 189-190, 398, 417, 443, 467, 499, et al.).

In the late twentieth century, as part of an integration dialogue between the Mennonite Church and the General Conference Mennonite Church, a new *Confession of Faith in a Mennonite Perspective* (1995) was compiled and adopted. The article on baptism likewise draws on 1 Peter, affirming that "Scripture also refers to baptism as a pledge to God (1 Pet. 3:21) and as a commitment to faithfulness and ministry (Rom. 6:1-11). Jesus' baptism can be seen in the light of this pledge. In the NT, baptism follows a person's faith. Baptism therefore is for those who are ready to enter into a faithful relationship with Christ and the church."

The Church as a Stewardship of Gifts

Dirk Philips in his essay "The Sending of Preachers or Teachers" (167) appeals to 1 Peter 4:10-11, as well as Romans 12, 1 Corinthians 12, and Ephesians 4, and comments:

> Out of these words it is easily understood in the first place, how God places his ministers in his congregations and distributes all kinds of gifts. In the second place, how necessary ministers are in the congregation and what their work and service is. In the third place, that the congregation (since it is one with Christ) has the power to choose teachers and ministers according to the Scripture. But which is the congregation of Christ, which has received such power from Christ (not only to choose teachers and leaders, but, what is more, to bind and loose, to forgive sins and to retain them), Scripture testifies clearly at many places, namely, that it is a gathering of believers, that is of living saints and born-again persons who believe the Word of God entirely, teach the same correctly, bear fruit with it, practice the sacraments of Christ fittingly, correctly maintain the ban, walk in love, and conduct and carry out all things according to the gospel. (Dirk: 220)

Pilgram Marpeck also, appealing to the same NT passages, including 1 Peter 4:10, speaks of the authority of believers to serve:

> Such authority is committed to all true believers by Christ, their Master. Christ also comforts them to act in all external commands in accordance with the gift and measure of faith that is given to each. Not all are apostles, not all are prophets, not all perform miracles, not all are teachers (1 Cor. 12:29). But none of these gifts of faith will be lacking to the believers in their need. For whoever believes that all authority has been given to Christ, attested by His words (Matt. 28:18), moves, speaks, and acts not out of his own authority but by the authorization of Christ. (Marpeck: 77)

Suffering for the Name of Jesus

Christian history also includes hundreds of accounts of "suffering for the name of Jesus." Somewhat less known than others are the stories of the Hutterites, who lived in Eastern Europe and now live in North America. *The Chronicle of the Hutterian Brethren* shows how they associated their experience with 1 Peter 4:12-19:

As soon as they stepped outside the door, they were abused and called Anabaptists, re-baptizers, new baptizers, schismatics, agitators, and all kinds of insulting names. People everywhere disparaged them and taunted them with gruesome lies, accusing them of eating children and other horrible things that would have shocked us deeply had we ever dreamed of them, much less done them. . . . The world hated and persecuted us solely for the sake of Christ's name and his truth, because we followed him, and for no other reason. And this was a sure sign. If someone traveled with only a staff in hand to show that he did not mean to harm anyone, or prayed before eating, he was called an Anabaptist, a heretic. Such is the stupidity of the devil. But if someone became unfaithful and walked according to the ways of the heathen, a sword at his side and a musket at his shoulder, from that moment on he was welcome to the world and "a good Christian" in their eyes. (Hutterian Brethren: 408)

Menno Simons in his "Reply to Gellius Faber" lists "True Signs" by which the church of Christ may be known. He includes the following: (1) unadulterated pure doctrine, (2) scriptural use of the sacramental signs, (3) obedience to the Word, (4) unfeigned and brotherly love, (5) bold confession of God and Christ, and also (6) oppression and tribulation for the sake of the Lord's Word, invoking 1 Peter 1:6; 3:14; 4:13; and 5:10 (Menno: 743). Earlier in the same document, Menno complains to Faber, a Roman Catholic leader who became Protestant but opposed the Anabaptists:

Although we testify by so many tribulations that we, in our poor weakness, sincerely desire to fear and follow the Lord, and that we seek the welfare of all men, yet they reproach without measure. They stir up the lords and rulers of cities and countries everywhere, peddling the idea that we are an ungodly sect and Anabaptists; that we seduce the people; that we plan to raise turmoil and rebellion, and more such turbulent inventions and slander, in order that they may thus obscure and extirpate and restrain the noble Word of God. (Menno: 627).

Christian Martyrdom in the Twentieth Century

Some may consider reflections on Christian martyrdom as irrelevant in our century. However, Susan Bergman notes that David Barrett and Todd M. Johnson count "40 million Christian martyrs across twenty centuries, and estimate 26,625,000 Christians who have been martyred in this century alone—more than in all other centuries combined" (Bergman, 1996b: 15). She cautions against misuse of such statistics. Nevertheless, "the current annual count of Christian martyrs' deaths by Barrett and Johnson's estimate runs to 290,000, as of 1990. If one is a bishop, evangelist, catechist, or missionary, the likelihood of being martyred this year is as high as 5 percent." We also acknowledge that it is sometimes difficult to distinguish between religious and political dissent in cases of martyrdom.

Among the descriptions of a courageous and hope-filled spirit on the part of such martyred missionaries, few would surpass the letter of Lizzie Atwater to her sister, written in China on August 3, 1900. Soon afterward she died in the Boxer Rebellion.

> Dear ones, I long for the sight of your faces, but I fear we shall not meet on earth. . . . I am preparing for the end very quietly and calmly. The Lord is wonderfully near, and He will not fail me. I was very restless and excited while there seemed a chance of life, but God has taken away that feeling, and now I just pray for grace to meet the terrible end bravely. The pain will soon be over, and, oh, the sweetness of the welcome above!
>
> My little baby will go with me. I think God will give it to me in Heaven, and my dear mother will be so glad to see us. I cannot imagine the Savior's welcome. Oh, that will compensate for all the days of suspense. Dear ones, live near to God, and cling less closely to earth. *There is no other way by which we can receive the peace from God which passes understanding.* . . . I must keep calm and still these hours. I do not regret coming to China, but am sorry I have done so little. My married life, two precious years, has been so very full of happiness. We will die together, my dear husband and I. . . . I send my love to you all, and the dear friends who remember me. (Bergman, 1996b:11).

This is surely the response called for in 1 Peter 4:19b. Such martyrs *entrust themselves to a faithful Creator, while continuing to do good.*

5:1-11

Leadership and Loyalty in the Suffering Church

PREVIEW

Having focused on the themes of hope and suffering in the first four chapters, Peter now brings his letter to a conclusion with special attention to the themes of leadership and loyalty. This concluding section begins with a direct address to the elders in these congregations, picking up again elements of the Household Codes by speaking first to *the elders* and then to *the younger*. Finally, he addresses *all* again, leaving the pattern of selecting a specific group within the larger community.

OUTLINE

The Call to Leadership and Loyalty, 5:1-5a

The Call to Humility and Trust, 5:5b-7

The Call to Watch and Resist Evil, 5:8-9

Benediction and Doxology, 5:10-11

EXPLANATORY NOTES

The Call to Leadership and Loyalty 5:1-5a

Peter first speaks to *elders*, identifying with them, *as an elder myself*. Earlier he had spoken of himself as *an apostle of Jesus Christ* (1:1) but now (5:1) literally as a "fellow-elder." He identifies himself further as *a witness (martus) of the sufferings of Christ*, and finally as *one who shares in the glory to be revealed*. Witness here is sometimes interpreted as "eye-witness" (as in *Living Bible*), and that may be the intended meaning. But *witness* is also used of one who bears witness to the sufferings of Christ, without having been "an eye-witness" of these sufferings. Nevertheless, this self-identification lends some support to the tradition of apostolic authorship of this epistle.

Participating or sharing in the yet-to-be-revealed *glory* not only reflects Peter's strong eschatological Christology (1:5, 7; 4:7, 11, 13) but anticipates 5:4, which speaks of the chief shepherd appearing and honoring faithful servants.

The word *elder (presbuteros)* has both a generalized and a particularized meaning. It commonly means "an older person," but in NT usage comes to denote a person entrusted with leadership responsibilities. Often, perhaps usually but not necessarily, these were older persons. The usage here as elsewhere in the NT clearly indicates a person carrying an understood role of congregational leadership (Acts 11:30; 14:23; 1 Tim. 5:17-19; Titus 1:5; 2 John 1; 3 John 1). This practice in the early church was taken over from Judaism, where civic-religious leaders were called *elders* and were commonly older persons (Luke 7:3) *[Images of the Church and Leadership]*.

The exhortation to the elders invokes the pastoral image of the shepherd. The shepherd imagery is already present in the prophetic literature (Isaiah, Jeremiah, Ezekiel) and is also claimed by Jesus in both the Synoptic and Johannine traditions. *Tend the flock of God, that is your charge, exercising the oversight* (5:2). This uses the image of the shepherd both in designating the church leader's task, to *tend* and to practice *oversight,* and in designating the people of faith as *the flock of God.* The word for *tend* is literally "to shepherd," which may well include "leading, feeding, and heeding." The same shepherd and flock image is used in Acts 20:28 of Paul instructing the elders in Ephesus. In both cases the meaning of *tend* is explicated to include *oversight.*

In 2:25 the author calls Jesus the *shepherd and guardian of your souls,* and describes people as straying sheep. The pastoral image is deeply imbedded in Peter's awareness. In 2:5 Peter has spoken of the church as the *household of God* and in 4:10-11 as *stewards of manifold gifts*. The image of *the flock of God* reminds us of the commission of Jesus to Peter in John 21:16, "Feed my sheep." There the sheep belong to Christ; here, in larger perspective, Christ is the Chief Shepherd, and the flock belongs to God.

This general appeal is followed by three somewhat parallel phrases that describe the shepherd's spirit, motivation, and leadership style, stated first negatively, then positively:

Negatively	Positively
not under compulsion	but willingly
not for sordid gain	but eagerly
not as lording	but as examples

The shepherding ministry of the elders is to be a voluntary service, not a response to conscription. The spirit is to be the same as in the practice of hospitality without complaining (4:9). Paul also warned the Corinthians that they are to give "not reluctantly or under compulsion, for God loves the cheerful giver" (2 Cor. 9:7). Peter adds the comment, *as God would have you do it,* indicating that the divine will, rather than their own willingness, is the ultimate measure of the shepherd's attitude.

A second antithesis, involving motivation, warns against serving because of greed. Peter's assumption is that the ministry of the elders is supported financially (Michaels: 283), but financial gain is not to become their motive for serving. This is similar to 1 Timothy 3:8; Titus 1:7; and more generally the warning against the "love of money" in 1 Timothy 6:6-10. Instead of serving motivated by greed, they are to serve *eagerly,* "with enthusiasm." This is a strong adverb to contrast with "greedily" and to enhance the meaning of *willingly* (Michaels: 285). This provides no comfort for a congregation supporting a pastor stingily. Neither does it give ground for church leaders to make salary a first consideration in a call to serve.

The third antithesis deals with the style of leadership. This is not to be one of being a *lord,* "domineering" over those for whom one has responsibility. This recalls Jesus' warning to his disciples in Mark 10:42-43. He used the same vocabulary to identify the leadership style his followers should exercise, in contrast with what prevails in the pagan world around them. Instead of *lording it over others,* elders are to *be examples to the flock.* In 2:21, Peter has already spoken of Jesus as an *example* in his way of responding to suffering. Here he uses a different word, *tupoi,* "model," also lived out by Paul, Timothy, and Titus (Phil. 3:17; 2 Thess. 3:9; 1 Tim. 4:12; Titus 2:7).

These church leaders are urged to model servanthood instead of dominance. They are to lead by being servant leaders, thus modeling for their people how to be servants of one another in Christian love.

Obviously, what Peter has asked of these fellow elders calls for humility and integrity as they reexamine their faithfulness to their task, their spirit, their motivations, and their style of leadership. As if anticipating that they might become discouraged, Peter reminds them, *And when the chief shepherd appears, you will receive the crown of glory that never fades away.*

The *chief shepherd* is Jesus Christ, whose appearing Peter has mentioned earlier (1:5, 7). Jesus had spoken of his appearing so that accounting can be given (Luke 12:8f. = Matt. 25:34ff.). As Goppelt says,

> The shepherds are to "receive," as all other believers, the goal of their faith, salvation. The shepherds are also to experience along with Peter (5:1) and all who suffer for the sake of discipleship (4:13, 14) participation in "glory." The shepherds will receive this participation as a *crown,* or "garland," that is, as a recognition of their faithfulness. (349)

This reward, in contrast to all other passing recognition, does not fade away, even as the eternal inheritance is unfading (1:4).

From his focus on the *elders,* Peter now addresses the *younger* ones. Continuing a pattern used in the Household Codes (3:1, 7), Peter says, *In the same way, you who are younger must accept the authority of the elders* (5:5). But who are the *younger* ones? Are these only younger church leaders? Are they all male? Or are they all the other believers who are not designated as elders or church leaders? Most commentators prefer the last option since the context has to do with the issue of church leadership and not simply differences in age (Goppelt: 351; Michaels: 289).

In 5:3, Peter has just admonished the *elders* not to misuse their appropriate authority over their congregations. This is now a balancing word to the people, calling on them to recognize and defer to the appropriate authority that church leaders do have. Without such a response to servant leadership, the ordered life within the community of faith breaks down.

The Call to Humility and Trust 5:5b-7

Immediately, Peter addresses *all,* both the *elders* and the *younger,* calling them to true humility. *All of you must clothe yourselves with humility in your dealings with one another.* Again Peter supports and motivates his admonition with a quotation from Proverbs 3:34: *God opposes the proud, but gives grace to the humble.* "Peter may have remembered the parable of Jesus about the Pharisee and the tax collector (Luke 18:9-14). Edmund Clowney comments, "The humility of which Peter speaks is like that of the tax-collector; it is not simply a winsome graciousness; it is the humility of repentance" (210).

Peter has already recognized the importance of humble-mindedness (3:8), commended also by Paul (Phil. 2:3; Col. 3:12; Eph. 4:2) and James (4:6-10). Goppelt notes,

> the virtue of humility was not honored in Greek-Hellenistic ethics but was considered the proper attitude for a slave, unworthy for one who is free. . . . In contrast, for OT and Jewish people and all the more for Christians, it is the elementary recognition of their true situation, especially that of their dependence on God as the Creator and Savior. (353)

Without humility, neither the church leaders nor the people will be able to manage the diversity of their gifts (4:11) nor practice the forbearing, forgiving, and serving love to which they have been called as they live in community. The image *clothe yourselves* has been vividly paraphrased: *Put on the apron of humility* (GNB).

The call to humility is underscored once more by Peter: *Humble yourselves therefore under the mighty hand of God, so that he may exalt you in due time.* This is best understood as Peter's application of Proverbs 3:34 to the situation faced by the churches of Asia Minor. James (4:6) uses the same quotation and makes an application in somewhat similar fashion (4:7-10). However, no one has proved that James or 1 Peter depends on the other. The language of exaltation has already been applied to Jesus Christ in 1 Peter 3:22 and is implied for faithful Christians in 4:13 and for church leaders in 5:4. It reappears in 5:10 for the suffering church as a whole.

Meanwhile, since the church lives in a situation of hostility and threat from the outside, Peter exhorts, *Cast all your anxiety on him, because he cares for you. Cast* translates a participle rather than a new imperative, indicating that this call to trust God fully is part of practicing humility. It is a strong word, however, meaning "throw," as one might decisively throw off a burden one has been carrying. What is to be cast away includes *all anxiety.* Once again Peter echoes what Jesus said about anxiety (Matt. 6:25-34; Luke 12:11, 22-32). Peter indicates that the basis for such action is that God cares for God's people. The Greek literally means, "It matters to God concerning you."

This is a central dimension of the grace of God, a theme pervading this letter. Goppelt has caught effectively the force of this passage:

> Worry, anxiety for oneself, and striving to secure one's own life, which are marked by fear, are lifted from those who are called to faith. . . . The casting off of fear is as necessary as submission: If a person does not succeed at separating himself or herself from fear, fear separates him or her from God. Affliction either drives one into the arms of God or severs one from God. (359)

The Call to Watch and Resist Evil 5:8-9

Peter is writing from within a common tradition of temptation, speaking of it as a "testing" by God (1:7; 4:12). Now he vigorously identifies another strand: evil destructively at work. Where God is active and redemptive, the evil one is also at work. He expresses this image concretely and dramatically.

Discipline yourselves, keep alert. Other appropriate translations are "Pay attention. Wake up" (Michaels: 297). Peter repeats the same language as in 4:7 in relation to prayer as vigil. The mode is eschatological, the vocabulary is vigorous, the imagery is powerful. The believers are to be aware that their ultimate enemy is not only real but dangerous. Peter says, *Like a roaring lion your adversary the devil prowls around, looking for someone to devour.* Notable is a threefold designation of the evil one: *roaring lion, adversary,* and *devil.*

The image of the evil one being like a roaring lion likely comes from Psalm 22:12-13. Elsewhere in the NT, the "lion" also stands for the Messiah (Rev. 5:5), but here it is identified with the devil. This lion appears already in motion, prowling around, and aggressively seeking someone to destroy. Thus it is urgent for believers to be watchful and alert.

The evil one is also their *adversary,* their opponent. Indeed, the hearers have many opponents who come in human form, but here opposition is perceived as coming ultimately from one source, the one who is also the enemy of God.

Finally, this one is called *the devil.* The Greek word *diabolos* is based on a verb that literally means "to throw over or across, divide, set at variance, accuse, bring charges, slander, inform, reject, misrepresent, deceive" (H. Bietenhard, *DNTT,* 3:468). As a noun, it is used in the NT 37 times, compared to 36 times for *Satan.* In the Gospels, the devil or Satan tempted Jesus (Mark 1:13; Matt. 4:1; Luke 4:2) and entered Judas (John 13:2). According to Ephesians, believers must avoid the devil because of his destructive power and by the power of God resist his wiles (4:27; 6:11). In Revelation 12:9 he is called "the Devil and Satan, the deceiver of the whole world." In Job 1–2, Satan brings accusations against Job, who is righteous (cf. Zech. 3:1-2; 1 Chron. 21:1).

This evil one is to be resisted. Here "nonresistance" does not apply! *Resist him steadfast in your faith, for you know that your brothers and sisters in all the world are undergoing the same kind of suffering.* Resisting the evil one is different from resisting human adversaries (Michaels: 299), as Jesus commands, "But I say to you, Do not resist an evildoer" (Matt. 5:39). The distinction between spiritual warfare and fighting against humans is made explicit in Ephesians 6:12 and 2 Corinthians 10:3-5.

The phrase *steadfast in your faith* describes the essential character of resistance to the evil one. Through that same faith in which believers humble themselves before God (5:6) and cast their anxieties on God (5:7), they now firmly resist the destructive power of the evil one.

Further resource for this resistance to the devil comes from the awareness that the suffering of Christians in a particular local situation is part of Christian experience universal in time and place. Peter speaks of *brothers and sisters*, inclusive language for the communities of faith *in all the world*. The important message here is that they are not alone in their sufferings. This does not necessarily indicate worldwide persecutions of Christians. They are the local participants in an experience shared by other believers in other parts of the world. We gain strength and courage when we know that we do not stand alone either in our faith or in our suffering for Christ's sake.

Resistance to evil and to the evil one has been a recurring theme in 1 Peter. Peter has admonished them:

- not to give in to the futile ways of their former lives (1:17).
- to abstain from the desires of the flesh (2:12).
- not to retaliate when mistreated (2:21-23).
- not to repay evil for evil, nor abuse for abuse (3:9).
- not to give in to terror (3:6, 14).
- no longer to do what the Gentiles like to do (4:3).

Peter's concern has been to empower them for the right kind of resistance.

Moreover, Peter has called them to live out their faith, hope, and love in appropriate respectful attitudes and conduct toward all humans and societal structures. They are to continue to practice their faith and bear witness to their faith and life in Jesus Christ, the ground of their living eternal hope.

Benediction and Doxology 5:10-11

Peter has called all to humility, mutual deference, deep faith, and firm resistance to the evil one. He has made them aware that the experience of suffering for Christ's sake is universal rather than only local. Now he blesses them with a promise: *And after you have suffered a while.* Their experience of suffering is temporary, in contrast to *the eternal glory in Christ.* In 1:6 Peter has mentioned the same temporary quality of suffering trials. This reflects again the eschatological nature of their hope.

The God of all grace, who has called you to his eternal glory in Christ—Peter identifies at least three dimensions of the divine reality: (1) the God of all grace, (2) the One who has called them, and (3) the God of eternal glory. To speak of God as God of grace is linked with 5:5, but also with the pervasive emphasis on grace in the epistle. To speak of God as the One who calls is linked with 2:9, on the vocation of the church. To speak of God as the God of eternal glory is linked with 1:7; 4:13; and 5:1.

This God of grace and glory *will himself restore, support, strengthen, and establish you.* These four verbs, all in future indicative, together constitute Peter's commentary on how God *gives grace to the humble* (5:5). God will vindicate the faithful followers of Jesus in the end, even as Jesus, the one who suffered innocently (2:22-23) and redemptively (2:24; 3:18) has already been vindicated (3:22) and will be further vindicated (4:13). The vindication of Jesus Christ and his faithful followers has both a present and a future dimension, an "already" and a "not yet" aspect. The emphasis in this passage, however, is future.

Meanwhile this God of grace is already given praise in a shortened form: *To him be the power forever and ever. Amen* (4:11). The word for *power* here means "might," echoing 5:6, *the mighty hand of God.* The brevity of this doxology is dramatic and powerful for persons who may well have felt overwhelmed by their circumstances and experiences.

5:12-14

Conclusion

The conclusion includes three elements:

How and Why the Letter Was Written and Sent, 5:12a
Exhortation to Stand Fast in the Grace of God, 5:12b
Greetings Enclosed, 5:13-14

Brief as it is, this conclusion carries considerable significance for a study of the background of the letter and its central purpose.

How and Why the Letter Was Written and Sent 5:12a

Through Silvanus, whom I consider a faithful brother, I have written this short letter. This reference to Silvanus has given rise to several theories about the relation of Silvanus or Silas to the writing of this epistle: (1) Silvanus was the scribe (amanuensis), recording the epistle, while the message came from Peter. (2) Silvanus was the bearer or carrier of the letter to the churches of Asia Minor, but was not involved in its composition. Or (3) Peter and Silvanus shared in the drafting of the epistle, but only Silvanus was involved in its delivery to Asia Minor. After years of discussion, the debate continues.

We have assumed that the primary writer was Peter, but this does not rule out the theory promoted by Selwyn (9-17) that Silvanus was directly involved in the drafting process. This third view has the advantage of helping explain why the Greek language used in some portions seems more refined or literary than we might expect of

Peter. It would also help to account for frequent similarities of this epistle's thought with that of the apostle Paul. Silvanus or Silas was one of Paul's co-workers (Eph. 6:21-22; Col. 4:7), some of whom join Paul in sending the letters (1 Cor. 1:1; 2 Cor. 1:1; Col. 1:1; Philem. 1). Silas had worked with Paul at Philippi (Acts 16:19, 25, 29), Thessalonica (Acts 17:4), Berea (Acts 17:10, 14) and Corinth (Acts 18:5; 2 Cor. 1:19; cf. Michaels: 307).

Exhortation to Stand Fast in the Grace of God 5:12b

The purpose of the letter is expressed: *to encourage you and to testify that this is the true grace of God.* Peter has earlier spoken of his writing as exhortation (2:11; 5:1), and he has also called himself a witness (5:1). Exhortation generally has to do with ethical matters, and witness relates to theological realities. Somewhat loosely, the two expressions together remind us of both the indicative and the imperative elements in the epistle. There is the witness to what is and will be, and the exhortation to a pattern of life consistent with that reality. However, there is a real issue: what does Peter mean by *this* and by *the true grace of God?*

Michaels helpfully outlines three options in understanding the meaning of the term *this* (308-309). The first is that Peter has in mind the eschatological sense of grace, what God has already done and will yet do through Jesus Christ. This would accentuate 1:10, 13; 5:4. A second option is to highlight 2:19, where the patient and forgiving response of abused servants to cruel masters is termed *grace;* that response is approved of God. A third option is to see *this* as meaning only the writing of the letter itself as an expression of grace.

Since this is described as *true grace* and followed by the exhortation, *Stand fast in it,* we read it as having a larger rather than a more limited intention. Peter is speaking of God's truly gracious dealings with humanity. This appears in the divine initiatives they have experienced, birthing them to a living hope and enabling the Spirit-empowered responses of forgiving abusers (as in 2:19). It also includes the ministries carried out by believers (4:10), including the writing of this epistle taken as a whole (5:12). God's grace is present and is to be seen in the whole of human experience. In this, they are to stand, both in faith and in faithfulness.

Greetings Enclosed 5:13-14

The epistle concludes with greetings of two kinds and a closing exhortation between them. First come the particularized greetings: *Your sister church in Babylon, chosen together with you, sends you greetings.* *Babylon* is commonly understood as a symbolic name for Rome, as shown in Revelation 14:8; 17:5, 9, 18; 18:2 (Goppelt: 374-375). The congregation of faith in Rome is designated as also the *chosen,* "the co-elect," along with the *chosen* of Asia Minor (1:1). Here Peter again underscores the linkage of Christian believers, whether they live in Rome or in Asia Minor (5:10).

The church in Rome joins Peter in sending greetings. The common word for church, *ekklēsia,* does not occur here but is assumed with the use of the feminine form of "the elect." It is considered a remote possibility that Peter may be speaking simply of one Christian woman instead of a congregation.

And so does my son Mark. For those rejecting apostolic authorship, this constitutes an enigma unless one assumes that a pseudonymous writer is using the tradition of a spiritual relationship between Peter and Mark to enhance the authority of his writing. To us, it seems more credible to identify this Mark with the one mentioned in Acts 12:12, there also named John. His mother was named Mary. In Acts 12:25, he becomes a companion of Barnabas. This Mark is also mentioned in Philemon 24, Colossians 4:10, and 2 Timothy 4:11. These texts indicate both Peter's and Paul's acquaintance of Mark.

Nevertheless, the precise meaning of *my son Mark* is somewhat problematic. Michaels dares to suggest: "With a little imagination, one could build a picture of Peter marrying Mark's widowed mother, so that Mark actually became his adopted son" (312). This is interesting, but simply not convincing. Papias, in the mid-second century, suggested that Mark was an interpreter of Peter, a disciple or follower. The precise relationship of Mark and Peter in this closing greeting remains unclear.

Peter continues with the word, *Greet one another with a kiss of love.* Similar expressions occur at the end of several of Paul's letters (Rom. 16:16; 1 Cor. 16:20; 2 Cor. 13:12; 1 Thess. 5:26). The expression *kiss of love* probably emphasizes the importance of sexual purity (Michaels: 313). Here the emphasis on love also picks up once more the theme emphasized in 1:22ff.; 3:8; and 4:8.

Peter gives his final word of blessing: *Peace to all of you who are in Christ.* This echoes the opening greeting: *May grace and peace be yours in abundance* (1:2). The word *peace* has not been prominent in the epistle, occurring only in 3:11 in an OT quotation, *Seek peace and pursue it.* Yet the concern for peace in relationships with hostile neighbors and even with enemies, along with the call to forgiving love, has been prominent throughout the letter. The expression *in Christ* is a final reminder of the basis of their living hope (1:3), the foundation of Christian community (2:4-8), the ground of their ethic (2:21), and the certainty of their destiny (4:13). These all find their reality in their relationship to Jesus Christ.

THE TEXT IN THE BIBLICAL CONTEXT
Church Leadership as Shepherding

The image of shepherding applied to church leadership has a long and rich biblical history. Nomadic backgrounds with the people's dependence on flocks of animals, whether cattle or sheep, made the pastoral image common. Even in classical Greek the word for herdsman or shepherd was figuratively applied to a leader or ruler of the people. "In the ancient East, *shepherd* at an early date was a title of honor applied to divinities and rulers alike. . . . Pastoral terminology was very much in vogue throughout the Hellenistic world" (E. Beyreuther, *DNTT,* 3:564).

Many OT passages use pastoral language to speak of Yahweh or God shepherding Israel (Gen. 48:15; 49:24; Isa. 40:11; Jer. 23:1-4; Ezek. 34:1-31; Zech. 11:7-17; Pss. 23; 80). The OT applies "shepherd" to a variety of human leaders in Israel: Moses, Joshua, kings, tribal leaders, and prophets (Num. 27:17; 2 Sam. 5:2; 7:7; 1 Chron. 11:2; Jer. 10:21; 12:10; 23:1-4). Texts sometimes speak of Israel's faithless shepherds (rulers) in contrast with the true Shepherd, Yahweh (1 Kings 22:17; Jer. 23; Ezek. 34). This imagery was also strong among the Essenes; the Dead Sea Scrolls speak of their overseer being "Guardian of the Congregation/Camp" (Community Rule 5; Damascus Document 13-15), "like a shepherd" (Goppelt: 344).

The same pastoral imagery is carried into the NT, where leaders are variously called overseers, shepherds, and/or elders; all three appear in Acts 20:17, 28-29. In 1 Peter also, these images merge: Jesus Christ is the *shepherd and guardian* (2:25) and *the chief shepherd* (5:4), to whom *the elders* are accountable as they *tend the flock, . . . exercising the oversight* (5:1-4). The image of Jesus as the true Shepherd appears in Matthew (9:36; 10:6; 15:24) and is implied in Luke (15:4ff.; 19:10). It is explicit and dominant in John 10:1-30 and again appears in 21:15-17, in the post-resurrection scene where Jesus commissions Peter: "Feed/tend my lambs/sheep." A fascinating question is whether Peter in his epistle is drawing on this experience.

Several actions are at the heart of the pastoral image applied to the church leader: knowing the sheep individually, caring for their welfare, providing protection in danger, giving direction and restoring those who go astray, and opening the way to an eternal and good destiny.

Wink wrestles with the problems of domination, which may arise when biblical concepts of leadership are ignored, misunderstood, or misapplied (as in Mark 9:35; 10:43-45; Luke 14:11; Matt. 18:4; 20:25-28; 23:8-12; Luke 18:14). He observes, "It is important to note that Jesus addresses his words to men, not women. They are an attack on male dominance, not an attempt to reinforce the servility of women. First Peter 5:2-3 continues this theme" (1992:356). Wink considers domination of others, the "domination system," wherever it appears, as a misrepresentation and abuse of the shepherd image (1992:361). He views the dismantling of worldly domination systems as one mark of the coming of God's kingdom.

The Theology of Humility

The call to humility, sounded clearly in the OT (Pss. 25:9; 37; Isa. 57:15; 66:2; 2 Chron 7:14; Zeph. 2:3), is a dominant theme in NT ethics. Several word families are employed by the writers. One (*praus*) word group means "gentle, humble, considerate, or meek" (as in 1 Pet. 2:18). Another (*epieikēs*) group means "mild, yielding, gentle, kind, or forbearing" (3:4). A third (*tapeinos*) group means "lowly or humble" (5:5). Strikingly, Peter uses samples from all three word clusters in speaking of humility, which he commends as part of Christian response to life in this world.

Concerning the third cluster, Esser observes, "The fundamental difference between the Greek and the biblical use of these words [is that] in the Greek world, with its anthropocentric view of [the human being], lowliness is looked on as shameful, to be avoided and overcome by act and thought. In the NT, with its theocentric view, . . . the words are used to describe those events that bring [humans] into a right relationship with God and . . . fellow-[humans]" (in *DNTT*, 2:260).

The first two word clusters (*praus* and *epieikēs*) are recognized as characteristic of the attitude and demeanor of Jesus in the NT. Paul and Peter commend them as especially appropriate for Christians. Peter has recognized that this may also be an attitude of a non-Christian master (2:18) but is indeed to be an expression of Christian love (3:4). It becomes particularly important when one is responding to hostility or persecution (3:16). In this, Peter concurs with Paul's counsel (Gal. 5:23; Phil. 4:5; Titus 3:2). Such teaching may come from Jesus himself. In Matthew 5:5 he says, "Blessed are the meek, for they shall inherit the earth." In Matthew 11:28-29 he invites, "Come, . . . learn from me; for I am gentle and humble in heart."

The third word group (*tapeinos*) occurs 34 times in the NT, but only four times in 1 Peter. Matthew 11:29 includes the word, and it is given prominence in Philippians 2:6-11, where the humility of Jesus Christ is extolled. It is picked up emphatically by both James (1:9f.; 4:6-10) and 1 Peter, with both writers appealing to Proverbs 3:34 (LXX) and earnestly urging such conduct. Peter thus expresses the same apostolic perspective seen also in James and in Paul.

Humility is not so much an ethic or an attitude to be achieved as a recognition of the reality of humanity in the presence of a loving, holy, and just God, whom we can trust completely, and on whom we depend.

Resisting the Evil One

Peter has much to say about how the Christian is to respond to hostility and abuse in society. Yet he has relatively little to say about the origin and nature of evil. Not till the final chapter does he introduce his understanding of the evil one. While Peter has much to say about God and even more about Jesus Christ, he has little to say about the devil. In what he does say, he contributes nothing unique but echoes what is expressed elsewhere in the NT on this theme.

Belief in demons and the demonic was widespread in the world of the Bible (Bietenhard, *DNTT,* 2:450). However, references to an evil one are primarily found in the Bible itself. The OT and NT include a number of terms for this evil one, such as *Satan, Beelzebul*, and *the devil*. In the NT, the word *devil* occurs 37 times, *Satan* 36 times, and *Beelzebul* 7 times. In addition, we find other designations: *the enemy, the evil one, the prince of this world, serpent, deceiver of the whole world*, and the *adversary*—a literal translation of the Hebrew word *Satan*, as in 1 Peter 5:8 (Bietenhard, *DNTT,* 3:468-469). This evil one is portrayed as the head of the demonic world and evil in character and intention, opposed to God's purposes.

First Peter uses both words *adversary* and *devil* to speak of this evil one. The adversary is an enemy or opponent. The devil is the accuser who casts something between, and thus separates or divides. In the OT, Satan is prominent in the book of Job as the adversary opposing God's people and the completion of God's will. Satan takes the role of an overzealous prosecuting attorney in God's heavenly court, trying to trip and tempt believers (Job 1–2; 1 Chron. 21:1).

Matthew 25:41 speaks of the devil and his angels being destined for punishment. In Luke 10:18, Jesus sees the downfall of Satan (cf. Rev. 12:9). Nevertheless, the devil is represented as alive and active. According to Ephesians 6:10-18, the devil is to be resisted with all the armor which God has placed at the disposal of the Christian. This is essentially the picture that Peter introduces when he speaks of this evil one as *your adversary*, a roaring lion, prowling around *like a roaring lion*, seeking persons *to devour* (5:8). As in Ephesians 6, Peter's call to *resist* the evil one builds on the perspective that those being addressed have a capacity to discern evil. With the resources of *faith* and fellow believers, they are not powerless in the presence of evil (5:9).

Satan can be resisted. Jesus saw Satan fall. In the power of the Spirit, believers are joined with Christ in faith, not only to believe in the ultimate downfall of evil, but also to take part in a cosmic resistance movement in the present.

THE TEXT IN THE LIFE OF THE CHURCH

Early Anabaptist Views of Church Leadership

Among Anabaptists, an early description of church leadership appears in the *Schleitheim Confession,* written by Michael Sattler and accepted by the believers assembled at Schleitheim, Switzerland, on February 24, 1527. Article 5 draws on the biblical imagery of shepherds:

> We have been united as follows concerning shepherds in the church of God. The shepherd in the church shall be a person according to the rule of Paul, fully and completely, who has a good report of those who are outside the faith. The office of such a person shall be to read and exhort and warn, admonish, or ban in the congregation, and properly to preside among sisters and brothers in prayer, and in the breaking of bread, and in all things to take care of the body of Christ, that it may be built up and developed, so that the name of God might be praised and honored through us, and the mouth of the mocker be stopped.
>
> He shall be supported, wherein he has need, by the congregation which has chosen him, so that he who serves the gospel can also live therefrom, as the Lord has ordered. But should the shepherd do something worthy of reprimand, nothing shall be done with him without the voice of two or three witnesses. If they sin they shall be properly reprimanded, so that others might fear.
>
> But if the shepherd should be driven away or led to the Lord by the cross, at the same hour another shall be ordained to his place, so that the little folk and the little flock of God may not be destroyed, but be preserved by warning and be consoled. (Sattler: 38-39)

Pilgram Marpeck, in a writing on "The Servants and Service of the Church," draws heavily on 1 Peter 5 when he declares,

> In this body, the gifts of the Holy Spirit are manifest in each member according to the measure of faith in Jesus Christ for service in the growth of the body of Christ. By this service the weakest, least and smallest members are strengthened, comforted, led, guided, and pastured by the strong, leading, and most able members. Thus they are trained, preserved, increased, and nourished until they reach the full maturity of Christ. For whoever would be the greatest must be the vassal and servant and not the ruler of all the others, says the Lord. Their service is not compelled or forced, not for the sake of shameful gain; rather, it flows voluntarily from an affectionate disposition. They do not rule over the heritage of God but become an example to the flock, says Peter. (Marpeck: 550)

Dirk Philips, writing on "The Sending of Preachers or Teachers," also appeals to 1 Peter 5:2 in seeking to help his readers discern truly called church leaders: "No one will be sent by the Lord nor correctly chosen by the congregation, except through the Holy Spirit, who must touch his heart, make him fiery with love, in order thus to voluntarily feed, lead, and send out the congregation of God, John 21:15, 1 Pet. 5:2" (Dirk: 203). Likewise, in denouncing false shepherds in the church, he admonishes, "For it behooves the shepherds to feed the sheep, just as Christ commanded Peter and Peter commanded the elders, John 21:17; 1 Pet. 5:2. But how is this to take place when the shepherds trample the precious pasture of the divine Word with their feet and then give the sheep to eat the same which they have trampled with their feet, Ezek. 34:18-19?" (212).

Menno Simons, who functioned as a priest before his conversion, had considerable to say about the role and function of pastors or shepherds. His understanding of church leadership, however, was broad, as suggested dramatically in his profusion of images of ministry:

> Once more, arm yourselves, for true teachers are called in the Scriptures, the angels of the Lord, and valiant soldiers. Therefore be [mature]; keep the commandment of God; hold fast and waver not.
> Watchmen and trumpeters are they. Therefore blow the trumpet on the right note; watch diligently over the city of God; watch, I say, and neither slumber nor sleep.
> Spiritual pillars are they. Oh, stand fast in the truth, bear your burden willingly, waver not, neither be faint.
> Messengers of peace are they called. Ah, . . . live up to your name, walk in peace, promote it and break it not.
> Bishops and overseers are they called. Oh, take great care of the flock of Christ. Take great care of them, I say, and neither destroy nor neglect them.

Shepherds are they called. Oh, keep and feed the lambs of Christ, leave them not nor disdain them.

Teachers are they called. Make known the Word and truth of Christ and neither hide it nor keep silence. Spiritual nurses and fathers are they. Oh, nourish and cherish your young children. Neither grieve nor thrust them away. Spiritual mother hens in Christ are they called. In Christ gather the little chicks and neither scatter them nor peck at them. Stewards of God are they called. Ah, dispense the mysteries of God aright; neither abuse nor disgrace them. . . .

Ministers are they called in Christ's stead. Ah, . . . serve but do not lord it.

Let no [one] glory in any gift, I beseech you. We are receivers, not givers, of grace; it is not of ourselves. Observe; we are servants and not lords. Ah, . . . bow and submit yourselves. (Menno: 996-997)

In the context of the times, this is a remarkable range of images of church leadership, calling for the spirit of servanthood rather than lordship, even as Peter did.

The Ambiguity of Humility

While Peter and other NT writers are emphatic about the importance of humility in Christian life and community, the expression of this grace is often ambiguous. Along with other Christian communities, Anabaptists have wrestled with the call to humility with considerable self-consciousness, which tends to complicate its true expression.

Schlabach (400-402) traces developing understandings of the nature and significance of humility in this faith tradition. He shows that as the heirs of this Anabaptist tradition gradually moved away from "a theology of suffering" that prevailed during times of persecution, they moved toward "a theology of humility." Humility became a dominant theme among some of the Mennonite groups (Mennonite Church and Amish) and gave them a defining characteristic, setting them apart from "the world" and even from other faith traditions in which they saw too much pride. Gradually this theology of humility gave way to a more aggressive commitment to witness and service.

Many Christians, not only those in the believers church tradition, still view pride as a basic sin. They thus lift up humility as a defining virtue. This might lead to failure in being actively involved in dynamic Christian evangelism or in ethically oriented political witness. If so, this may be a limiting vestige, from overemphasizing a "theology of humility," as Schlabach suggests. "The quiet in the land" may be quiet about their faith in Jesus Christ and about their strongly felt convictions against injustice, abuse, and violence. If so, they have moved beyond the balance which Peter suggests between "the quiet spirit"

(3:4) and giving a clear reason for one's hope (3:15) in word and in lifestyle.

C. S. Lewis, in another perspective, reflects perceptively on the ambiguity of humility: "A man [or woman] is never so proud as when striking the attitude of humility" (14). "If anyone would like to acquire humility, I can, I think, tell him the first step. The first step is to realize that one is proud. And a biggish step, too. At least, nothing whatever can be done before it. If you think you are not conceited, it means you are very conceited indeed" (114). Lewis also speaks of the genuinely humble person as "one who seems to enjoy life easily. He will not be thinking about humility: he will not be thinking about himself at all" (114).

In other words, to humble oneself before God means becoming so aware of the greatness and reality of God that the self falls into its proper perspective, certainly not at the center, but infinitely worthy and precious because God is fully present and in control. This runs counter to a common current convention that the human self must "take control."

Petersen (1993) gives this tribute to Peter as a leader in the early church, embodying true humility:

> In the early church, his influence was enormous and acknowledged by all. By virtue of his position, he was easily the most powerful figure in the Christian community. . . . The way Peter handled himself in that position of power is even more impressive than the power itself. He stayed out of the center, didn't "wield" power, maintained a scrupulous subordination to Jesus. Given his charismatic personality and well-deserved position as the head, he could easily have taken over, using the prominence of his association with Jesus to promote himself. That he didn't do it, given the frequency with which such spiritual leaders do exactly that, is impressive. Peter is a breath of fresh air. (486)

The Call to Resistance Today

One needs to read 1 Peter 5 as a culmination of the epistle, rather than considering 1 Peter 5:1-11 as a miscellany of concluding exhortations. Then we hear an urgent call to resist the devil and all forms of compromise with evil today, standing firm in faith and good conscience, whatever the cost.

This call to resist evil, even at the cost of life, is a renewed call to "martyrdom." An updating of Foxe's *Book of Martyrs* and Thieleman J. van Braght's *Martyrs Mirror* has recently been undertaken by James and Marti Hefley in *By Their Blood: Christian Martyrs of the Twentieth Century* and by Susan Bergman, *Martyrs:*

Contemporary Writers on Modern Lives of Faith.
Bergman defines a martyr as someone who believes "that something matters more than life."

> In our century, there are clear records of Christians being put to the choice between faith and life in Pakistan, the former Soviet Union, Armenia, Sudan, China, Chile, Iran—the list goes on. More often though, a martyr's determination has been complicated by the layering of political and racial differences over the issue of direct spiritual opposition, and the choice is whether to follow a spiritual call and remain in known danger or to cease, whether to stay in the place of jeopardy or to move to another place. . . . (1996a: 20)
> Archbishop Oscar Romero of El Salvador could have chosen to leave but stayed and died. Martin Luther King could have muted his message, but continued his civil rights cause, [and] declared at a funeral for martyred children at the Sixteenth Street Baptist Church in Birmingham, on Sept. 15, 1963, possibly in a premonition of his own fate:
> "I hope you can find some consolation from Christian affirmation that death is not the end. Death is not a period that ends the great sentence of life but a comma which punctuates it to more lofty significance. Death is not a blind alley that leads the human race into a state of nothingness, but an open door which leads [humans] into life eternal. Let this daring faith, *this invincible surmise*, be your sustaining power during these trying days." (1996a: 25).

Peter's call to resist evil, whether in the form of prejudice or destructive compromise or some other betrayal of Christian faith or ethics, is surely a contemporary expression of his call to resist the devil. That roaring lion is seeking also in our time *someone to devour.* Some Christians currently, as was the case in Peter's day, do face the call to martyrdom. Resistance to evil does not happen without costly discipleship.

We remember the Boxer Rebellion in China and the testimony of Lizzie Atwater, one of 150 missionaries and children killed. We remember the five missionaries to the Auca Indians massacred in Ecuador in early 1956. We remember Dr. Paul Carlson in the same year, shot by the Simbas in the Congo, leaving in his pocket the date and the word "Peace."

We remember many others who resisted the *adversary* to the end, determined not to give up their faith or their ministry. We remember the irresistible witness of the martyrs, who continue to speak from Peter's time until now (cf. Heb. 11:1–12:4, esp. 11:4 and 12:4). Their experiences encourage us to stay *alert* and *steadfast* in the *faith* (1 Pet. 5:8-9). This we can do with strength from the *God of all grace*, who calls us to *eternal glory in Christ* (5:10).

Outline of 1 Peter

The Opening Greeting   **1:1-2**

Name and Title of the Writer	1:1a
Designation of the Readers	1:1b
Their Spiritual Status	1:2a
Grace and Peace Be Yours	1:2b

The Celebration of Christian Hope and Its Impact 1:3-12

The Ground and Assurance of Christian Hope	1:3-5
The Ground of Hope	1:3
The Assurance of Hope	1:4-5
The Joyful Benefits of Christian Hope	1:6-9
In Experiences of Trials	1:6-7
In Anticipating the Completion of Salvation	1:8-9
The High Privilege of Christian Hope	1:10-12
Hope Fulfills the Prophetic Search	1:10-12a
Hope Attracts the Attention of Angels	1:12b

The Changed Lifestyle of Hope   **1:13—2:3**

Hope Changes the Lifestyle	1:13-21
The Alignment of the Mind	1:13
Obedient Children of a Holy God	1:14-16
Reverent Fear in Redeemed People	1:17-21
The Call to Holy Love	1:22—2:3
Heart with Loving Heart United, Purified and Newborn	1:22-25
Putting Off Malice; Craving Nourishment as Babes	2:1-3

The Community of Hope   **2:4-10**

Come to the Living Stone   2:4-5
As Understood in Scripture   2:6-8
You Are God's Own People   2:9-10

Christian Witness in Hostile Society   **2:11—3:12**

True Witness of Maligned Believers   2:11-12
Witness as "Citizens" Under a Hostile State   2:13-17
Witness as Mistreated Servants Following Jesus   2:18-25
    The Situation of Mistreated Servants   2:18-20
    The Pattern of Responding: The Cross   2:21-25
Christian Witness in Marriage   3:1-7
    Christian Wives of Unbelieving Husbands   3:1-6
    Christian Husbands Who Show Consideration   3:7
Witness of the Unified and Forgiving Community   3:8-12

Christian Response to Suffering for Righteous Living   **3:13—4:19**

Christian Suffering in Light of Christ's Suffering   3:13—4:6
    Christian Witness While Suffering   3:13-17
    The Vicarious Suffering and Exaltation of Christ   3:18-22
    The Value of Suffering Like Christ   4:1-6
Christian Suffering in View of Coming Judgment   4:7-19
    The Loving and Serving Community Facing the End   4:7-11
    Facing Suffering for the Sake of Christ   4:12-19
       Expect Suffering   4:12
       Rejoice in Suffering   4:13-14
       Examine Yourselves in Suffering   4:15
       Glorify God in Suffering   4:16-18
       Trust God and Keep On Doing Good   4:19

Leadership and Loyalty in the Suffering Church   **5:1-11**

The Call to Leadership and Loyalty   5:1-5a
The Call to Humility and Trust   5:5b-7
The Call to Watch and Resist Evil   5:8-9
Benediction and Doxology   5:10-11

Conclusion   **5:12-14**

How and Why the Letter Was Written and Sent   5:12a
Exhortation to Stand Fast in the Grace of God   5:12b
Greetings Enclosed   5:13-14

Essays for 1 Peter

AUTHORSHIP   The debate over the authorship of 1 Peter continues among biblical scholars. The posture taken in this commentary is to assume the apostolic authorship on the basis that this long tradition has not been decisively disproved. Even so, it also is not possible to prove Petrine authorship to the satisfaction of all biblical scholars.

I. H. Marshall summarizes the present state of the debate as follows: (1) Those considering 1 Peter as having been written by the apostle include: Benetreau, Clowney, Cranfield, Grudem, Hunter, Michaels (with some hesitation), Neugebauer, Schelke, Selwyn, Spicq, Stibbs, and Walls. To this list we could add Bigg, Kistemaker, Hiebert, and McKnight. (2) Those considering 1 Peter as pseudonymous or not from Peter: Beare, Best, Brox, Goppelt, Schutter. We add Elliott. (3) Undecided: Kelly (21). We add Achtemeier (43).

The internal evidence includes the author's self-designation as *Peter, an apostle of Jesus Christ* (1:1); Peter's claim in 5:1 that he is a *fellow elder and a witness of the sufferings of Christ;* and the conclusion in 5:12-13 that refers to Silvanus and Mark—and presumably also the church of believers in Rome. The external evidence that the early church accepted the epistle as authentic and apostolic includes 1 Clement (ca. A.D. 95), who cites almost verbatim the greeting in 1 Peter, refers to "the precious blood of Christ" (1:19), and uses two of 1 Peter's OT quotations (Prov. 10:12; 3:34). Furthermore, Polycarp, writing to the Philippians, seems to be quoting from 1 Peter 1:3 and 8.

By A.D. 185, Irenaeus quotes 1 Peter 1:8 with the introduction "and Peter says in his Epistle." In the following century, Clement of Alexandria and Tertullian both quote from 1 Peter and name Peter as the writer. Also, the church historian Eusebius mentions that Papias, an early-first-century bishop in Asia Minor, "used quotations from the First Epistle of John and likewise also from that of Peter" (Kistemaker: 6).

In spite of rather impressive evidence for the traditional apostolic authorship, biblical scholars have raised at least five significant challenges (I. H.

Marshall: 22), which I describe with some counter considerations:

1. It is argued that the quality of Greek used in 1 Peter is better than one could reasonably expect of the Peter who came to Jesus as a fisherman. This, however, underestimates the potential of multilingualism in the biblical world and in Peter's life. Even if 1 Peter was written as early as A.D. 62-64, Peter could have had over twenty-five years of considerable transcultural contacts to learn to speak Greek well. As suggested in the synoptic Gospels, much of this time he may have been in Galilee, where the Greco-Roman influence was strong. Beyond this, however, the possibility that Silvanus may have played an assisting role in literary composition makes the linguistic and stylistic argument moot.

2. Externally, we lack evidence establishing the apostle Peter's contacts with the Christians of Asia Minor. How could Peter presume to write with pastoral sensitivity and apostolic authority to congregations he did not know well, without even mentioning Paul, who had evangelized in those areas? This is puzzling. However, Paul also writes a letter, Romans, to a community of believers he has not yet visited. Goppelt has argued well that both Paul and Peter already had wide apostolic status, even beyond the regions where they had personally served. Thus for Peter to write such a letter, or for a letter to be written in the name of Peter, would be considered appropriate and appreciated because of their recognized though sometimes challenged status (Goppelt: 9).

3. The "worldwide" persecution of Christians assumed in the letter (4:16; 5:9) did not take place until after Peter's death, it is alleged. However, a more careful reading of the text of 1 Peter indicates that the persecution in view may have been more local than throughout the Roman empire or worldwide. It may have come from hostile neighbors rather than being state ordered or organized. Some of this persecution came in non-Christian households where it was feared that the changes being introduced would undermine the social order and eventually challenge the empire. Peter thus correctly surmised that the persecutions would become worse and more widespread.

Moreover, as Michaels has carefully stated, the tradition about Peter dying in Rome during the Neronian persecution (in 64), while assumed in this commentary, is not fully established. It is simply based on a long-held tradition (Michaels: lvii-lxi). In short, we lack evidence that Peter died before 1 Peter was written.

4. "The letter shows no concrete characteristics of Peter, such as eyewitness recollections of Jesus," it is said. On the other hand, it is not the purpose of this letter to characterize Peter or to describe his activities. However, echoes of his eyewitness experience with Jesus can be perceived at various points, as indicated in the comments on 3:9, 15; 5:1. In any case, we know too little of Peter to say with confidence what Peter could have or should have included or excluded.

5. "The letter shows a religious idiom that developed against a background of Hellenistic Judaism rather than Palestinian Judaism." But if we take the portrayal of Peter in Acts 10–15 seriously, Peter, along with Paul, was being influenced by Hellenistic Judaism. In Acts, Peter is presented as a slow learner. Yet he makes tremendous changes in his perspectives and activities. Schroeder suggests that it would take only one Christian living in a non-Christian household for the church to have to contend with Hellenism.

In short, we agree with I. H. Marshall that "none of the arguments for pseudonymity, therefore, is able to refute the impression made by the letter itself" (23). We also agree with Michaels: "The traditional view that the living Peter was personally responsible for the letter as it stands has not been, and probably in the nature of the case cannot be, decisively shaken" (lxvi-lxvii).

CHRISTOLOGY According to the tradition of the synoptic Gospels (Mark 8:27—9:8 and //), as well as in the Johannine tradition (John 1:40-41; 6:66-69; 13:1-20; 21:1-23), Peter the disciple was centrally involved in discerning Jesus as the Messiah. Given our perspective on the issue of authorship, the Christology of 1 Peter becomes especially significant.

First Peter does not develop a systematic Christology. Instead, Peter invokes the person and work, the life, suffering, death, and resurrection of Jesus Christ to guide and motivate Christian faith and life. God is spoken of directly thirty-nine times, Christ appears twenty-two times, Jesus Christ nine of these times, and Lord Jesus Christ once (1:3). In 1 Peter, the relationship between God and Jesus employs family imagery, with God called Father (1:2) and Jesus, by implication, Child or Son. Michaels observes, "If God is the Actor in the work of human salvation, Jesus Christ is the Agent and therefore the one with whom the theology is most directly concerned" (lxviii). Achtemeier (37) notes that God's lordship in this letter "is expressed exclusively through Christ," who is superior to all other powers (3:22).

In 1 Peter, Jesus Christ is centrally involved in *revelation*. Though Jesus is invisible to the readers (1:8), he is the One to be revealed (1:7, 13). He is the One who has appeared (1:20) and also the One who will appear, as Chief Shepherd (5:4). His revelation involves both salvation (1:5) and glory (4:13; 5:1).

Moreover, Jesus Christ in 1 Peter is centrally involved in *redemption*. He is presented as the innocent and sinless One (1:19; 2:22, using Isa. 53:9). Jesus is described as a sacrificial *lamb* offering (1:18-19) and as the abused, nonretaliating servant who is to be followed (2:21-23). He is declared to be the atoning Savior whose death brings about our healing from sins (2:24; 3:18) so that we may live for God. This emphasis on the suffering of Jesus as prelude to his exaltation is the core of Peter's Christology (Achtemeier: 37).

In 2:4-10, Jesus Christ is the Living Stone on which the community of believers is built up, the decisive One who determines destiny, rejected by disobedient unbelievers, but approved by God and made into a cornerstone of the people of God in worship and mission.

Basic to this exalted view of Jesus Christ is his *resurrection* which, according to Peter, is the ground of our living hope (1:3). Christ's resurrection gives validity to our baptism (3:21) and makes possible both faith and hope (1:21). Michaels notes, "If the cross is the basis of Christian ethics, the resurrection is the basis of Christian experience" (lxxii).

Peter, however, also speaks of the ascension and the exaltation of Jesus Christ over all *angels, authorities, and powers* (3:22). Moreover, Christ is to appear in the future (5:4) to consummate in glory God's purpose with believers and their leaders (4:13; 5:1, 4).

In the presence of this understanding of Jesus Christ, Peter calls us to come to Christ (2:4), believe on him (2:7), obey him (1:2), and especially to follow him (2:21), acknowledging and relating to Christ as Lord (3:15). In this relationship, we are called to eternal glory (5:10) and even now experience peace (5:14).

For contemporary reflections of Anabaptist perspectives on Christology, see Erland Waltner, editor, *Jesus Christ and the Mission of the Church*. This book includes leading papers and findings of a study conference on Christology sponsored by the Mennonite Church, the General Conference Mennonite Church, the Mennonite Brethren Church, and the Brethren in Christ Church, held at Normal, Illinois, on August 4-6, 1989. These perspectives move in a different direction than those of Robert W. Funk, *Honest to Jesus*, representing the Jesus Seminar in its quest for "the historical Jesus." See also Luke Timothy Johnson, *The Real Jesus*.

ESCHATOLOGY Peter H. Davids says, "The whole of 1 Peter is characterized by an eschatological, even an apocalyptic focus. It is not really possible to understand the work without appreciating this focus" (15). By *eschatological*, we mean a perspective that sees human history moving toward a purposeful end. By *apocalyptic*, we mean that something now hidden is to be revealed, often shown in a symbolic portrayal of the triumph of the good and the destruction of evil.

Both in 1:5 and in 1:20, Peter speaks of the *last times*. In 2:12 he mentions a future time of God's visitation, and in 4:17 the present time for *judgment to begin with the household of God*. In 4:7 he declares that *the end of all things is at hand*. In 4:13 and 5:10 he speaks of *eternal glory*.

Davids (15) reminds us that most of these references indicate the *temporal* dimension of this apocalyptic eschatology in 1 Peter. Peter, who has spoken of *the foundation of the world* (1:20), perceives of temporal reality as including the long past, the present, and also the future. Thus what happens in the present needs to be understood in this broad eschatological context. Especially, suffering happening now has precedents in the past, and its meaning is to become clear in a glorious future. Hence, the nature and work of Jesus Christ and the experience and mission of the church of believers must be seen in this eschatological framework. Peter shares the Pauline view that "the sufferings of this present time are not worth comparing with the glory about to be revealed to us" (Rom. 8:18).

Davids (16) further reminds us that there are also *spatial* dimensions of this framework in 1 Peter. The text speaks of an inheritance *reserved in heaven* (1:4), of the Holy Spirit *sent from heaven* (1:12), and of Jesus Christ having *gone into heaven* (3:22). Jesus' ministry to *the spirits in prison* (3:19) represents also "another world" sometimes identified with hell or Hades. In short, readers are to understand that the sufferings and other crises of their present lives are to be understood in a much larger framework, one that is eschatological. More specifically, Peter's perspective is one in which God's purposes finally triumph.

This is a significant aspect of the living hope which now belongs to believers because they have followed a living Lord, who was resurrected from the dead, and who is destined for ultimate and triumphant glory (4:13), together with those who walk and suffer with him (5:10). The ethic of a nonviolent response to evil, as taught in this epistle, is grounded in this robust and pervasive eschatology.

THE HOUSEHOLD CODES   In his rigorous 1945 commentary on 1 Peter, Selwyn traces what he called the "Code of Subordination" in the NT. In the chart on page 181, I have adapted some of his material, aligning it with nuances of meaning developed above. This topic has received considerable and diverse attention by subsequent scholars. It also shows that while the presence of these codes in 1 Peter is prominent, their use in the NT is much more extensive.

The varied interpretations of the significance of these codes for Christian ethics are most important for us. Goppelt (162-179) gives an extensive discussion on the nature, sources, and uses of these Household Codes (what Luther called *Haustafeln*). He prefers to call them "Station Codes" (*Ständetafeln*). They consist of directives given to persons who find themselves in different roles or stations in life, such as slaves and masters, husbands and wives, parents and children, rulers and citizens, older and younger, leaders and learners. Goppelt notes that various types can be identified, some of which are closer in spirit to the Stoic codes, with an emphasis on duty. Others, with an element of grace and voluntarism, reflect more clearly the influence of Jesus and Paul.

Achtemeier observes that the Greco-Roman Household Codes "represent the basic social and economic mode of existence in the ancient world. . . . Based on the premise that men are more rational, women least rational, children prerational (or immature), and slaves irrational—such codes portrayed the order of authority and submission for each of the classes" (52). A challenge to this order would ultimately be seen as a challenge to the Roman political order. Balch has argued that 1 Peter advises accommodation to this perspective and ideology, but Achtemeier notes that 1 Peter and other NT passages warn against such accommodation (53). Such passages as Galatians 3:28-29 emphasize the new order in Christ. Ephesians 5:21 insists on mutuality in subordinating oneself to another. These emphases run counter to the system represented by the pagan Household Codes.

Christians living in the Greco-Roman world, however, needed to face the same issues of social relationships involved in the Household Codes, since the church was seen as a new house or household. How do pairs handle their relationships, slave and master, wife and husband, parents and children? How do believers relate to rulers?

Schroeder argues that the answers given in the NT point to "another way" than that given by the codes of the pagan world. This new way arises out of believers' new life in Christ, new freedom in Christ, new ethic of holy love, and new community. Believers want to relate to each other as sisters and brothers in God's family, and as missionaries witness helpfully to non-Christians, sometimes even in their "old" household. In these "household" relationships, there is also a place for a new kind of "authority and submission." But it is on the borderline of the faith community with a pagan world that these social relationships become particularly crucial and admittedly difficult. Here the NT seeks to provide counsel by giving illustrations of a Christian nonretaliatory response when abuse occurs. To grasp Peter's intentions with the Household Codes, this commentary has followed the perspectives of Achtemeier and Schroeder rather than those of Balch.

Elisabeth Schüssler Fiorenza also notes that while the NT writers do not make a direct critique of either slavery or patriarchy, the image of "a disci-

Household Honor Codes in the New Testament

1 Peter	Romans	Colossians	Ephesians	1 Timothy	Titus	James & Hebrews
a. 2:13-17 Honor all created ones, esp. civil rulers.	a. 13:17 Recognize & honor civil authority.	e. 3:12 Practice humility.	e. 5:21 Honor one another.	a. 2:1-8 Pray for all, e.g., kings and all in authority.	c. 2:4, 5 Wives, honor husbands. f. 2:6 Younger, be self-controlled.	g. James 4:6 Practice humility (Prov. 3:34). h. James 4:7, 10 Practice humility toward God.
b. 2:18-25 Servants, honor masters. Follow Jesus Christ.		c. 3:18 Wives, honor husbands.	c. 5:22-24 Wives, honor husbands (as church to Christ).	c. 2:9-11 Women, honor men in the church (Gen. 2).	b. 2:9, 10 Servants, honor masters.	h. Heb. 12:9 Honor God.
c. 3:1-6 Wives, honor husbands as OT Sarah.		c[1]. 3:19 Husbands, love wives. No harshness.	c[1]. 5:25-33 Husbands, love wives (as Christ the church).	b. 6:1, 2 Servants, honor masters.	a. 3:1 Honor civil authority.	f. Heb. 13:17 Honor church leaders.
c[1]. 3:7 Husbands, honor wives. Be considerate.		d. 3:20 Children, honor parents.	d. 6:1-3 Children, honor parents (5th commandment).			
e. 3:8 All be humbleminded.		d[1]. 3:21 Fathers, do not provoke children.	d[1]. 6:4 Fathers, do not provoke children, but nurture and discipline them.			
f. 5:5 Younger, honor elders.		b. 3:22-25 Servants, honor masters.	b. 6:5-8 Servants, honor masters.			
g. 5:5 Practice humility reciprocally.		b[1]. 4:1 Masters, treat servants justly & fairly.	b[1]. 6:9 Masters, honor servants. Do not threaten.			
h. 5:6 Practice humility toward God.						

Key to Relationships

a. With all and rulers.
b. Servants and masters.
c. Wives and husbands.
d. Children and parents.
e, g, h. Humility.
f. Younger ones and elders as church leaders.

Adapted from Edward G. Selwyn, The First Epistle of Peter, 423. Grand Rapids: Baker Books, 1981 reprint.

pleship of equals," particularly as expressed in Galatians 3:28, remains as a basic ethic (205ff.). That is the goal toward which God moves. The conversion of slaves and wives to Christianity, however, in itself became a challenge to the prevailing social structures. Thus this new faith was sometimes feared to be subversive. Pagans expected that a wife would share the religious faith of her husband. Hence, the very existence of Christian women who had non-Christian husbands was in itself already a threat to the social order. Peter certainly does not tell such wives to adopt the faith of their husbands. Instead, he speaks of attitudes and patterns of speech and behavior that may result in the conversion of husbands to Christian faith.

Characteristic of these codes in the NT, however, is the call to "subordinate yourselves," which is different from urging people to "obey" (used in 1 Peter only in 3:6). Strikingly, this call to subordination is applied to all persons, not just to slaves or women (Eph. 5:21; 1 Pet. 2:13). Over recent decades, the more precise understanding of this imperative to "subordinate yourselves" has changed significantly in scholars' discussions. Strongly influenced by scholars such as Cranfield, Goppelt, Michaels, Davids, Schroeder, and Achtemeier, we now understand that Peter views believers as "free" in Christ (2:16). Even so, some may occupationally be "household slaves."

Given the circumstances and their station in life, believers are urged to adopt voluntarily appropriate Christian social attitudes and behaviors, "for the Lord's sake," so that both their integrity as followers of Jesus and their missionary witness might not be destroyed. The Stoics emphasized duty as motivation. Wendland (in Goppelt: 170) emphasizes that, on the other hand, the codes in the NT essentially call for an application of "the commandment to love one's neighbor and brother in the *oikos* [house] and among the membership of the household."

Currently, we understand Peter's call in using the Household Codes to be "to acknowledge authority" or "to respect" or "to defer to," even as one follows Jesus in a path of nonretaliating and forgiving love. The positive dimension of this is always "doing good" or "doing right," while trusting God for eschatological vindication and justice. In this discernment process, questions are still relevant: What did Jesus do? What would Jesus do? What is the counsel of fellow believers?

Nonretaliation, however, does not preclude, in appropriate context, criticism of an unjust order or action, or working toward a more just and merciful order in fallen society. On occasion, Jesus confronted hypocrisy and evil in his world with prophetic insight and directness. He calls his followers not to bless an unfair or unjust status quo. Instead, they are to seek a nonretaliating way of allowing God to bring about social transformation. Liberation theologies, including feminist theology (Fiorenza, 1983:260-266), make a significant contribution to our understanding of the present applicability of the Household Codes.

We must not sanction or perpetuate oppressive and abusive relationships, either in employment or family or church or community contexts, by misusing the "submission texts." On the contrary, we must recognize the particular missionary stance in the context of hostile Hellenistic paganism. We see Peter's own underlying missionary concern that includes ultimate justice (1:17; 2:23; 4:5, 17; 5:10). Moreover, we need to see that the call to continue in "doing good" and "doing right" includes appropriate action to bring true human freedom (2:16) and true justice, as God intends for all, and the peace which the gospel brings (1:2; 3:11; 5:14; cf. Schertz: 282-284). This is a far cry from servile, passive compliance and moves toward the kind of civil respect and confrontation that God can use to change both individuals and eventually social structures.

We support such a commitment to nonretaliation in responding to oppressive situations while continuing an active practice of confronting and forgiving enemy love, as taught by Peter. It finds expression in the writings of Swartley (1983, 1992, 1996), Schertz, Schroeder (1990), Yoder (1972), Zerbe, and others.

IMAGES OF THE CHURCH AND CHURCH LEADERSHIP In 1960 Paul Minear identified no less than 96 significant images applied in the NT to the people of God. Sixteen of these are found, explicitly or implicitly, in 1 Peter: the elect, exiles, the Diaspora, the people of God, a chosen race, a holy nation, the flock of God, the holy temple, a priesthood, fighters against Satan, the ark, the name, the sanctified, followers, servants of God, house hold of God, brotherhood. We can add to Minear's list: children of God (1:14), living stones (2:4), aliens (2:11), and free people (2:16). This gives us a clue to the rich imagery of the nature and mission of the church in this epistle.

In 1997, John Driver has provided a significant update reflecting on the nature and mission of the church, particularly in Anabaptist perspective.

The images for church leadership are fewer but no less intriguing: apostle (1:1), prophet (1:10), evangelist (1:12, 23), good steward (4:10), elder (5:1), shepherd (2:25; 5:2-4), guardian (or bishop, exercising oversight; 2:25; 5:2), example (5:3), speaker (4:11), and servant (4:10). Each image illuminates a slightly different aspect of servant leadership in the church.

The primary passages that help communicate Peter's image of the church and its ministry are 2:4-10; 4:7-11; and 5:1-10. Ross Bender's book *The People of God* is significant in drawing on imagery of the church in 1 Peter and the whole NT, and applying that imagery to theological education.

Images of the church that continue to have special appeal include the portrayal of the people of God as "pilgrims" or as "resident aliens." John Elliott has tapped into the "household image" in his appealing title, *A Home for the Homeless.* John H. Yoder has two books using images from 1 Peter: *The Priestly Kingdom* and *The Royal Priesthood.*

Here are some basic elements in Peter's understanding of the church and its leadership:

1. The church is perceived essentially as a people, rather than a movement or an organization. This people is made up of persons who are born anew to faith and hope and a changed style of ethical living, characterized particularly by love toward fellow believers and respectful attitudes toward nonbelievers. Some of the latter may be abusing believers. An external mark of this people is their baptism, described as *a pledge to God from a good conscience.*

2. Jesus Christ is clearly the foundation of this believing people, the foundation stone on whom the church is built. He is the once-rejected stone who has now become a true *cornerstone.* Christ has redeemed this people, at the cost of innocent blood, so that they may live for God, prayerfully and ethi-

cally. He is the one from whom the church derives the "right angles" for its faith and its ethical life.

3. The church is a priesthood in the sense that all believers participate in both the benefits and responsibilities of those in the family of God. The church is to exercise a stewardship of God's manifold grace. To the church have been given gifts, spoken of broadly as gifts of speaking and gifts of serving, so that it may perform its priestly functions. These include especially worship, witness, and ministry.

4. The church experiences suffering in many forms, not only as individual members suffer, but also because persecution comes to them for bearing the name of Jesus. This suffering with and for the sake of Jesus Christ and the gospel, however, moves on to eschatological vindication and glory for believers.

5. To the church on earth is given leadership so that its life may be nourished, its faith may be sustained and guided, and its hope remain strong and clearly focused. These leaders, whether called shepherds, overseers, or elders, are "undershepherds" who themselves follow the Chief Shepherd, Jesus Christ, and are accountable to him. They are servant leaders who do not exercise their authority as do the "lords" of secular society; instead, they embody the shepherding love of Jesus Christ in themselves and in their ministering relationships to the people entrusted to their care.

6. The church is to be a household (2:5; 4:17), a true family (5:9), whose stewardship includes hospitality (4:8-11). Thus the church is the true *home.* The people of God, as pilgrims and sojourners, are not at home in this world. The church is indeed a "Home for the Homeless" (Elliot), engaged in mission (Driver), inviting, welcoming, nurturing, and caring and creating space for those who come into this community of faith, hope, and love. For further excellent discussion, see Driver.

A THEOLOGY OF SUFFERING In one perspective, 1 Peter does not offer "a theology of suffering," yet this theme is inescapably pervasive. It can be seen as the central concern or at least the central setting for its message of hope. In 1 Peter (NRSV), some form of the word *suffer* appears at least twenty times.

Peter Davids has devoted special attention to a careful review of this theme in 1 Peter. In current usage the word *suffer* has a wider range of meanings than in 1 Peter. Contemporary dictionary definitions of *suffering* range from undergoing "pain or grief or damage or disablement" to undergoing "martyrdom" (Davids: 30). In trying to understand the biblical text, we need then to give special attention to the context and meanings of biblical terms.

In reviewing the understandings of suffering in the OT, the NT, and in church history, Davids briefly traces changing "theologies of suffering" having to do with the relation of sin and suffering, the perceived ultimate origin of suffering (from God or Satan), the possible meaning and even the benefits of suffering, and its ultimate end. He pleads correctly that 1 Peter must be read first of all in terms of its own understanding of suffering, not our presuppositions.

Most of the OT associates sin and suffering. Suffering is perceived as a consequence of sin. God is commonly viewed as bringing suffering. Thus suffering is seen either as punishment or at least chastisement designed to bring people back to God. Often such suffering takes place at the hands of enemies, especially enemy nations. The grand exception to this view is in the book of Job, which seeks to break the direct connection between personal sin and human suffering. Job does not portray suffering as a purifying or character-building experience. Satan rather than God becomes the principal agent, though with God's "permission."

In the Suffering of God, Fretheim offers another perspective, reinterpreting the OT and tracing how indeed God is also perceived as suffering. God is not only, as some have read it, the one who causes or allows people to suffer. Throughout the OT, God is portrayed as one who suffers because of, with, and for God's people, anticipating NT perspectives.

In the NT, Jesus also disconnects a direct relationship between sin and suffering (John 9:3; Luke 13:1-5), particularly in the matter of physical health. Moreover, the concept of the innocent or the righteous suffering comes into play and finds its ultimate expression in Jesus as the innocent and even sinless sufferer. Suffering is perceived as a testing of faith (James 1:1-4, 12-15) and as discipline (Heb. 12:2-11). Beyond these perspectives, the concept of vicarious redemptive suffering, drawn especially from Isaiah 53, becomes significant.

In 1 Peter itself, the theme of suffering is pervasive. The particular Greek vocabulary of suffering comes from the paschō cluster of terms rather than thlipsis, "oppression, affliction" (Davids: 31). Of the 42 times paschō appears in the NT, twelve of these are in 1 Peter. It is clearly a dominant word in this epistle, though other expressions for suffering are also used. As indicated above (notes on 1:18-21; 2:21-25; 3:18-22; 4:13ff.), the suffering of Jesus Christ has a most significant role in this epistle.

However, about half the references deal with the suffering endured by the followers of Christ. They suffer trials and the testing of their faith (1:6). They are falsely accused as evildoers (2:12). Some are treated harshly and unjustly by their masters (2:18-20). Some wives have unbelieving husbands (3:1). Believers experience evil or abuse from others (3:9). Former associates blaspheme because the believers have changed their lifestyle (4:4). More profoundly, they share in Christ's sufferings (4:13) and are reviled in the name of Christ (4:14). They may implicitly be considered either murderers, thieves, criminals, or mischief-makers (4:15). They simply suffer as a Christian (4:16). Moreover, they face the attack of the devil, sharing in the suffering of many sisters and brothers in all the world (5:9).

Peter indicates that their suffering may indeed be in accordance with God's will (4:19). But this does not imply that God intends or blesses what cruel masters do to their slaves (2:18-20), what unbelieving or inconsiderate husbands do to their wives (3:1-7), or the evil or abuse done in the Christian community or by pagans (3:9). In Peter's perspective, God is aware of what is happening, and we ought to be aware of God's presence (2:19-20).

Believers are to examine their lives to see whether they are simply suffering as a result of their own misdeeds (4:15). Thus they may try to avoid suffering that God cannot bless. Suffering which God can bless includes (1) the challenge of their faith (3:15), (2) the abuse they suffer for Christian behavior (3:16; 4:4), and (3) suffering because they bear the name of Christ (4:14). In this context, the Christian's response to suffering harm or abuse becomes a significant part of Christian witness.

First Peter does not deal specifically with the question of suffering physical illness. *By his wounds you have been healed* (2:24c) is a statement to be understood metaphorically (Michaels: 149-150), both in Isaiah as well as in 1 Peter. Peter is speaking of their conversion to Christ and the healing that brings, as shown in 2:25. He is not making explicit reference to the literal wounds inflicted on Jesus during his trials or the abuse that cruel masters have given slaves. The healing, "making whole," is essentially the capacity to live in God's strength and do God's will in God's way. This in no way excludes the healing, spiritually and also physically, that God brings to the believer and to the Christian community when God's power to heal is acknowledged and sought for in prayer.

The larger perspective in 1 Peter is that the Christian responds to suffering in the light of Christ's suffering, understood as both example and atonement, and in the light of coming judgment, as developed in the commentary notes (above).

Our understanding of Peter's view of suffering includes the following:

• Suffering is not what God ultimately desires for Christ or Christians or anyone else, though God may allow and even include it in God's sovereign or permissive will. Instead, suffering happens, often with causes not fully understood, and Christ and his followers are to respond discerningly, seeking God's support, grace, and glory (5:10). God's ultimate desire is healing and life, including righteousness, justice and peace.

• Suffering is not to be sought by Christians. It is to be avoided unless the endurance of it is truly *a participation in the sufferings of Christ* (4:13) and thus has redemptive or liberating possibilities through the working of God's grace.

• Suffering by the innocent or the righteous is virtually inevitable in a sinful world, as is seen supremely in the suffering of the innocent Jesus. Christians can endure it with an awareness of God's presence and approval when they follow Jesus in their response to necessary or inevitable suffering.

• The suffering of Jesus Christ becomes the decisive embodiment of God's transformation of suffering in the design of human redemption from sin, abuse, and violence. It thus is the focal center for the Christian in facing life's painful experiences and the anticipation of God's ultimate righteous judgment.

• The suffering and death of Jesus took place precisely in the context of his own "doing right" and "doing good," as 1 Peter 2:21-23 indicates. This innocent and nonretaliatory way of the cross was not an accident of history. According to Peter, it was *destined before the foundation of the world* (1:19-20). In Peter's theology of the cross, this innocent suffering and dying for the redemption of the unrighteous belongs to the eternal purpose of God. Even on the cross, Jesus prays the forgiveness of God for those who crucified him, not knowing what they were doing (Luke 23:34).

• The Christian's response to suffering in 1 Peter becomes a crucial measure of faithfulness in discipleship and in Christian witness. This response moves beyond the usual human responses of acquiescence to evil on one hand, or on the other hand violent attack on evil. A truly Christian response seeks to find a constructive, creative, nonviolent, Spirit-empowered, and Spirit-guided alternative.

• The resurrection of Jesus is God's profound approval of the faithfulness of Jesus (2:20-21). His death is not the victory of the unrighteous enemies of God. It is the victory of Jesus, the Righteous One, over suffering and death that gives Peter a basis for a living hope (1:3). When followers of Jesus participate in suffering because of identification with Jesus Christ, they likewise participate in the glory of Christ's resurrection and exaltation (4:13; 5:1, 10).

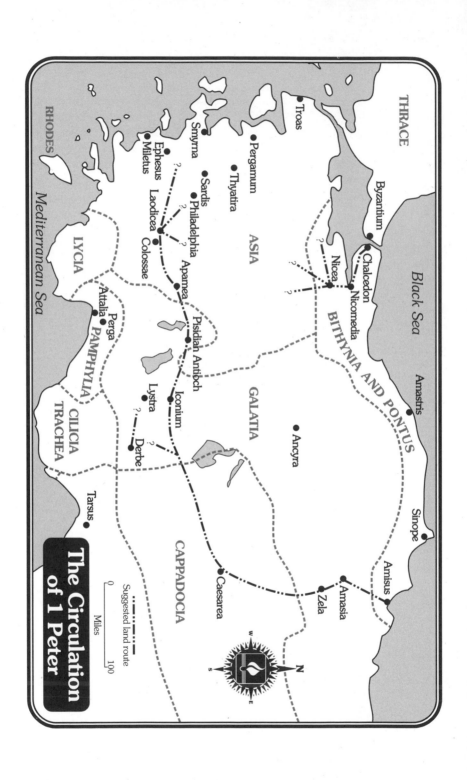

The Circulation of 1 Peter

Bibliography for 1 Peter

ABD   Ed. D. N. Freedman et al.
   1992   *The Anchor Bible Dictionary.* 6 vols. New York: Doubleday.
Achtemeier, Paul J.
   1996   *1 Peter.* Hermeneia. Minneapolis: Fortress.
Arichea, Daniel C. and Eugene A. Nida
   1980   *The Translators Handbook on the First Letter from Peter.* New
          York: United Bible Societies.
Balch, David L.
   1981   *Let Wives Be Submissive: The Domestic Code in 1 Peter.*
          Chico, Calif.: Scholars Press.
Barclay, William
   1958   *The Letters of James and Peter.* The Daily Study Bible. 2d ed.
          Edinburgh: The Saint Andrew Press.
Barth, Karl
   1962   *The Epistle to the Philippians.* Richmond, Va.: John Knox.
Beasley-Murray, G. R.
   1962   *Baptism in the New Testament.* Grand Rapids: Eerdmans.
Bechter, Steven Richard
   1998   *Following in His Steps: Suffering, Community, and
          Christology in 1 Peter.* Society of Biblical Literature. Atlanta:
          Scholars Press.
Bender, Ross T.
   1971   *The People of God: A Mennonite Interpretation of the Free
          Church Tradition.* Scottdale, Pa.: Herald Press.
Bergman, Susan
   1996a "In the Shadow of the Martyrs." *Christianity Today* 40
          (Aug. 12): 18-25.
Bergman, Susan, ed.
   1996b *Martyrs: Contemporary Writers on Modern Lives of Faith.* San
          Francisco: Harper.

Berkhof, Hendrik
    1971   *Christ and the Powers.* Trans. J. H. Yoder. Scottdale, Pa.:
           Herald Press.
Best, Ernest
    1971   *1 Peter.* New Century Bible. Greenwood, S.C.: Attic Press.
Bigg, Charles
    1905   *A Critical and Exegetical Commentary on the Epistles of St.
           Peter and St. Jude.* International Critical Commentary. New
           York: Charles Scribners Sons.
Brown, Alexandra R.
    1995   *The Cross and Human Transformation: Paul's Apocalyptic
           Word in 1 Corinthians.* Minneapolis: Augsburg Fortress.
Brown, Raymond E., Karl P. Donfried, and John Reumann, eds.
    1973   *Peter in the New Testament.* Minneapolis: Augsburg.
Cahill, Lisa Sowle
    1994   *Love Your Enemies: Discipleship, Pacifism, and Just War
           Theory.* Minneapolis: Fortress.
Charlesworth, James H., ed.
    1983   *The Old Testament Pseudepigrapha.* Vol. 1: *Apocalyptic
           Literature and Testaments.* Garden City, N.Y.: Doubleday &
           Company.
Chergé Christian de
    1996   "Last Testament." *First Things* 65:21.
Clowney, Edmund
    1988   *The Message of 1 Peter: The Bible Speaks Today.* Downers
           Grove, Ill.: InterVarsity.
Confession of Faith in a Mennonite Perspective
    1995   Scottdale, Pa.: Herald Press.
Corley, Kathleen E.
    1994   "1 Peter." In *Searching the Scriptures: A Feminist Commentary,*
           2:349-359. Ed. Elisabeth Schüssler Fiorenza. New York:
           Crossroad.
Craddock, Fred B.
    1995   *First and Second Peter and Jude.* Westminster Bible Companion.
           Louisville: Westminster John Knox.
Cranfield, C. E. B.
    1950   *The First Epistle of Peter.* London: SCM.
Crook, John
    1967   *Law and Life of Rome.* Ithaca, N.Y.: Cornell University Press.
Cross, Frank L.
    1954   *1 Peter, A Paschal Liturgy.* London: Mobray.
Davids, Peter H.
    1990   *The First Epistle of Peter.* The New International Commentary
           on the New Testament. Grand Rapids: Eerdmans.
Dirk Philips
    1992   *The Writings of Dirk Philips.* Trans. and ed. Cornelius J. Dyck,
           William E. Keeney, and Alvin J. Beachy. Classics of the Radical
           Reformation. Scottdale, Pa.: Herald Press.
DNTT
    1975-78 *Dictionary of New Testament Theology.* Vols. 1-3. Ed.

Colin Brown. Trans. and augmented from *Theologisches Begriffslexicon zum Neuen Testament*. Grand Rapids: Zondervan.

Driver, John
1997 *Images of the Church in Mission*. Scottdale, Pa.: Herald Press.

Dyck, Cornelius J.
1995 *Spiritual Life in Anabaptism*. Scottdale, Pa.: Herald Press.

Ehrman, Bart D.
1997 *The New Testament: A Historical Introduction to Early Christian Writings*. New York: Oxford University Press.

Elliott, John H.
1981 *A Home for the Homeless: A Sociological Exegesis of 1 Peter, Its Situation and Strategy*. Philadelphia: Fortress.
1992 "First Epistle of Peter." In *ABD*, 5:169-278.

Fields, Sue Wagner
1997 "SueZann Bosler: I Forgive." *The Messenger* (Church of the Brethren): Nov. 1997:12-17.

Fiorenza, Elisabeth Schüssler
1983 *In Memory of Her: A Feminist Theological Reconstruction of Christian Origins*. New York: Crossroad.

Fiorenza, Elisabeth Schüssler, ed.
1994 *Searching the Scriptures*. Vol. 2. New York: Crossroad.

Frend, William H. C.
1978 "Blandina and Perpetua: Two Early Christian Heroines." In *Les Martyrs de Lyon*, 167-177. Ed. M. LeGlay et al. Paris: Editions du Centre National de la Recherche Scientifique.

Fretheim, Terence E.
1984 *The Suffering of God: An Old Testament Perspective*. Overtures to Biblical Theology. Philadelphia: Fortress.

Fromm, Erich
1973 *The Anatomy of Human Destructiveness*. New York: Holt, Rinehart & Winston.

Funk, Robert W.
1996 *Honest to Jesus: Jesus for a New Millennium*. San Francisco: Harper.

Gaster, Theodor H.
1959 *The Dead Sea Scriptures in English Translation*. Garden City, N.Y.: Doubleday & Co.

Goppelt, Leonhard
1993 *A Commentary on 1 Peter*. Ed. Ferdinand Hahn. Tr. and aug. by John E. Alsup. Grand Rapids: Eerdmans.

Grudem, Wayne
1988 *1 Peter*. Tyndale New Testament. Grand Rapids: Eerdmans.

Harder, Leland, ed.
1985 *The Sources of Swiss Anabaptism*. Classics of the Radical Reformation. Scottdale, Pa.: Herald Press.

Hays, Richard B.
1996 *The Moral Vision of the New Testament: Community, Cross, New Creation*. San Francisco: Harper.

Hefley, James C., and Marti Hefley
   1996 *By Their Blood: Christian Martyrs of the Twentieth Century.*
         Grand Rapids: Baker Books.
Hiebert, D. Edmond
   1984 *First Peter.* Chicago: Moody Press.
Hubmaier, Balthasar
   1989 Balthasar Hubmaier, Theologian of Anabaptism. Trans. and ed.
         H. Wayne Pipkin and John H. Yoder. Classics of the Radical
         Reformation. Scottdale, Pa.: Herald Press.
Hunter, Archibald M.
   1957 "The First Epistle of Peter." In The Interpreter's Bible, 12:75-
         159. Nashville: Abingdon-Cokesbury.
Hutterian Brethren
   1987 *The Chronicle of the Hutterian Brethren,* vol. 1. Trans. and ed.
         the Hutterian Brethren from *Das grosse Geschichtsbuch der
         Hutterischen Brüder.* Rifton, N.Y.: Plough Publishing House.
Hymnal: A Worship Book
   1992 Ed. Rebecca Slough et al. Scottdale, Pa.: Mennonite Publishing
         House.
Jenco, Lawrence Martin
   1995 *Bound to Forgive: The Pilgrimage to Reconciliation of a Beirut
         Hostage.* Notre Dame, Ind.: Ave Maria Press.
Jensen, Anne
   1996 *God's Self-Confident Daughters: Early Christianity and the
         Liberation of Women.* Louisville: Westminster John Knox.
Johnson, Luke Timothy
   1996 *The Real Jesus: The Misguided Quest for the Historical Jesus
         and the Truth of the Traditional Gospels.* San Francisco:
         Harper.
Jones, L. Gregory
   1995 *Embodying Forgiveness: A Theological Analysis.* Grand Rapids:
         Eerdmans.
Kelly, J. N. D.
   1969 *A Commentary on the Epistles of Peter and Jude.* Thornapple
         Commentaries. Grand Rapids: Baker Books, 1981 reprint.
King, Martin Luther Jr.
   1986 *A Testament of Hope: The Essential Writings of Martin Luther
         King, Jr.* Ed. James Melvin Washington. San Francisco: Harper
         & Row.
Kistemaker, Simon J.
   1987 *Peter and Jude.* New Testament Commentary. Grand Rapids:
         Baker Books.
Kivengere, Festo, and Dorothy Smoker
   1977 *I Love Idi Amin.* Old Tappan, N.J.: F. H. Revell Co.
Klassen, William
   1984 *Love of Enemies: The Way to Peace.* Overtures to Biblical
         Theology. Philadelphia: Fortress.
Koontz, Ted, ed.
   1996 *Godward: Personal Stories of Grace.* Scottdale, Pa.: Herald
         Press.

Kreider, Alan
  1987   *Journey Towards Holiness.* Scottdale, Pa.: Herald Press.
Lewis, C. S.
  1989   *The Quotable Lewis.* Ed. Wayne Martindale and Jerry Root.
         Wheaton, Ill.: Tyndale House.
Luther, Martin
  1982   *Commentary on the Epistles of Peter and Jude* [1523]. Ed.
         John N. Lenker in 1904 and Peter W. Bennehoff in 1982. Grand
         Rapids: Kregel Publications.
Maas, Robert, and Gabriel O'Donnell
  1990   *Spiritual Traditions for the Contemporary Church.* Nashville:
         Abingdon.
Marpeck, Pilgram
  1978   *The Writings of Pilgram Marpeck.* Trans. and ed. William
         Klassen and Walter Klaassen. Classics of the Radical Reformation.
         Scottdale, Pa.: Herald Press.
Marshall, I. Howard
  1991   *1 Peter.* The IVP New Testament Commentary. Downers Grove,
         Ill.: InterVarsity.
Marshall, Paul
  1997   *Their Blood Cries Out.* Dallas: Word.
Martin, Clarice J.
  1991   "The *Haustafeln* (Household Codes) in African American Biblical
         Interpretation: 'Free Slaves' and 'Subordinate Women.'" In *Stony
         the Road We Trod: African American Biblical Interpretation.*
         Ed. Cain Hope Felder. Minneapolis: Fortress
McKnight, Scot
  1996   *1 Peter.* The NIV Application Commentary. Grand Rapids:
         Zondervan.
Meeks, Wayne A.
  1986   *The Moral World of the First Christians.* Library of Early
         Christianity. Philadelphia: Westminster.
Menno Simons
  1956   *The Complete Writings of Menno Simons.* Trans. L. Verduin.
         Ed. J. C. Wenger. Scottdale, Pa.: Herald Press.
Mennonite Encyclopedia, The
  1955-59, 1990 Vols. 1-4 ed. H. S. Bender et al. Vol. 5 ed. C. J. Dyck
         and Dennis D. Martin. Scottdale, Pa.: Herald Press.
Metzger, Bruce M.
  1971   *A Textual Commentary on the Greek New Testament.* New
         York: United Bible Societies.
Michaels, J. Ramsey
  1988   *1 Peter.* Word Biblical Commentary. Waco: Word Books.
Minear, Paul S.
  1960   *Images of the Church in the New Testament.* Philadelphia:
         Westminster.
MM
  1938   *Martyrs Mirror.* Compiled by Thieleman J. van Braght. Trans.
         Joseph F. Sohm. Scottdale, Pa.: Herald Press.

Moltmann, Jürgen
1967 *The Theology of Hope.* New York: Harper & Row.
1983 *Following Jesus Christ in the World Today.* Occasional Papers,
      4. Elkhart, Ind.: Institute of Mennonite Studies.
1997 *The Source of Life: The Holy Spirit and the Theology of Life.*
      Minneapolis: Fortress.
Mounce, Robert H.
*1982 Born Anew to a Living Hope: A Commentary on 1 and 2
      Peter.* Grand Rapids: Eerdmans.
Musurillo, Herbert, ed. and trans.
1972 *The Acts of the Christian Martyrs:* Oxford: Clarendon.
Neill, Stephen
1964 *The Interpretation of the New Testament 1861-1961.* London:
      Oxford University Press.
Nouwen, Henri J. M.
1972 *The Wounded Healer.* Garden City, N.Y.: Doubleday.
O'Connor, Elizabeth
1979 *Letters to Scattered Pilgrims.* San Francisco: Harper.
Pankratz, Theodora
1993 *Living with Fringe Benefits from Here to There.* Mountain
      Lake, Minn.: The Author.
Perkins, Pheme
1995 *First and Second Peter, James, and Jude.* Interpretation.
      Louisville: Westminster John Knox.
Petersen, Eugene H.
1993 *The Message: The New Testament in Contemporary
      Language.* Colorado Springs: Navpress.
Phillips, J. B.
1958 *The New Testament in Modern English.* New York: Macmillan.
Philips. *See* Dirk
Piper, John
1979 *"Love Your Enemies:" Jesus' Love Command in the Synoptic
      Gospels and in Early Christian Paraenesis.* Society for New
      Testament Studies, 38. New York: Cambridge University Press.
1980 "Hope as the Motivation for Love: 1 Peter 3:9-12." *New
      Testament Studies* 26:212-231.
Ramsay, William
1893 *The Church in the Roman Empire.* London: Hodder &
      Stoughton.
Reike, Bo
1964 *The Epistles of James, Peter, and Jude.* The Anchor Bible.
      Garden City, N.Y.: Doubleday & Co.
Richardson, Alan
1950 *A Theological Wordbook of the Bible.* London: SCM.
Riedemann, Peter
1999 *Peter Riedemann's Hutterite Confession of Faith.* Trans. and
      ed. John J. Friesen. Classics of the Radical Reformation.
      Scottdale, Pa.: Herald Press.

Sattler, Michael
 1973   *The Legacy of Michael Sattler.* Trans. and ed. John H. Yoder.
        Classics of the Radical Reformation. Scottdale. Pa.: Herald Press.
Schertz, Mary H.
 1992   "Nonretaliation and the Haustafeln in 1 Peter." In *The Love of
        Enemy and Nonretaliation in the New Testament,* 258-286.
        Ed. Willard M. Swartley. Studies in Peace and Scripture.
        Louisville: Westminster John Knox.
Schlabach, Theron F.
 1990   "Humility." In *The Mennonite Encyclopedia,* 5:400-401. Ed.
        C. J. Dyck and Dennis D. Martin. Scottdale, Pa.: Herald Press.
Schmidt, Orlando, ed.
 1979   *Sing and Rejoice.* Scottdale, Pa.: Herald Press.
Schroeder, David
 1959   "Die Haustafeln des Neuen Testaments: Ihre Herkunft und ihr
        theologischer Sinn." Dissertation, Hamburg.
 1976   "Lists, Ethical." In *The Interpreter's Dictionary of the Bible,*
        Suppl. Vol., 546-547. Ed. Keith Crim et al. Nashville: Abingdon.
 1987   "The New Testament Haustafel: Egalitarian or Status Quo?" In
        Perspectives on Feminist Hermeneutics. Occasional Papers
        10:56-65. Ed. Gayle Gerber Koontz and Willard Swartley.
        Elkhart, Ind.: Institute of Mennonite Studies.
 1988   *First Peter: Faith Refined by Fire.* Faith and Life Bible Studies.
        Newton, Kan.: Faith & Life.
 1990   "Once You Were No People . . ." In *The Church as Theological
        Community: Essays in Honour of David Schroeder,* 36-65. Ed.
        Harry Huebner. Winnipeg: Canadian Mennonite Bible College.
Schüssler. *See* Fiorenza
Selwyn, Edward Gordon
 1946   *The First Epistle of St. Peter.* 2d ed. Thornapple Commen-
        taries. Grand Rapids: Baker Books, 1981 reprint.
Simons. *See* Menno
Swartley, Willard M.
 1983   *Slavery, Sabbath, War, and Women: Case Issues in Biblical
        Interpretation.* Scottdale, Pa.: Herald Press.
 1994   *Israel's Scripture Traditions and the Synoptic Gospels: Story
        Shaping Story.* Peabody, Mass.: Hendrickson.
 1996   "War and Peace in the New Testament." In *Aufstieg und
        Niedergang der römischer Welt (ANRW),* Principate II, vol. 26,
        part 3, pages 2298-2408. Ed. Wolfgang Haase and Hildegard
        Temporini. New York: Walter de Gruyter.
Swartley, Willard M., ed.
 1992   *The Love of Enemy and Nonretaliation in the New Testament.*
        Studies in Peace and Scripture, 3. Louisville: Westminster John
        Knox.
TDNT
 1964-76 *Theological Dictionary of the New Testament.* 9 vols. Ed. G.
        Kittel et al. Trans. and ed. G. W. Bromiley. Grand Rapids:
        Eerdmans.

Thuren, Lauri
    1995   *Argument and Theology of 1 Peter: The Origins of Christian
            Paraenesis.* Journal for the Study of the New Testament:
            Supplement Series, 114. Sheffield: Sheffield Academic Press.
Toews, John E.
    1977   "The Law in Paul's Letter to the Romans: A Study of Romans
            9:30—10:13." Dissertation, Northwestern University, Evanston, Ill.
Vermes, G.
    1962   *The Dead Sea Scrolls in English.* New York: Penguin Books.
Volf, Miroslav
    1996   *Exclusion and Embrace: A Theological Exploration of
            Identity, Otherness, and Reconciliation.* Nashville: Abingdon.
    1994   "Soft Difference: Theological Reflections on the Relation
            Between Church and Culture in 1 Peter." *Ex Auditu* 10 (1994):
            230-248.
Waltner, Erland, ed.
    1990   *Jesus Christ and the Mission of the Church: Contemporary
            Anabaptist Perspectives.* Newton, Kan.: Faith & Life.
Washington, James Melvin. *See* King
Watts, Gary
    1999   *Painful Questions.* Scottdale, Pa.: Herald Press.
Weir, Ben and Carol, with Dennis Benson
    1987   *Hostage Bound, Hostage Free.* Philadelphia: Westminster Press.
Wink, Walter
    1986   *Unmasking the Powers: The Invisible Forces that Determine
            Human Existence.* Philadelphia: Fortress.
    1992   *Engaging the Powers: Discernment and Resistance in a World
            of Domination.* Minneapolis: Fortress.
Yoder, Eldon T., and Monroe D. Hochstetler, compilers
    1962   *Biblical References in Anabaptist Writings.* LaGrange, Ind.:
            Pathway Publishers.
Yoder, Elizabeth G., ed.
    1992   *Peace Theology and Violence Against Women.* Occasional
            Papers, 16. Elkhart, Ind.: Institute of Mennonite Studies.
Yoder, John Howard
    1972   *The Politics of Jesus.* Grand Rapids: Eerdmans.
    1984   *The Priestly Kingdom: Social Ethics as Gospel.* Notre Dame,
            Ind.: University of Notre Dame Press.
    1994   *The Royal Priesthood: Essays Ecclesiastical and Ecumenical.*
            Grand Rapids: Eerdmans. Scottdale, Pa.: Herald Press, 1998.
Zerbe, Gordon M.
    1993   *Non-Retaliation in Early Jewish and New Testament Texts:
            Ethical Themes in Social Contexts. Journal for the Study of
            Pseudepigrapha,* Supplement Series, 13. Sheffield, England:
            Sheffield Academic (JSOT) Press.

Selected Resources for 1 Peter

Achtemeier, Paul J. *1 Peter*. Hermeneia. Minneapolis: Fortress, 1996. A scholarly comprehensive exegetical commentary useful for pastors, Bible teachers, and biblical scholars.

Davids, Peter H. *The First Epistle of Peter.* The International Commentary on the New Testament. Grand Rapids: Eerdmans, 1990. Theologically conservative commentary giving special attention to the theme of suffering in this epistle.

Elliott, John H. *A Home for the Homeless: A Sociological Exegesis of 1 Peter, Its Situation and Strategy.* Philadelphia: Fortress, 1981. Explores seriously (not always convincingly) the sociological context of this epistle.

Goppelt, Leonhard. *A Commentary on First Peter.* Edited by Ferdinand Hahn. Translated and augmented by John E. Alsup. Grand Rapids: Eerdmans, 1993. First appearing in German, this landmark study opened the way for more sociological interpretations that influenced Mennonite scholars like David Schroeder, who did his doctoral study with Goppelt.

Hiebert, D. Edmond. *First Peter*. Chicago: Moody Press, 1964. Mennonite Brethren biblical scholar presents an evangelically oriented commentary.

Kelly, J. N. D. *A Commentary on the Epistles of Peter and Jude.* Thornapple Commentaries, 1969. Grand Rapids: Baker Books, 1981 reprint. Long used as a standard commentary in college and

seminary studies of the Petrine Epistles and Jude. Still valuable.
Marshall, I. Howard. *1 Peter*. The IVP New Testament Commentary.
Downers Grove, Ill.: InterVarsity, 1991. Especially helpful in sur-
veying and evaluating critical judgments on such issues as author-
ship. Works from evangelical perspectives.
McKnight, Scot. *1 Peter*. The NIV Application Commentary. Grand
Rapids: Zondervan, 1996. User-friendly commentary focusing on
application to contemporary life.
Michaels, J. Ramsey. *1 Peter*. Word Biblical Commentary. Waco,
Tex.: Word Books, 1988. Comprehensive and scholarly, this
commentary helpfully wrestles with critical and exegetical issues in
depth. It contributes significantly to a better understanding of the
subordination codes.
Perkins, Pheme. *First and Second Peter, James, and Jude*.
Interpretation. Louisville: Westminster John Knox, 1995.
Intended to help church leaders in their preaching ministry.
Illustrative and contemporary in style.
Schertz, Mary H. "Nonretaliation and the Haustafeln in 1 Peter." In
The Love of Enemy and Nonretaliation in the New Testament,
258-286. Edited by Willard M. Swartley. Studies in Peace and
Scripture, 3. Louisville: Westminster John Knox, 1992. Using her
skills in biblical literary studies, the author sees and presents
1 Peter as a document for making peace.
Schroeder, David. "Once You Were No People. . . ." In *The Church
as Theological Community: Essays in Honor of David
Schroeder*, 36-65. Edited by Harry Huebner. Winnipeg:
Canadian Mennonite Bible College, 1990. Schroeder wrote his
doctoral dissertation on 1 Peter under Leonhard Goppelt and here
contributes some of his profoundest insights.
Zerbe, Gordon. *Non-Retaliation in Early Jewish and New
Testament Texts: Ethical Themes in Social Contexts*. Journal
for the Study of the Pseudepigrapha, Supplement Series, 13.
Sheffield: Sheffield Academic (JSOT) Press. Helpful study by a
Mennonite scholar on nonretaliation, including 1 Peter.

Erland Waltner

For over sixty years Erland Waltner, the writer of the commentary on 1 Peter, has served as pastor, Bible teacher, preacher, church conference leader, and administrator in church institutions and agencies. He grew up on a farm near Freeman, South Dakota. Upon baptism, he became a member of the Salem Mennonite Church.

Waltner graduated from Bethel College, North Newton, Kansas, in 1935. He finished his pastoral training at the Biblical Seminary in New York in 1938, and then at his home church was ordained for leadership ministry.

While serving as pastor of the Second Mennonite Church of Philadelphia in 1938-41, he pursued graduate biblical and theological studies at Princeton Theological Seminary, Temple University, and Eastern Baptist Theological Seminary, where he completed two degrees, master of theology (1940) and doctor of theology (1948).

During 1941-49 Waltner served as pastor of Bethel Mennonite Church, Mountain Lake, Minnesota. In 1949 he began teaching Bible and religion courses at Bethel College.

During the summer of 1954, he taught "Petrine Epistles" in a joint summer school of Goshen (Ind.) College Biblical Seminary and Mennonite Biblical Seminary. Through this experience, he became involved in explorations to establish the Associated Mennonite Biblical Seminaries (now Seminary) at Elkhart, Indiana.

From 1958 to 1978, Waltner served as president and professor at Mennonite Biblical Seminary, then continued at AMBS part-time. In retirement, he was executive secretary of the Mennonite Medical Association for twelve years. During 1956-62 he served as president of the General Conference Mennonite Church, and in 1962-72 as president of the Mennonite World Conference.

He is married to Mary Winifred Schlosser, daughter of missionaries to China, and they are active members of the Hively Avenue Mennonite Church in Elkhart. They are richly blessed by four daughters: Mary, a psychiatric social worker in San Diego; Irene, a public school teacher in Elkhart; Kathy, a professional counselor at the University of Guelph; and Rose Elaine, an ordained chaplain in eastern Pennsylvania. Seven grandchildren and two great-grandchildren grace the family circle.

2 Peter, Jude

J. Daryl Charles

Preface to 2 Peter, Jude

While writing my master's thesis on John the Baptist years ago, I was struck by how important the cultural factor is in understanding and appreciating the documents of the NT. A consideration of John the Baptist, about whom we know little, inevitably leads one into the world of Judaism that is contemporary to the advent of the Christian community. In terms of its literature, this is a world of apocalyptic visions and angelic messengers. It is a world depicted in stark terms, a world of darkness and light, and a world in which the wicked conspire against the righteous, who cry out to God for vindication.

Backgrounds are exceedingly important for understanding works such as 2 Peter and Jude. The epistle of Jude is generally acknowledged to be framed against the backdrop of Palestinian Jewish-Christianity. Not surprisingly, the author's denunciations as well as exhortations are apocalyptic in tenor. Backgrounds are important in 2 Peter but for a different reason. As Tord Fornberg demonstrated in his important study of 2 Peter (*An Early Church in a Pluralistic Society*, 1977), the recipients of 2 Peter appear to live amid a pagan, Gentile social environment. This assumption has significant implications for our interpretation of the letter. Ethics rather than doctrine are in the author's purview.

Historical-critical scholarship, with few exceptions, has assumed that 2 Peter mirrors a second-century background, in which Gnostic heresy is being countered; if so, the epistle cannot be considered authentic, coming from the letter's namesake, the apostle Peter. What are the implications of such presupposed backgrounds?

Whatever position we take regarding the letter's background, then, determines the trajectory of any interpretation that proceeds.

In addition to NT backgrounds, I am also fascinated by the relationship between eschatology and ethics. The NT has nothing to say if it says nothing about ethics. Most of the Pauline epistles, known for their theological content, devote a considerable portion of the text to ethical concerns. The general epistles are almost wholly devoted to ethical concerns. It is remarkable that scholarly books on NT ethics all but ignore 2 Peter and Jude as resources.

To illustrate, consider the conspicuous silence of important works published in the last fifteen years. Willi Marxsen's *New Testament Foundations for Christian Ethics* (English trans., 1993) contains not a single reference to 2 Peter. Two massive (untranslated) German volumes—*Neues Testament und Ethik* (1989), edited by Helmut Merklein; and *Neutestamentliche Ethik* (1987), edited by Siegfried Schulz—together have 1,251 pages but allot only six pages to 2 Peter, and none to Jude. Wolfgang Schrage's *The Ethics of the New Testament* (1987) is hailed by Victor Paul Furnish (*Theological Ethics in Paul*) as "the finest recent treatment of ethics in the New Testament I have read." Yet it devotes only seven pages to 2 Peter and Jude in passing, and this at the conclusion of 1 Peter.

We could cite more. Jack T. Sanders' *Ethics in the New Testament* devotes just over a page to Jude and 2 Peter. Ceslas Spicq's imposing two-volume *Théologie morale du Nouveau Testament*, Rudolph Schnackenburg's *The Moral Teaching of the New Testament*, and R. H. Marshall's *The Challenge of New Testament Ethics* all contain no discussion of ethics in 2 Peter. Finally, Wayne Meeks's probing of the early Christians' moral grammar, *The Moral World of the First Christians*, also omits any reference to 2 Peter. Alas, the reader begins to see the problem.

This conspicuous absence raises an obvious question. Why do textbooks on NT ethics uniformly fail to include 2 Peter and Jude in their discussions? Surely the reason is not because of an absence of moral vocabulary in these two works. Moral grammar, as it turns out, is most dense in the general epistles, and 2 Peter and Jude are not excepted.

Yet a third motivation, not unrelated to the second, accounts for my interest in these two brief epistles, and that is their relative obscurity. While the average believer spends little time in the general epistles, even less—if any!—is spent in sorting out those cryptic references to fallen angels, Balaam, and company in 2 Peter and Jude. It is no understatement to say that these two writings together constitute the "Rodney Dangerfield" of the NT! This relative lack of respect toward 2 Peter and Jude, it seems to me, beckons the church, whatever its form and confessional distinctives, to rediscover and reexamine these invaluable documents.

Contained within these epistles are important pastoral insights. Pressing to the fore are issues of holy living in a pagan cultural setting, communal accountability and discipline, spiritual authority, moral formation, and the relationship between doctrine and ethics, or belief and practice. The church ignores 2 Peter and Jude at great peril; they call the church to reappropriate resources that for too long have been ignored and neglected.

My sincere thanks go to Willard Swartley, who has patiently worked with me on this project; and to Elmer Martens, whose kind words and recommendations were helpful along the way. David Garber, Herald Press book editor, has also ably assisted the editorial process.

Now to him who is able to keep you [and me] from stumbling and [who is able] to present you [and me] in his glorious presence without fault and with exceeding joy, to the only wise God our Savior, through Jesus Christ our Lord, be glory, majesty, dominion and authority, before all ages, now and forever. Amen (Jude 24-25).

—*J. Daryl Charles*
Department of Religion and Philosophy
Taylor University
Upland, Indiana

Overview of 2 Peter

The Misunderstood Epistle

While Jude is considered the "neglected" epistle of the NT, 2 Peter is in many ways the misunderstood epistle. This misunderstanding is due largely to the assumptions NT scholarship has brought to the letter itself. From the beginning, few books of the Bible have had more difficulty gaining widespread acceptance in the canon. This does not mean, however, that no consensus existed in the early church. Doubts did exist in some parts of the early church, yet by the end of the second century, 2 Peter was generally held to be canonical.

Assumptions traditionally informing the interpretation of 2 Peter have tended to be driven by modern skepticism. Inevitably, the chief battle surrounding 2 Peter has been whether the letter is authentically Petrine. In the main, few scholars—whatever their theological orientation—have been willing to attribute the letter to its namesake, the apostle Peter. If it is believed that the epistle is not the work of the apostle, one is then left to choose from various theories of pseudonymity to explain the contents of the epistle.

In the notes, 2 Peter 1:12-15 and 1:16-21 receive some comments on authorship, date, origin, and literary character. However, a fuller discussion of these matters is reserved for an essay [Authorship]. This format lets the epistle's message unfold directly, without neglecting issues of scholarship traditionally associated with the text of 2 Peter.

In 2 Peter 1 the author clarifies his purpose in writing. There can be no claims to Christian spirituality apart from possessing a virtuous lifestyle. The readers have been given full knowledge of their inheritance in Christ and are to add to this base by cultivating an ethical pattern of living in the face of unethical cultural forces. Some members of the community, sadly, have forgotten that they were utterly cleansed of their sins. Second Peter 2 is devoted to a portrait of those fueling the apostasy, while 2 Peter 3 constitutes a call to moral vigilance.

Thus the author must confront the problem of *apostasy*, people leaving the Christian way of life and faith. The apostle, shortly before his martyrdom, is pressed in the Spirit to remind them both of their spiritual resources and their moral obligations. The pastoral situation cries out for a prophetic-apostolic word of authority. The readers, in accepting or rejecting this word, accept or reject the very word of God.

Themes in 2 Peter

Several related themes interweave in 2 Peter: (1) a call to virtuous living, knowing the certainty of our salvation; (2) a warning to beware of those who lead others into apostasy; and (3) a reminder that God will fulfill his divine purpose by judging those who do evil and vindicating the faithful.

Second Peter reads as a strong exhortation to a Christian community struggling in a pagan social environment (Fornberg: 111-124). Against the flow of traditional commentary, one need not locate 2 Peter in second-century Gnosticism, with its cosmological dualism, dichotomy between the material and the spiritual, and denial of the resurrection. As we read the epistle, we can easily imagine ourselves living in Corinth of the mid-first century. Consider, for example, the many parallels in 1 Corinthians and 2 Peter.

"Knowledge" is important in both (1 Cor. 1:5; 8:1-3, 7-11; 12:8; 13:2, 8; 14:6; 2 Pet. 1:2, 3, 5, 6, 8). Sexual ethics is a theme central to both (1 Cor. 5:1-13; 6:12-20; 7:1-7; 2 Pet. 1:4; 2:2, 6-10, 14, 18; 3:3). In both letters, factions are preoccupied with a false sense of freedom (1 Cor. 7:21-24; 8:9-13; 9:1-23; 10:29; 2 Pet. 2:19). Both letters suggest abuses of the love feast (1 Cor. 11:17-34; 2 Pet. 2:13). Also, both letters develop the significance of Christ's return, to counter a particular error affecting the thinking of some in the community (1 Cor. 15:23-28; 2 Pet. 3:3-13).

In sum, what we encounter in 2 Peter could just as readily reflect conditions in mid first-century Corinth addressed by Paul. The parallels are further suggested by the writer of 2 Peter himself: *Our beloved brother Paul wrote to you, . . . speaking of this as he does in all his letters* (3:15-16). The epistle may well be written to counter first-century moral skepticism and ethical lapse, as suggested by Mounce (97-99), Green (34-35), and Charles (1997:44-75). Hence, it becomes less a tract to affirm doctrinal orthodoxy than a passionate exhortation toward virtuous living.

The Audience of 2 Peter

A unitary reading of 2 Peter leads to the view that ethical lapse and apostasy plague the community to whom the epistle is addressed. The combined ingredients of literary style and paraenetic (exhortatory) language, Stoic and mystic categories, the catalog of virtues, moral typology, and caricatures of the adversaries all add up to a cultural setting permeated by Hellenistic influence. Moral corruption, licentiousness, antinomianism (rejection of moral standards), and irreverence— all these vex the church immersed in a pluralistic society. For this reason, moral skepticism rather than dissatisfaction with orthodoxy (against Kelly: 305) is the prime object of the author's highly stylized polemic.

A main premise of most commentaries on 2 Peter is that doctrine, especially countering false doctrine, represents the chief burden of the writer. It is true that the writer includes in his closing exhortation a reminder of the certainty of the Lord's return. Yet this allusion serves an *ethical* and not doctrinal purpose. The issue at hand is scoffing on the part of people indulging in their own lusts. The writer's concern is not to proffer a particular eschatological viewpoint. Instead, he reminds his readers that the *fact* of the destruction of the godless is certain beyond doubt. Ethics rather than doctrine is the taproot of fermentation within the community.

Given the community's need for orthopraxy, right living, which in turn informs the author's literary strategy, the introductory material in 2 Peter presents a window into the social location of the audience. Throughout, the epistle strongly confronts a fundamental denial of moral self-responsibility. In its advanced stages, this denial has resulted in the apostasy of certain members of the community. It is true that theological justification (heresy) necessarily accompanies any departure from the faith. Nevertheless, the author chiefly addresses apostasy, an ethical departure from the moral truth of Christian revelation, which is the scourge of this community. This apostasy is the fruit of renunciation of the faith and abandonment of their previous loyalty. The present situation calls for a roundly prophetic and eminently pastoral word of exhortation. The apostle's foremost aim is to enunciate the ethical foundations of the Christian faith.

2 Peter 1:1-21

The Author, His Audience, Purpose for Writing, and Authority

PREVIEW

Three general concerns can be detected in the introductory part of the epistle. The *first* of these is ethical. The author takes pains to observe that divine resources are available to the Christian for living a godly life. Divine power and promises have been provided so that the readers might escape moral corruption in the world around them. This escape, it is emphasized, depends not merely on the promises themselves (great as they are), but on the ethical response of the Christian. To this end, the author employs a Hellenistic rhetorical device, a catalog of virtues, to exhort his readers to reach a higher ethical plane. Human cooperation with God, while it does not cause righteousness, nevertheless will *confirm* the believers' *call and election* (1:10).

A *second* concern of note is reflected in the writer's terminology. He intends *to keep on reminding of these things,* even though the readers *already know them and are established in the truth that formerly had come* to them (1:12). In the short time he has to live (before his martyrdom, if the letter is genuinely Petrine), the author

209

deems it necessary to refresh the memory of his readers. He seeks to *make every effort* in admonishing them *to recall these things* (1:15).

Precisely what are the things that should be recalled? The answer lies in the urgent call to an ethical lifestyle. The catalog of virtues, with several commonly cited Stoic features *[Virtue as a Theme]*, reflects a pagan social environment in which the Christian community finds itself. Theirs is not a faith that is void of the moral life. Instead, the distinctly Christian ethic is to shine forth in bold contrast to surrounding pagan culture. The readership, we may conclude, has disregarded the divine promises. Tragically, they have *forgotten* their *cleansing from past sins* (1:9).

A *third* emphasis in 2 Peter 1 is the issue of authority. Much commentary on 2 Peter tends to be derivative, owing to the long-standing assumption that the epistle was written in the second century— several generations removed from the apostles. Thus it is generally supposed that the writer, in need of invoking ecclesiastical authority for the purpose of countering second-century heresy, lays claim to the name of Peter. Not only does he ascribe the epistle to an apostle, he also lays claim to apostolic experience—notably, Peter's experience on the mountain during Jesus' transfiguration (1:16-18).

If, however, the apostle Peter is actually writing, as few commentators will allow (Green and Mounce excepted), his authority is attested to not only by his eyewitness account of Christ's glory but also by the prophetic spirit (1:19). The prophetic message, after all, is one birthed and carried by the Holy Spirit. The same prophetic anointing that applied to the prophets of the old covenant applies to Christ's apostles. They speak not on their own but under the inspiration of the Spirit of God. The present needs of the community call for nothing less than a strong prophetic-apostolic word.

OUTLINE

Introduction and Address, 1:1-2

Purpose in Writing, 1:3-11
1:3-4	Divine Resources Available
1:5-7	Catalog of Virtues
1:8-11	Exhortation to Return

Prophetic Reminder, 1:12-15

Prophetic Testimony, 1:16-18

The Prophetic Word, 1:19-21

EXPLANATORY NOTES
Introduction and Address 1:1-2

As in 1 Peter, the author of 2 Peter identifies himself as the apostle Peter. The author also expresses the same wish for his readers, that *grace and peace be multiplied to you* (1:2). The two letters differ in their opening address to the extent that 1 Peter names a geographically specific group of believers, whereas the addressees in 2 Peter are undesignated—*To those who have received a faith as precious as ours* (1:1).

Although the origin and the destination of the letter elude certainty, it is plausible that it was written in Rome shortly before the apostle's martyrdom. This lack of concrete evidence, however, contrasts with the character of the epistle, which contains clear indications of a concrete local situation in which grave pastoral needs are found. The letter is clearly addressed to a particular congregation or community where serious problems are already established. In this sense, then, 2 Peter is not a "general epistle," which by definition is broader or "catholic" in its scope.

The use of *Simeon* (Greek: *Sumeōn*), appearing with the nickname *Peter*, is reminiscent of the Gospel narratives and Acts 15:14 (all of which suggest a Palestinian setting). Used here, however, it strikes the reader as unexpected. Commentators who reject 2 Peter as inauthentic tend to regard the allusion to *Simeon* as a "deliberate archaizing touch by a pseudonymous writer" (Bauckham: 166-167) seeking the mark of authenticity. Admittedly, one would rather expect an opening similar to that of 1 Peter 1:1, "Peter, an apostle of Jesus Christ." Bauckham, rejecting Petrine authorship, suggests that *Simeon* may reflect a writer who was part of a "Petrine circle" in Rome that included Mark and Silvanus as well as other Jewish-Christian leaders (167).

A more plausible explanation, assuming the writer to be the apostle, lies with a first-century pastoral situation that requires denunciation, rebuke, and correspondingly strong exhortations, not unlike one finds in Jude. The writer is thus in a position of having to "present his credentials" (Green: 67). "Simeon" was involved in the formal process of the Jewish Council (Acts 15). Here he is at another point in his life when apostolic authority must be brought to bear on the Christian community, in this case both apostolically and prophetically (2 Pet. 1:16-18; 19-21) and not merely as a pastorally minded elder (cf. 1 Pet. 5:1).

The present letter gives precise credentials. The writer is said to be a *servant and apostle of Jesus Christ* (1:1). This twofold self-description once more resembles Jude, where passionate denunciation of the ungodly as well as affirmation of the faithful stand side-by-side. The strong nature of the prophetic word in 2 Peter mirrors a local situation calling for a vigorous application of spiritual authority rooted in the apostolic office. Yet, significantly, in both 2 Peter and Jude, deep humility clothes the one who speaks with prophetic force. As a *bondslave* (*doulos*, 1:1) *of Jesus Christ*, the writer shows evidence of being a seasoned man of God, tempered by divine dealings, much as one finds in 1 Peter: *Let all of you clothe yourselves with humility, for God opposes the proud but gives grace to the lowly* (1 Pet. 5:5).

The readers are described as *those of equal standing who have received faith* (1:1). Some commentators see in this formula a Jewish-Gentile factor (a faith equally accessible to both groups). However, a closer reading of 2 Peter 1 suggests that the issue is not so much one of ethnic inclusion, as suggested by Bauckham (167). Instead, it stresses that God's grace is open and accessible to all, apostles and nonapostles. This reading is confirmed by what follows: *Everything has been given to us* (1:3). *Through these he has given us precious and very great promises* (1:4). This common provision, available to all, has been made *on the basis of the justice-righteousness of our God* (1:1). In accord with this justice, no partiality exists in the salvation issuing from the *Savior Jesus Christ.* God's justice provides the believers' equal standing.

The phrase at the end of verse 1, *the righteous of our God and Saviour Jesus Christ,* could technically be understood as designating Jesus Christ as God and Savior. Taken together with the doxology to Jesus Christ in 3:18, we might regard these statements as an inclusio or set of bookends for this epistle, depicting the exalted status of Christ (cf. Titus 2:13; John 1:1; 20:28; Jude 25). On the other hand, the expression may simply be intended to identify Jesus as the full manifestation of God's saving righteousness-justice. In this case, the phrase functions as a parallel to a similar phrase at the end of verse 2, *in the knowledge of God and of Jesus our Lord,* where both *God* and *Jesus our Lord* are together the content and the focus of the believers' *knowledge.*

The salutation, *May grace and peace be multiplied to you* (1:2), is similar to the greeting in 1 Peter 1:2. It is not "in fact copied from 1 Peter," contrary to Kelly (298), who sees here initial evidence of pseudonymity *[Authorship].* Rather, it is one of numerous important touch-points between the two epistles. In 2 Peter, the key ingredient in receiving God's grace is the full knowledge of God and Jesus our Lord.

There is room for speculating with Green (70) that *knowledge*, a catchword in 2 Peter (appearing seven times), has something of a rhetorically polemical edge. The author is likely reclaiming the word to oppose those who misuse it. As employed by the author, *full knowledge* (1:2) reflects an understanding of the grace of God at work in our lives. Armed with this knowledge, the Christian community is prevented from moral lapse, and ultimately, apostasy. With all believers having equal access to this grace through knowledge of Christ, all are on equal footing and therefore without excuse.

Purpose in Writing 1:3-11

Much in contrast to 2:1ff., the tone of which is combative, condemnatory, and apologetic, the language of 1:3-11 is optimistic and gracious. From an interpreter's standpoint, the combativeness of 2:1ff. can easily cause the reader to miss the writer's intent, which is to call the Christian community to a higher ethic.

Rhetorically, this strategy consists initially of a review of the provisions available for Christian living (1:3-4), followed by an exhortation to ethical rejuvenation through the use of a catalog of virtues (1:5-7). It concludes with the reassurance that these promises are sufficient for the ethical life (1:8-11). The Petrine formula for this provision lies in the *knowledge* of God, as already noted. A *full knowledge* (1:2) of him who has called us *through his own moral excellence* is the total sufficiency for a godly life (1:3). The result is that, stated negatively, the readers might escape the world's corruption rooted in fleshly lust and, stated positively, they might *partake in the divine nature*.

Commentators differ as to the precise function of being *participants in the divine nature* (1:4). The language is broadly recognized to have been common in the ancient world, particularly in the pagan mystery religions. Mystery cult initiates understood themselves as being absorbed gradually or later into deity. In 2 Peter, however, the concept is to be understood solely in Christocentric terms: our union with Christ, based on grace, enables us to resist lust and live godly lives of goodness and moral excellence.

The author's appeal in 2 Peter 1 is above all a call for holy living. Verses 3-4 are clothed in the language of "decree," an official declaration by which the benefactor, beneficiaries, and benefits are enumerated (Danker: 64-66). This admonition to holiness in the form of a decree is based on both the divine provision and human cooperation. God's provision: *through these he has given to us precious and very great promises.* Human cooperation: *so that through them you might escape the world's corruption that comes through lust.*

In the epistle, there is no overemphasis on a predestination that circumvents human moral agency. Neither is there a doctrine of human perfectibility divorced from grace. Instead, both the gracious promises of God *and* human moral freedom are a part of the ethical equation. On one hand, the divine provision covers every conceivable contingency for the purpose of moral growth. On the other hand, development of moral character is contingent on one's willingness to grow. In 2 Peter, the emphasis is clearly placed on our responsibility.

The writer has established the accessibility of supernatural resources—resources that are considerable and of exceeding value (1:4). He proceeds to place the accent on human moral accountability. For this reason, the readers are to apply themselves fully, *making every effort* to respond to the ethical task at hand (1:5a). That the verb *spoudazein*, "spare no effort," appears three times in chapter 1 (1:5, 10, 15) is highly instructive; it reflects the overt pastoral need existing among the readers. Theirs is the challenge of exhibiting moral character amidst pagan culture. This requires willingness and determination, both of which at the present may be lacking.

A catalog or listing of particular virtues *[Ethical List]* shows the contours of the moral effort the readers are to make: *For this very reason, make every effort to add virtue to your faith, and to virtue [add] knowledge, and to knowledge self-control, and to self-control endurance, and to endurance godliness, and to godliness brotherly affection, and to brotherly affection love* (1:5-7). This catalog is designed to have a rhetorical effect. It mirrors a discussion of virtues commonplace among Hellenistic philosophers (Deissmann: 317-318), with the notable exception of *pistis*, Christian *faith.*

The Christian ethical distinctive is that one's faith is a response to divine grace and an acceptance of that grace. Hence, one's motivation is in the direction of demonstrating, through our works, a lifestyle of gratitude that pleases God. That 2 Peter speaks of no "works-righteousness" is made clear by the epistle's very introduction. The letter is addressed *to those who have received a faith through the righteousness of our God and Savior Jesus Christ* (1:1). Righteousness has been received; it is a gift imparted by God through Christ. The important Petrine theme of *righteousness* is foundational to a proper understanding of Christian ethics (1 Pet. 2:24; 3:12, 14, 18; 4:18; 2 Pet. 2:5, 7, 8 [twice], 21; 3:13; see Waltner commentary on

1 Peter passages, above). The secular ethic wholly misses this foundation of righteous faith; on this foundation, believers are to supply a repository of confirming virtues, manifesting a righteous life.

This *supply* of virtue presents the reader with a vivid image. The verb used here, *chorēgein* ("*to add, supply*, or supplement") originally conveyed the sense of "lead a chorus," and more technically, "pay the expenses for training a chorus"; in time it came to denote "defraying the expenses of something" (Bauer: 883; cf. also Josephus, *War* 1.625). Typically, Greek theater proceeded on the generosity of a wealthy local benefactor, the *chorēgos*, who saw to it that actors, props, musicians, and dancers were paid.

Hence, the picture presented in 2 Peter is colorful and pregnant with meaning: God, in his infinite glory and kindness, has covered, through his Son, the cost of provisions necessary for a life of godliness. On the basis of this exceeding generosity, the readers are to build, ethically speaking. In corresponding fashion, Christians are to be lavish in the way they invest themselves in the development of moral character, striving to offer the world the best window for viewing God's grace. As Hillyer observes, this approach to Christian life is far removed from the cynicism that views the Christian experience as an "initial spasm followed by chronic inertia" (165).

Faith, in the Petrine scheme of things, results in *virtue* or *moral excellence*. Commonly employed in Stoic lists, virtue is the quality of life and centerpiece of classic pagan textbook morality (Kelly: 306). It is moral goodness toward which all humanity strives. Moral excellence, in turn, supplies *knowledge*. Hereby, the intellectual element of belief is affirmed. Knowledge can never harm the true seeker—knowledge, that is, which is perceptive, understanding, and desirous of wisdom. Knowledge, in turn, supplies *self-control*, a quality highly prized among Greek moral philosophers. As a pagan virtue, knowledge is equated with mastery over one's lusts and appetites.

True knowledge, then, leads not to license, but rather to self-control. Herein an expressly Christian faith distinguishes itself: a system of belief divorcing content from ethics, and separating belief from practice, demonstrates itself as wrong teaching and inauthentic. True knowledge, on the other hand, will tend toward self-restraint, not libertinism, unrestrained living. This is especially important for the fledgling Christian community as it is dispersed throughout first-century Hellenistic culture.

Self-control, in turn, supplies *endurance* or *perseverance*. Self-mastery and discipline have the effect of producing the ability to endure, literally to be patient under the weight of adversity.

Endurance is the mark of maturity, since superficial faith will *not* endure. Doing what is ethically right, in spite of surrounding culture, is the ethical challenge to endure. For the Christian, this is undergirded by a deeper awareness of God's sovereignty (Calvin: 363); thus, unlike its pagan ethical counterpart, it is not fatalistic or cynical.

Perseverance, in turn, supplies *godliness* or *piety*. Piety entails both vertical and horizontal duties. It is simultaneously reverence toward deity and a sense of duty toward people. It comes to expression most completely in the Christian community. Godliness, in turn, supplies *mutual affection*. While filial affection is an important virtue in broader Hellenistic culture, it acquires new significance in a Christian context.

Finally, brotherly/mutual affection is to be topped out with *love*, the "crown" of moral development (Bauckham: 187; Green: 80). It is the ultimate expression of Christian belief (1 Cor. 13:13) and the fruit of genuine faith (Gal. 5:6). The catalog of virtues in 2 Peter 1 uses language similar to a Stoic model, but nonetheless is distinguished from its secular counterpart by its foundation, which is faith, and its goal, which is love.

In sum, the author's concern, highlighted by the catalog of virtues, is to counter a view of life in which faith is independent of ethics. The form of the ethical catalog, originating from the Hellenistic diatribe (Fornberg: 98), spread in usage to Greek-speaking Jews. It bears close connection to the form present in Stoic literature, Philo, and Hellenistic writings. The final virtue, love, is the crowning and thus uniquely Christian virtue in its origin, encompassing all others.

The context of bearing fruit ethically *in the knowledge of our Lord Jesus Christ* stands in contrast to the ineffectual life (1:9), described in terms of nearsightedness, blindness, and forgetfulness. It calls to mind the metaphor used in Revelation 3:14, 17-18, of the Laodicean church. Indeed, forgetting one's *cleansing from past sins* (1:9) is the beginning of all apostasy (Green: 82).

Therefore, brothers and sisters, be all the more desirous . . . For this reason, it is all the more urgent that [the readers] confirm [their] calling and election; in so doing, [they] will never stumble (1:10). Ethics offers proof of one's election, and hence, one's faith. Orthodoxy and orthopraxy, correct belief and becoming conduct, go hand-in-hand. The readers will not stumble in this life; they will also inherit the next life (1:11). In the coming age, it is the Lord Jesus who is the lavish supplier. In 1:11 the verb *epichorēgein*, "to supply lavishly," is used again, this time of the Lord, who supplies entrance into his *eternal kingdom*.

Prophetic Reminder 1:12-15

Much like Jude, 2 Peter uses a conspicuous reminder terminology. Repetition in the Christian life is crucial, so the writer employs the language of recall: *I intend to keep on reminding you; you already know [these things]; I consider it right . . . to refresh your memory . . . so that you . . . may recall these things.* Mindful of both his apostolic duties and limited time yet to live, the writer reemphasizes the basics; here the purpose of the letter is clarified.

Frequently the role of the Christian teacher or preacher is to remind the audience of what they already know, to exhort them in the truth they already possess. The metaphor of the tabernacle (1:13), used in the context of the writer's personal reflections, speaks of the transitory nature of life both for Israel of old and the readers in the present. The Christians have need of being reminded that they are pilgrims on a journey (Hillyer: 172).

Two interpretive options present themselves in these verses *[Authorship]*. Either the apostle Peter is reflecting on his approaching death, or a literary convention, the farewell speech, "has provided the author of 2 Peter with a model, using the example of the apostle Peter, who is said to be at the point of departure from life" (Chester and Martin: 139). For most commentators, the testamental character of the epistle is one of the clearest indications of its post-Petrine setting. The language used here, however, is reflective—that of an eyewitness of the Lord, not one writing generations removed from the apostolic era. The writer recalls the striking prophecy of Jesus years earlier (John 21:18-19; cf. 13:36) concerning Peter's death. Green's observation captures the drama contained within the writer's admonition in 1:12-15:

> There may be something poignant in his use of the word "established" to describe his hesitant and wavering readers. For that is the word which Jesus used of him on one memorable occasion when, although so fickle, he was sure that *he* was established in the truth and could not possibly apostasize (Luke 22:32). It seems to have become a favorite word of this turbulent man who now really was established. He uses it in his final prayer at the end of 1 Peter (5:10), and a similar word occurs in a significant context in 2 Peter 3:17. (87-88)

Painfully aware of what it means to waver in the faith and deny the Lord, the apostle reminds his audience with great earnestness of Christian "first things." Inasmuch as they are presently *established in the truth* (1:12), apostasy (ethical lapse and denial of the faith) is the present danger, not heresy or wrong teaching.

Prophetic Testimony 1:16-18

The issue of authority presses to the fore in these verses as the author's focus is sharpened. The clash, in the mind of the writer, is nothing less than between error (*cleverly devised myths*) and truth: *we made known to you the power and coming of our Lord Jesus Christ*; and *we were eye-witnesses of his majesty* (1:16). That the author can write *we made known to you the power and coming of our Lord Jesus Christ* validates the assertion that he indeed is one of the apostles.

The writer appears to be keenly aware of the uniqueness of apostolic authority. Apostolic preaching, that proclamation which initially brings the reader to the place of faith, is rooted in and flows out of historical events. Specifically, it is grounded in one's relation to Jesus and one's witness to the resurrection. This experience qualified an individual to preach the Christian message firsthand.

At the time of this writing, Peter must exert his authority in light of the pressing pastoral problem. This is achieved by his testimony as an eyewitness (*epoptēs*) of the Lord's glory. The use of *epoptēs* in 2 Peter is the sole appearance of the word in the NT. It normally designates those who had been initiated into the highest grade of mysteries in Hellenistic mystery cults (Bauer: 305; cf. Col. 2:18; Martin: 120-121). The most memorable, transforming event in Peter's life, suggested by the synoptic Gospels, was on the Mount of Transfiguration (Mark 9:2-8; and par.). With this mark of apostolicity, the prophetic message is abundantly verified (1:19).

The revelation and resulting full perception of *honor and glory* bestowed by God the Father on Jesus doubtless left a permanent mark on Peter and remains etched in his memory throughout his life. In this revelatory and transforming context, the eyewitnesses on the mountain were made to understand the unique relationship between the Father and the Son: *This is my beloved son, with whom I am well pleased. Listen to him!* (Matt. 17:5; Mark 9:7; Luke 9:35). Of the disciples assembled on the mountain, it was especially for Peter's sake that the command *Listen to him!* was given. Peter had rebuked Jesus for his teachings that the Son of Man would suffer and be killed and rise again (Mark 8:32-33; and par.).

Moreover, this revelation was conveyed in language reminiscent both of Israel's beloved David and the Isaianic "Servant of the Lord": "I will proclaim the decree of the Lord: He said to me, 'You are my Son; today I have become your Father'" (Ps. 2:7, NIV). "Here is my servant, whom I uphold, my chosen one in whom I delight" (Isa. 42:1, NIV).

The language of self-witness in 2 Peter 1:12ff. is both earnest and emphatic. It heightens the personal nature of the writer's testimony: *We ourselves heard this, . . . while we were with him* (1:18). The significance of this testimony should not be lost on the readers. It reinforces his authority before he proceeds in chapter 2 to censure the morally corrupt and in chapter 3 to exhort the faithful in the community. More immediately, as Hillyer (176) correctly notes, the writer wishes to stress the solidarity between the prophetic message of the past and that of the present, the latter being borne by the apostles (1:19-21).

The Prophetic Word 1:19-21

Most discussions of 1:19-21, especially conservative commentary on 1:19, assume an overarching thesis of Scripture interpretation. Commentators read into this text a scenario in which the Scriptures are being read amiss, apart from the illumination of the Holy Spirit. This reading, however, misses the contextual flow of the material in 2 Peter 1–2. Authority is being asserted, and quite probably is being denied by some. What was received from the prophets of old was taken to be the authoritative word of God. This same norm, confirmed by apostolic witness, is to continue to be the Christian's guide.

The true sense of these verses has to do with inspiration and authentication, not interpretation (Green: 101). Peter's concern is not proper interpretation of the Scriptures; it is authentication of the prophetic voice. We may assume a background to 2 Peter in which Peter's apostolic authority is being denied, or at the least called into question. His response, which serves as a necessary introduction to chapters 2–3, is that prophetic speech originates with God, even when spoken by human agents. The OT Scriptures are inspired and prophetic; thus, they come to the reader as the Word of God.

Needed in the present situation is the application of apostolic authority for the purposes of countering certain influences injurious to the Christian community: doubt, hostility, mockery, or hardness toward truth. Perhaps Christian truth is being wholly derided; perhaps Peter himself is being ridiculed. In essence, the writer is saying that to deny Simon Peter's apostolic authority (cf. 1:1) is to deny the OT and the prophets themselves.

THE TEXT IN BIBLICAL CONTEXT

From the outset, the reader is struck with the emphasis on *knowledge* and *knowing* in 2 Peter. This language is strategic, serving an important function. On one hand, a *full knowledge* stands over against any claims made by the apostate themselves; knowledge of God assures escape from defilements of the world. On the other hand, *full knowledge* functions to remind the faithful of the first things of the faith into which they have been immersed.

The language of knowing is prominent elsewhere in the NT— notably in the Gospel of John, the epistle of 1 John, and the Corinthian correspondence. This terminology is integral to the OT as well as Hellenistic Jewish apologetic literature, in which the knowledge of God is contrasted with pagan ignorance of the true God. Such language is carried over into the NT, as its writers develop an apologetic for members of the Christian community dispersed throughout Greco-Roman culture.

In light of this cultural challenge, the affinities between 2 Peter, 1–2 Corinthians, and 1 John are worth noting. Each of these letters reflects a pagan Gentile social environment in which theoretical knowledge and personal knowledge of God in Jesus Christ are held in stark contrast. Furthermore, this knowledge of God and of Jesus Christ has decidedly strong ethical implications for the readers.

As in 2 Peter, 1 Corinthians is devoted primarily to ethical issues within the community, teaching needed because of strife and division, sexual immorality, and boasting over freedom, all of which are detrimental to the corporate life. First John resembles 2 Peter to the extent that the knowledge of Jesus Christ comes through the eyewitness testimony of the writer (1 John 1:1). First John also opposes a strong element of denial, an advanced form of lawlessness and apostasy in which obedience and the reality of sin are being rejected (1:5—2:5; 3:4-10, 22; 5:16-17), the things of the world are loved (2:15-17), and Jesus' humanity and lordship are being disavowed (2:22-23; 4:1-6, 15).

In the language of 2 Peter, it is precisely the *full knowledge* of our second nature—our righteousness in Christ (1:1)—that is emphasized as the antidote to sin. Righteousness constitutes the absence of sin, just as sin constitutes the absence of righteousness (Jeschke: 43), and yet it is more. Righteousness is first of all positive and not penal (Augsburger: 107), a call for deeds that are an extension of an inner life. Hence, Christian discipleship is characterized by an ethic of freedom.

What then is a "biblical" approach to ethics and virtue? Peter's tactic is instructive: he borrows a secular (Stoic) catalog of virtues for literary-rhetorical purposes. To this list, he adds distinctly Christian virtues and puts the whole catalog in a Christian framework that builds on *faith* and is completed with *love*. Pagan ethics is not the equivalent of Christian ethics. Yet pagan virtues need not be simply discarded without examination. Believers need to test them to determine what can be useful or reconceived to fit a Christian faith and worldview. In relation to 2 Peter 1:5-7, the Stoic ideal of *self-control* means to avoid excesses; the Christian goal is to discipline oneself to avoid *lust* and sin (1:4; 2:10—3:3), yet to practice hilarious and extravagant self-giving motivated by *mutual* affection and *love* (cf. 2 Cor. 9; John 15:13). The Stoic idea of *endurance* is rather fatalistic; the Christian idea of *endurance* means to persevere in faith and godly living.

Because human beings are stamped with the image of God, many such virtues are recognized by most cultures and societies as good and true (Gen. 1:26-27; Rom. 2:15; Henry: 477). What is flawed in the pagan system of ethics is its motivation, not the virtues in and of themselves, when rightly understood. By comparison, in Christian faith, God's *grace* empowers human beings to live virtuous lives and to redefine individual virtues. Biblical ethics, hence, is the highest ethical system; it is based not on degree but on being a different *kind* of ethics. Christian ethics not only presents a standard, the righteous life as exemplified in Jesus Christ (1:1); it also enables believers to fulfill the ethical demands of that standard. Indeed, charity or love is the source and the goal of the Christian practice.

The biblical ethic serves to remind surrounding culture of human sinfulness; indeed, we fall short of moral excellence (cf. Rom. 3:23). The motivation undergirding this ethic, however, comes from grace. It is by no means an accident that the metaphor of redemption from the slave market is frequently employed by biblical writers to communicate in everyday terms the reality of God's grace. Saints have received a faith as precious as ours *through the righteousness of our God and Savior Jesus Christ* (1:1). Therefore, *grace and peace may be multiplied* to the readers *through the full knowledge of God and Jesus our Lord* (1:2).

While virtuous living in a pagan culture requires habits of self-control, perseverance, godliness, and brotherly affection (1:6-7), it is all based on a full awareness of the divine provision (1:3-4), *grace*. The Christian ethic, in the end, is no mere "works-righteousness," as the full weight of Scripture indicates (cf. Eph. 2:8-10).

The synoptic Gospels each contain an account of Peter's experience of the transfiguration of Jesus (Matt. 17:1-8; Mark 9:2-8; Luke 9:28-36). This episode comes at a strategic time in the lives of the apostles. Matthew exquisitely captures the timing of this event. Following a preview of his own death, Jesus stresses the necessity of self-denial and the way of the cross (Matt. 16:21-28). Immediately preceding this part of the narrative is Peter's confession of Jesus as Messiah and Son of the living God (16:13-20). Peter will have a leadership role in establishing the fledgling Christian community (16:18-19).

While Peter's confession mirrors true faith as one of the Lord's chosen, he is not yet ready to face the great test of faith that lies ahead (Matt. 16:22-23). Six days later (17:1), the revelation of Jesus' glory on the mountain is utterly crucial for confirming this faith and equipping him for the coming day of trial.

Now, many years later and on the eve of his own martyrdom, Peter can write the flock of God with a faith and authority that are fully matured as a result of joint sufferings in Christ (1 Pet. 2:18-25; 3:8-22; 4:12-19; 5:1). In what may be his last will and testament, Peter musters the full weight of apostolic authority to address a severe pastoral need. It is possible that both the message of Christian grace and his own apostolic authority are being denied. For this reason, given the cancerous nature of apostasy and the late hour in his life, he reflects on his eyewitness experiences with the Son of God. The high point of Jesus' self-revelation was his transfiguration in the presence of Peter, James, and John. Second Peter is dramatic testimony to this occasion.

Paul writes to the Christians in Ephesus that the church, the household of God, is *built upon the foundation of the apostles and prophets,* with Jesus Christ as the head cornerstone (Eph. 2:20; 3:5; 4:11). In the NT Apocalypse, John indicates the same (Rev. 18:20). Indeed, the introduction to most of the NT letters mirrors this fact about the church (Rom. 1:1; 1 Cor. 1:1; 2 Cor. 1:1; Gal. 1:1; Eph. 1:1; Col. 1:1; 1 Tim. 1:1; 2 Tim. 1:1; Tit. 1:1; 1 Pet. 1:1; 2 Pet. 1:1).

The distinctive mark of apostolicity is that one has been an eyewitness to the suffering and resurrection of Christ (cf. 1 Pet. 5:1; 1 John 1:1; 1 Cor. 15:5, 7-9). The authority of the apostle validates the Christian message once Jesus has returned to the Father, as well as later in the subapostolic period. Just as any building is as strong as the foundation upon which it rests, so the church, founded on the apostles and prophets, is established and safeguarded by the Lord's apostles.

First Corinthians 4 and 9 provide striking testimony of an apostle's self-defense (cf. 2 Cor. 11–13). In Corinth, Paul's authority may be under attack. At least he encounters disrespect for the apostle's role. Defense of his role as an apostle is not mere rhetorical flourish, though it contains that. Paul is exercised in spirit because of the sheer arrogance of some in the church (1 Cor. 4:7, 19; 5:2, 6; 8:1-2). Certain individuals within the Christian community are undermining or even rejecting apostolic authority. His response is poignant: *What would you prefer? Shall I visit you with a rod, or with love in a spirit of gentleness?* The kingdom of God, he reminds them, is confirmed not just by words but by spiritual power—power that on occasion involves severe discipline (4:21; 5:3-5, 12-13).

The need for authority is doubtless aggravated by the church living in a pagan social climate that accommodates varieties of pluralism. This conflict between pluralism and Christian exclusivism has two effects: it may induce persecution of the church from the outside, and it may breed a moral laxness inside the community of believers. In response, a hint of a twofold "Petrine strategy" surfaces in 1 Peter, a tract written with despised Christians in view, and in 2 Peter, which exhorts believers to ethical living. The readers are reminded that Christ suffered and was despised before they have experienced suffering (1 Pet. 2–4).

In 1 Peter, part of the reason believers are persecuted comes from their imitation of their Master; they follow in his way. Part of it, however, is for the church's refinement and purging of sin. For this reason, *the time has come for judgment to begin with the household of God, since if it is hard for the righteous to be saved what will become of the ungodly and sinners?* (1 Pet. 4:17-18).

The theme of judgment, while only mentioned in passing in 1 Peter, presses to the fore in 2 Peter. It is clear by the tone of 2 Peter that apostasy has progressed, affecting the Christian community in profound ways. Because of this context, the church needs supreme moral authority, the authority vested in the apostolic-prophetic office.

Authority in 2 Peter is viewed not merely as an office or a function of the institutional church, though it is that. Even more, it is vested in the very Word of God, which contains the prophetic message itself (1:19). It is moral authority through which the prophets of old have spoken and attested to its truth. It is written, inscripturated, for the benefit of successive generations of Christians (1:20-21; cf. 2 Tim. 3:16-17).

THE TEXT IN THE LIFE OF THE CHURCH

It is a general pattern that heresy, advancing false teaching in an attempt to justify one's departure from the faith, follows an ethical departure, apostasy, which means abandoning what one has believed in. Typical of such flight is a teaching emphasis that denies our sinful nature. This feature has characterized the great debates throughout church history—from Augustine and Pelagius, Athanasius and Nestorius, to the Reformation and beyond.

The tension between human freedom and human restraint, reflected in the systematic teaching of virtues, by no means begins with the Christian community. So-called cardinal virtues emerge in both religious and secular ethics. Among Socratic philosophers, ethical lists come into full bloom. In his *Nicomachean Ethics*, Aristotle gives considerable attention to the "cardinal virtues" of prudence, temperance, fortitude, and justice, as well as to corresponding vices.

These foundational virtues are also extolled in the wisdom literature of the OT (notably in Proverbs) and in Jewish wisdom literature of the intertestamental era: "If anyone loves righteousness, [wisdom's] labors are virtues; for she teaches self-control and prudence, justice and courage" (Wisd. of Sol. 8:7).

With a background in pagan philosophy before his conversion, Augustine approaches the subject of virtues with some reservation: "The virtues themselves, if they bear no relation to God, are in truth vices rather than virtues" (*City of God* 19.25). Gregory of Nyssa is more optimistic: "The goal of a virtuous life is to become like God" (*De beatitudinibus* 1 [Migne, *PG*, 44.1200D]). Thomas Aquinas is noted for wedding the cardinal Hellenistic virtues with the theological virtues of faith, hope, and love (*Summa Theologiae* IIa-IIae.49-89). Both medieval scholastic theologians and mainline Protestants, in the view of theologian Carl Henry, attempt to mix oil and water in their efforts to wed Christian ethics with secular philosophy (476).

Menno Simons responds to a similar challenge of his day (*Spiritual Resurrection,* 1536; *Reply to Micron,* 1556). He remarks that 2 Peter 1:4 *(you are partakers of the divine nature)* clearly indicates the coexistence of two natures—one sinful, born of Adam, and one redeemed, quickened by the Holy Spirit through the new birth (Menno: 61, 901-902). The tone of Menno's response, on par with Reformation rhetoric, strikes the modern reader as accusatory. From Menno's standpoint, however, Micron represents a serious threat to the life and health of the Christian community. He stands accused as one who has departed from the faith and is leading others astray. Menno seems aware of the grave issue at hand and the psychology of apostasy. A denial of biblical truth inevitably seeks its own justification.

In his book, *Christian Behavior,* C. S. Lewis, the twentieth century's most beloved apologist, assesses the relationship of the four cardinal or pivotal virtues—prudence, temperance, fortitude, and justice—to the three theological virtues: faith, hope, and love. Even in his own day, Lewis lamented conventional wisdom that seemed to be marked by a relentless call for removing Victorian restraints (26).

Ethicist Paul Ramsey speaks of the primacy of *agapē* (love) as the crowning Christian virtue in terms that reflect an unconscious debt to 2 Peter 1. Love, Ramsey points out, creates a moral bond; it is a "promissory" agreement from the heart that breeds social cohesion (140). Since Ramsey, a renewed interest in virtue and moral theology has been evident, especially over the last two decades. In *Ethics from a Theocentric Perspective*, James Gustafson clarifies to what extent ethics issues out of one's worldview and values (215).

In his seminal work *After Virtue*, Alasdair MacIntyre traces the systematic study of ethics from Homer to the present. In considering the moral life, MacIntyre observes that virtues are defined in relation to what society considers to be internal "goods" (176-186). Gilbert Meilaender, in his primer *Faith and Faithfulness: Basic Themes in Christian Ethics*, underscores the singularity of the Christian ethos. The moral life furnishes society with stability. While it must constantly adjust to cultural changes, it must not disintegrate. The chief danger, however, according to Meilaender, is not collapse but its gradual degeneration (4).

The thesis of Oliver O'Donovan's important volume *Resurrection and Moral Order* is that Christian ethics is above all "evangelical" ethics. "Moralism" is to be regarded as moral conviction apart from the good news. The "evangel," the distinctly Christian ethic, depends on the resurrection of Jesus Christ from the dead (13). Christian morality, O'Donovan reminds the church, is rooted in objective historical and transcendent reality (76).

Published in 1992 (1994 in English), the *Catechism of the Catholic Church* also contains discussion of virtue and its relation to faith. The *Catechism* stresses that the overarching guide for the ethical life is charity, based on the assertions of Paul (1 Corinthians 13). Accordingly, the practice of all the virtues, "cardinal" or "theological," is inspired by charity, which "binds everything together in perfect harmony" (Col. 3:14) and orders the ethical life (nos. 1822 1829).

Few writings of the NT find more touchpoints to contemporary culture than 2 Peter, with its stress on virtuous living, Christian ethics, and passionate critique of moral skepticism that fuels religious apostasy. In 2 Peter we find reflections of a social environment in which the Christian tradition appears to be taken for granted, Jewish influence is negligible, and pagan Hellenistic cultural winds are pervasive. The letter contains similarities to what Francis Schaeffer has called a "post-Christian" culture.

Much has been written on the church's relation to surrounding culture. A classic text is H. Richard Niebuhr's *Christ and Culture*, published in 1951. Niebuhr's burden, as he sought to avoid the extremes of fundamentalism and degenerate liberalism, was to consider how the gospel "transforms" culture. Another model of the church in the world was offered by Swiss theologian Karl Barth, roughly contemporary to Niebuhr. Barth was reacting to fresh memories of a church co-opted by National Socialism. His model suggested that the Christian church be a social example to surrounding culture, whether or not any transformation might occur (124-142). Christian ethicist Stanley Hauerwas presents a similar approach: the Christian community faithfully interprets God's ways to secular culture and exhibits distinctly Christian character. Faithfulness rather than "success" is to be the mark of the church (5-12).

What these models offer us is a reminder that the church is simultaneously in the world yet not *of* it (John 15:18-25; 1 John 4:4-6). Inherent in this calling is a necessary tension: the church is to relate to the world by means of sacrificial love, based on the cross. The fact of the cross is already established. The readiness with which we accept this fact, however, as James William McClendon Jr. observes, is the primary question (239). For this reason, 2 Peter is an invaluable witness to Christian social ethics. It charts, in the most practical terms, a strategy for the Christian community that seeks to be "in the world but not of it" (John 17).

Second Peter reads much like a tract for late twentieth-century Christians living in a decadent society where Judeo-Christian influences have receded or are absent. The present situation calls for a reaffirmation of the "Peter principle": virtuous living that weds classic Christian confession with biblical ethics in response to apostasy. What, concretely, is the Petrine strategy for the Christian community?

Part of the church's strategy at the threshold of the third millennium is to lay hold of Christian "first things," to *confirm your calling and election*. In so doing, the Christian disciple *will never stumble* (1:10). To confirm our Christian calling in a markedly unchristian cultural environment, we need to wrestle with a theological tension. This tension issues out of two complementary but not antithetical poles—divine sovereignty *(His divine power has given us everything needed for life and godliness*, 1:3) and human moral freedom (*so that you might escape the corruption that is in the world*, 1:4).

Christian ethics, not unlike the character of God, can be described in terms of different polarities or complementarities (Burke: 27-45). These polarities must be in tension. Examples are holiness and love, freedom and responsibility, transcendence and immanence, law and principle. The apparent tensions in truth show underlying interdependencies. There is, understandably, a natural human tendency for Christians to emphasize one pole in this tension, frequently at the expense of the other. Historically, Calvinists have been prone to stress God's sovereignty, human election, and the believer's predestination. Arminians and Roman Catholics, in contrast, favor a view of divine grace that places accent on human cooperation with that existing grace.

Anabaptists and most Baptists are partakers of the Reformation heritage who stress the necessity of personal piety and a holy lifestyle. They have traditionally possessed a high view of both grace and freedom. It is this balance that is urgently needed in the church as a whole (cf. Eph. 2:8-10; Phil. 2:12-13).

If we emphasize grace and election in a way that minimizes human moral freedom, we miss the value of 2 Peter. Christians are exhorted to persevere in the midst of a morally skeptical and even nihilistic environment. We are to *make every effort to add to our faith* the virtues of moral excellence, knowledge, self-control, endurance, brotherly affection, and sacrificial love. The one professing faith *who lacks these things is nearsighted and blind, forgetful of having been cleansed from past sins.* Clearly communicated in 2 Peter is not only the possibility but the reality of apostasy. Regarding religious apostasy, Jeschke captures the right balance: it is not proper to speak of the unpardonable sin, only an unpardonable *sinner* (40). The difference here is the attitude of the person, not the qualitative measure of the act. The possibility lies within every person to repent, embrace God's forgiveness, and walk in obedience to the Lord.

A strict predestinarian view that denies the possibility of apostasy is a distortion of Christian ethics, as in the slogan "once saved, always saved." The Christian disciple is morally "free" to walk in the way of faith. At any point, the church member can choose to embrace or disregard the commandments of the Lord. When we read seriously and heed the message of 2 Peter, we heed Menno's warning in "The Spiritual Resurrection": "We have two natures, two opposing predispositions, each of which grows or diminishes based on whether it is fed. Only at the final Resurrection will we be ultimately transformed" (Menno: 61).

Calvin's contention that even perseverance comes from God (373) needs to be kept in its proper perspective. It is certainly true that God initiates. Nevertheless, humans must appropriate what is available. Luther concurs: necessity implies moral responsibility (185). Second Peter warns us not to neglect the human side of this mystery, our responsibility.

Going hand-in-hand with Christian ethics in a post-Christian culture is the issue of authority, moral as well as ecclesiastical. One feature of turn-of-the-millennium Western culture is its rejection of any definitive guideline for addressing matters of right and wrong. A post-Christian society is one in which the church has lost its moral authority and *all forms* of authority are viewed with extreme skepticism. Moral discourse in society is stifled by reigning pluralistic, secular assumptions. Contemporary culture is adamant in asserting that there is no such thing as fixed or absolute truth. Instead, truth is understood to be multiple, personal, and subjective. Moral choices are based on personal preferences rather than enduring moral canons that are binding for successive generations.

The church is surrounded by severe moral skepticism. How does it relate to a society that denies its fundamental beliefs? Its view of a moral universe? Its assumptions about life?

As we head into the third millennium, the church is called upon to reaffirm its apologetic "first things." This will require theological integrity and confession of the substance of historic Christian truth (classic orthodoxy). We also need to find culturally relevant ways to clothe that truth (J. D. Charles, 1995a: 234-246). Many present-day evangelicals have had difficulty in preserving the tension between the poles of theological substance and cultural relevancy.

We have tended either toward personal piety that retreats from cultural conflict, or toward an uncritical acceptance of assumptions undergirding secular society around us. Both responses, however, are to be avoided. The church has a cultural mandate (J. D. Charles, 1995b: 38-39). The church's moral authority will be shown by the degree to which it "reaffirms its call" and the degree of ethical integrity exhibited before a watching world. In short, the times call for a new commitment to the "Peter principle."

2 Peter 2:1-22

Profile of Apostasy

PREVIEW

Just as the contextual link between 1:19-21 and 2:1ff. is clear, so is the contrast. Men and women of God, moved by the Holy Spirit and speaking prophetically, find their antithesis in false teachers who bring destructive heresy, deny the Lord Himself, and use guile to influence others. While chapter 1 of the epistle speaks of truth, holiness, and authority, chapter 2 is devoted to an entirely different profile, one in which error, falsehood, sexual license, and defilement are depicted. Second Peter characterizes Peter's adversaries bleakly. They have been ethically compromised. They introduce heresy, operate covertly via deceit and corruption, and encourage moral abandonment. Apparently, theirs is a significant following.

The material in 2 Peter 2 shows the greatest degree of literary relationship to Jude (see Mayor: i-xxv). The links in style, vocabulary and substance demonstrate a literary dependence that typically is the centerpiece of most commentaries on Jude and 2 Peter [Authorship]. In contrast to the readers, who are called, elected, and established in the truth (2:12), the opponents are consigned to inescapable judgment. Their fate is sure, based on three paradigms, three examples of ruin: the fallen angels, the contemporaries of Noah, and Sodom and Gomorrah.

What unites these examples in 2 Peter? What is the lesson to be learned? Verses 4-10a constitute one unbroken sentence with a four-fold structure: For if God did not spare, . . . and if he did not spare, . . . yet protected, . . . and he condemned, . . . and he rescued, . . .

[then] the Lord knows how to deliver. . . . . The lesson in these examples is twofold: (1) judgment of the ungodly is certain (*God did not spare*), and (2) deliverance of the righteous, even in the worst of circumstances (such as Lot experienced), is equally assured.

The thread uniting the three similar examples in Jude 5-7 is judgment, with no emphasis on the preservation of the righteous. In Jude, the context suggests a similar historical situation though with a different accent: all three sets of characters reflect a peculiar departure from truth, and they are condemned. In 2 Peter, the historical models, two of which are borrowed from Jude, serve to highlight *both* judgment of the wicked *and* deliverance of the righteous.

Issues of authority and sexuality constantly surface in 2 Peter. True Christian discipleship shows itself in a wholesome attitude toward authority in general and a bridled sexuality in particular. Peter's opponents, in contrast, manifest precisely the opposite. They flaunt their rejection of spiritual authority and their sexual uncleanness. Both of these dispositions justify the graphic and denunciatory portrait of Peter's adversaries that unfolds in chapter 2. Presumptuous, self-willed, reviling, deceptive, debauched, carousing, spiritually adulterous, seductive, covetous, and dangerous—these are the descriptions of Peter's opponents. Taken together, they remind us of one noted character in the OT, Balaam, *who loved the wages of evil* (2:15).

With Balaam as their spiritual model, the apostates are vividly depicted in a striking double-metaphor—a dog returning to its vomit and a pig that can only return to the mud (2:22). A sketch outlining the pastoral problem emerges. Former believers are being censured by the apostle. They have had prior knowledge of the truth and *have escaped the defilements of the world through . . . Jesus Christ . . . but are again entangled and overpowered, so that the last state is worse than the first* (2:20). What's more, they are now beginning to lead others astray, thus earning the designation of *false teachers* (2:1).

OUTLINE

Peter's Opponents: An Introduction, 2:1-3

Peter's Opponents: Three Precedents, 2:4-10a

2:4	The Fallen Angels
2:5	Noah and His Contemporaries
2:6-10a	Lot Amidst Sodom and Gomorrah

Peter's Opponents: A Closer Look, 2:10b-22

EXPLANATORY NOTES

Peter's Opponents: An Introduction 2:1-3

Chapter 2 continues the allusion to the OT introduced in 1:20-21. Central to the OT story are both true and false prophets, those who uphold the truth and those who deny or actively suppress the truth. With this transition, Peter shifts the focus to his adversaries.

Commentators disagree on the identity of Peter's opponents. Kelly (229-231) and Cranfield (183) see here the doctrinal shortcomings and ethical libertinism of second-century Gnostics, given the combative tone of the epistle and the use of the catchword *knowledge*. Such a reading, however, depends more on questionable assumptions of a late dating [Authorship] than on the text itself.

A closer reading of 2 Peter suggests that an ethical rather than doctrinal departure lies at the root of the opponents' behavior (Desjardins: 89-92). Generally speaking, first comes apostasy, meaning sinful behavior that shows rejection of the truth. Then heresy or doctrinal error follows, as justification for the bad conduct. Peter's opponents are foremost sexual libertarians, as confirmed by the portrait that follows (2:2, 6-7, 10, 14, 18-20, 22) and Peter's prior accent on moral virtue and self-control. Danger is confronting the Christian community: it is being influenced by the outside world.

Peter does not designate these current individuals as *false prophets*. Instead, that term is applied to deceivers who *arose among the people,* Israel of old. What Peter *does* say is *that there will be false teachers among you.* The tense is important, for it suggests that the Christian community will need to be on guard in the future.

Contrary to traditional scholarship that places 2 Peter in the early or mid-second century, this description fits well in a mid-sixties scenario in the first century. Ethical lapse has visited the church as it takes root in Gentile culture. This occurs long before the noted (Gnostic) heretical schools of the second and third centuries are established. The appearance in 2:1 of the term *haireseis,* from which we derive the English word *heresies,* has further fed the misconception that 2 Peter mirrors a late date—a date in which heresy is growing or already widespread. However, Paul, writing in about 55, also uses the term in the sense of "faction" or "division" rather than heretical teaching (1 Cor. 11:18). *Heresies of destruction* or *destructive opinions* (2:1) means that the opinions or teachings of Peter's opponents lead ultimately to their own ruin (Bauckham: 239-240).

The slave-market metaphor appears in 2:1: *They will deny the Master who bought them.* It reappears in 2:19. As in Jude 4, Peter's opponents *deny the Master who purchased them.* What sort of denial might this be? As with Jude's adversaries, these people have apparently made a confession of faith at one time and now have departed from the faith (Jude 4). The denial, as Green observes, is primarily ethical and not intellectual in character (107). The slave metaphor of redemption, appearing in 2:19, confirms this suspicion.

Tragically, these individuals appear to be apostate former believers who have disowned their Lord. Not doctrine but the fact of *their licentious ways* (2:2), a "hardened immorality" (Green: 107), constitutes the root of their apostasy and subsequent judgment. Pagan skepticism and a resulting lapse into pagan ways have solidified into apostasy (Bauckham: 241).

The charge that *because of these the way of truth will be blasphemed* (2:2) is reminiscent of Paul's condemnation in Romans 2:24. By breaking the commandments "the name of God is blasphemed because of you" (Rom. 2:24). Such an indictment is nothing short of scandalous. Sexual immorality gives Christianity a bad name in surrounding culture. Given the natural hostility of pagans toward Christians to begin with, this ethical scandal is all the more reprehensible.

Peter states that the opponents are deceptive in their use of *fabricated words* (2:3a). He then announces that their condemnation is *not inoperative,* their destruction is *not idle* (2:3b). This declaration may be a flat rebuke of the opponents' skepticism toward divine judgment (Bauckham: 247; Neyrey, 1980:415-416).

In sum, the nature of apostasy is such that it works covertly, it negates Christ's lordship, it is characterized by ethical lapse, it denies the truth, and it inevitably exploits others. Because of its cumulative negative effect on the body of Christ, the church, Peter announces condemnation of the faithless in no uncertain terms. At the same time, he affirms that a righteous remnant will be preserved.

Peter's Opponents: Three Precedents 2:4-10a

2:4 The Fallen Angels

Two of Jude's examples of judgment appear in Peter's list. One of these, the fallen angels, is depicted in much the same terms (cf. notes on Jude 6). The allusion to the fallen angels in 2 Peter, as in Jude, is somewhat veiled. Yet subtle nuances in language are worth noting and reflect in minor ways on the pastoral need in the community, and thus on the purpose of the letter. Jude notes that they *did not keep their position but left their dwelling* (6). The emphasis in

2 Peter is placed on the fact that God did not spare the angels. Already in the first of three moral types, the tension between judgment and deliverance begins to emerge.

Another detail distinguishing the portrait in 2 Peter from Jude is the use of the Greek term *Tartaros,* the subterranean abyss and place of punishment in classical Greek mythology, or hell. The writer is sensitive to the social environment of the readers and borrows imagery without endorsing Greek mythology itself. Jude, on the other hand, seems to presuppose a Palestinian social setting.

Second Peter, like Jude, does not identify the precise sin of the angels, only that they sinned and have consequently been reserved for judgment. The shocking nature of this illustration is not to be lost on Peter's audience: the exalted ranks of angels themselves were not immune to rebellion and its eternal consequences. Even the angels were not spared (cf. notes on Jude 6 and 9, and the TBC thereon).

2:5 Noah and His Contemporaries

A second precedent *of not having been spared* is cited, a precedent not mentioned in Jude. This second illustration of catastrophic judgment, unlike the first, exhibits an important bifurcation. The writer states that God *did not spare the ancient world . . . when he brought a flood on the world of the ungodly.* He notes parenthetically, *however, that God did rescue Noah, a herald of righteousness, with seven others.*

The generation with which this righteous herald is compared is described in the biblical narrative in the following terms:

> The Lord saw how great man's wickedness on the earth had become, and that every inclination of the thoughts of his heart was only evil all the time. . . . Now the earth was corrupt in God's sight and was full of violence. God saw how corrupt the earth had become, for all the people on earth had corrupted their ways. (Gen. 6:5, 11-12)

In contrast, Noah is depicted in the Genesis narrative as a *righteous man, blameless in his generation* (Gen. 6:9). In Ezekiel 14:12-23, Noah stands alongside Daniel and Job as a paradigm of faithfulness amidst a generation facing inescapable judgment.

Similarly, the proverbial days of Noah are alluded to in Jesus' teaching on watchfulness (Matt. 24:36-44; Luke 17:22-27). In 1 Peter 3:8ff., the days of Noah are described as a time when "God waited patiently," at the end of which "eight persons were saved through water" (1 Pet. 3:20). Noah also appears in the catalog of faithful believers recorded in Hebrews 11. By heeding the divine warning and building the ark, he thus "condemned the world and became an heir to the righteousness that is in accordance with faith" (Heb. 11:7). The biblical account is unified in its portrait of Noah as a model of righteousness and faithfulness.

Postbiblical interpretations of Noah, while assuming the Genesis narrative, freely embellish him as a hero (as in Jub. 10:13-14; 21:10; 1 Enoch 65-67, 106-107; Philo, *Congr.* 90; *Post.* 48, 173, 174; *Quaest. et Sol. in Gen.* 2.33, 34; *Leg. Alleg.* 3.77). In Philo, for example, Noah is lauded as being perfect from birth, having acquired all the virtues and having committed no deliberate wrong (*Leg. Alleg.* 3.77; *De Abr.* 34; *De Vit. Mos.* 2.59). Though the OT does not explictly state (as in 2 Pet. 2:5) that Noah preached to his generation, he is accorded this role by diverse strands of Jewish tradition (e.g., Josephus, *Ant.* 1.3.1; Gen. Rab. 30:7; Eccl. Rab. 9:15; Babyl. Talmud, Sanh. 108; see J. P. Lewis).

In 2 Peter, attention is drawn both to judgment befalling the *world of the ungodly* (2:5) and to the salvation of Noah and his family. This dual emphasis resonates with the readers, encouraging them to remain faithful in the midst of their own seemingly overwhelming social challenges.

It is surely not coincidental that in 2 Peter, Noah and the fallen angels appear together in the same context. In apocalyptic literature, the Flood is bound together with the elaborate story of the fall of "the Watchers" or fallen angels (e.g., Test. Naph. 3:5; cf. 2 Pet. 2:4). Significantly, too, the reference to the days of Noah in 2 Peter has a notable and fascinating parallel in 1 Peter.

One of the more difficult passages in the NT, 1 Peter 3:18-22 rivals portions of 2 Peter and Jude for obscurity. In these verses the reader passes from Christ's suffering, a central theme of 1 Peter, to Christ's victory. The contextual flow of 2:18ff. traces the psychology of the believer's suffering for Christ in a pagan and hostile world, a theme picked up again in 3:13ff. The writer shows the effects of Christ's work in terms of complete and utter triumph. Jesus goes into heaven and is enthroned at the right hand of God, with all angelic powers subject to his authority (3:22). Parenthetically, 1 Peter notes that "Christ went and made proclamation to the imprisoned spirits, who in former times did not obey, when God waited patiently in the days of Noah" (3:19-20).

The interpretive difficulties with this passage are numerous and complex (see Waltner commentary on 1 Peter, above). Yet an important pastoral need is met by this cryptic allusion both to Christ's preaching to "imprisoned spirits" and to the days of Noah when God was forbearing. It is meant to encourage the Christian community. Despite the hostility aimed by surrounding society at believers, Christ has triumphed, and he has done so unconditionally. In this proclamation to the evil spirits, Christ announces his completed conquest of them and their doom, without hope.

Even the demon hosts are subjugated to the rule of Christ. Therefore, Christians living in Asia Minor (the first audience of 1 Peter), enduring suffering inflicted by pagans, should take comfort. Christ the victor sits enthroned at the right hand of Almighty God (1 Pet. 3:22). Their lot is in Christ's hands. The 1 Peter text corresponds to 2 Peter, with the allusion to Noah and his contemporaries having a similar effect. It is simultaneously intended to promise retribution and to comfort the righteous remnant.

Noah's generation is used in Jesus' teaching for the purposes of a moral lesson. In Matthew's Gospel, the context resembles that of 2 Peter—watchfulness in the midst of a perverted generation (Matt. 24:37-38). In Luke, Noah is an example of endurance surrounded by contemporary skepticism (Luke 17:25-27). Hebrews 11, another catalog of historical examples, salutes Noah as an archetype of faith (11:7). Finally, 1 Peter 3:20 portrays Noah as one of eight persons saved by the ark in the context of divine judgment.

Noah serves as a symbol to the Christian community of faithfulness in spite of overwhelming obstacles. In 2 Peter, attention is drawn both to the Flood which God brought upon the world and deliverance of a righteous remnant—Noah plus seven others. As Hillyer (188-189) notes, the pastoral side of Peter presses through. His readers are encouraged to remain faithful to God in their present situation, in spite of difficult cultural circumstances.

2:6-10a Lot Amidst Sodom and Gomorrah

The third example also incorporates motifs of both judgment and salvation. It is instructive insofar as it exploits comparison for a notably pastoral effect. Because God reduced the cities of the plain to ashes, *thereby making them an example of what is to visit the ungodly* (2:6; cf. Jude 7), punishment for Peter's opponents is certain.

What is striking, however, about Peter's contrast is that Lot, depicted in Genesis 19 as morally tainted, is called righteous (*dikaios*) three times. He is cast as a victim of surrounding cultural licentiousness, one whose *righteous soul was tormented day after day by the lawless* things that he saw and heard (2:8). Lot thus is *righteous* not by example but by comparison to surrounding debauchery. The clause *If God rescued Lot* confirms this comparative picture: Peter's audience should take heart in the throes of their present social context. If they have it difficult confronting pagan immorality, Lot had it even harder.

The Flood typology in 2 Peter 2, conspicuously absent from Jude, is intended to be prototypical of eschatological judgment. In 2 Peter, Noah and Lot become types of faithful Christians who, in spite of enormous social obstacles, expect God to bring *deliverance* (*salvation, rescue; phulassō*, 2:5; *rhuomai*, 2:7, 9). The catchword *Savior*, occurring five times in the epistle, has more than a christological thrust (1:1, 11; 2:20; 3:2, 18). God saves a righteous remnant:

> For in this way abundant entrance has been provided for you to the eternal kingdom of our Lord and *Savior* Jesus Christ. (1:11)
> For if, after having escaped the defilements of the world through the knowledge of our Lord and *Savior* Jesus Christ, they are again entangled . . . (2:20)
> Remember the past words spoken by the holy prophets and the commandment of the Lord and *Savior* spoken through your apostles. (3:2)
> Grow in grace and knowledge of our Lord and Savior Jesus Christ. (3:18)

The message of 2 Peter, unlike Jude, is not mere condemnation. Instead, it is the assurance of rescue from the midst of the cultural "furnace." Important touchpoints exist between the social environment of the readers and the days of Noah and Lot. Hillyer (188-189) captures the sense of these verses:

> Peter thus maintains his pastoral purpose of encouraging his readers to keep faith with God in their own situation. Such a loyal stand will neither go unnoticed nor fail to attract a similar divine protection from the consequences of sin of the godless. . . . Yet, as God kept Noah and his family from perishing in the Flood which carried off the wicked of those times, so the same God will protect believers who remain faithful to him in later generations.

The theme of righteous rescue, introduced in the second example, is magnified in the third. The Lord knows how to rescue the godly from trial. The *trial* from which rescue can be expected is disillusionment and the temptation to lapse ethically (2:9; Kelly: 335). Emphasis is placed on the hardened character of immorality that surrounds the Christian community. The licentious nature of lawless society *torments* the righteous soul. Moral promiscuity no longer shocks many people. Their consciences become dulled to sin and moral parameters. Judgment, therefore, is a necessity, *especially* for *those who indulge their flesh in depraved lust, and who despise authority* (2:10a).

In summarizing the moral types in 2 Peter 2:4-10a, we may draw an important pastoral conclusion. Noah, Noah's family, and Lot are instructive in the writer's thinking. They illustrate the fact that God is not indifferent toward the moral challenges of his people. Particularly for those living in a pluralistic Hellenistic environment, this reminder is crucial. Although Lot and Noah are worlds apart in terms of their personal ethical example, both are objects of God's redeeming and unmerited favor.

Peter's audience, doubtless, can identify with both characters. Noah faithfully endured many years of scorn and derision. Lot, whose character based on the Genesis narrative leaves much to be desired, nevertheless was delivered from God's judgment. The readers should take courage, even though the sensuality and skepticism of their social environment conspire against their faith. In response, Peter offers a prophetic reminder: the life of sin and debauchery will not go unpunished. The faithful may anticipate divine rescue, as epitomized in the stories of Noah and Lot.

Peter's Opponents: A Closer Look 2:10b-22

Structurally and stylistically, these verses bear notable similarity to Jude—down to minute detail. The obvious literary relationship has occupied NT scholarship considerably (commentary on Jude, below). In both letters, a portrait of the ungodly contains a litany of descriptions and accusations, and follows the writer's use of historical examples. The individuals under indictment are compared with the angels. Whereas angels, *though greater in might and power, do not bring a railing judgment against them before the Lord,* these individuals, in their bold blasphemy, *are not afraid to slander the glorious ones,* the angels (2:10b-11). This statement by the author is less a theological assertion about angels than it is a simple and startling comparison: the apostate have no reverential fear that inhibits them; they blaspheme what they do not understand (2:12).

Moreover, these people are *irrational beasts; they are mere creatures of instinct, born to be caught and killed* (2:12). They are further described as spots and blemishes in the love feasts (implied, 2:13; cf. Jude 12), like *Balaam,* the notorious apostate (2:15-16), and *waterless clouds* for whom is reserved *the deepest darkness* (2:17).

Despite notable literary parallels, however, the portrait in 2 Peter distinguishes itself from Jude by far greater detail given to the moral cesspool. The opponents have *eyes that are full of adultery* (literally, "full of an adulteress") and *insatiable for sin* (2:14a). These individuals seduce unstable souls and have *hearts trained in greed* (2:14b). As apostates, they *have abandoned the straight way and have gone astray, following the way of Balaam*, who *loved the wages of wrongdoing* (2:15). Indeed, so entrenched in a moral stupor was Balaam, so overcome by *madness*, he had to be restrained by an ass speaking with a human voice (2:16).

The description accorded the adversaries in 2:10b-21 contains significant parallels to Jude and is differentiated by a notable expansion of the Balaam typology (2:15-16). The moral corrosion that characterizes these individuals in 2 Peter is breathtaking. They act as irrational beasts, they slander, they revel in their corruption. They are boastful, irreverent, disobedient, and scornful. They are adulterous, insatiable in their appetite for sin, and actively seducing others.

Only a brief standardization of this type appears in Jude ("the error of Balaam," 11). However, in 2 Peter these individuals are more fully developed as a type and depicted as *having abandoned the upright way and gone astray, following the road of Balaam son of Bosor, who loved the wages of wrongdoing* (2:15). This language points to apostasy. In Jewish tradition, Balaam becomes a paradigm of self-seeking and greed (Vermes: 127-177). More important for 2 Peter, he was seduced by pagans, the fruit of which meant apostasy for Israel (Num. 22–25). Balaam is prototypical of some in the community addressed by 2 Peter. With Balaam, these are said to *love the rewards of wrongdoing*.

Two strains of tradition exist in the OT concerning the prophet who led Israel astray. On one hand, he is viewed as a villain, corrupt and seducing. On the other, he is depicted as a tragic hero. Numbers 22–24 offers a mixed review. In other texts, Balaam is portrayed as a strictly negative memorial, one who was hired to curse and who led Israel astray (Num. 31:16; Deut. 23:4-5; Josh. 13:22; 24:9; Neh. 13:2).

Traditional hostility toward Balaam in Jewish tradition appears to come from Numbers 31:15-16; Deuteronomy 23:5-6; and Joshua 13:22. Balaam is a bad example of self-seeking and greed. More important, he led Israel into idolatry and immorality at Baal-Peor. He was a fascinating subject for Jews, as reflected by Josephus: "This was the man to whom Moses did the high honor of recording his prophecies. And though it was possible for him [Moses] to claim credit for them himself . . . , he has given Balaam his testimony and deigned to perpetuate his memory" (*Ant.* 4.6.13).

The point of emphasis in 2 Peter 2:15-16 is that it took an ordinarily *dumb* (*speechless*) beast, Balaam's donkey, speaking *with a human voice*, to put an end to *the prophet's madness* (Num. 22:21-35).

The downfall of a prophet of God is a singular phenomenon, and one that is highly instructive. Over time, Balaam became ethically divorced from the message he bore. The psychology and character of apostasy are such that a moral skepticism and cynicism lead one to loathe what was formerly embraced. In the end, one *loves the rewards of wrongdoing.* Such a tragic case is a possibility that can befall the individual. It is also a cancer that threatens everything around it.

One recurring description of Peter's opponents is that they deceive, entice, or seduce others (1:16; 2:1, 3, 14, 18). It is moral depravity more than doctrinal error that afflicts the community. False doctrine or heresy is no doubt present, but the fact that some *deny the Master who purchased them* (2:1) points foremost to an ethical dilemma. Central to the apostates' rhetorical strategy is the *promise* of *liberation* (2:19). Yet they themselves are *slaves* to moral *corruption.*

Ultimately, people are slaves to whatever rules them (2:19c), even their own *bombastic nonsense* (2:18). The slave imagery was suggested already in 2:1. The apostate *deny the Master who had bought them* (cf. Acts 20:28). These persons emphasize and use the catchword *freedom* (2:19), with all its seductive attraction. Their abuse first of all is ethical. They value freedom—freedom from moral restraint and from divine retribution (Bauckham: 275; Neyrey, 1980: 407-412).

Two vivid pictures from the natural realm sum up the state of the apostate (2:22), *who in the past had escaped the defilements of the world,* yet had *again* become *entangled and overwhelmed* therein (2:20). Both images communicate actions that fit *irrational beasts* and *mere creatures of instinct* (2:12). Yet these images have the effect of shocking the readers when applied to their faith.

If people return to the world's defilement after rescue through the knowledge of Jesus Christ, they enter *a state that has become worse for them than the first* (2:20). It would have been better, Peter writes, if they had *never known the way of righteousness than, after knowing it, to turn back from the holy commandment passed on to them* (2:21). In relative terms, ignorance of *the way of righteousness*, according to the apostle's logic, is better than apostasy from it (Green: 130). Apostasy is extremely serious business.

Green perceptively draws from the text that the first stage in apostasy is the rejection of the category of law. This is why Peter alludes to *the holy commandment* (2:21; cf. 3:2). Moreover, by the singular law (*entolē*), Peter demonstrates that he is contending for the general function of law, not the detailed prescriptions of the law (Green: 131). Orthopraxy necessarily flows out of orthodoxy; ethical living must validate one's beliefs. Bold, willful, presumptuous, and blasphemous, the apostate intuitively seek to be released from the moral restraints of law. *Lawless deeds* (2:8) characterize the spirit that prides itself in being above law. Rejection of God's law can thus be seen as the initial step in rejecting God's authority (Green: 131). Because God is holy, he commands that his people be likewise (Lev. 11:44-45; 19:2; 20:26; 1 Pet. 1:16).

The common proverbial imagery depicting two unclean animals mirrors the sobering fact that God gives us over to that which we choose: the dog returning to its vomit, and the pig to its mud (cf. Matt. 7:6; Rev. 22:15; Rom. 1:18-32). Peter draws attention to two disgusting habits of these creatures, one of which finds its parallel in the OT. The fool in Proverbs is likened to the dog that returns to its vomit (Prov. 26:11). This dog, moreover, is the *kuōn*, the wild scavenger of the streets, not the *kunarion*, the house dog (Matt. 15:26-27). Similarly, the proverb of the pig finds its analogue in the Egyptian Story of Ahikar: "My son, you were to me like a pig which had been in a hot bath, . . . and when it came out and saw a filthy pool went down and wallowed in it" (*APOT*, 2:772).

The rhetorical effect is to shock his readers into seeing the folly of reverting to the moral squalor of pagan culture, from whence they came and were washed. The proverbs serve a dual purpose (2:22). They clinch the earlier argument that the opponents are *irrational beasts* (2:12), not unlike the prophet gone mad (2:16). These proverbs further suggest that the opponents have formerly been *washed* and clean (2:22). The effect is to jolt the audience into seeing the sobering nature of apostasy: a willful departure from revealed truth.

THE TEXT IN BIBLICAL CONTEXT

Attention has already been drawn to the marked change in tone that distinguishes 2:1ff. from 1:1-21. The character of the pastor, elder, and witness to Christ's sufferings (cf. 1 Pet. 5:1ff.) presses to the fore in chapter 1; the apostle-prophet emerges in chapter 2. The writer has a passion for truth and holiness. This passion infuses his denunciation of the apostates, depicted as exercising notable influence in the community.

In the commentary on Jude (below), the literary relation between Jude and 2 Peter is observed. Most NT scholars assume a literary and not merely oral connection between the two documents. Scholarship is divided as to which source employed which. We might also consider an alternative explanation, that both Jude and 2 Peter are using a common source. The frequency of parallels as well as the common order in which they appear lends credence to such a view. Nevertheless, 2 Peter 2 distinguishes itself from Jude in several ways.

Jude displays rampant use of triplets to describe people or events; this literary tendency is absent in 2 Peter. For example, only Balaam is highlighted as a type of the lawless, but Jude adds Cain and Korah to the narrative. Moreover, there may be some significance to the fact that Peter arranges his material in a historically chronological order, unlike Jude (Hillyer: 14). Also, the depiction of the fallen angels in 2 Peter locates them in *Tartaros*, a term absent from Jude (cf. notes on Jude 6). The former would suggest a Gentile social location, unlike the Palestinian Jewish-Christian context in Jude.

The antecedents of the false teachers being denounced in 2 Peter are the false prophets of the OT, who stand in naked contrast *to men moved by the Holy Spirit [who] spoke from God* (1:21). Three prominent traits of the *pseudoprophētai* are the following: they lacked divine authority (Deut. 18; Jer. 14); their message often was peace and prosperity rather than impending judgment (Jer. 6; 23; Ezek. 13); they themselves were judged by God (Deut. 18; Jer. 28; cf. Bauckham: 243).

In his letters to Timothy, Paul admonishes his student three times that deceit, hypocrisy, rejection of sound teaching, and departure from the truth would characterize the "last days" (1 Tim. 4:1-3; 2 Tim. 3:1-9; 4:3-5). For this reason, Timothy is to be sober and vigilant, carrying out fully his appointed ministry (2 Tim. 4:5).

In his parabolic teaching, Jesus on numerous occasions hinted at the reality of apostasy from the faith. It is implicit in the parable of the sower (Matt. 13:1-23; Mark 4:1-12; Luke 8:4-10), the parable of the weeds (Matt. 13:24-30), the parable of the net (Matt. 13:47-52), the parable of the tenants (Matt. 21:33-46; Mark 12:1-12; Luke 20:9-19), and the parable of the wedding banquet (Matt. 22:2-14; Luke 14:16-24). The eschatological parables of Matthew 25 relate to preparedness and readiness: the ten virgins, the talents, the sheep and goats. All suggest the possibility of catastrophic surprise. Some do not enter the kingdom of heaven. Watchfulness, faithfulness, and Christian ethics are lessons to be drawn from each of the three parables.

As already noted, 2 Peter is no predestinarian tract. It is not advancing human autonomy at the expense of God's grace. Both divine promises and moral imperatives are part of the Petrine formula. The epistle retains a theological balance between divine sovereignty and human moral agency that all Christians, whatever their confessional commitments, need to acknowledge.

Nevertheless, 2 Peter emphasizes appropriating what grace has made available for the ethical life. Ultimately, the reputation of God and of God's people hangs in the balance. Either God is blasphemed by apostates who trample on divine truth, or God is glorified by a thorough purging of the church's ranks. The authority of the prophetic voice is urgently required to address the pastoral needs at hand.

THE TEXT IN THE LIFE OF THE CHURCH

At many times throughout the history of the church, the epistle of 2 Peter has been one of the most relevant documents the church has possessed. The letter's message calls not only for sound interpretation but reflection and application as well.

With the language and imagery of apostasy in 2 Peter 2, we may wonder about the precise nature of apostasy and how it occurs. The letter's depiction of Peter's opponents as *false teachers* is arresting. They are compared to the *false prophets* of ancient Israel (2:1). In what sense are these individuals false? In their claims and authority, or in their message? Green is likely correct to argue that it is both: they do *not* speak with authority, their message is spurious, and they do stand under divine judgment (105).

The latter part of chapter 2 confirms this appraisal. These are apostate individuals, persons in the mold of Balaam, *who loved the wages of evil* (2:15) and who *were again entangled in them and overwhelmed* (2:20). The verdict handed down for them suggests a frightening possibility: *It would have been better for them never to have known the way of righteousness than, after knowing it, to turn back* (2:21). It has happened to them, the apostle writes, according to the common proverb: *the dog returns to its own vomit, and the pig returns to the mud from whence it was washed* (2:22). Peter places responsibility for their departure from the faith squarely on their shoulders.

Let us look at the whole scene. Some measure of *apostasy* must occur before heresy can set in, for heresy is the theological justification for a lifestyle that has rebelled against and rejected divine truth. Departure, it should be observed, does not take place overnight; neither does it announce its arrival. Instead, it works covertly, manifesting itself through the will, which in small steps rejects the light of the Holy Spirit. The Spirit's function is to convict the individual of sin, righteousness, and divine judgment (John 16:7-11).

Thus the essential character of apostasy appears as apostates suppress the truth. In so doing, they deny Christ's lordship. To use Peter's words, they *deny the Master who bought them* (2:1). Inevitably, apostasy will lead to exploiting others, as the epistle warns. It cannot remain a private affair. For this reason, Peter is profoundly exercised in his spirit. If sin and the resultant departure from the faith are merely a singular, private phenomenon, the Christian community will not suffer. But apostasy is like cancer and will spread. It eats away at the body's healthy cells, leaving destruction and rot in its wake, often before people are fully aware of its advanced stages.

Apostasy, then, is primarily ethical in its initial character. It begins and matures by reason of the will. It is volitional in constitution and not primarily intellectual. Typically, apostasy leads to moral lapse, and in time will express itself in two ways: rejection of authority in any form and sexual deviation (2:2, 6, 8-10, 14, 18). The freedom with which apostates boast of themselves is in reality not freedom at all; instead, it is a return to slavery (2:19). This slavery, however, is not merely the standard variety. It is a more degrading form of bondage, since they have willingly forsaken the redeeming power they have known. In the end, they reach a state worse than the original (2:20).

It simply will not do to maintain that biblical warnings against turning away from the truth are merely hypothetical. These warnings are addressed to people professing faith; therefore, we must heed them. It is true that we are kept by the power and grace of God (John 10:28-29; Jude 24). It is also true that there are threats—very real threats—to our perseverance. Perhaps for this reason, books such as Jude and 2 Peter have not fared well in terms of popularity. It is not easy to reconcile these two strands of biblical teaching that stand in tension: God's ability to keep us, and our ability to reject truth and consequently subvert God's keeping. The human tendency, as one esteemed biblical theologian has noted, is to push beyond the biblical evidence to some logical system overemphasizing one theological pole, whether divine sovereignty or human freedom (Marshall: 12).

The psychology of apostasy, when its presence is very real to believers, is generally underestimated by the Christian church. It is real because believers must *continually* choose the way of discipleship. Christian discipleship shows itself to be the polar opposite of Petrine-defined apostasy. It exhibits a wholesome attitude toward authority in general, whether religious or nonreligious. Furthermore, it is characterized by a bridled sexuality, in strong contrast to pagan culture surrounding the church.

For the discerning Christian, then, apostasy in the contemporary church should not be difficult to identify, even when it is increasingly hard to denounce. It rejects religious or ecclesiastical authority, and it carries with it physical uncleanness in human relationships. In postmodern Western culture, it is increasingly true that people despise authority of any type and are licentious to the core. Thus it stands to reason that in the face of contemporary social pathologies, the Christian community is in dire need of the prophetic word contained in 2 Peter. Neglected and misunderstood, the message of this epistle cries out to the church in our contemporary situation.

2 Peter 3:1-18

Exhortation to the Faithful

PREVIEW

In chapter 2, Peter has focused sharply on the apostates. Now he returns to the faithful, who are in the throes of a dilemma and in need of a reminder. From the beginning of their spiritual sojourn, they have been forewarned of the perilous nature of moral skepticism. The pastoral side of the apostle now emerges once more as the faithful struggle to reconcile God's seeming indifference to their lot, and the moral challenges presented by pagan society.

Peter's response to this quandary is to remind his readers of God's dealings in the past, using the imagery of water and fire. Water was the means by which the antediluvian world came under judgment. Fire is the means through which divine judgment will again be manifest. The Christian community is called to adopt the posture of Noah, who endured years of scorn and derision while being faithful to God. When judgment eventually did fall on Noah's contemporaries, it fell suddenly and catastrophically. It came as "a thief in the night" (cf. 1 Thess. 5:2; 2 Pet. 3:10).

OUTLINE

Apostolic Repetition and Exhortation, 3:1-7

The Economy of God, 3:8-13

Final Exhortation and Doxology, 3:14-18

EXPLANATORY NOTES

Apostolic Repetition and Exhortation 3:1-7

With the material in chapter 3, Peter revisits his reason for writing. He must remind his readers of the apostolic "first things." The language here is strongly motivational: *I stir in you a sincere mind by way of reminder that you remember* . . . It is a call to moral purity, to be unmixed and untainted in a moral sense. This exhortation follows on the heels of material in 2:1-22 that is presented in the strongest terms, almost harshly. Given the contaminated moral environment in which the readers find themselves, like Noah and Lot, they are to remain uncontaminated.

Once again the writer states that there is continuity between the OT prophets, who prefigured Christian discipleship, and *the commandment of the Lord and Savior* (cf. 1:1, 11), conveyed through apostolic teaching (3:1-2). Paul also views the words of the prophets and the apostles as the foundation of the gospel (Eph. 2:20; 3:5-6). As in 1:19-21, emphasis is given to the link between past and present, between the word of God spoken by the prophets and that spoken by the apostles. They are the ones to whom the word of God has been spoken and entrusted.

One cannot speak of an authoritative "word of God" apart from the concept of apostolicity and the apostolic tradition (cf. 1 Cor. 15:3-7). The apostle is authoritative inasmuch as he stands in direct relation to Jesus, and thus is a deputized representative. Matthew's Gospel captures the close link between Peter's confession (Matt. 16:13-20) and his experience of Jesus' transfiguration, "while we were with him on the holy mountain" (2 Pet. 1:18): "Six days later Jesus took with him Peter, James and his brother John and led them up a high mountain, by themselves . . ." (Matt. 17:1-8). The implications of the apostolic office are weighty. Apostolic witness is not merely personal testimony; instead, it is "infallibly authoritative, a legally binding deposition, the kind that stands up in a law court" (Gaffin: 176).

Believers are urged to recall foundational Christian teaching; in fact, this is the *second [such] letter* (3:1-2) written by the apostle, exhorting his audience onward. Whether we have here a reference to 1 Peter or another writing is unclear (cf. 1 Cor. 5:9). What is certain is that the author is writing again, reiterating the apostolic "first things." In the present context, this is meant to invoke authority for the purpose of drawing out the moral implications of Christian faith.

Considerable speculation characterizes traditional scholarship as to the identity of the *second letter*. While this allusion naturally suggests 1 Peter as its predecessor, those who view 2 Peter as the work of a later writer using Peter's name dismiss 1 Peter as the intended reference. Accordingly, they take 3:1-2 as a transparent mark of forgery *[Authorship]*. Kelly states that this reference is "only another prop in the apparatus of pseudonymity" (353). Given the contents and style of 2 Peter, however, it is possible that 3:1-2 is an allusion to another, unknown epistle.

Nevertheless the suggestion that the author of 1 Peter "had no close personal link" with his audience (Green: 134), while geographically probable, does not militate against the same author for 1 and 2 Peter. Indeed, both letters are written by an individual who is intimate and passionate with his readers. "Beloved" occurs in 1 Peter 2:11 and 4:12 as well as in 2 Peter 3:1, 14, 17. Furthermore, both epistles reflect a detailed knowledge of the local situation: considerable suffering and trial in 1 Peter, and the cancerous growth of apostasy in 2 Peter. Both 1 and 2 Peter also are penned by a man of God, seasoned in his ways, writing late in life (1 Pet. 5:1-5; 2 Pet. 1:12-18).

One need not regard the reference to *your apostles* (3:2) as something which "inadvertently betrays that the writer belongs to an age when the apostles have been elevated to a venerated group who mediate Christ's teaching authoritatively to the whole Church" (thus Kelly: 354). Rather than suggesting a generation removed from the early apostles, as is broadly assumed by critical scholarship, *your apostles* may be understood as "the apostles whom you ought to trust" (Bigg: 290), with a present and not future emphasis.

The author speaks of *your apostles* through whom the Lord has spoken. The *apostles* are those "who preached the gospel to you and founded the churches in your area" (Green: 137), over against the apostates. They have in view what is best for the community. When truth is being sacrificed, apostolic authority is needed to redirect the local situation. At least, we may legitimately theorize about a local situation in which authority is being denied. Second Peter 3:3-7 supplies further information about those causing dissension.

Peter's description of *the last days* (3:3) is intended to reflect on the local situation, characterized by scoffing, indulging in lust, and moral skepticism. Most commentators, in their interpretation of chapter 3, are predisposed to view the material as a theological treatise on eschatology. However, such an approach ignores both the contextual flow throughout chapters 1 and 2 and the interpretive clues contained in chapter 3. Cynical, carnal, and law-mocking people are in the writer's view. Their skepticism of truth and right is what sets them apart and makes them dangerous. Self–indulgence, rooted in nihilistic hedonism, undercuts moral absolutes at the most basic level.

Consider their method of reasoning: they say, *Where is the promise of [Christ's] coming? For . . . all things continue as they were from the beginning of creation* (3:4). Peter's opponents are denying any divine interference in human affairs. To this assertion of moral relativity, the apostle responds with a cosmological argument. It is an argument based on the creation of a moral universe. The lesson of the flood is above all a moral lesson. Water was the means by which judgment came initially (cf. 1 Pet. 3:19-20). On the final day of reckoning, judgment will come through fire (2 Pet. 3:5-7). Peter's concern is chiefly with the apostates' basic predisposition, hardened skepticism that breeds a relativistic ethic.

NT scholarship is inclined to see in 2 Peter 3 a large debt to Jewish apocalyptic literature of the intertestamental period, with its theme of cosmic upheaval. The combative tone and allusion to fiery judgment does indeed offer two points of resemblance. However, the social environment of the readers is pagan and Gentile. Jewish apocalyptic lacks the resonance that it might possess in Jude, where a markedly Palestinian Jewish-Christian setting is mirrored. Citing pagan sources and popular proverbs (cf. notes on 2:22), while employing a Stoic catalog of virtues (1:5-7), achieves a greater effect, fitting the social context in which Peter's audience finds itself.

The Economy of God 3:8-13

The writer's focus now shifts. He follows the counterargument that judgment, foreshadowed by the past, is being reserved for the ungodly. The faithful may be perplexed by the delay in divine judgment. Surfacing here are touchpoints to Noah and Lot, used as models in chapter 2. A delay in God's action calls for reassurance that the faithful have not been and are not being forgotten, even when it appears that God is not intervening in human affairs. Thus it is necessary to address the readers once more as *dear friends* (*agapētoi*; cf. 3:1).

Traditional commentary sees the purpose of the letter and especially the material in 2 Peter 3 as refuting *doctrinal* error. The problem aggravating the writer of 2 Peter is generally thought to be a rejection of the doctrine of the second coming. A rhetorical question is hence viewed as the clue: *Where then is the sign of his coming?* (3:4). Commentators assume that the writer is generations removed from the apostolic era. It follows that the church is struggling with false doctrine, a denial of the eschatological hope of Christ's return.

Thus far we have argued that the tenor of 2 Peter is foremost ethical. In this light, 2 Peter 3 can be seen not so much as a theological response to a rejection of right doctrine (orthodoxy); rather, it is chiefly an apologetic and an affirmation of the certainty of divine rewards in a moral universe. This interpretive distinction determines how one reads the letter. It also reveals differing assumptions that inform the interpreter's starting-point.

If one assumes that 2 Peter is a second-century tract to bolster the morale of the church, generations removed from the apostles, then the "problem" of 2 Peter takes on a doctrinal cast. Thus Kelly's assertion that the writer's "concern for the orthodox interpretation of Scripture (1:20ff.; 3:15ff.) and for the apostolic tradition (e.g., 2:21; 2:2) smacks of emergent 'Catholicism' rather than of first-generation Christianity" (235). If, however, the epistle is written to counter first-century moral skepticism and ethical lapse, the epistle becomes less a tract to affirm doctrinal orthodoxy than a passionate exhortation toward virtuous living.

The skeptics mock the fundamental notion of being called to account for their deeds. In contrast, the faithful are to reflect on the ways of God in the past as they touch human affairs. For the faithful, a proper perspective of God's dealings is crucial. Believers often have trouble seeing any bad results coming in the present to others who deny the truth and have moral skepticism. Hence, they struggle with the question of apparent delay in God's response.

Why does God not act? Where is his retribution? Why do the righteous suffer disgrace in the eyes of the world? Why is God lax concerning his promises? (3:9). If believers are to persevere in faith amidst social decay and moral skepticism, they need to recognize the difference between the human and divine perspective (3:8-9). Consider the plight of human beings, framed so vividly by the psalmist:

How long, O Lord? Will you forget me forever?
How long will you hide your face from me?
How long must I wrestle with my thoughts
    and every day have sorrow in my heart?
How long will my enemy triumph over me? (Ps. 13:1-2, NIV)

The apostolic wisdom applied to this quandary is rooted in an adjusted perspective—the divine perspective. To the Lord, a day is like a millennium and a millennium like a day. This language, reminiscent of Psalm 90:4 and surfacing in several intertestamental Jewish texts, is not chronological but comparative in function. Psalm 90, a prayer ascribed to Moses, is a meditative reflection on the transient nature of our days: "They quickly pass, and we fly away" (90:10c, NIV). This contrasts with the Lord dwelling in eternity: "From everlasting to everlasting, you are God" (90:2b, NIV). Bauckham cites several examples of rabbinic literature showing that Psalm 90:4 was used to contrast human perception of time with God's (307-10).

Significantly, not only time's relativity but time's importance is an integral part of Psalm 90. This may be why 2 Peter 3:8 restates Psalm 90:4: "With the Lord one day is as a thousand years, and a thousand years are as a day." After the psalmist observes that our days pass quickly, flying away (90:10), he offers this prayer: "Teach us to number our days accordingly, so that we might acquire a heart of wisdom" (90:12).

In stressing both the relativity and significance of time, the author appeals to the character of God. One aspect of the Godhead that distinguishes divine from human nature is the quality of forbearance. In truth, the Lord is *not slack* or *slow* concerning his *promise*, as it may seem to humans. Instead, at the heart of the issue of "delay" is divine patience. The object of this forbearance is people. *All* persons are given the opportunity to bow the knee and make room for *repentance*. Here again the central motif of 2 Peter surfaces: human moral agency. While a day of judgment is reserved for the godless (3:7), it is not God's will that they perish. These, rather, have brought condemnation upon themselves. Divine sovereignty does not cancel out their freedom to make moral decisions.

This forbearance, however, should not be misconstrued as divine indifference. Mercy and not impotence is the reason for the delay. Delay in no way suggests nonfulfillment (Green: 148). *The day of the Lord will come like a thief* in the night (cf. Matt. 24:43; Luke 12:39; 1 Thess. 5:2, 4; Rev. 3:3; 16:15). That is when the ungodly are to be judged, with full disclosure of deeds that humans have committed (3:10).

To counter any distortions about the ultimacy of divine judgment, the writer expresses the day of the Lord in cataclysmic terms. It is sudden, decisive, cosmic, and final in its nature. The *thief* motif underscores the fact that few will be prepared for this event. Destruction of the cosmos by *fire*, alluded to in 3:10-13 (*puroomai*, "melt with fire"), mirrors the Stoic belief that the universe has gone through periodic renewal by means of burning (*ekpurōsis*). This was understood to take place over and over again, without end. The author of 2 Peter, however, does not endorse the Stoic view of the universe; rather, he advances an apocalyptic eschatological perspective (cf. Mal. 3:2-5; 4:1; 2 Thess. 1:8; Heb. 10:27). In doing so, he is making use of a Stoic motif. What is important from the writer's standpoint is that the deeds of all will be laid bare. Individuals cannot avoid a day of moral reckoning.

These things should serve both to encourage the righteous and warn the apostates. For believers, the certainty and finality of God's act of judging the wicked should cause them to lead lives characterized by *holiness and godliness* (2 Pet. 3:11). In this way, the saints can *eagerly anticipate and hasten the coming of the day of God* (3:12). They are to wait for the *day of God*, and *new heavens and a new earth, where righteousness is at home* (3:13).

In the teaching of 2 Peter, eschatology and ethics are indivisible. The certainty of judgment, the inevitability of a day of moral reckoning, prods believers on to holy living. Christians by nature are future-oriented rather than looking only at the present. Creation and all of life point to a climax in the purposes of God. Outside the faith community, from the perspective of nihilism and self-indulgent living, there is nothing ultimately for which to live. Therefore, it matters not how we live our lives.

From the Christian's perspective, the passing of everything in this age unveils the reality of the coming age, all in accordance with God's promise. The writer closes out his eschatological exhortation just as he has introduced his letter, with the keyword *righteousness* (cf. 1:1): the new home to be anticipated is one *where righteousness dwells*.

Final Exhortation and Doxology 3:14-18

In the saints' present struggle to discern God's timing and forbearance, Peter's audience is to strive toward three aims:

- Be spotless and without blemish (cf. Jude 24).
- Be at peace in the Lord.
- View God's long-suffering as leading to the salvation of others (3:14-15).

While the reader may not automatically see a connection between these three imperatives, they hinge on each another.

The first priority is foundational and affects one's ability to realize the other two: the saints are to remain pure in an impure, vulgar world. In spite of seemingly insurmountable cultural obstacles facing the Christian community, *everything for life and godliness* has already been provided, based on God's grace (1:3-4). The resources are there; what remains to be determined is the saints' willingness. It is no coincidence that the same language occurs again, used earlier to describe those troubling the community. Those indulging in their flesh and despising authority (2:10b) are characterized as *blots and blemishes* (2:13). Peter's concluding exhortation is that the faithful, in contrast, be without *blot or blemish* (3:14). Christian truth-claims are only as authoritative as the vessels who bear them.

The second and third priorities relate to the first. The human tendency is to question God: "Where are you, God? How long, Lord?" Hence, at the heart of the ethical imperative lies the challenge of finding the place of God's peace, bearing in mind that others' salvation is lodged within the heart of God (3:15). The Lord, after all, is not willing that any should perish (3:9). The day of the Lord is a day of vindication and justice. Yet, since God's timing and purposes are beyond human comprehension, believers are challenged to find the place of rest and peace as they wait on God's activity.

Meanwhile, it will mean enduring hardship as disciples of Christ, and this in a world at cross-purposes with its Creator. To endure is to manifest Christian virtue, to be godly in character (1:6). Human perseverance is born out of the deep conviction that God perseveres on our behalf: The Lord wishes none to perish. God takes into account human moral agency and does not restrict it.

Here it is not Peter the theologian who is speaking. Rather, it is Peter the pastor and apostle. Paul was the acknowledged theologian: *According to the wisdom given to him, he has written to you, as he has in all his epistles, about these things*, that is, about the nature of salvation and the long-suffering of God (3:15-16). It is true, Peter grants, that these mysteries are *hard to understand*, causing some to distort and pervert them for their own purposes. The faithful, however, stand in bold contrast; they are prepared for these distortions and in steadfastness refuse to be carried away by the error of the wicked (3:17).

Concluding his letter, Peter reminds his readers once more that indeed it is possible for them to be affected by the lawless and thereby *to lose your own stability*. If the angels, who were exposed to incomparable glory, fell from that place of glory (2:4), then the lesson is clear: the community must take moral agency seriously. They are responsible and accountable. It is possible to be exposed to the truth, as Peter had the utmost privilege of doing years earlier (1:16-18; Matt. 17:1-8; Mark 9:2-8; Luke 9:28-36), and yet negate that truth, as Peter is personally and painfully aware (Matt. 26:69-75; Mark 14:66-72; Luke 22:54-62). This denial of the truth may happen through fear, self-centeredness, or immorality. The man writing knows whereof he speaks; his is a poignant, lifelong memory of confession followed by denial (cf. Matt. 16:13-20 and 26:69-75). Thus the Petrine admonition has a decided ring of authority, an authority fashioned out of painfully difficult experience through the years: *Beware that you are not carried away . . . and lose your footing.*

Fittingly, the antidote to this possibility is stated again in the letter's concluding statement just as it had appeared in the greeting (1:2): *Grow in grace and knowledge of our Lord and Savior Jesus Christ* (3:18).

THE TEXT IN BIBLICAL CONTEXT

The material in 2 Peter 3 expresses several points of theological tension that run throughout the Scriptures. The reader's frequent and thorough identification with the psalmist releases the Psalms to be heard with force and poignance for the human experience. Typical of numerous psalms is the lament of the writer who observes with great agony the seeming triumph of the wicked. Many such laments are so framed in Psalms 6, 10, 13, 22, 31, 38, 69, 73, and 88: Where is the Lord's vindication of the righteous? Why do the righteous suffer so? Where is the Lord's justice? Why do evil people seem to prosper? How long, O Lord, will you remain silent in the face of agonizing trial and tribulation?

In light of such perplexing questions, the text of 2 Peter 3 gives readers a condensed statement of the economy of God. Consider the pattern: self-indulgent scoffers mock the very idea of moral accountability. They ignore both God's intervention in history through judgment, and the coming day of reckoning by which God has chosen to judge the world through his Son. That eschatological judgment, foretold by the prophets again and again, is reaffirmed in the context of Christian discipleship in a fallen world.

Second Peter 3 caricatures the hardened moral skeptic, while reminding the faithful of past acts of judgment that foreshadowed the coming day of the Lord. At the same time, the writer is sensitive to the quandary of perseverance and, like the psalmist, reminds his readers of a different and higher perspective. This delay points to the fact that God wants to be merciful to all (3:9; Rom. 11:32). God the

Savior "desires everyone to be saved and to come to the knowledge
of the truth" (1 Tim. 2:4).

The day-of-the-Lord imagery derives generally from the prominence of God as Judge in the OT. It is especially employed in the
prophetic writings (as in Isa. 13:9; Jer. 46:10; 50:31; Ezek. 30:2;
Joel 1:15; 2:31; Amos 3:13; 5:20; Obad. 15; Zeph. 1:14; Zech.
14:1; Mal. 4:5). The judge of the whole earth (Gen. 18:25; Ps. 9:7-
8; Rom. 3:6) judges both individuals (Gen. 16:5) and nations (Judg.
11:27; Ps. 110:6; Amos 1–2). The great day as a day of judgment is
alluded to in every prophetic book, from Isaiah to Malachi. The OT
writers understood this judgment as occurring within history.

The "day of judgment" also occurs frequently in Jewish intertestamental writings (e.g., Jth. 16:17; Wisd. of Sol. 3:18; 4 Ezra =
2 Esd. 7:38ff.; 1 En. 22:4, 13; 97:3; Jub. 22:21). Particularly in
these writings, vindication of the righteous is an important element in
the unfolding of eschatological events. This is due in part to Israel's
exile and dispersion among the nations.

While the term "day of the Lord" is emphasized less in the NT, it
is not a neglected theme. There are numerous and explicit references
to judgment in the NT (e.g., Matt. 10:15; 11:22; 12:36, 41-42; Luke
10:14; 21:34-35). In addition, much of Jesus' parabolic teaching
assumes in one form or another a coming day of judgment. The
expressions "day of the Lord, "that day," or "day of judgment"
appear in many texts (e.g., Acts 17:31; Rom. 2:16; 1 Thess. 5:2-4;
2 Thess. 2:2; 2 Tim. 1:18; 4:1-8; 2 Pet. 2:9; 3:10-12; Jude 6;
1 John 4:17). Reference to Christ judging the world is both explicit
and frequent (e.g., Acts 17:31; Rom. 2:16; 1 Cor. 1:8; 3:10-15; 6:2;
2 Cor. 1:14; 2 Tim. 4:1; 1 Pet. 2:12; 4:5; Rev. 6:10; 11:18; 19:11;
21:27).

The day of judgment is characterized several times in the NT as a
day coming like a "thief." In each of these allusions, it appears with
a moral imperative. Jesus used the image in the Olivet Discourse to
underscore the need for watchfulness (Matt. 24:36-44; cf. Luke
12:35-40). Moreover, the description of the Second Advent has a
familiar ring to it for the reader of the Petrine epistles:

> For as the days of Noah were, so will be the coming of the Son of Man.
> For as in those days before the flood they were eating and drinking, mar-
> rying and giving in marriage, until the day Noah entered the ark, and they
> knew nothing until the flood came and swept them all away, so too will be
> the coming of the Son of Man. (Matt. 24:37-39)

Paul also borrows this motif as he reflects on the coming of the
Lord:

Now concerning the times and the seasons, brothers and sisters, . . . you yourselves know very well that the day of the Lord will come like a thief in the night. When they say, "There is peace and security," then sudden destruction will come upon them, as labor pains come upon a pregnant woman, and there will be no escape! But you, beloved, are not in darkness, for that day to surprise you like a thief; for you are all children of light and children of the day; we are not of the night or of darkness. (1 Thess. 5:1-5)

In the NT Apocalypse, we also encounter the thief imagery in the context of watchfulness (Rev. 3:3; 16:15). A strong exhortation is given to the church at Sardis, containing reminder language like that in 2 Peter:

Wake up, and strengthen what remains and is on the point of death, for I have not found your works perfect in the sight of my God. Remember then what you received and heard; obey it, and repent. If you do not wake up, I will come like a thief, and you will not know at what hour I will come to you. (Rev. 3:2-3)

Finally, in the context of the outpouring of God's wrath, the words of Jesus constitute a call for vigilance in the face of deception throughout the world: "See, I am coming like a thief! Blessed is the one who stays awake and is clothed, not going about naked and exposed to shame" (Rev. 16:15).

All of the eschatological warnings found in the NT have doctrinal implications, yet they are motivated by an ethical imperative. Jesus gives his warning about the last days because his followers need to be faithful, to watch and wait, and thus, to persevere.

Similarly, John writes from his exilic post on Patmos, relaying his visions and auditions (Rev. 1:9-11). He stresses faithfulness and endurance in the midst of intense persecution (e.g., 2:10, 19; 3:10; 7:14; 13:10; etc.). John is acutely aware that Christian believers in the provinces are suffering for their faith, enduring the oppressive weight of Roman domination and slandering or scoffing neighbors (2:9; cf. 2 Pet. 3:3-4).

In the Apocalypse, John promises that in God's timing, the tables will be turned: believers "will reign on earth" (Rev. 5:10; cf. 2:26-28; 3:21; 20:6; 22:5; Matt. 19:28; 20:21, 23; Rom. 8:17; 1 Cor. 6:3; 2 Tim. 2:12). Indeed, they already are "a royal house, to serve as the priests" of God (Rev. 1:6, REB); "a royal priesthood," as Peter says in his first epistle (2:9; cf. Exod. 19:6).

However, the exhortations regarding apostasy or faithfulness do not always describe the future state of affairs. They concern themselves first with present realities of faith and faithlessness. The prophets repeatedly warn Israel, the people of God, to repent and seek the ways of the Lord. Following the ebbs and flows of Israel's spiritual life in the OT is like riding a roller-coaster. It is the habit of human nature, though not its *predestination*, to depart from the truth.

Consider what sadness the apostles endured when former professing believers departed the faith. Among such individuals, Paul lists Demas, who is "in love with this present world [and] has deserted me" (2 Tim. 4:10). He also mentions Hymenaeus and Alexander, who "by rejecting conscience, . . . have suffered shipwreck in the faith" (1 Tim. 1:19).

Hence, the realities of Christian discipleship are such that some choose to reject the truth. The admonition of 2 Peter is to persevere in spite of overwhelming obstacles. Under the old covenant, God often took generations to consummate his purposes. Frequently the righteous had to wait while the unrighteous died off (Num. 32:13; Deut. 1:35; 2:14). From Moses to Job, Jeremiah, and the prophets of the Exile—the true people of God were united in a common cry to the Lord their vindicator: "Lord, how long? Lord, when will you visit your people?" (cf. 2 Pet. 3:4, 13-14; Rev. 6:10). In the end, the Lord is not slack concerning his promises. At the same time, God does not want anyone to perish (2 Pet. 3:9; cf. 1 Tim. 2:4; Rev. 9:20-21; 16:9-11).

THE TEXT IN THE LIFE OF THE CHURCH

What one believes truly affects how one lives. Evidence of this reality is found in 1 John 3:3: "All who have this hope [of Christ's full revelation] purify themselves, just as he is pure." The argument of 2 Peter 3 is founded on this assumption. In the words of Michael Green, the moral imperative follows the eschatological indicative (152). Indeed, anticipation of the Lord's return has the effect of spurring us on to holy living: *Since all these things are to be dissolved in this way, what sort of persons ought you to be in leading lives of holiness and godliness, waiting for and hastening the coming of the day of God* (2 Pet. 3:11-12)? The link between eschatology and ethics is crucially important (cf. Yoder, 1998:143-167).

In terms of Christian faith, 2 Peter 3 confronts the church with a theological dilemma. Two seemingly opposite poles are held in tension: God's holiness in contrast with his long-suffering; God's justice in contrast with his compassion. Due to our finite perspective, we tend to react in one of two ways. Either we dissolve the tension by negating one of the poles, ending with a reduced view of God; or we view the poles as opposites, adopting an equally skewed understanding of God's character. We should avoid both tendencies.

Being affirmed in 2 Peter are both the justice and the long-suffering of God. The same God hates evil and judges sin, all the while exhibiting forbearance toward a sinful and wayward generation that has lost its moral sense. The Christian community readily identifies with the audience in 2 Peter. Surrounded by hostile cultural forces, the righteous look for God's hand of righteous judgment. Their cry, much like that of their spiritual forbears, issues from the wounds that culture has inflicted: "Lord, how long? Why is the Lord slack concerning his promises?" Meanwhile, God is long-suffering, desiring that all who are hardened by moral skepticism might come to a place of brokenness and repentance.

Learning to live within the tension of judgment and repentance is both the privilege and the obligation of the Christian disciple. At Athens, Paul addresses intellectual and moral skeptics as well as cultural idolatry (Acts 17:16-34). Likewise, the church must learn how to relate Christian moral truth to those who refuse to acknowledge any moral authority higher than themselves.

> While God has overlooked the times of human ignorance, now he commands all people everywhere to repent, because he has fixed a day on which he will have the world judged in righteousness by a man whom he has appointed, and of this he has given assurance to all by raising him from the dead. (Acts 17:30-31)

The epistle of 2 Peter is not a message solely of judgment, however. It has much to suggest regarding Christian living. For this reason the Christian community does well to reflect on the Petrine doctrine of the Christian life. Believers are those who have received a precious faith through Christ's righteousness. They have been redeemed and given exceedingly great and divine resources for a godly life. This life, above all else, is to be characterized by Christian virtues. Continually growing in grace and knowledge, believers persevere, even in the face of immense cultural obstacles and opposition to the faith.

Although apostasy is acknowledged as a real possibility, the author does not lose sight of the grace of God that enables saints to persevere. His rationale for the need to persevere is informed by the divine perspective: God himself perseveres toward all people, *not wanting any to perish* (2 Pet. 3:9). This suggests two divine attributes:

on one hand, the mercy of God extends to all individuals; on the other, there are limits to the long-suffering of the Lord.

Located between these two poles is the life of faith, in which believers persevere and rest in the sovereign hand of Almighty God.

Outline of 2 Peter

The Author, His Audience, Purpose for Writing,
Authority   **1:1-21**
  Introduction and Address   1:1-2
  Purpose in Writing   1:3-11
    Divine Resources Available   1:3-4
    Catalog of Virtues   1:5-7
    Exhortation to Return   1:8-11
  Prophetic Reminder   1:12-15
  Prophetic Testimony   1:16-18
  The Prophetic Word   1:19-21

Profile of Apostasy   **2:1-22**
  Peter's Opponents: An Introduction   2:1-3
  Peter's Opponents: Three Precedents   2:4-10a
    The Fallen Angels   2:4
    Noah and His Contemporaries   2:5
    Lot Amidst Sodom and Gomorrah   2:6-10a
  Peter's Opponents: A Closer Look   2:10b-22

Exhortation to the Faithful   **3:1-18**
  Apostolic Repetition and Exhortation   3:1-7
  The Economy of God   3:8-13
  Final Exhortation and Doxology   3:14-18

Essays for 2 Peter

AUTHORSHIP OF 2 PETER   Two views of authorship collide in the epistle of 2 Peter. Either the apostle Peter is writing shortly before his death, by himself or with the help of a secretary (cf. 1 Pet. 5:12); or someone is using a pseudonym in attempting the apologetic equivalent of a home run. In the main, biblical scholarship of the 1800s and 1900s has held 2 Peter to be pseudonymous. Indeed, no NT document has had as much difficulty in achieving canonical acceptance. Writing in the early fourth century, Eusebius (*Church History* 3.3.1-4; 25.3) mirrors doubts raised about the letter in the patristic era. Until the fourth century, 2 Peter was relatively neglected. In spite of the early church's consensus that the epistle belongs to the NT canon, Erasmus, Luther, and Calvin pondered doubts concerning its authenticity.

According to the more-conventional view of 2 Peter, the writer is aiming for a most impressive and solemn reception by casting it in the form of a farewell address or testament (thus, Reicke: 146; Kelly: 311; Bauckham: 194-203), not unlike the Testaments of the Twelve Patriarchs (second century B.C.; cf. farewell speeches in Gen. 49; Deut. 32–33; John 14–17). Representative of this view is Kelly, who holds any discussion of the author being the apostle Peter to be "unrealistic" (314): "Scarcely anyone nowadays doubts that 2 Peter is pseudonymous" (235).

Kelly rationalizes the prophecy of 1:13-14: "It came naturally to Christians to believe that the heroes of the faith received premonitions of their approaching martyrdom. . . . The same motive was probably at work here, and it is fruitless to hunt around for any particular incident, historical or legendary" (314). The great majority of commentators reject the attempt to connect the writer directly with the Lord's prophecy as "fruitless" and "unrealistic." They do this because of basic assumptions ruling out genuine predictive prophecy.

The case for pseudonymity, which bears directly on our interpretation of the letter, rests on the following claims:

- 2 Peter's literary relation to *Jude*.
- A style and vocabulary that differ from 1 Peter.
- A style and vocabulary that are not the product of an illiterate Galilean fisherman.
- The assumption that the apostles belong to a past generation (3:2, 4).
- The letter's lack of universal attestation in the early church.
- A doctrinal emphasis that differs from 1 Peter.
- The assumption that the hope of the second advent has been abandoned (3:4).
- The numerous second-century pseudonymous works attributed to Peter, collected with the NT Apocrypha (e.g., the Letter of Peter, the Acts of Peter, the Apocalypse of Peter, the Travels of Peter, and the Gospel of Peter).

Pseudonymity is "a polite way of saying that the letter was written by someone else other than Peter and then assigned to the apostle" (Mounce: 98). It appears to bring assumptions *to* the text (*eisegesis*, reading things into the text that are not there) rather than deriving meaning *from* the text itself (*exegesis*). Significantly, no evidence is to be found in the NT to suggest pseudonymity as legitimate in the eyes of the biblical writers. On the contrary, Paul seems to be aware of false attempts among contemporaries to ascribe writings to authentic persons: "I, Paul, write this . . . with my own hand. This is the mark in every letter of mine; it is the way I write" (2 Thess. 3:17). "We beg you . . . not to be quickly shaken, . . . either by spirit or by word or by letter, as though from us. . . . Let no one deceive you in any way" (2 Thess. 2:1-3).

Bauckham, whose commentary on 2 Peter is among the richest and most impressive, seeks to give credence to the use of the testament genre in 2 Peter on the basis of (1) the hero's imminent death and (2) the hero's wish to have his teaching remembered after his death (194). (These two features are on display, for example, in 2 Apocalypse of Baruch 78-86, and Josephus' account of Moses' death in *Antiquities* 4.309-19.) Bauckham notes that the author does not, as do some authors of pseudepigraphal writings, imagine fictitious readers. Instead, the audience consists of actual Christian communities that the historical Peter knows (196). Moreover, the author's reference "as our Lord Jesus Christ revealed to me" (1:14) is described by Bauckham as "a piece of specifically Petrine tradition" (200). He concludes:

> Behind the fictional device which made it possible for Peter to be represented as addressing them many years after his death, they would have understood the real author's intention of providing a "reminder" and defense of the apostle's message for his own time. By writing in Peter's name, the author disclaims any desire to present a new teaching of his own. The literary device of the "testament" is a valid vehicle for his message insofar as he wishes only to preserve the apostolic message, while interpreting and defending it in terms appropriate to his readers' situation. (203)

Bauckham is by no means the first to advance a theory of pseudonymity for 2 Peter. However, he is a most-eloquent spokesman for it. Plausible as

Bauckham's explanation is, it nevertheless imports assumptions into the text that are alien to the spirit of the NT. Would the apostles have naively condoned the use of "fictional devices"? Would the readers have naively "understood the real author's intention," simply because he meant well? To "preserve the apostolic message" through the literary device of a testament is valid, but not to the extent that proponents of the pseudonymity theory might think. Largely ignored in discussions of authorship is the crucial element of apostolicity, which does not extend to well-meaning "interpreters" several generations removed from the apostle.

That the documents of the NT resist our attempts to be classified with nonapostolic pseudepigrapha is by no means an arbitrary ecclesiastical verdict. Rather, it brings us to the heart of the *a priori* character of Christian faith and the authority upon which this faith rests. The Christian community from the beginning has recognized that the NT documents are bound up with revelation that is imparted within history. In precisely what does this authority initially consist?

One cannot speak of the NT as authoritative apart from the concept of apostolicity and the apostolic tradition (cf. 1 Cor. 15:3-7). Apostles are authoritative inasmuch as they are witnesses to the life, death, and resurrection of Jesus. "You are Peter, and on this rock I will build my church" (Matt. 16:18) is not a statement to Peter in the abstract; rather, it is a declaration that confirms his confession: he is representative of the apostles. In light of Christ's once-for-all redemptive act, there can be "no other foundation" (1 Cor. 3:11), as Paul seeks to impress upon the church at Corinth.

How aware of this authoritative foundation were the writers of the NT? Or the apostolic fathers? Modern biblical scholarship broadly assumes that this awareness, if it existed, had limited bearing on the church's literary canon. Yet the implications of the apostolic office are weighty. Strictly speaking, "apostolic pseudepigrapha" is a contradiction in terms, since not even well-intended literary motives, expressed under the name of an apostle generations removed from the earthly ministry of Jesus Christ, warrant apostolic authority. Given the role of the apostle in the early church, "scholars cannot have it both ways. They cannot identify apostolic letters as pseudepigrapha and at the same time declare them to be innocent products with a right to a place in the canon" (Ellis: 224).

That an epistle such as 2 Peter might come from the apostle in the historical setting illuminated by the text is not to say *how* it might come from him. It is perfectly reasonable to suggest, with E. I. Robson (296) earlier this century, that the work of an amanuensis or secretary helps to account for purported "inconsistencies" between 2 Peter and "the authentic Petrine tradition." Writes G. J. Bahr:

> The influence of the secretary would be even greater if he were left to compose the letter himself along the general lines laid down by the author. The result would be that the letter might represent the basic thought of the author, but not necessarily his terminology or style. . . . It may be that the discrepancy between what Paul wrote and what he spoke was due to the abilities of a secretary who was expert in the composition of letters. (475-476)

Indeed, evidence of the involvement of an amanuensis in the formation the NT's documents is credible based on statements found in the Pauline, pastoral, and Petrine epistles (Rom. 16:22; 1 Cor. 16:21; Gal. 6:11; Col. 4:18; 2 Thess. 3:17; 2 Tim. 4:1; Philem. 19; and 1 Pet. 5:12).

For Jerome, writing in the late fourth century, the difference in style and expression between 1 and 2 Peter could be accounted for on the basis of different amanuenses (Letter 120, "To Hebidia," p. 224). We recognize that 2 Peter, despite its difficulties, was ultimately accepted and confessed by the church fathers as canonical, while other works in the end were deemed spurious. Hence, the theory of an amanuensis rather than pseudonymity would be more in line with historic Christian tradition.

Pseudonymity theory ranges from a flat rejection of Petrine authorship—the conviction of most scholars over the last 150 years—to a view represented by Bauckham, who claims that 2 Peter reflects the apostle's message recast after his death by a faithful interpreter in the form of a last testament. Yet, as Green rightly notes, it is asking too much of us to believe that a pseudepigraphon was surreptitiously inserted into the canon of a church built on eyewitness testimony of the apostles (34). After all, we possess no other clearly orthodox pseudepigrapha. If the literary convention of pseudonymity was widespread in the first century, then it is difficult to understand why personal marks of authentication, such as one finds in 2 Peter 1:13-14, were employed in the first place. After all, such marks were prominent among heretical sects.

Guthrie summarizes our dilemma. Ultimately, the interpretive choice appears to be between two alternatives. Either the epistle is genuinely Petrine, with or without the aid of an amanuensis or secretary; or it is pseudonymous, in which case the historical situation and motive are obscured (840-841). If 2 Peter is indeed pseudonymous, its author, as Green has observed, must have been sophisticated in the extreme to produce so delicate a touch (89). That 2 Peter, in the end, has achieved universal acceptance (and thus canonicity) reflects acknowledgment both of its apostolic content as well as apostolic authorship. This consensus, until relatively recently, has been that of the church since the end of the second century. Because the epistle mirrors a situation not unlike that of Jude, it requires no date that is much later (Beasley-Murray: 85).

THE ETHICAL LIST AS A TEACHING DEVICE The ethical vocabulary of 2 Peter 1:5-7 presents us with a fascinating glimpse into the moral thought-world of Hellenistic culture. Although the grouping of ethical values into lists surfaces in diverse cultures of antiquity, the rhetorical use of ethical lists comes into full bloom in the moral doctrine of the Socratic philosophers, and particularly in the teaching of the Stoa. The use of the ethical catalog by NT writers derives from its function in Hellenistic and Jewish literature. With some exceptions, the theological motivation behind use of the catalog is owing primarily to the thought world of Hellenistic Judaism, in which the dualism of the righteous and the unrighteous comes to expression. In the NT, both strands—Hellenistic form and Jewish theological assumptions—merge in the Christian ethical tradition.

The recording of ethical lists in the Hellenistic world extends formally from the Homeric era. Preliterary types of the catalog that can be cited include crime registers, lists of character traits of those born under certain constellations, memorials to the deceased, and decrees of honor. A large number of inscriptions, especially gravesites and memorials, list virtues in honor of the said individual. Honors were typically bestowed upon military generals, doctors, judges, and officeholders.

The emergence of ethical catalogs in the Hellenistic period can be seen initially within an "academic" context and later in a more popular one. The ethical list has a decisive rhetorical function. It is a form of speech intended to instill praise or shame in the hearer or listener and incite to action. Vice and virtue lists perform this practical function equally in pagan Stoic as well as Christian usage. Because the Christian message was formed against the backdrop of Greco-Roman moral-social conditions, touchpoints between Stoic thought and the NT are numerous (e.g., Acts 17:16-34). While the two systems are radically different in the way each perceives the *means* to the ethical life, they nonetheless share common ethical terms, though the religious contexts in which they appear provide them with important nuances of meaning.

As a pedagogical device, the ethical catalog derives its force from a standardization of human or behavioral types. Over time, popular moral philosophers expanded the form of ethical catalogs to include new elements, especially additional vices. Preaching moral uplift in the marketplace, peripatetics found ethical lists to be a practical and effective rhetorical tool. In popular usage, the lists were far from the convoluted philosophical constructs that had been employed by "scholastic" moral philosophers. Practical needs of the masses propelled the use and extension of ethical lists in a popular format. People saw themselves in these lists, whether by vice or virtue.

In their form, Stoic ethical catalogs do not possess a rigid hierarchy of virtues so as to suggest a moral progression leading to an ethical climax, even when all the virtues stand in close connection with each other and constitute a natural unity. No particular order or arrangement of virtues came to characterize popular usage of lists, although a play on words was frequently achieved through the word order. Further, Stoic vice or virtue lists were not meant to be all-inclusive. The presence or absence of particular virtues in the list simply reflected the values or particular emphasis of the author.

Vice and virtue lists in the NT function in different ways. They may be used for the purpose of antithesis (e.g., Gal. 5:19-23; James 3:13-18), contrast (Titus 3:1-7), polemics (1 Tim. 1:9-10; 6:3-5; 2 Tim. 3:2-5), or instruction (2 Pet. 1:5-7). Occasionally, though not necessarily, alliteration or assonance, cadence, and inclusio (two similar terms bracketing a section) enhance their descriptions. A unified structure is hard to detect, and rhetorical motivation is not always apparent, with the notable exception of Philippians 4:8. In other texts, the virtues listed seem to build on one another and demonstrate a progression of sorts (2 Cor. 6:4-10; Gal. 5:22-23; Eph. 4:2-6; Col. 3:12-14; 2 Pet. 1:5-7).

In the Petrine catalog, faith can be seen as the foundation of the Christian ethic and love as the climax. The NT writers may be understood to appropriate a standard device for underscoring the necessity of the moral life as proof of one's profession, both to the community and to the world.

While the form and function of the ethical list is borrowed by NT writers, it should be emphasized that the intellectual element of Greek philosophical reflection is not carried over into the NT by its writers. The reason for this can be traced to the fundamental divergence of Stoic and Christian outlooks. To the Greek mind, ethical requirements do not issue from a source of transcendent moral authority; instead, they are the fruit of rational education and knowledge, by which one comes to realize the fullness of human nature. Acquiring virtue for the Stoic is an absolute good, a goal in and of itself. Hence, the categories of sin and guilt—constituting the core of Hebrew and Christian theological understanding—have no real place in Stoic thought. While the Stoic is called to reflect, the Christian is called to repent and be redeemed. That is something the human mind is incapable of producing by itself.

VIRTUE AS A THEME OF 2 PETER We have considered the relative abundance of ethical language and categories employed in the epistle. The writer is burdened that his readers cultivate an ethos which "offers proof" (1:11) of a virtuous lifestyle. This proof is both to the one who has provided abundant resources for life and godliness (1:3-4, 11) and to the moral skeptic (3:3-7). *What sort of persons should you be in holy conduct and piety?* (3:11). That is the ringing question the readers, in the end, are left to ponder.

Tracing the theme of the moral life throughout the letter helps us see the unity of 2 Peter, and consequently, the author's purpose in writing. Following the greeting, which accentuates received righteousness and grace, a catalog of virtues (1:5-7) is introduced. This list uses terms that also appear in philosophic and pagan religious formulations. Significantly, the language of the mysteries surfaces again in 1:16, where the writer speaks of himself as *epoptēs, an eyewitness* of the Transfiguration, *while we were on the holy mountain.* It is noteworthy that in spite of three Synoptic narratives recording the Transfiguration, 2 Peter 1:16 is the only NT appearance of the word *epoptēs.* The reason may lie in the fact that the term is used in a technical sense for the highest degree of enlightenment in the Eleusinian mysteries. If 2 Peter is addressed to an audience in Asia Minor, use of the term *epoptēs* may also have a strategic rhetorical effect.

The catalog of virtues itself (1:5-7), meant to outline the contours of Christian *life and godliness* (1:3), includes several commonly cited features that appear in standard Stoic virtue lists and are adapted to the Christian tradition of exhortation. Although Stoic terms are used, they serve a distinctly Christian purpose, and their content is to be understood in a framework of Christian faith. The letter's greeting clarifies and highlights grace, an acute departure from the Stoic understanding of fate and ultimate things. Both Stoic and Christian moral traditions urge styles of moral progress. The latter, however, are less rigid and based on divine grace and self-discipline, rather than on human achievement alone.

The writer claims that if believers possess these virtues (1:8-9), they will prevent ineffective and unfruitful living. If they lack the virtues, however, they are *blind* and neglecting truth (1:9). At issue is moral responsibility.

The language of exhortation presses to the fore throughout 2 Peter 1: *for this reason* (1:5); *if these things are yours* (1:8); *anyone lacking these things* (1:9); *if you do these things* (1:10); *for this reason I intend to remind you, even though you know them already and are established in the truth that has come to you* (1:12); *I think it right to stir you up* (1:13); *recall these things* (1:15).

Second Peter 1 reflects a markedly Gentile social environment in which the Christian community finds itself. The rhetorical effect of this ethical terminology, easily lost on the modern reader, would have been unmistakable to its intended audience. Theirs is not a faith that is void of the moral life. Instead, the distinctly Christian ethic is to shine forth in bold contrast to surrounding pagan culture.

Tragically, in the view of the author, some have disregarded the divine *promises* (1:4; implied in 1:9, 12, 15). As a result of accommodation to the world, they have *forgotten* their *cleansing from past sins* (1:9). These are to confirm their election through a robust Christian ethic (1:10). Worse yet, some are even aggressively announcing that there is no moral authority to which they must give account (2:1; 3:3-5).

Second Peter features the use of moral types and graphic sketches of the opponents. The defining features of the pastoral problem, outlined in 2:10b-18 immediately following examples from the past, are *licentiousness* [twice], *defiling passion, squalor, moral depravity, corruption, seduction,* and *lawlessness.* The examples of 2:4-10a are united by the moral depths to which the people sank. They are relevant to the present, given the description of the reprobates who appear to be reveling in a like condition (2:13).

The Noah and Balaam typology indicate that not doctrinal strife so much as ethical lapse is the focus of the writer's polemic. This combines with two further clues (2:19; 2:20-22) as to the source of the pastoral problem. The opponents are antinomian in character (rejecting moral standards) and boast of their freedom from moral constraints. In casting off divine moral authority, these individuals actually become *slaves* (2:19) to their own *lusts* (2:18) and *pleasure* (2:13).

The same combination (claiming to be free but really enslaved) was well-known in Hellenistic ethics. Christians, in looking back on their preconversion state, see even greater meaning in this combination than the Greek moralist. Second Peter 2:19, as 2:20-22, describes moral degeneration that characterizes pagan lifestyle, a decidedly pre-Christian condition. The implication for the readers, rhetorically speaking, is that even moral pagans are better off than some in the community who have claimed to be believers.

As already noted, traditional commentary has read 2 Peter 3 through the lens of an eschatological framework, normally interpreting this material to be evidence of doctrinal deformation in need of adjustment. Viewed structurally, 3:1-13 consists of the following components: reminder terminology, a caricature of the hardened moral skeptic, the declaration that moral accountability is beyond dispute, and pastoral remarks concerning theodicy (the ways of God in dealing with people).

Viewed theologically, the opponents are not questioning the *timing* of the parousia (second coming of Christ); instead, they deny that it is even coming at all. They reject accountability and coming judgment. The writer vigorously asserts that Christ is surely coming. The day of moral reckoning and death, as aptly stated by Mayor (211), removes the skeptic from the realm of illusion and into the sphere of reality. On this basis, hortatory language can be inserted once more, to warn the saints. The writer thus concludes, *I am arousing you by way of reminder; . . . what sort of people should you be?*

(3:11). *Therefore, . . . make every effort . . .* (3:14).

The affirmation of cosmic renewal in 3:13 mirrors interplay of pagan and Judeo-Christian cosmology, behind which stands a fundamental question: What is the relationship of human beings to matter? Behind this question stands an even more fundamental question: What is the relationship of *moral* human beings to matter? Yet in the strictest sense, cosmology and eschatology are not being showcased. Instead, the author's purpose is to develop a response to a caricature of the moral skeptic (3:4). Because the opponents are championing moral self-determination (2:1-2; [implicit in 2:4-10a;] 2:13, 15, 18-19), they must justify their ethical departure. In this context, the caricature in 3:3-5 presents the moral question from the standpoint of someone on the outside.

What's more, they *deliberately ignore* past examples of divine retribution (2:5-6), which typologically point to the ultimate day of moral reckoning (3:7). The occurrence twice in chapter 3 of the verb *heuriskō*, "to find out" (3:10, 14), is significant. In 3:10, the text reads: *and the earth and all deeds done on it will be revealed.* The point of the teaching is not so much to adjust theology; instead, it is to stress that judgment will be the expression of a *judicial* process and a *moral* reckoning.

A unitary reading of 2 Peter brings us to an important determination. What plagues the community hearing this epistle are ethical lapse and apostasy, and not the doctrinal emphasis (on the delay of the parousia) presupposed by "early Catholic" proponents. Such apostasy appears already before the second century. The combined ingredients of literary style and hortatory language, Stoic and mystic terms, the catalog of virtues, moral typology, and caricatures of the adversaries—these all add up to a cultural setting permeated by Hellenistic influence. Moral corruption, licentiousness, antinomianism, and irreverence vex the church set within a pluralistic society. For this reason, moral skepticism rather than dissatisfaction with orthodoxy (against Kelly: 305) is the object of the author's highly stylized polemic.

Given the community's need for orthopraxy or right living, which in turn informs the author's literary strategy, the introductory material in 2 Peter may be understood as presenting a window into the social location of the audience. Throughout the epistle, the writer is exposing a fundamental denial of moral self-responsibility. In its advanced stages, this denial has resulted in the apostasy of certain members of the community. It is true that "theological justification" (heresy) necessarily accompanies any departure from the faith. Yet apostasy—an ethical departure from the moral truth of Christian revelation—is the scourge of this community. The present situation calls for a roundly prophetic and eminently pastoral word of exhortation. This exhortation is aimed foremost at enunciating the ethical foundations of the Christian faith.

Bibliography for 2 Peter

APOT. *See* Charles, R. H.

Aristotle
1986 *Nicomachean Ethics*. Trans. M. Ostwald. New York: Macmillan.

Augsburger, Myron S.
1990 *The Christ-Shaped Conscience*. Wheaton: Victor.

Bahr, G. J.
1966 "Paul and Letter Writing in the First Century." *Catholic Biblical Quarterly* 28:475-476.

Barth, Karl
1960 "The Christian Community and the Civil Community." In *Community, State, and Church*, 124-142. Ed. W. Herberg. Garden City, N.Y.: Doubleday (Anchor).

Bauckham, Richard J.
1983 *Jude, 2 Peter*. Word Biblical Commentary, 50. Waco: Word.

Bauer, W., W. F. Arndt, and F. W. Gingrich
1979 *A Greek-English Lexicon of the New Testament and Other Early Christian Literature*. Chicago: Univ. of Chicago Press.

Beasley-Murray, G. R.
1965 *The General Epistles: James, 1 Peter, Jude, 2 Peter*. London: Lutterworth; New York: Abingdon.

Bigg, Charles
1922 *A Critical and Exegetical Commentary on the Epistles of St. Peter and St. Jude.* International Critical Commentary. New York: Scribner.

Burke, Thomas J.
1986 "The Fundamental Principles of Biblical Ethics." In *The Christian Vision: Man and Morality*, 25-46. Ed. T. J. Burke. Hillsdale, Mich.: Hillsdale College.

Calvin, John
1959 *Commentaries on the Catholic Epistles*. Trans. J. Owen. Grand Rapids: Eerdmans.

Charles, J. Daryl
1995a "Engaging the (Neo) Pagan Mind: Paul's Confrontation with Athenian Culture as a Model for Cultural Apologetics." *Trinity Journal* 16/2:115-134.
1995b "The Scandal of the Evangelical Mind: A Symposium." *First Things* (March): 38-39.
1997 *Virtue Amidst Vice*. Sheffield: Sheffield Academic Press.
1998 "The Language and Logic of Virtue in 2 Peter 1:5-7." *Bulletin of Biblical Research* 8:55-73.
Charles, R. H.
1913 *The Apocrypha and Pseudepigrapha of the Old Testament*. 2 vols. Oxford: Clarendon.
Chester, Andrew, and Ralph P. Martin
1994 *The Theology of the Letters of James, Peter, and Jude*. Cambridge: Cambridge Univ. Press.
Cranfield, C. E. B.
1960 *I and II Peter and Jude*. Torch Bible Commentary. London: SCM.
Danker, Frederick W.
1978 "2 Peter 1: A Solemn Decree." *Catholic Biblical Quarterly* 40:64-82.
Desjardins, Michel
1987 "The Portrayal of the Dissidents in 2 Peter and Jude: Does It Tell Us More About the 'Ungodly' than the 'Godly'?" *Journal for the Study of the New Testament* 30:89-102.
Ellis, E. E.
1992 "Pseudonymity and Canonicity of New Testament Documents." In *Worship, Theology and Ministry in the Early Church: Essays in Honor of R. P. Martin*. Journal for the Study of the New Testament Supplement Series, 87. Sheffield: JSOT Press.
Fornberg, Tord
1977 *An Early Church in a Pluralistic Society: A Study of 2 Peter*. Coniectanea biblica, New Testament, 9. Lund: Gleerup.
Gaffin, Richard B., Jr.
1988 "The New Testament as Canon." In *Inerrancy and Hermeneutic: A Tradition, a Challenge, a Debate*, 165-183. Ed. H. M. Conn. Grand Rapids: Baker Books.
Green, Michael (E. M. B.)
1960 *2 Peter Reconsidered*. Tyndale New Testament Commentaries. London: Tyndale.
1988 *The Second Epistle General of Peter and the General Epistle of Jude*. Tyndale. Rev. New Testament Commentaries. Leicester: Inter-Varsity; Grand Rapids: Eerdmans.
Gustafson, James M.
1981 *Ethics from a Theocentric Perspective*. Chicago: Univ. of Chicago Press.
Guthrie, Donald
1990 *New Testament Introduction*. Leicester: Apollos; Downers Grove: InterVarsity.

Hauerwas, Stanley
    1981   A Community of Character. Notre Dame: Univ. of Notre Dame
            Press.
Henry, Carl F. H.
    1982   Christian Personal Ethics. Grand Rapids: Baker Books (reprint).
Hillyer, Norman
    1992   1 and 2 Peter, Jude. Peabody: Hendrickson.
Jerome
    1954   Nicene and Post-Nicene Fathers. Early Church Fathers. Ser. 2,
            vol. 6. Grand Rapids: Eerdmans.
Jeschke, Marlin
    1988   Discipling in the Church. Scottdale, Pa.: Herald Press.
Käsemann, Ernst
    1982   "An Apologia for Primitive Christian Eschatology." In Essays on
            New Testament Themes, 169-195. Philadelphia: Fortress.
Kelly, J. N. D.
    1969   A Commentary on the Epistles of Peter and Jude. London:
            Adam & Charles Black.
Lewis, C. S.
    1946   Christian Behavior. New York: Macmillan.
Lewis, J. P.
    1968   A Study of the Interpretation of Noah and the Flood in Jewish
            and Christian Literature. Leiden: Brill.
Luther, Martin
    1957   The Bondage of the Will. Trans. J. I. Packer and O. R.
            Johnston. Westwood: Revell.
MacIntyre, Alasdair
    1981   After Virtue: A Study of Moral Theology. Notre Dame: Univ. of
            Notre Dame Press.
Marshall, I. Howard
    1969   Kept by the Power of God: A Study of Perseverance and
            Falling Away. Minneapolis: Bethany Fellowship.
Martin, Ernest D.
    1993   Colossians, Philemon. Believers Church Bible Commentary.
            Scottdale, Pa.: Herald Press.
Mayor, J. B.
    1907   The Epistle of St. Jude and the Second Epistle of St. Peter.
            New York: Macmillan.
McClendon, James William Jr.
    1988   Ethics: Systematic Theology, vol. 1. Nashville: Abingdon.
Meade, David G.
    1986   Pseudonymity and Canonicity: An Investigation into the
            Relationship of Authorship and Authority in Jewish and Earliest
            Christian Tradition. Tübingen: Mohr.
Meilaender, Gilbert
    1991   Faith and Faithfulness: Basic Themes in Christian Ethics.
            Notre Dame: Univ. of Notre Dame Press.
Menno Simons
    1956   The Complete Writings of Menno Simons. Trans. L. Verduin.
            Ed. J. C. Wenger. Scottdale, Pa.: Herald Press.

Migne, J. P., ed.
    1857-66 *Patrologia Graeca*. Paris: Migne.
Mott, Stephen C.
    1982 *Biblical Ethics and Social Change*. New York and Oxford: Oxford Univ. Press.
Mounce, Robert H.
    1982 *A Living Hope: A Commentary on 1 and 2 Peter*. Grand Rapids: Eerdmans.
Neyrey, Jerome N.
    1980 "The Form and Background of the Polemic in 2 Peter." *Journal of Biblical Literature* 99:407-431.
    1993 *2 Peter, Jude: A New Translation with Introduction and Commentary*. Anchor Bible, 37c. New York: Doubleday.
Niebuhr, H. Richard
    1951 *Christ and Culture*. New York: Harper & Row.
O'Donovan, Oliver
    1986 *Resurrection and the Moral Order*. Leicester: Inter-Varsity; Grand Rapids: Eerdmans.
Ramsey, Paul
    1967 *Deeds and Rules in Christian Ethics*. New York: Charles Scribner's Sons.
Ratzinger, Joseph Cardinal, et al.
    1994 *Catechism of the Catholic Church*. Washington, D.C.: U.S. Catholic Conference.
Reicke, Bo
    1964 *The Epistles of James, Peter, and Jude*. Anchor Bible. Garden City: Doubleday.
Robson, E. I.
    1917 "Composition and Dictation in New Testament Books." *Journal of Theological Studies* 18:228-301.
Sidebottom, E. M.
    1967 *James, Jude, and 2 Peter*. New Century Bible. London: Nelson.
Simons. See Menno
Soards, Marion L.
    1988 "1 Peter, 2 Peter, and Jude as Evidence for a Petrine School." In *Aufstieg und Niedergang der römischen Welt. Geschichte und Kultur Roms im Spiegel der neueren Forschung*. Principate II, vol. 25, part 5, pages 3826-3849. Ed. W. Hasse. Berlin and New York: Walter de Gruyter.
Vermes, Geza
    1973 "The Story of Balaam." In *Scripture and Tradition in Judaism*, 127-177. Leiden: Brill.
Yoder, John Howard
    1996 "How H. Richard Niebuhr Reasons: A Critique of *Christ and Culture*." In *Authentic Transformation: A New Vision of Christ and Culture*, 31-89. Ed. Glen H. Stassen. Nashville: Abingdon.
    1998 "Peace Without Eschatology?" In *The Royal Priesthood: Essays Ecclesiological and Ecumenical*, 143-167. Scottdale, Pa.: Herald Press.

Selected Resources for 2 Peter

Bauckham, Richard J. *Jude, 2 Peter*. Word Biblical Commentary, 50. Waco, Tex.: Word, 1983. A rich, comprehensive exegetical commentary and necessary part of every scholar's and pastor-teacher's library.

Charles, J. Daryl. *Virtue Amidst Vice*. Journal for the Study of the New Testament Supplemental Series. Sheffield: Sheffield Academic Press, 1997. An in-depth examination of the virtue motif in 2 Peter. Includes an appendix on the nature of apostasy and the relationship between predestination and perseverance.

Chester, Andrew, and, Ralph P. Martin. *The Theology of the Letters of James, Peter, and Jude*. Cambridge: Cambridge Univ. Press, 1994. A helpful and concise treatment of theological themes. A welcome addition to the scholar's and layperson's library.

Fornberg, Tord. *An Early Church in a Pluralistic Society: A Study of 2 Peter*. Coniectanea biblica, New Testament. Lund: Gleerup, 1977. An excellent study of the epistle. Considers evidence from the text that suggests a Gentile social location of the audience.

Green, Michael (E. M. B.). *2 Peter Reconsidered*. London: Tyndale, 1960. Provides a re-examination of the traditional scholarly consensus that 2 Peter is pseudonymous. Argues for the epistle as authentically Petrine.

Green, Michael (E. M. B.). *The Second Epistle General of Peter and the General Epistle of Jude*. Revised. Tyndale New Testament

Commentaries. Leicester: Inter-Varsity; Grand Rapids: Eerdmans, 1988. Along with Bauckham, a must for the personal library of both the scholar and the layperson. Written from an evangelical perspective.

Hillyer, Norman. *1 and 2 Peter, Jude*. Peabody: Hendrickson, 1992. Useful commentary with additional exegetical notes. Written from an evangelical perspective.

Kelly, J. N. D. *A Commentary on the Epistles of Peter and Jude*. London: Adam & Charles Black, 1969. See Selected Resources for 1 Peter.

Neyrey, Jerome N. *2 Peter, Jude: A New Translation with Introduction and Commentary*. Anchor Bible Commentary, revised edition. New York: Doubleday, 1993. Exegetical commentary that reads 2 Peter using the interpretive rubric of praise and shame.

Reicke, Bo. *The Epistles of James, Peter, and Jude*. Anchor Bible. Garden City: Doubleday, 1964. Standard, valuable commentary representing historical-critical scholarship.

Overview of Jude

The Neglected Epistle

The message and world of Jude are strangely unfamiliar to modern readers. Whether among lay people, pastors, teachers, or seminarians, this unfamiliarity is conspicuous. With good reason, the letter of Jude has been called "the most neglected book in the NT" (Rowston: 554). Most readers of the Bible, puzzled by cryptic references to Enoch, Michael the archangel, the devil, and a slate of OT characters, are acquainted at best with the letter's doxology.

Although most of the NT epistles mirror something of the historical situation and pastoral needs lying behind their writing, Jude offers little in the way of clues. Comprehensive neglect of Jude extends even to serious students of the NT. In the main, biblical scholarship has bypassed a thorough treatment of the letter. Where it is studied, Jude is usually lumped together with the other catholic (general) epistles or subsumed under the study of 2 Peter, because of parallel material in the two letters. The assumption typically follows that Jude and 2 Peter reflect nearly identical historical occasions, with the later writing—normally held to be 2 Peter—presumably exhibiting either a considerable lack of literary originality or the need to "smooth out" particular features in Jude.

The epistle of Jude is an impassioned exhortation to a church that is being compromised. The writer's concerns, while touching on doctrine, are foremost ethical in nature. Posing a threat to the Christian community is a self-indulgent group that spurns spiritual authority and arrogantly appropriates its own authority.

The reader finds it impossible to identify precisely who these schismatics are. Nevertheless, Jude grants us insight into the dangers they pose. They retain a religious guise while supporting a lifestyle of licentiousness. Jude further assumes a minimal acquaintance among his readers with Jewish apocalyptic tradition that is characteristic of the intertestamental period [Apocalyptic Literature]. For this reason, the fate of the ungodly is spelled out in apocalyptic terms. To this end, the writer employs themes rooted squarely in the OT—election, predestination and divine foreknowledge, apostasy, theophany (a visible manifestation of God), judgment by fire, the day of the Lord, and divine kingship.

The literary form of Jude is just as important as its message. Effective literature embodies meaning in a way that allows the reader to experience it. With passion and great eloquence, Jude engages his audience. He effectively exploits the imaginative and sensory dimensions of language. Taken together, graphic symbolism, wordplay, frequent alliteration, parallelism, the use of triplets, typology, midrash (explanation), and woe-cry all add force to the writer's burden as he addresses pastoral needs of the Christian community. The modern reader becomes witness to a literary-rhetorical artist at work (Watson: 32-76; Wolthuis: 126-134; J. D. Charles, 1993b: 25-48)—all this within the incredibly brief span of only twenty-five verses.

Structure of the Epistle

In considering the structure of Jude, one is struck by the writer's repeated use of particular catchwords. These terms are rhetorically significant and not arbitrarily chosen (Bauckham, 1983:3-6; J. D. Charles, 1993b: 30-32). In a mere twenty-five verses, nine terms occur five times or more, with five of these appearing seven or more times (J. D. Charles, 1993b: 30). Consider the following survey of vocabulary, based on the Greek text:

- ungodly/ungodliness: Jude 4, 15 (3 x), 18
- you: 3 (3 x), 5 (2 x), 12, 17, 18, 20 (2 x), 21 (yourselves), 24
- keep/guard: 1, 6 (2 x), 13, 21, 24
- these: 4 (some), 8, 10, 11, 12, 14, 16, 19
- Lord: 4, 5, 9, 14, 17, 21, 25
- holy: 3, 14, 20 (2 x), 24 (blameless)
- love/beloved: 1, 2, 3, 12, 17, 20, 21
- mercy/show mercy: 2, 21, 22, 23
- judgment/condemnation: 4, 6, 9, 15

A conspicuous use not only of catchwords but conjunctions as well reflects conscious deliberation on the part of the writer in the structuring of his material. Consider the logical progression of Jude's argumentation within sections of material as well as between them:

- Jude 1-2, greeting: To those who are called, . . . beloved . . .
- 3-4, occasion/purpose: For certain individuals have slipped in . . .
- 5-19, illustrative: Now I wish to remind you . . .
    paradigms, reminder: for the Lord destroyed . . .
                                       and the angels who did not keep . . .
                                       but rather abandoned . . .
                                       just as Sodom and Gomorrah . . .
                                            gave themselves over . . .
                                       Yet in the same manner,
                                            these dreamers also defile . . .
                                       But Michael did not dare . . .
                                       but rather he said . . .
                                       yet these blaspheme . . .
                                       for they walk . . .
                                       Indeed, Enoch . . . prophesied . . .
                                       but you, beloved, remember . . .
                                       for they said . . .
- 20-23, exhortation: But you, beloved, build yourselves . . .
                                       pray . . .
                                       keep yourselves . . .
                                       and . . . be merciful . . .
                                       and save . . .
                                       and show mercy . . .
- 24-25, closing: Now to the One is able . . .

Literary Character

In its own right, Jude is a remarkable piece of literature. Rich and original in style and vocabulary, this short letter is "filled with flowing words of heavenly grace" (Origen, *Comm. in Ev. Sec. Matt.* 17.30 [Migne, *PG*, 13.1571]). It not only displays an astounding brevity but a thorough acquaintance with and calculated use of Jewish literary sources. The literary milieu of Jude is chiefly Palestinian Jewish-Christian. For his purpose, the writer marshals extracanonical source material—notably, 1 Enoch (mid-second century B.C.–A.D. first century) and the Assumption of Moses (first or second century)—as well as OT figures. He frames it all in a concise, well-conceived polemic that exhorts the faithful and warns the unfaithful.

Although not a single explicit citation from the OT is to be found in Jude, the letter is nonetheless replete with prophetic typology. No fewer than nine subjects—unbelieving Israel, the fallen angels, Sodom and Gomorrah, Michael the archangel, Moses, Cain, Balaam, Korah, and Enoch—are employed against ungodly figures of this type. The ungodly have "wormed their way in" (Kelly: 248) among the faithful and thus pose a danger to the believing community. It is these unfaithful (Jude 4, 8, 10, 12, 14, 16, 19) who are the focus of Jude's invective.

The epistle of Jude bears some similarity to the commentary on the OT found in the *pesharim* or commentaries of the Qumran community (Ellis: 226; Bauckham, 1983:4-5,46-47; 1988:303 305). Jude links types from the past with corollaries in the present, to confront need prophetically and pastorally. This is achieved logistically, as already noted, by the use of catchwords—e.g., *these, keep, ungodly, judgment, error, blaspheme*—which form links in Jude's polemical argument.

Commentators have traditionally focused attention on both the notable literary parallels in Jude and 2 Peter as well the order in which these appear:

- a greeting of peace being multiplied (Jude 2 // 2 Pet. 1:2)
- denial of Christ's lordship (1 // 2:1)
- fallen angels imprisoned in chains of darkness, awaiting judgment (6 // 2:4)
- Sodom and Gomorrah (7 // 2:6)
- defiling flesh, despising authority, blaspheming angelic beings (8 // 2:10-11)
- angelic restraint before the Lord (9 // 2:11)
- blasphemers as brute beasts, ignorant of what they speak (10 // 2:12)
- following the way of Balaam (11 // 2:15)
- spots/blemishes in the love feasts (12 // 2:13)
- clouds and water (12 // 2:17)
- blackest darkness (13 // 2:17)
- great, swelling speech (16 // 2:18)
- lust of the flesh (16 // 2:18)
- being foretold by the apostles (17 // 3:2)
- scoffers in the last days (18 // 3:3)

Since Jude appears like an abstract of 2 Peter, most commentators explain the parallel material by holding that 2 Peter used (and supplemented) Jude, rather than vice versa. Some, however, hold to a third view, that both epistles employ a common written source (Reicke, 1964:192-194; Hillyer: 13-14). Such an explanation is plausible.

In any case, the use of the material in Jude differs from its use in 2 Peter. One survey of this literary dependence has shown that of the total number of words in both epistles, 70 percent of the vocabulary is different (Guthrie: 925). This observation lends support to the notion that the historical situations behind Jude and 2 Peter are different and unique, and thus the intents of the two writers.

Copying a literary source, while editing 70 percent of the material in the process, seems rather unlikely. Furthermore, two different social situations are indicated by the epistles. Evidence of this includes Jude's reference to *James*, his use of material from the OT and Jewish tradition, and his rampant use of triplets. On the other hand, 2 Peter employs a Hellenistic rhetorical device (a catalog of virtues), a conspicuously pagan-mystical vocabulary, a reference to *Tartaros*, common proverbial imagery, and chronological ordering of historical examples.

Authorship and Date

Scholarship has traditionally considered Jude to be of pseudonymous authorship, a reflection of the subapostolic era, and thus assigns a relatively late date to it. This dating has ranged from the late-first century to mid-second century. Several factors have contributed to this scholarly consensus: Jude's literary relationship to 2 Peter (normally viewed as second-century), the lack of historical markers in the epistle, the strident nature of Jude's warnings against antinomians (people rejecting moral standards), and the assumption that Jude exemplifies a second-century response to Gnosticism. The view of Mayor a century ago is representative: "The communications of the Apostles had now ceased, either by their death or by their removal from Jerusalem" (cxlv).

The literary relationship between Jude and 2 Peter, rather than determining authorship, raises important questions about the author's purpose in writing and his selection of material. Both epistles may be drawing from a third document or source, in much the same way that Paul, writing in the first century, could make use of traditional material on occasion from pagan proverbs, poets, apocryphal legends, and Stoic or Epicurean philosophers.

Recognizing the amount of the epistle that focuses on denouncing the unfaithful (Jude 5-19), some have concluded that Jude reflects a later period when the church is encountering mature forms of heresy. In the second century, however, the writer would be less likely to allude to OT characters and intertestamental Jewish sources because of the church's expansion in the Gentile world, where fewer people would know them. In a first-century Palestinian environment, on the other hand, these would be pregnant with meaning. It is a notable tendency of the NT writers—especially in Matthew, James, Hebrews, Jude, 1 and 2 Peter—to quote or allude to the OT.

An "early Catholic" interpretation of Jude and 2 Peter has been broadly assumed by NT scholars, owing greatly to the theological assumptions expressed in 1952 by Ernst Käsemann. Along with other theologians, Käsemann sought to explain the church's reaction to incipient gnosticism. Käsemann's "early Catholicism" presupposes the existence of an ecclesiastical hierarchy several generations after the apostles. The chief rationale for an "early Catholic" reading is the belief that a "creedal" faith had emerged, guarded by the growing prominence of church leaders, to counter heresy and a fading hope in Christ's return (1952: 272-296). This, it is argued, was necessary in order to bridge the gap between the apostolic and postapostolic eras.

Yet, as one NT commentator has noted, "early Catholicism" wrongly assumes what it seeks to prove (Green: 53). Nothing in Jude requires an "early Catholic" reading of the epistle. Moreover, the character of Jude's dispute with the opponents is more one of moral obligation than doctrinal heterodoxy (Bauckham, 1983: 9) [cf. Virtue as Theme, essay for 2 Peter].

In the second and third centuries, Gnosticism had developed into sophisticated schools of thought, with elaborate myths appearing in various documents. However, its seeds were already evident by the mid-first century (Martin: 289-290). First Corinthians and Colossians provide ample evidence of church leaders' efforts to counter gnostic tendencies. Furthermore, Jude alludes to what the apostles have said (legein) and not what they have written (graphein). Nothing in Jude requires a considerable chronological gap between the apostolic and subapostolic era.

In spite of its brevity, Jude is rich in Christology, particularly its lordship Christology (Jude 4, 9, 14, 17, 21, 25). The readers are eagerly awaiting the appearance of Christ's mercy and eternal life (23). The hope for the Lord's return (the parousia) is very much alive in Jude, contrary to the supposition of most scholars. Hence, the language of lordship and the focus on the Lord's return clearly place Jude squarely within a first-century NT environment, alongside writings such as the Corinthian and Thessalonian correspondence.

Finally, all of the exhortations in the epistle are addressed to the hearers. Not a word is present that indicates the need for church officials to intervene, as one would expect in the second century. Jude's readers themselves are to deal with the problem at hand. They are to keep themselves in the love and mercy of God. Hence, finally, an "early Catholic" reading of Jude is found wanting.

At the advent of the Christian era, the name Jude *(Ioudas)* was commonplace among the Jews. The writer identifies himself as *a brother of James* (Jude 1). The NT mentions several men with the name *James:* James the son of Zebedee (Matt. 10:2), James the son of Alphaeus and one of the twelve (Matt. 10:3), James the brother of Jesus (Matt. 13:55), James the younger and son of Mary (Mark 15:40), James the father of Judas the apostle (Luke 6:16; Acts 1:13), and James the author of the NT epistle (James 1:1).

Matthew 13:55 links James and Jude as brothers of Jesus: "his brothers James and Joseph and Simon and Judas." Thus, there is good reason to identify the James of Jude 1 with the brother of Jesus. According to tradition (cf. Acts 15:13-21; Gal. 2:9; 1 Cor. 15:7), this James became a leader in the Jerusalem church and was stoned by the Sanhedrin in the year 62 (Josephus, *Ant.* 20.200). If Jude was younger than James, a date of composition falling in the 60s or 70s is likely.

Clement of Alexandria tells us that the author of this epistle is Jude, the brother of James, the Lord's brother. The same claim is made by Origen, Athanasius, Jerome, and Augustine. Given Paul's allusion in Galatians 1:19 to "James the Lord's brother," it is a reasonable assumption that the Lord's brothers were widely known, particularly in Palestine.

In his *Church History,* Eusebius relates a story told by Hegesippus: the grandsons of "Jude the brother of the Lord" had been accused by the emperor Domitian (81-96) of being revolutionaries (3.19-20). The grandsons, according to Hegesippus, eventually became bishops in the church. Some commentators, favoring a second-century composition of the letter, use this as evidence to support the claim that Jude the Lord's brother would not have lived long enough to be the author. Nevertheless, this tradition related by Eusebius does in fact square with NT chronology. Mayor, earlier this century, showed that Jude could have been in his early 70s at the beginning of Domitian's reign. After our weighing of all these matters, the epistle of Jude mirrors no inherent conflict with NT chronology.

Jude 1-4

The Author, His Audience and Purpose for Writing

PREVIEW

The introductory verses contain little in the way of historical indicators. They nevertheless supply the reader with a backdrop against which Jude finds it necessary to write. Jude's choice of words is concise and deliberate, his tone is impassioned, and his burden is highly pastoral. We can assume that urgent needs in the Christian community have come to his attention. They require an immediate response that is far more hortatory than he had originally intended (Jude 3).

Of the twenty-seven books of the NT, *twenty* are epistolary in genre, with two of the remaining seven—Acts and Hebrews—containing epistolary material. The epistolary genre is an important literary form of the NT, even though over half of the New Testament consists of the Gospels and the nonepistolary parts of Acts, Hebrews, and Revelation. More than any other genre, it mirrors a genuine, heartfelt relationship between writers and readers. Students of the NT benefit greatly from becoming better acquainted with ancient letter writing, for it plays an important role in ancient rhetoric (Malherbe: 1-6). In this regard, Jude, despite its brevity, is a classic illustration. *How* a message is expressed cannot be separated from the *what* of its content. Meaning is conveyed and contextualized by means of literary form. NT writers, just as secular counterparts of their day, incarnated their message in literary forms that demand careful scrutiny.

The epistle of Jude serves to cultivate faithfulness among true believers who are surrounded by apostasy. Both intimate pastoral concern and vehement denunciation are present in the letter. The faithful are strengthened and exhorted by means of graphic depictions of the ungodly as well as by direct admonitions. Following the greeting, the body of the letter recalls the fate of examples from the past whose lapses resulted in divine judgment. In the epistle's greeting, the readers are necessarily reminded of their *true identity*. Thereafter, they will be reminded of the sure and binding power of apostolic teaching that undergirds them.

OUTLINE

Opening Salutation, Jude 1-2

Occasion for Writing, Jude 3-4

EXPLANATORY NOTES
Opening 1-2

Most of the letters of the NT conform to the pattern normative in ancient letter writing. The threefold introductory formula, "from A to B, grace," was in broad use from the third century B.C. until the third century A.D. (Exler: 61-62). We find this pattern in Jude (as well as in numerous NT epistles): *Jude, to those called, . . . beloved . . . and kept. . . Mercy, peace, and love be multiplied to you* (Jude 1-2).

One of the primary stylistic features of the epistle, already noted, is Jude's frequent use of triplets. Not one or two but three elements combine to define, illustrate, or underscore truth. The writer's self-designation is *Judas, servant, brother*. In addition, special attributes are ascribed to his audience: *beloved, kept, called*. Three elements, moreover, are contained in the greeting: *mercy, peace, love*. These are but several among the extraordinary twenty sets of triplets in a mere twenty-five verses (J. D. Charles, 1991a: 107-109). Stylistically, the writer begins in a thoroughly calculating fashion.

A curious ingredient in the introduction is the choice of descriptions the writer uses to identify himself—*servant of Jesus Christ* and *brother of James*. If he is in fact the brother of the Lord and Messiah, why not derive authority by writing *brother of the Lord Jesus*? Yet, this confession of humility, remarkable for someone who was a skeptic before the resurrection (John 7:5), illustrates the nature of paradox inherent in the Christian faith. Bond-service brings freedom, abandonment yields blessing, and humble submission grants authority. Out of humility, neither Jude nor James (cf. James 1:1) make any reference to their blood kinship with Jesus.

Jude designates his audience three ways: *those who are called, who are beloved of the Father and kept by Jesus Christ.* These terms are not merely chosen at random. Together they strengthen the believers' confidence in God to fulfill his purpose. Bauckham suggests that these three derive from the Isaianic Servant Songs, with Jude applying them eschatologically to the church (1983:25). Two of the three terms, *beloved* and *kept*, are perfect participles, implying that divine love and keeping power, having been once and for all bestowed, remain in force for those who are called. This is especially important if Jude is to counter any element of apostasy at work within the community by reminding his readers of their high privilege.

Verses 1-2 and 24-25 (the doxology) are like a pair of bookends, an inclusio that effectively reminds the audience of God's ability to preserve. Although divine action in no way negates the element of human responsibility, the faithful can be encouraged. God preserves them for their appointed end; their inheritance is secure. *Keep* is an important catchword throughout the epistle. It occurs five times in twenty-five verses: *tērein* in 1, 6 (2 x), 13, and 21; and *phulassein* (a strengthened form of "guard") in 24.

The triad of virtues listed in verse 2—mercy, peace, and love—is imparted by divine grace alone. Jude's prayer is that his readers abound in these, that they receive them in abundance. Despite the letter's seemingly harsh tone, both mercy and judgment are highlighted in Jude. Those who choose to depart incur certain judgment; those who choose to be *kept* can anticipate mercy. Both elements reflect the character of God and are not antithetical. As noted by Green (170), one can hardly imagine a more comprehensive greeting than the fullest measure of mercy, peace, and love.

Occasion for Writing 3-4

The clause *I had to write,* following his original intention to write on a common theme, suggests that Jude is under constraint to write due to an urgent need. His first intention to enlarge on a theme of salvation is likely eclipsed by news of problems in the Christian community. His imperative has a ring of urgency to it: the readers are to *contend earnestly* (*epagōnizesthai,* a strengthened form of "agonize") *for the faith.* Here Jude employs an athletic metaphor that derives from the gymnasium. The image calls to mind a wrestling bout and implies that the Christians are presently engaged in an intense moral struggle over truth. With "all the energy and watchfulness of an athlete in the arena" (Plummer: 387), they should "agonize" over the Christian faith.

The *faith which was once for all delivered to the saints* is that Christian teaching handed down to the Christian community by way of apostolic tradition; it is normative. This apostolic deposit establishes what is authoritative Christian truth, not what is currently theologically fashionable. This once-for-all character of Christian truth is eternally bound up with the nonnegotiables of the historic Christian faith: the self-disclosing and transcendent Creator God, the incarnation of Jesus Christ, the atonement, the resurrection, future judgment, the absolute lordship of Christ. Because divine revelation has been historically mediated, apostolic witness is central to the unique and once-for-all quality of Christian claims. Hence, the test of Christian character is faithfulness to the apostolic witness.

Jude's exhortation against moral laxness and breaking the law finds many parallels in Paul's epistles. The antinomian spirit, which leads to ethical compromise, is a perversion of the Christian gospel. Paul's first letter to the Christians at Corinth is primarily devoted to ethical lapse within the Christian community. This lapse is scandalous, for it negates the objective reality of Christ's lordship.

The reason Jude's audience must *wrestle earnestly* for the faith lies in the subtle method of his opponents. Certain individuals have used stealth in attaching themselves to the community. They have crept in virtually unnoticed; the sense is that a spy or crook is at work, infiltrating the church (Bauckham, 1983:35). The identity of these individuals is not known, although commentators normally attribute to them an itinerant ministry, such as one finds in Didache 11-12 or in Ignatius' Epistle to the Ephesians 9:1 (both of which are early second century). Since three examples of prototypical rebellion appear in Jude 5-7, the *intruders* seem to be apostate believers.

An intriguing depiction of the ungodly accompanies: *those whose judgment was written down long ago.* Keeping in mind the Palestinian Jewish-Christian milieu represented by Jude, readers may best interpret this description along the lines of standard apocalyptic genre. A common feature in the OT and intertestamental apocalyptic literature is the notion of heavenly books of life and of judgment. In them were understood to be written the names and deeds of the righteous and of the wicked, as seen in the following examples:

Exod. 32:32-33; Pss. 40:7; 56:8; 69:28; 139:16; Isa. 4:3; Jer. 22:30;
Dan. 7:10; 12:1; Mal. 3:16; 1 Enoch 47:3; 81:1-2; 89:62, 70-71;
90:14, 17, 20, 22; 104:1, 7; 108:3, 7; 2 Enoch 52:15; Test.
Jacob 7:27-28; 2 Baruch 24:1; 4 Ezra (2 Esdras) 6:20; Joseph and Aseneth
15:4; Jubilees 30:20-22; cf. Mishnah Aboth 2:1; 3:3, 20; Luke 10:20;
Phil. 4:3; Heb. 12:23; Rev. 3:5; 5:1, 7, 8; 10:8-11; 13:8; 20:12;
21:27.

These heavenly books reflect a religious self-understanding basic
to Hebrew thought. The divine purpose, though hidden from human
view, is revealed in history and certain to be fulfilled. The heavenly
books point to the divine foreknowledge by which the chosen people
(Israel, and now the church) have been called as God's own possession.

The essence of the verb used in Jude 4 is juridical (*prographein*,
"to mark out in former times"). This is paralleled in the OT: Malachi
3:16, "A scroll of remembrance was written in his presence concerning those who feared the Lord and honored his name" (NIV); and
Jeremiah 22:30, "This is what the Lord says: 'Record this man' "
(NIV). The verb carries a specific penal sense, that of a public accusation against criminals (Fuchs: 159). *Prographein* also corresponds
in tone and meaning to the verbs *proephēteusen* ("prophesied") in
Jude 14, and *proeirēmenōn* ("predicted") in 17. The past speaks
prophetically to the present, and in Jude it finds fulfillment in the
ungodly who presently are threatening the community.

Jude casts his opponents as ungodly antitypes, for whom judgment has long since been prescribed and has already been appointed
(as shown by the perfect participle of *prographein*). Jude views judgment as being fulfilled in his adversaries and to be confirmed at *the
great Day* (7). Their appointed end, just as that of past unfaithful, is
sure.

THE TEXT IN BIBLICAL CONTEXT

As reflected in the catchword *keep/kept* (Jude 1), an important theme
of the letter is immediately introduced. In the OT, apostasy is no
minor focus. The OT places considerable emphasis on the fact of
communion between the God of Israel and the Israelites themselves.
Disobedience to the laws of God constitutes corporate apostasy, on
account of which the prophets are raised up again and again.

Although sin by its inherent character leads to judgment, Yahweh
does not always judge. Mercy and loving-kindness are exalted again
and again as attributes of Israel's God. Repentance provides the

means by which the people of God avert judgment. Yahweh himself takes initiative in restoring his own. Ultimately, as predicted by the prophet Jeremiah (31:31), the answer lies in a "new covenant."

In the last half-century, the Dead Sea Scrolls have served as an extraordinary impetus for the study of the NT. The scrolls are important because they depict the life and convictions of a strand of intertestamental Judaism believing that apostasy had corrupted Israel as a nation. For the sectarian members of Qumran, the prophets' messages took on current meaning: hidden therein were predictions of contemporary events. The sect believed that in their number God had preserved a faithful remnant, a covenant community. The rest of apostate Israel would be destroyed (see, for example, the Community Rule [1QS] and the War Rule [1QM, 4QM]).

In the NT, the Gospels present readers with teaching of the kingdom of God and the demands of Christian discipleship, to which a human response is required. Not only are the disciples called to be with Jesus; they are also called to persevere as a new community. Jesus' teaching, especially in Matthew, depicts a surrounding milieu of mixed composition, wheat and tares, sheep and goats, faithful and faithless, sheep and wolves (Matt. 13:24-43; 24:23-24; 25:31-46; 7:15-20). Even those who say "Lord, Lord" may be "evildoers" (Matt. 7:21-27). Temptation and stumbling-blocks in the Gospel narratives are viewed as an ever-present reality for the disciple. Error and deception pose a genuine threat.

Correspondingly, pastoral care for the flock is developed notably in the Matthean Gospel. The possibility of sin against a brother presupposes the need for discipline and adjustment (Matt. 18:15-19), even to the point of excommunication. Moreover, in Matthew the notion of watchfulness, faithfulness, and perseverance are developed at considerable length (e.g., Matt. 24–25).

Although Luke is not concerned to highlight the dangers of apostasy in Acts, he does report two highly suggestive episodes involving Ananias and Sapphira (5:1-11) and Simon Magus (8:9-25). This suggests the need for discernment and perseverance. The narrative of Acts 5:1-11 is particularly instructive, though seemingly harsh and unqualified to the modern reader. Both instances, tantalizing in the way they withhold details from the reader, nevertheless teach believers and motivate them strongly.

The sin of Ananias and Sapphira was that, in the setting of shared possessions and human need within the Christian community, they feigned what was not true and lied to the Holy Spirit. Simon presumed that the power and ministry of God could be humanly bought and managed. In the eyes of Peter, this constituted a notable wickedness of heart that required thoroughgoing repentance.

In the writings of Paul, salvation is clearly the initiative of God. Strong emphasis is given to election and predestination. God is again and again depicted as faithful to his people. Several warnings in the Pauline epistles, however, are worthy of mention: the danger of falling through sexual sin (1 Cor. 5–7; 1 Thess. 4), idleness (2 Thess. 3), living in the flesh (1 Cor. 3; Gal. 5), and profaning the eucharist (1 Cor. 11). Israel of old is an ongoing paradigm, warning the church against falling away (1 Cor. 10). Apostasy in the church is a subtheme in 1 Timothy, along with the pastoral realities of discipline and excommunication (cf. also Titus 3). Nevertheless, throughout Paul's epistles, repentance and restoration are the ultimate goal of discipline.

Several passages in Hebrews are famous for difficulty as well as implication. In chapters 4, 6, and 10, the language of disobedience, hardening of the heart, falling away, repentance, and perseverance is employed to show that apostasy is a real danger.

> It is impossible to restore again to repentance those who have once been enlightened, and have tasted the heavenly gift, and shared in the Holy Spirit, and have tasted the goodness of the word of God and the powers of the age to come, and then have fallen away, since on their own they are crucifying again the Son of God and are holding him up to contempt. (Heb. 6:4-6)

Ultimately, the writer of Hebrews concludes that believers are to *fear* God, who is a consuming fire:

> Ground that drinks up the rain falling on it repeatedly, and that produces a crop useful to those for whom it is cultivated, receives a blessing from God. But if it produces thorns and thistles, it is worthless and on the verge of being cursed; its end is to be burned over. (6:7-8)
>
> For if we willfully persist in sin after having received the knowledge of the truth, there no longer remains a sacrifice for sins, but a fearful prospect of judgment, and a fury of fire that will consume the [Lord's] adversaries. (10:26-27)

Although it is not expressly stated in Hebrews at what point a person crosses a spiritual boundary and thus cannot return, the emphasis is that a limit does exist in the economy of God. The argument by some that the writer to the Hebrews is speaking hypothetically is unconvincing.

The NT presents us with the mysterious intersection of divine sovereignty and human moral freedom. It also gives witness to one certain antidote to apostasy: repentance and confession of faith in the God who is faithful. Seen as such, faith is no mere human achievement or the exercise of raw willpower (Marshall: 154). Instead, it is the conviction that God transcends all human limitations and impediments.

Jude urges his readers to contend strongly against perversions of the Christian faith (Jude 3). While disaster awaits the faithless (5-19), the faithful receive encouragement. Several aspects of persevering are listed (20-23). In the end, God is able to prevent anyone from falling (24). The Christian community can rest in the assurance of God's staying power.

Christians tend not to recognize the necessary tension inherent in biblical paradoxes. Sensing this tension, human beings are inclined to wipe out one side of a paradox. The human mind frequently pits grace and divine initiative against human responsibility. We may see mercy as the opposite of judgment and justice. We may take suffering and hardship to mean the absence of divine blessing. In reality, a necessary tension must be preserved between opposite theological poles, since both sides of the theological coin exist in the economy of God.

THE TEXT IN THE LIFE OF THE CHURCH

The matter of God keeping believers, as claimed in the letter's greeting (Jude 1), raises potential theological controversy. Apostasy or error entails a level of denial and rejection of the lordship of Christ (Jude 4) and thus presents the church with an eminently pastoral problem. How does the Christian community deal with its own who fail to persevere or who compromise truth?

Our first concern is not with psychological or sociological data, although both dimensions are involved. Those fulfilling pastoral callings are faced with a theological dilemma, an age-old dilemma. How are the promises of grace and election to be reconciled with the realm of human responsibility? The church should take care not to overemphasize the dangers associated with apostasy. Yet the church also must take seriously scriptural warnings against compromising Christ's lordship, both doctrinally and ethically.

As heirs of the Reformation, Calvinists and Arminians have continued a debate in one form or another that has raged since the subapostolic period. This debate over the seeming antithesis of predestination and free will is not about to be resolved. Both poles are needed in the theological equation, for there exists truth on both sides.

The exalted language of election and predestination found in Ephesians 1 must stand alongside the sober warnings of Hebrews 6. The riches of a sure inheritance in Christ are the lot of the Christian, just as are the grave possibilities that go with disavowing the mysteries and grace of God.

In the letter of Jude, the seemingly opposite poles of this theological tension appear at the same time. Both the faithful and the apostate have their future reward. Divine sovereignty and human freedom coexist. Jude, with extraordinary brevity and apocalyptic imagination, preserves this tension.

It may not appear easy to reconcile the seemingly contradictory strands of Jude's teaching: election and apostasy, sovereignty and freedom. Because of human nature, the history of the church reads like a seesaw in recording the excesses both of what passes as hyper-Calvinism and extreme Arminianism. Some years ago, British evangelical theologian I. Howard Marshall suggested, in a study of related biblical passages, that the church's responsibility is to move past the rigidity of various theological models and thoroughly examine NT evidence (26). The epistle of Jude is an indispensable piece of such evidence. The paradox of grace and free will remain just that—a paradox. To emphasize one to the exclusion of the other is to negate an important part of the economy of God.

Samuel Taylor Coleridge once commented that heresy is not an error of the understanding but an error of the will. With this, Coleridge properly noted the *human* factor, the will. In Jude, the reader is confronted with the possibility of moral decisions to reject truth and embrace behavior incompatible with that truth.

The question arises whether the epistle of Jude deals specifically with the matter of heresy or apostasy. The relationship between the two can perhaps best be illustrated by the relationship between doctrine and ethics, both of which are suggested in Jude 4. *Heresy* may be formally defined as doctrinal deviance from orthodox belief (Greek: *haeresis*, "a choosing," a dissension, faction, sect; 1 Cor. 11:19). *Apostasy* constitutes the behavioral or ethical side of rejecting religious dogma (*apostasia*, a "withdrawing," a "wandering away"; 2 Thess. 2:3). In Jude, both doctrine and ethics, belief and practice, are at work. The unfaithful *deny lordship,* and they *pervert grace* (Jude 4). Both doctrinal erosion and moral error compromise the integrity of the Gospel and the believing community.

Seen pastorally, a doctrinal denial is often first shown in the individual's life by a moral failing or ethical compromise. Sooner or later, the individual deals with "conflicting thoughts" (Rom. 2:15) and tries to find theological justification for the adopted lifestyle. This rationale regularly means a denial of fundamental tenets of historic Christian faith, which has always required a faithful lifestyle of obedience and believing. The steady link between ethics and doctrine was noted by Menno Simons in his reflections on the record of Israel's faithfulness:

> Thus also it is with some at the present day. Those that have been enlightened by the word of the Lord, have tasted the heavenly gift, have partaken of the Holy Spirit . . . and the power of the world to come, . . . do not reckon with the Lord but with their own sinful, disobedient, evil flesh, which always seeks its own pleasure; and will not willingly bear the cross of the Lord. . . . They . . . choose for themselves here and there a leader, false prophet, or teacher who . . . leads them back to Egypt. (Menno: 356).

Menno notes further that "all heresy, seduction . . . and hypocrisy can be . . . defended with Scripture" (663). His observation is worth pondering.

The well-known axiom of Dietrich Bonhoeffer also bears repeating: Christianity without discipleship is always Christianity without Christ (68-70). Faith is only real when it manifests itself in obedience. Historically, this has been a hallmark of the believers church tradition. A righteous walk with the Lord follows true repentance. The disciple holds fast to the word of God.

One sociologist describes modernity as making place for widespread heresy. He observes the increasing secularization of religion in American life (Berger: 1-3). To contemporaries, picking and choosing becomes an imperative, with people turning inward and claiming absolute authority for their own experience. Religion and theology thus increasingly become an individual and human phenomenon. They lose their sense of transcendent moral authority. In the end, heresy is little more than private opinion.

However, how can we be sure that our experience is true or faithful? One's own religious experience must be rooted in Christ's sovereign lordship (Jude 4). Furthermore, apostolic teaching which has been received and passed on remains authoritative and binding for the church of any age (Jude 17). The Christian community, taught and led by the Holy Spirit, must reaffirm its theological-moral foundation again and again. It does not subsist in a cultural vacuum. Instead, it operates within culture to infiltrate and ultimately *transform* culture. Jude's prophetic burden, which should be the church's as well, is that evils from the surrounding culture have infiltrated the church. The Christian community must sit up and take notice.

Jude 5-19

Profile of the Unfaithful

PREVIEW

Typology is integral to the sometimes knotty question of the NT's use of the OT. Apostolic preaching reflects the underlying premise that the OT points beyond itself, finding completion in the NT (Goppelt: 17-18). For the first-century Jew, it was entirely natural to view past episodes in Israel's history as a shadow of the future, to view the significance of the present in terms of the past. By means of typology, the NT writers apply a deeper and often christological sense of present truth. A type presupposes a purpose in the linear movement of history. It bears out a spiritual correspondence and historical connection between people, events, or institutions (Lampe: 39-40).

Typological interpretation grows out of the conviction that the biblical history of Israel contains all the principle forms of divine activity pointing to the ultimate purposes of God. The theological center of this is the life, death, and resurrection of Jesus Christ. In Christ, much of what constitutes OT institutions, events, and offices is fulfilled. Beyond christological typology, however, lies moral typology. OT characters or events project themselves in ways that allow them to serve as paradigms or models in the Christian moral tradition. It is the abundance of the moral type that makes the general (catholic) epistles such a rich and distinct contribution to the NT canon.

The effect of moral typology is to comfort, exhort, and warn. The end is certain, though in some respects hidden and unannounced. In Jude, examples from the past are marshaled chiefly to warn against the cancer of apostasy. The past explains the present and thus foreshadows the future.

The pattern found in Jude 5-19 is type, explanation, type, explanation. It constitutes a form of midrash or commentary on the fate of the ungodly (Ellis: 221-236; Bauckham, 1983:4-5). Jude is skillful in reworking OT material, applying religious tradition for the sake of his readers. Like Jewish apocalyptic writers (and the writer of the NT Apocalypse), Jude alludes to OT characters or events without formal citation. Jude, moreover, possesses several features of a Jewish-Christian midrash: (1) relating OT tradition material prophetically to the situation at hand; (2) modifying the text to suit the present need; and (3) using catchwords to form rhetorical links in the polemic. The intended audience clearly belongs to a distinct cultural milieu, Palestinian Jewish-Christianity.

Two sets of triplets (Jude 5-7; 11) are employed as paradigms or models of ungodliness leading to destruction. In verses 5-7, unbelieving Israel, the rebellious angels, and the cities of the plain illustrate catastrophic loss through divine judgment. A second triad of deserting types appears in verse 11: Cain, Balaam, and Korah are united by a woe-cry. Each of the three, notably, is signified by a formula: *the way of Cain, the error of Balaam, the rebellion of Korah.* This gives the appearance of a standard type, already formulated in intertestamental and first-century circles of Judaism.

Together the two sets of triplets underscore the realities of divine fiat, both to the Christian community and to those who pose a threat.

OUTLINE

Tales of Woe, Part 1: An Intolerable Triad, Jude 5-7
5   Unbelieving Israel
6   The Fallen Angels
7   Sodom and Gomorrah

Marks of the Apostate, Part 1, Jude 8-10

Tales of Woe, Part 2: An Intractable Triad, Jude 11
11a   Cain
11b   Balaam
11c   Korah

Marks of the Apostate, Part 2, Jude 12-13

Judgment of the Ungodly, Jude 14-15

Marks of the Apostate, Part 3, 16-19

EXPLANATORY NOTES

Tales of Woe, Part 1: An Intolerable Triad   Jude 5-7

5 Unbelieving Israel

Jude 5 contains the first of a triplet of ungodly examples. Such lists belong to popular Jewish tradition. Similar catalogs are found in writings of mainstream and sectarian Judaism, as in Sirach, Jubilees, 3 Maccabees, the Testaments of the Twelve Patriarchs, the Damascus Document of the Qumran community (CD), and the Mishnah. All typically occur in literary contexts dealing with hard-heartedness, apostasy, or disregard for the Torah.

Several examples of apocryphal and pseudepigraphal writings are sufficient for illustration. In Sirach 16:5-15, the writer provides a catalog of historical examples that include Korah, Assyria, giants, Sodomites, Canaanites, and unbelieving Israel. The context of 3 Maccabees 2:3-7 is a prayer for Israel against a Ptolemaic ruler. It lists Pharaoh, Sodomites, and giants as evil characters. In the Testaments of the Twelve Patriarchs (Test. Naph. 2:8—4:3), the writer draws lessons from the Flood, the Watchers (angels), Sodom, and the Gentiles.

Jude's interest in the initial illustration is Israel, God's chosen. Allusion to the OT covenant community suggests that the opponents in view are former believers, those who had experienced divine redemption. Note the emphatic terminology in Jude 5. Since the readers *already know all things*, Jude wants to remind them of Israel of old. Accounts of Israel's unbelief in the wilderness, after miraculous deliverance from Egypt, are found in Numbers 11, 14, 26, and 32. The Lord let that "evil generation" die out before Israel crossed into the Promised Land (Num. 32:13; Deut. 1:35; 2:14). Throughout the OT, there is a constant prophetic reminder of Israel's deliverance, and of its severance from Egypt. In the account of the old covenant, Yahweh delivered Israel, who promised to obey him and be his special people. After they repeatedly and persistently failed to obey the Lord, he did not deliver them. Instead, he judged them through destruction and exile.

By implication, Jude is saying the same applies to those who threaten the community. Some formerly experienced redemption and have denied the Lord (4). The same will be judged at Jesus' second coming. The contrast before the readers concerns two divine acts, one of mercy and one of judgment. The present need calls for a prophetic reminder: *You know all things.*

6 The Fallen Angels

The fall of the angels is a further case illustrating the gravity of spiritual lapse in Jude. Perhaps sensing great interest in angels among his readers, the writer strategically chooses a second example, a heavenly one, to complement his instructive allusion to Israel. The issue is clearly the utter seriousness and mystery of falling away.

The angels are said to have *deserted* their heavenly home (note the prefix *apo-* in the participle *apolipontas*, which denotes movement away). They fell from a domain of divine liberty and light to imprisonment and darkness. Angels in the OT figure prominently in certain historical narratives. During and following Israel's exile, they acquire increasing importance and a more clearly defined function (e.g., Ezek. 9:2ff.; 40:3ff.; 43:6ff.; Dan. 3:28; 4:13; 6:22; 7:16; 8:13; 10:5ff.; 12:1ff.; Zech. 1:8ff.; 2:1ff.; 3:1ff.; 4:1ff.; 5:1ff.; 6:1ff.). Jewish intertestamental literature depicts angels far more systematically and states names and functions for some.

Virtually all commentary, past and present, has related Jude (and 2 Pet. 2:4) to Genesis 6:1-4 in some form or another. This interpretation of "the sons of God," following the lead of Clement of Alexandria, has two chief sources: (1) a mistaken linking of the angels in Jude 6 with Sodom and Gomorrah in Jude 7, and (2) the association of demons with Genesis 6:1-4 that began to emerge in second-century B.C. Jewish interpretation. For example, in the book of Enoch, chapters 6-16 (second and first centuries B.C.), we find perhaps the most elaborate expansion of this connection between the angels' fall and sexual promiscuity.

The sin of the angels, though veiled to humans, was very real. The point of Jude's witness, however, is not the precise *nature* of their sin. Instead, the angels of Jude 6, mentioned parenthetically, share something in common with Israel of verse 5 and the cities of the plain in verse 7: a radical disobedience and total disenfranchisement. Yet Jude, in using apocalyptic motifs, stresses certain things and omits others.

Contrary to the view of many commentators, there is nothing about angels in Genesis 6 that is mentioned in Jude. Instead, the conceptualization of the angelic realm in Jude is simply an extension of what emerged during the intertestamental era. In apocryphal and pseudepigraphical works of that era, apocalypticists tended to incorporate features of pagan mythology into their conceptualizations of the angelic world. Biblical writers, on the other hand, were generally more radical in rejecting a framework of pagan mythology. They wrote from a divine revelatory and prophetic viewpoint, even when they used an apocalyptic literary mode and language.

Jude employs clearly apocalyptic motifs without necessarily embracing Jewish apocalyptic theology. The center point of his illustration involving the angels is the fact *that* they were dispossessed, not specifically *how* or *why* they were dispossessed. This basic interpretive premise is confirmed by the grammar and syntax of Jude 6. The issue at hand is apostasy, not fornication (J. D. Charles, 1993b: 108-116). All three examples of Jude 5-7 underscore the fact of enduring loss. Any speculation as to the particular nature of the sins of the angels, though intriguing, is of secondary importance. The point of Jude's allusion to the angels is that they wrongly exercised their free will, to their own discredit.

Neither the OT nor the NT makes any explicit statements as to the fall of the rebellious angels. At most, the NT states that Satan, a fallen angel chief among many (cf. Eph. 2:2), was cast down (Luke 10:18; John 12:31; Rev. 12:4, 7, 9, 10). Yet the NT gives no clear time or explanation for the fall. Some, like Origen, hold Jesus' words in Luke 10:18 to refer to an original fall (*Paedagogus* 3.2). Others believe the statement to be a dramatic way of expressing Satan's certain ruin (Aulén: 111; Boyd: 39). Still others view the fall as coinciding with Jesus' earthly ministry (Caird, 1965:31).

Corresponding typology to the fallen angels of Jude might be drawn from several prophetic oracles in the OT, oracles giving graphic illustrations of fall or ruin: Isaiah 14:5-23, a taunt against the king of Babylon; 24:21-22, a symbolic representation of Yahweh's judgment; and Ezekiel 28:1-19, a prophetic funeral dirge against the king of Tyre. The oracles in Isaiah 14 and Ezekiel 28 reflect, as in Jude, utter fall from glory.

Significantly, several elements are present in all three sources. First, there is a conspicuously abrupt transition from the earthly to heavenly plane. Second, there is a correlation between the earthly and heavenly realm in each case. Third, the objects of condemnation all tumble from the heavens as "stars." Falling from glory, whether as an arrogant king or those to whom truth has been committed, has an extraordinary antecedent in the heavenly realm.

The imprisonment of spirits, undefined in the OT, is a prominent theme in Jewish apocalyptic literature, notably in such writings as 1 Enoch, 2 Baruch, and Jubilees (see notes on 1 Pet. 3:19, above), and surfaces in the NT Apocalypse. Within the apocalyptic tradition, a frequent pattern emerges: (1) war erupts in heaven, often depicted in astral terms; (2) this rebellion against God spills over to earth; (3) it culminates in ultimate vindication of the King of heaven, who punishes the rebels (Hanson: 208).

Jude's readers are to be mindful of the lesson of the angels: punishment is proportionate to privilege. In heavenly realms, the angels were exposed to great light. Now they are consigned to the gloom of *darkness*. They chose not to keep their unique and exalted status. Consequently, they are being *kept in chains of darkness*, awaiting *the judgment of the great Day* and a terrible destiny that should cause humans to shudder. Like Israel of old, they departed from their *allotted place*, their *proper dwelling*. Apostasy in the Christian community has both earthly and heavenly antecedents.

7 Sodom and Gomorrah

Consistently throughout OT and Jewish literature, the example of the cities of the plain stands out (Gen. 19). Sodom's overthrow is cited again and again.

> Deut. 29:23; 32:32; Isa. 1:9-10; 3:9; Jer. 23:14; 49:18; 50:40; Lam. 4:6; Ezek. 16:49-59; Amos 4:11; Hos. 11:8; Zeph. 2:9; Jub. 16:5, 6, 9; 20:5; 22:22; 36:10; Wisd. of Sol. 10:6-7; Sir. 16:8; Test. Asher 7:1; Test. Naph. 3:4; 3 Macc. 2:5; Gen. Rab. 27:3; Mishnah Sanh. 10:3; Aboth 5:10.

The OT strikingly depicts how Sodom flaunts its sin and is given a permanent judgment. The prophet Jeremiah declares that no person will henceforth live there (49:18; 50:40). In intertestamental Judaism, Sodom remains the classic Jewish example of immorality and a model of certain and consuming divine judgment.

According to the rabbis, seven groups would have no portion in the coming world: the generation of the Flood, the generation of the Diaspora, the spies who brought back evil reports of the land of Canaan, the generation in the wilderness, the congregation of Korah, the ten tribes (Northern Kingdom), and the men of Sodom (Mishnah Sanh. 10:3). For Jude, Sodom and Gomorrah are the type par excellence for the finality of divine judgment.

Three times Genesis 18–19 notes the anguished outcry of those oppressed by Sodom (18:20-21; 19:13). Their cry mandates a divine visitation. The Abraham account in Genesis is painstaking to show that God is absolutely just. As in Jude's account, the fate of these cities is continually open to exhibit. In the first century, Philo (*De Abrahamo* 140-141) and Josephus (*De vita Mosis* 2.56) indicate that later generations are to learn from the example of Sodom and Gomorrah. Even though the sin of Sodom is linked in several apocryphal Jewish sources to the fallen angels, Jude's intention is to link

Sodom with the angels *and with Israel.*
The Jewish apocalypticist was inclined to explain the state of the world in unseen, angelic terms. Jude, however, in line with the OT prophetic tradition, focuses on the *human* face of evil. Moreover, his qualification *in the same manner* as *these* speaks not to the nature of sin but to the same end met by Israel, the angels, and Sodom and Gomorrah. We may translate Jude 7 as follows: . . . *just as Sodom and Gomorrah and the surrounding cities in the same manner as these, who have given themselves to utter sexual immorality and perversion, are an ongoing example of those undergoing the punishment of eternal fire.* This rendering does justice to the context of Jude 5-7. All three examples display unnatural rebellion (Green: 166-167). Taken together, they characterize the opponents of Jude who are despising normal life and perverting the good.

Several evil types from the past regularly appear in Jewish extrabiblical lists: Sodom and Gomorrah, the fallen angels or "Watchers," giants, the Flood, and unbelieving Israel. In similar fashion, Jude 5-7 presents evidence compounded against the guilty: exhibits A, B, and C.

Marks of the Apostate, Part 1   Jude 8-10

Between Jude 8 and 9, the contextual link and contrast between the character of the *dreamers* and Michael is significant. Verse 9 begins, *But when Michael the archangel.* Building upon the implied notion of demonic conflict, Jude assumes his readers' acquaintance with an apocryphal tradition on an angelic dispute over Moses' body. We learn first from Origen (*De principiis* 3.2.1) that this tradition is in the Assumption of Moses, a pseudepigraphal Jewish writing of the early first century (part of which is lost).

The tradition about Moses' body proliferated in mainstream and sectarian Judaism. Philo and Josephus allude to it; Philo writes that Moses was buried by angels. Clement of Alexandria adds that Joshua and Caleb witnessed Moses' ascension to heaven while his body was being buried in the mountains.

The OT background for the tradition is in Deuteronomy 34:5-6 and Numbers 27:12-13. Imagery from Daniel 10:4-21; 12:1; and Zechariah 3 is also incorporated. In Zechariah, Joshua the high priest is standing before the angel of the Lord, with Satan rising up to accuse him. While a Targum (an Aramaic paraphrase) on Deuteronomy 34 and several rabbinic sources bring the reader a bit closer to the background of Jude's illustration, they do not inform us that Satan and Michael fought over Moses' body.

The contextual flow begins in Jude 8 with a portrait of Jude's opponents, a portrait drawn from the preceding historical antecedents. The opponents carry three identifying marks: moral defilement, rejection of authority, and shocking irreverence. They resemble Sodom and Gomorrah in their sexual practices. They also bear resemblance to the angels, who astonishingly, chose to rebel against heaven's authority and as a result were disenfranchised.

The archangel Michael is meant to stand in stark contrast to these wicked spiritual beings (cf. Dan. 10:13, 21; 12:1). Though Michael was superior and could have railed at the prince of darkness, he declined to do so. Conversely, the unfaithful of Jude consider themselves superior but really are inferior; they *slander the glorious ones*, the angels.

Jude 9 is framed in the language of legal disputation. In light of the accusation raised by the devil, Michael appeals to the Lord's judgment and *rebuke*, not his own authority. Note the contrast between the arrogant, quick-to-slander people of verse 10 (cf. 4, 8) and Michael's refusal to slander, linked with his humble appeal to God. The implication of Jude 9, which portrays the devil in an accusatory mode, is consistent with both OT and NT portraits of the prince of darkness.

The devil's role is foremost that of an accuser or an overzealous prosecutor (e.g., Job 1–2, 1 Chron. 21:1; Zech. 3:1; Matt. 4:1-11; Mark 1:12-13; Luke 4:1-13; 2 Cor. 2:11; Rev. 2:9; 12:10). What is striking about the few OT allusions to Satan is that he seems to fall into the same category as the "sons of God" who are part of the heavenly council (as in Job 1:6; 2:1, RSV; cf. Gen. 6:2; 1 Kings 22:19). Yet, in several other OT passages, the reader finds faint traces of hostility orchestrated against God.

The serpent in Genesis 3, for example, is endowed with a peculiar cunning, doing more than merely acting as one of Yahweh's "court lawyers." Indeed, he contradicts God's statements, in the end waging war against the woman's seed (cf. Rev. 12:13-17). First Chronicles 21, a slight variation on 2 Samuel 24, finds David tempted to number Israel. According to the Chronicler, the influence of this "accuser" is not neutral. Before all is said and done, seventy thousand of Israel's men have died.

The motif of spiritual warfare, vaguely hinted at in similar OT passages and developed broadly by NT writers, is assumed by Jude in his polemic against the apostates. Jewish traditions that grew out of the OT account of Moses' death are employed by Jude to underscore the corrupt and brutish nature of those he is opposing. Their denial of the lordship of Christ is plainly manifest in their insubordination, rebellion, antinomianism, and despising of spiritual authority. They too have a heavenly antecedent.

Tales of Woe, Part 2: An Intractable Triad   Jude 11

A second triplet of OT paradigms appears in Jude 11. These are the object of a woe-cry, a prophetic denunciation. Having blasphemed and rejected authority (8), the opponents have brought themselves under a divine curse.

Genesis 4:3-4 says that Cain brought as an offering to the Lord the "fruit" of the earth, while his brother Abel brought "firstlings" of his flock. The Lord then looked upon Abel and not Cain with favor. To the Jewish mind, Cain represents the epitome of wickedness, the archetype of an ungodly person. He is the first individual in the Hebrew Scriptures to intentionally defy God and despise a fellow human being; hence, he is prototypical. Interestingly, the rabbis, taking note of the wording of Genesis 4:10 ("your brother's bloods cry out"), charge Cain with destroying a whole world. The Scriptures indicate "both his blood and the blood of his succeeding generations" (Mishnah Sanh. 4:5). In the words of Philo, Cain is the type and teacher of ungodliness (*De posteritate Caini* 38).

Numbers 22–24 gives the account of Balaam, son of Beor. These three chapters offer a mixed review of the foreign priest-diviner. The OT portrays Balaam chiefly as a negative memorial for his role in betraying Israel (Num. 31:16; Deut. 23:4-5; Josh. 13:22; 24:9; Neh. 13:2; Mic. 6:5). While being possessed of greed, he more importantly led Israel into idolatry and immorality at Baal-Peor (cf. Num. 31:16). To the rabbis, Balaam constituted an antithesis to Abraham (Mishnah Sanh. 5:19). The "deception of Balaam" is deception for selfish profit (Kelly: 268). Balaam typically loved the wages of wickedness (2 Pet. 2:15).

Third in this prophetic triad of Jude 11 is Korah, perhaps the most arresting illustration of insubordination in all the OT. He and a band of ringleaders challenged the authority of Moses, the man of God; they despised the Lord and were consequently swallowed up by the earth (Num. 16). Siding with Korah were some 250 men among Israel's leaders, who were consumed by fire from the Lord (Num. 16:17, 35). Along with the men of Sodom, Korah and his following, according to the rabbis, would find no place in the world to come (Mishnah Sanh. 10:3). Korah's fate fits his deed.

Cain, Balaam, and Korah are linked in Jude by means of a woe-oracle. The woe-cry in the OT is found in several contexts: a call for attention (as in Zech. 2:6), mourning for the dead (1 Kings 13:30; Jer. 22:18), a cry of excitement (Isa. 55:1; Zech. 2:10), a cry of revenge (Isa. 1:24), and the announcement of doom (Isa. 3:9, 11; Jer. 13:27; Ezek. 13:3, 18; Hos. 7:13; Amos 6:1; Mic. 2:1). The vast majority of incidents fall under the heading of doom declared.

In the minds of the prophets, to whom the primary use of "woe" (hoy) is restricted, the warning of judgment is synonymous with judgment itself (Clifford: 464). Perhaps initially derived from a funerary setting (Clifford: 459-463; Janzen: 2-26), the woe-cry came to incorporate a vengeance pattern. For Jude's purposes, the trio of verse 11 foreshadows the fate of those who rebel and blaspheme (Jude 8, 10). With a cry of condemnation and threat of divine vengeance hanging over their heads, Jude's opponents await the execution of irrevocable judgment.

Marks of the Apostate, Part 2   Jude 12-13

In these two verses the writer piles metaphor upon metaphor to express his indignation over the apostates. These individuals are dangerous, self-absorbed, deceptive, and doomed. Mention of the "love feast" here (cf. 2 Pet. 2:12-13) has normally led commentators to conclude that Jude reflects a second-century milieu, since the love-feast is first otherwise mentioned in subapostolic literature.

The meal evidently became independent of the eucharist fairly early, perhaps because of its corruption and dilution, as suggested by Clement of Alexandria (Stromata 3.2). In the Didache, a subapostolic writing contemporary with the Epistles of Ignatius (early second century), the character of a "true prophet" is described in relation to the "meal," somewhat reminiscent of Jude and 2 Peter (Did. 11.9). Nevertheless, defilement of the Lord's table, as reflected in 1 Corinthians 10:17-34, was a mid-first-century problem.

The double meaning of spilades, "spots/blemishes" and "rocks," may account for differences in translations of Jude 12. Both are plausible and fit the context. On the one hand, Jude is concerned about the apostates polluting and defiling the faithful in the community (8, 23-24). On the other hand, the metaphor of shipwreck due to hidden rocks is equally fitting, since Jude's opponents pose unseen dangers to the faithful. Inasmuch as it is impossible for the faithful to avoid the faithless, the former stand in peril.

The adversaries as clouds without rain reveal their lack of true substance. They disappoint, they promise but do not deliver (cf. Prov.

25:14). Some commentators (e.g., Osburn: 296-303) see traces of the book of Enoch in Jude at this point. In 1 Enoch both rain and fruit are linked together (80:2-3). With explicit reference in Jude 14 to 1 Enoch 1:9, this connection is indeed possible.

Jude's description of his opponents as *fruitless trees in late autumn, twice dead and uprooted,* has elicited a wide range of interpretations. *Late autumn* has commentators divided: some suggest this is the end of the harvest, while others argue that in the Mediterranean region, harvest comes in late summer, well before late autumn. At the very least, late autumn suggests no expectation of fruit, with winter approaching.

The term *twice dead* also finds no unified interpretation. The metaphor seems to carry eschatological significance, like Matthew 7:19; 15:13; and John 15:5. It also speaks of barrenness, a chief element in Jesus' preaching. If in fact the adversaries of Jude are apostate from the faith, then the imagery is pregnant with meaning. Salvation is not to be spurned; apostates await the second death (Rev. 21:8). Given the *once for all* language used for Israel in Jude 5, this interpretation seems to be consistent with Jude's purpose.

Mayor (43) thinks the images in Jude 13 are progressive, depicting the false profession of the faithless, their true condition, shamelessness, and eventual fate. These images are reminiscent of those found in Greek mythology. One commentator has suggested that *the wild waves of the sea, foaming up their shame,* refers to the grotesque account of Aphrodite's birth in Hesiod's *Theogony* (188-206), literature dated 730-700 B.C. (Oleson: 492-503). By this ancient account, Kronos, a son of Mother Earth, uses a sickle to castrate Uranos, the Sky. The severed genitals are thrown into the sea and covered with foam (*aphros*). Out of the foam, Aphrodite is nurtured, the "Lady of Cyprus" and protectress of sailors at sea. The foam then washes her ashore.

Conceived as such, the apostates are the waves that bring to the shore the vile state to which they have returned. In the Aphrodite tradition, the opponents of Jude have a notable antecedent. According to pagan mythology, Aphrodite is not merely associated with love. There is a dark side to her as well: wantonness and sexual perversion. In Jewish-Christian apocalyptic terms, the opponents of Jude are *wandering stars, for whom the gloom of darkness has been forever reserved* (13).

Jude's imagery, then, is meant to conjure up a graphic portrait of the opponents. They have antecedents, in Israel's past and in pagan mythology. There can be no doubt as to their true nature.

Judgment of the Ungodly Jude 14-15

The engaged reader discovers numerous touchpoints between Jude and Jewish sectarian literature of the late intertestamental period. Several such examples are the apocalyptic mode, a reinterpreting of Israel's past history for the present, and the use of Jewish tradition. At this point, the book of Enoch requires some discussion. First Enoch, parts of which are dated second century B.C. (R. H. Charles, 2:170; Isaac: 6-7), is Palestinian in origin. It was in use at Qumran around the same time as the emergence of the Christian church. The work was likely well-known in the early Christian community, particularly in the region of Judea. While Jude is the sole NT writer who quotes directly from it, the writer of 1 Enoch and the writers of the NT share a common thought-world, even when their theological orientation differs drastically (cf. Isaac: 8-10).

Jewish literature of the second century B.C., especially the parts reflecting a Palestinian milieu, was fervently anti-Hellenistic in character and frequently took on the literary form of apocalypses or testaments. At the time of the Maccabean Revolt (167-164 B.C.), we find the "assembly of the pious," the "Hasidim," as a clearly defined Jewish sect (cf. 1 Macc. 7:13; 2 Macc. 14:6). The Hasidim are significant for two reasons. They are thought to be the common root of both the Essenes and the Pharisees, and their theological agenda is mirrored in the earliest parts of 1 Enoch, dated to this time (Hengel, 1:175-176).

The deep crisis emerging out of Hellenistic reform (Elias: 357-368) is explained by the conviction of the devout that this is a period of apostasy. Thus Enoch is depicted in this apocalypse as a messenger of repentance and judgment, sent to call the people of God back to the faith. Many statements to this effect are found in the pseudepigraphal Testaments of the Twelve Patriachs (around second century B.C.). Various Jewish texts of the time reflect the agenda of the Hasidim (Nickelsburg: 19-39).

In similar fashion, Jude passionately exhorts his audience to *fiercely struggle* against the apostates, who have perverted the faith *once for all delivered to the saints* (Jude 3). These *ungodly* people (15, *asebeis,* an important catchword in Jude) furnish a notable parallel between Enoch and Jude. Thus a statement found in 1 Enoch, shaped by conditions which helped birth a pre-Christian "repentance" movement, rings prophetically true:

> Behold, he comes with myriads of his holy ones in order to execute judgment upon all, and he will destroy all the ungodly and will reprove all flesh on account of all their ungodly works which they have done and for the harsh things which ungodly sinners have spoken against him. (1 En. 1:9)

Jude 14-15, citing 1 Enoch 1:9, is the language of theophany (divine manifestation) and judgment. It is patterned after numerous similar statements in the OT, such as in the following texts:

Deut. 33:2; Judg. 5:4; Ps. 18:9; 46:8-9; 68:17; 76:9; 96:13; Isa. 19:1; 31:4; 40:10; 66:15; Jer. 25:31; Dan. 7:10; Amos 1:2; Joel 3:2; Mic. 1:3; Hab. 3:3; Zeph. 1:7-9,12; Hag. 2:22; Zech. 3:8; 9:14; Mal. 3:3-5.

This prophetic denunciation serves to remind Jude's readers that the Lord comes to judge the ungodly. The fate of the faithless is certain.

Tertullian in his commentary on the epistle held that Jude was alluding to Enoch, the antediluvian patriarch. Contrarily, the expression "the seventh from Adam" also occurs in 1 Enoch (60:8; 93:3), in Philo (*De Posteritate Caini* 173), and in rabbinic literature (Lev. Rab. 29:11). The OT does not call Enoch "the seventh from Adam," though it can be inferred from the list of generations following Adam (Gen. 5:3, 6, 9, 12, 15, 18). Thus we seem to be dealing with a Jewish literary convention of about the same time as the NT writings.

Moreover, the Enoch prediction can be understood as "prophecy" in the same way as a Cretan poet is a "prophet" in Titus 1:12. Viewed as such, Jude 14-15 is a citation of 1 Enoch due not so much to Jude's respect for the work itself as to its impact on Jude's audience. Given the Jewish-Christian character of the epistle, it is likely that Jude's readers are products of a Palestinian religious-cultural milieu. Thus a popular sectarian Jewish work, not necessarily viewed by Jude as "inspired," is cited strategically for edifying usage. Similar circumstances stand behind both writings. The literary strategy and the pastoral agenda of Jude call for vigilance and repentance.

Marks of the Apostate, Part 3   Jude 16-19

Consistent with the Israel and Korah typology, the adversaries are *grumblers* and *complainers*. Jude underscores the pernicious nature of sowing discord among the community of faith. The fate of Israel in the wilderness was not ambiguous; they perished. The Testament of Moses, a work with which Jude was likely acquainted, alludes to the malcontent and to "bombastic speech" (esp. Test. Moses 7:7, 9). Jude's opponents are *scoffers* (Jude 18). Apostasy thus appears to be a prime issue in Jude.

Furthermore, Jude's opponents have cast aside moral law and self-restraint. As *sensual* persons (Jude 16), these libertines hold the constraints of moral law in wholesale contempt. Though claiming to have the Spirit, they are in truth devoid of it, as shown by their carnal state (cf. 1 Cor. 2–3).

Remember the words of the apostles. Commentators often assume this statement to reflect a distance of several generations between Jude and the apostles of the first century (e.g., Kelly: 281). This assumption, however, does not come from the text. Attention in Jude is given to what the apostles *said,* not what they *wrote.* What is significant here is the reality of authoritative, prophetic speech, not a chronological distance.

Jude himself is not one of the chief apostles, given his somewhat late conversion (John 7:5). For him, the antidote to faithlessness is the sure anchor of apostolic teaching, just as it was for the apostle Paul (cf. Rom. 16:7; 1 Cor. 12:28; 15:9; 2 Cor. 8:23; Gal. 1:17, 19; Eph. 2:20; 3:5; 4:11). Remembering what the saints first believed was the urgent and ongoing need. Discipleship entails pressing on, reaffirming the all-important foundations. Believers are to recall spiritual foundations, not simply earlier generations.

The opponents are guilty in both word and deed. Likely the verbal sins they have committed stand in relation to their rejection of authority and lustful indulgence (Jude 16, 18). They are grumblers and discontents, engaging in bombast, and selfishly flattering others (16). In bald contrast to this profane speech stands the word of the apostles, through which the believers were grounded in the faith. The faithful are to remember the foundational teaching given to them. Reminder terminology plays an important role in both 2 Peter and Jude. As Israel of old (Jude 5), the tendency toward forgetting God's commands is typically human, but inexcusable.

Summary

Jude 5-19 marshals evidence against those who, according to the writer, have *wormed their way in* and have had a corrosive effect on the community (Jude 4). The opponents are condemned in dramatic and emphatic terms. Theirs is a doom that is sealed, a doom foretold (4, 17). Artfully and with almost breathtaking precision, Jude describes this fate.

Three examples of disenfranchisement in Jude 5-7 underscore the fact that wickedness has both human and superhuman antecedents. All three examples are linked by their rejection of norms or constraints, and their subsequent loss in the present life. Three further paradigms in verse 11 emphasize the progressive nature of apostasy: first one departs, but eventually one perishes.

Jude further embellishes his teaching with several instances from pseudepigraphal traditions. The notion of imprisoned spirits is veiled in the Scriptures. Extra traditions surrounding the burial of Moses surface only in extracanonical Jewish writings. Yet these traditions serve Jude's overall polemic. To illustrate, in Jude 14-15 we encounter a near-verbatim citation from 1 Enoch 1:9, found in the context of theophany and judgment. This allusion to Enoch reminds us of the religious and literary milieu of which early Christians were a part.

An important touchpoint can be detected between Jude and much intertestamental Jewish literature: the theme of apostasy. The use of extracanonical material in Jude reflects a common thought-world uniting Palestinian Judaism and the early Jewish-Christian community. It is unnecessary to ascribe to these extracanonical writings sacred or inspired status. Yet, to suit his theological-pastoral purpose, Jude makes inspired use of these writings, respected in sectarian Judaism. They are directly applicable in the present, and all the more so if the readers already know this literature.

THE TEXT IN BIBLICAL CONTEXT

The broader neglect of Jude, noted earlier, stretches from the early patristic era down to the modern period. Traditionally, several factors have contributed to this state of affairs. Among these are (1) a lack of internal evidence as to the historical setting; (2) the language, symbolism, and literary-rhetorical style of the writer; and (3) the writer's use of traditional material from both the OT and extracanonical sources. In particular, surviving Jewish literature from the last three centuries B.C. and first century A.D. is decisive in helping to explain the religious thought-world of Jude.

Jude's use of the book of Enoch and the Testament of Moses reflects a common cultural milieu of shared theological concepts and apocalyptic literary conventions. Jude is by no means the only NT writer who shares the Palestinian Jewish-Christian heritage. A century ago, Robert H. Charles showed many similarities between phraseology from 1 Enoch and portions of the Gospels, the general epistles, Revelation, and even in Paul's letters (1:180-181). It is clear that the writers of the NT do not think and speak in a religious and cultural vacuum.

The way Jude exploits popular literature and tradition, on display in verses 5-19, is not unique in the NT. There are other such examples. While in Athens, Paul demonstrates an ability to converse with ancient literary and cultural traditions known by his Athenian contemporaries (Acts 17:16-34). While addressing the council of the Areopagus, he quotes two noted Greek poets: "In him we live and move and have our being" (Epimenides); and "We are his offspring" (Aratus). Further, the apostle cites the legend of the altar "to the unknown god," a tradition several centuries old. He then declares that he will proclaim this unknown God to the Athenians (on this, see Faw: 195-196).

Paul's knowledge and use of contemporary Jewish source material also surfaces in the NT. As a former student of Gamaliel (Acts 22:3), he doubtless had recourse to much in the way of rabbinic traditions. Evidence of this appears in 1 Corinthians 10:1-5, a midrash or commentary on the "rock that followed" the Israelites in the wilderness. The apostle builds on a Jewish legend, commonly ascribed to popular rabbinic tradition. According to the tradition, a rock was moving with the wilderness generation during their forty-year sojourn. Without evaluating this familiar legend, Paul simply uses it to underscore spiritual truth about the rock being a symbol of Christ.

Second Timothy 3:1-9 contains another instance of Paul's use of Jewish tradition for purposes of illustration. In characterizing the "last days," the apostle depicts the ungodly as in the type of two figures in Jewish midrash but unknown in the OT, Jannes and Jambres. These two are identified with Pharaoh's court magicians who opposed Moses (Odeberg: 192-193). Whether Paul depends on written or oral tradition, the names of these two rebels come to us from numerous sources: Jewish pseudepigraphal writings, rabbinic literature, Origen, Eusebius, and even several pagan writers.

Titus 1 includes instruction on the character required of an elder. There Paul alludes to a Greek poet recognized by the locals in Crete. The context here is an outline of what the elder is *not* to personify. This portrait owes its significance to the fact that Cretans were notorious for being gluttons, liars, and drunks. The ancient writer Polybius, in *Histories*, confirms a portrait of greed, duplicity, and wantonness, for which Cretans had become proverbially known. As in Acts 17, Paul uses a familiar maxim, accommodating even a secular viewpoint by attributing the tradition to a poet (Epimenides) considered on a popular level to be a "prophet."

An important though difficult text found in 1 Peter deserves comment as we consider the use of extrabiblical sources in the NT. Since it relates to the study of Jude, a brief discussion of 1 Peter 3:18-22 is appropriate (cf. Waltner, above). In these verses the reader passes from Christ's suffering, a central theme of the epistle, to Christ's triumph. The material in 1 Peter 2:8ff. traces the psychology of the believer's suffering for Christ in a pagan and hostile world. In 3:18-22 the author views the effect of Christ's work in terms of conquest.

Jesus Christ goes into heaven and is enthroned at the right hand of God, with all (hostile) angelic powers "made subject" to his authority.

Structurally and rhetorically, Jesus' enthronement in 1 Peter 3:22 is an important corollary to 3:18, the "proclamation" of Christ's triumph "to the spirits in prison," the disobedient (3:19) and fallen angels (Waltner, above). The writer exhorts and confronts his audience with the reassurance that nothing in the cosmos is outside the reign of Christ. As judgment fell on the ancient world of Noah's era, so God's judgment has come through Christ, who "suffered for sins once for all," and whose conquest over hostile spiritual powers is manifest.

The history of interpretation of these verses is notorious, and commentaries may be consulted (for a summary of approaches, see Waltner, above; J. D. Charles, 1993b: 134-142). What connects with the study of Jude is the writer's allusion to fallen angels ("imprisoned spirits"), developed extensively in Jewish apocalyptic literature and the book of Enoch in particular, in which we read of Enoch's commission to go and preach to them (1 Enoch 12).

Bo Reicke (1946:52-70) has demonstrated a clear link between the Jewish intertestamental notion of "imprisoned spirits" and corollaries in 2 Peter and Jude. On this view, 1 Peter is in essence depicting Christ as an "end-time Enoch," who has proclaimed judgment over the fallen spirits. While no specification of the angels' sin is made in 1 Peter 3 (or in 2 Peter 2:4 or Jude 6), one assumption is made: a revolt broke forth among angelic creatures (cf. John Milton, *Paradise Lost*, book 1).

The likely allusion in 1 Peter 3 to extracanonical Jewish tradition serves the greater purpose of hortatory teaching on Christ's victorious conquest over the demonic realm. In a modified fashion, Peter makes inspired use of a tradition known to some in his audience to illustrate the effects of Christ's redemptive activity. He thereby pastorally encourages his audience in a way that is scarcely appreciated by the modern reader.

Careful attention given to Jude 5-19 yields an important conclusion. Literary sources are best understood as they relate to the epistle's central purpose. They unveil a literary strategy at work, a conscious and deliberate manipulating of literary bricks and mortar by the writer. What is Jude's chief concern? He is seeking to exhort and strengthen the *faithful* by highlighting in graphic terms the fate of the *unfaithful*. The illustrations in Jude have one thing in common: they point to a place of lapse and dispossession. Unbelieving Israel, the disenfranchised angels, Sodom and Gomorrah, Cain, Balaam, and Korah—all *departed* in some respect, and all were judged accordingly.

Most commentators assume that the unfaithful in Jude represent a less-advanced state of apostasy than the "false teachers" of 2 Peter 2:1. In Jude, the unfaithful are not described in specific terms; they are merely said to operate by stealth (Jude 4) and mingle with true believers (12). Jude is less concerned with a detailed description of their present status than with the reality of their sure fate. For him, their lifestyle is an open contradiction of earlier confessed faith (cf. also 1 Tim. 5:8; 2 Tim. 3:5; Titus 1:16). Though claiming to possess the Spirit, these individuals are in fact spiritually barren (Jude 19).

Jude's perception is that these opponents have fallen away through calculation and willful disobedience. Yet the Christian community need not be shaken by the parade of sobering examples from history. On the contrary, the faithful are free to choose a pattern of obedience, as Jude 20-23 teaches.

THE TEXT IN THE LIFE OF THE CHURCH

The illustrations of Jude 5-19 show the possibility of apostasy from genuine faith. In this regard, the history of Israel as recorded in the OT leaves little room for doubt. Faith and faithlessness are always options for the people of God throughout their checkered history. The prophets are an abiding testimony to the record of both. The promises of God have always been, and continue to be, contingent upon faith and covenantal obedience. Seen as such, the framework for fellowship with God remains unchanged. Human response to God's initiative is required.

We are thus confronted with an age-old, knotty theological problem: Does the biblical teaching of predestination and election exclude the possibility of apostasy and need for perseverance of the saints? Stated conversely, how do apostasy and perseverance bear upon the doctrines of grace and election?

One view of the divine economy is that God already has chosen those who are to attain salvation in Christ. Accordingly, it is impossible for the elect to become unfaithful and ultimately apostate, since faith in the human heart issues out of the irresistible compulsion of God himself. Only those chosen beforehand are spiritually quickened. The strength of this view is its perception of the role of sovereignty and divine initiative in the believers' lives. It correctly sees the danger residing in arrogant or inflated claims to human autonomy. The believers' predestined inheritance is rooted in divine faithfulness.

An opposing view of God's dealings with his people rests upon

the assumption that there are genuine threats to Christian perseverance. Biblical injunctions toward steadfast faith and obedience, therefore, are treated with sobriety, recognizing that spiritual apostasy is a
real danger.

Historically, it has been common for representatives of these two
contrasting camps to deemphasize the biblical basis on which the
opposing view is built. The early-fifth-century controversy between
Augustine and Pelagius set the stage for what would be an ongoing
theological debate in Christendom. Pelagius insisted that the human
will acts in a sovereign way in bringing about salvation. Augustine
stressed the impossibility of even "the beginning of faith" without the
gift of prevenient grace. According to the Augustinian model of "double predestination," the elect could not in any way fall away from
faith. The unregenerate either never professed faith or professed faith
but were in fact never true believers.

Theologians of the early scholastic era generally tended to avoid
both extreme forms of Augustinianism and Pelagianism. In the period preceding the Protestant Reformation, the status of the doctrine
of grace was "superficial" (Jackson, 9:196), with a growing view that
the elect could fall from grace. Consequently, in the Reformation era
the doctrines of election and perseverance were strengthened in the
systems of both Calvin and Luther. Reformed confessions of the late
sixteenth and seventeenth centuries took both rigid and milder forms.
Disciples of Jacobus Arminius, as well as later Lutherans, rejected the
five essentials of Calvinism formulated at Dort, the fifth of which was
final perseverance.

Churches of the Anabaptist tradition were in many respects suffering churches, on certain key points at odds with the theological climate out of which they arose (Klaassen: 85-86). The disciple's suffering was to be viewed as participation in the suffering of the cross.
All of God's elect, past and present, have suffered hardship and
humiliation, patiently endured, and stood in need of forgiveness.
Implicit in the saints' election is the sharing of Christ's sacrifice. The
saints are called to persevere. To profess the merits of Christ yet continue in sin is blasphemous. If one continues in the old life, one does
not truly believe. Though Christ died for all, not all choose to embrace
his work.

Both in England and the New World, Puritans adopted a
Calvinistic stance, with its assumption of final perseverance or "eternal security." A century later, John Wesley, reacting to extreme versions of Calvinism in his day, opposed the doctrine of final perseverance, although he acknowledged the reality of and need for Christian

perseverance as a norm in believers' lives.

Polarized theological debate has characterized much of the church's history. Hence, the epistle of Jude stands as a much-needed antidote to lengthy arguments advanced by proponents of two theological poles: eternal security of the saints, and the possibility of apostasy from the faith. The responsible student of the Scriptures, whether pastor or teacher or lay person, should strive to reach beyond this historical controversy to a stance that does justice to the full weight of biblical data. We need to acknowledge the strengths and weaknesses of each side.

Jude stresses the reality of God's election and keeping power, while at the same time assuming the real possibility of departing from the faith once for all delivered to the saints. Specifics regarding the handling of disciplinary matters within the Christian community will follow in the next section (Jude 20-23). Yet we must see that Jude 5-19 plainly presumes a (pastoral) distinction between the faithful and the unfaithful.

Lessons from the past serve an instructional and prime pastoral function in the present. Those who chose to depart proceed onward to a matching doom. The irresistibility of grace is not such that a person is infallibly kept from sinning. Two opposite extremes in the Christian mind-set are to be avoided: viewing the Christian life as one of natural causation, and viewing it as one of divine determinism. Danger accompanies either extreme.

On a practical level, orthodox faith surely manifests itself in a lifestyle that honors God rightly (orthos, "correctly"; doxazein, "to honor, magnify or glorify"). It is one thing to be pagan and ignorant. It is quite another to be apostate, to have known salvation (Jude 5) and yet departed from it. Thus the reader should not miss the full force of the writer to the Hebrews, who describes the sober consequences of trampling upon the grace of God, after one has already tasted of it (Heb. 6:4-6).

Highly cultured people living in a modern and even post-Christian era have a hard time acknowledging heresy or apostasy as a reality, both theologically and morally. For many today, the categories are irrelevant. The idea seems fixed in the minds of most that orthodoxy is dull, unimaginative, and restrictive, while some tend to think of heresy as bold, courageous, and creative.

Hence, Jude's tone strikes modern readers as unusually forceful and even "insensitive." In a culture where "tolerance" has practically achieved status above God, we see intolerance for truth, morality, and religious authority. The fact remains, however, that certain doctrines and lifestyles are true, and some are false. The latter, from Jude's prophetic standpoint, lead to disaster. Thus the distinction between orthodoxy and heterodoxy is not merely academic or passé. Instead, it has consequences both for the present life and for *eternal* destiny, *forever* (Jude 6-7, 13, 21, 25).

Not to be tolerated in the Christian community are discord, discontent, murmuring, divisiveness, or moral laxity. These must be dealt with because of their corporate effect: they despoil, they act as cancer in the body, they destroy faith and community, even while their perpetrators don an air of "spirituality" and "raised consciousness." Jude condemns those who question spiritual authority, and those resisting any authority (Sidebottom: 87).

Culturally speaking, apostasy is a foremost social phenomenon (Swensen: 267). It is undergirded by a deep-rooted questioning and denying of authority that is both religious and moral in nature. Moreover, it manifests itself in moral laxness and its antinomian character. These are the trademarks of the modern spirit. Apostasy produces cleavage, division, and departure from the faith; it contaminates and corrupts as it goes. Jude's illustrations from the past have a teaching function: they remind the Christian community that compromising the truth is serious business. Above all things, Christians are supposed to be stewards of the truth (1 Cor. 4:1-2; 1 Pet. 4:10; 2 Pet. 1:12). Those who compromised in the past met their day of reckoning. The lesson should not be lost on Jude's audience. It is dangerous to keep sinning and also count on God's grace.

The language of faith and truth should not be misconstrued as intolerance or bigotry. There exists a divinely revealed standard by which we are to measure our lives. Any compromise or denial spoils the church's integrity. This is one of the great lessons of the epistle of Jude.

G. K. Chesterton expressed it well. Right is right, even when nobody does it; wrong is wrong, even if everybody is wrong about it (1956:166-167). In the "great silent collapse" of modern Western culture previewed by Chesterton (1905:320), we are prone to speak of "freedom," "rights," and "liberation," while eschewing or even mocking what is good and moral.

With the advent of a new paganism in Western culture, the church needs to reaffirm its calling, seeking to avoid two extremes: either escaping mainstream culture through pietistic retreat, or becoming merely social-political activists (Dulles: 29-55). We must reaffirm the importance of absolute truth, a doctrine of "ultimate things," which is both theological and moral in character.

Jude 20-23

Profile of the Faithful

PREVIEW

Structurally, the epistle of Jude moves back and forth between the present danger posed to the Christian community and past examples of apostasy. This is achieved by means of typology. The past models of ungodliness speak forcefully in the present.

Jude 3-4	I felt constrained to write . . . , since certain individuals . . .
5	But I want to remind you . . .
8	Likewise, these . . .
9-11	Yet Michael . . . Woe to them . . .
12	These . . .
14	But Enoch . . .
16	These . . .
17	But you . . .
19	These . . .
20	But you . . .

But you (17) begins Jude's final rhetorical response to these individuals who threaten the spiritual vitality of the Christian community. The marks of the faithful stand in bold contrast to those of the unfaithful. The latter are sensual, divisive, and devoid of the Spirit. But the truly Christian community builds itself up in its faith, prays in the Spirit, keeps itself in the love of God, and awaits Christ's mercy. By these practical steps, the believer can develop the spiritual life and remain *kept* (1, 24) by God and *keep* themselves (21). Not only do they guard themselves; they also have the moral obligation to rescue those who have become morally tainted.

To this point, the writer has used rhetorical flare, graphic imagery, and apocalyptic warnings. Now, in reflecting genuine pastoral concern, he waxes practical, suggesting in concrete terms what believers can do humanly speaking to be *kept* "by the power of God" (Jude 1, 24; 1 Pet. 1:5). The paradox of divine keeping and human responsibility remains intact. On the one hand, God is ultimately responsible for the care of his people; on the other hand, the believers themselves are obliged to remain actively in that place of divine keeping.

OUTLINE

The Faithful Reaffirming Their Foundation, Jude 20-21

The Faithful Dealing with the Unfaithful, Jude 22-23

EXPLANATORY NOTES

The Faithful Reaffirming Their Foundation
Jude 20-21

Bauckham has rightly observed that these verses are no appendix to the letter, but rather a climax (1983:111). They constitute the strategy for contending for the faith, as announced in Jude 3. Jude's pastoral burden is felt at this point, and he addresses his audience for the third time as *beloved* (3, 17, 20). The Christian community must grasp not only the sobriety of the moment but also the reality of God's sure provision.

There is a pastoral dimension to Jude's burden. He links four admonitions to underscore the believers' responsibility: (1) *Building yourselves up in your most holy faith*, (2) *praying in the Holy Spirit*, (3) *keep yourselves in the love of God*, while (4) *anticipating the mercy of our Lord Jesus Christ*.

Several features strike readers of this fourfold admonition to edify, pray, remain, and anticipate. One is the involvement of the Trinity. Each person of the Godhead is at work. Another feature is the recurrence in Jude 21 of the catchword *keep (tērein;* cf. 1, 6 [2 x], 13). Of the four verbs in 20-21, three are participial, *building, praying, awaiting;* and one is imperative, *keep*. The believers are to remain rooted in the love of God. While God is the one who calls and initiates (1), the emphasis here is clearly on human responsibility. Obedience is the fundamental imperative.

Furthermore, the believer anticipates mercy to be revealed in Jesus Christ. Here again we encounter in Jude the link between eschatology and ethics. Jesus, through whom mercy was originally extended, metes out that final judgment. Jesus is no less than the sovereign Lord. In addition, believers demonstrate the genuine presence of the Holy Spirit, in contrast to Jude's opponents (19), by cultivating a rich prayer life. Life in the Spirit is not borne out by inflated claims, but rather by dependence on God and corresponding fruit.

The fourth admonition, listed first in most English translations, draws from a metaphor common in early Christian tradition (e.g., Matt. 16:18; Acts 15:16; 1 Cor. 3:9-15; 2 Cor. 6:16; Gal. 2:9; Eph. 2:19-22; Col. 2:7; 1 Pet. 2:5): *building yourselves up in your most holy faith*. This foundation of faith, upon which the Christian community is built, is *most holy*. The contrast between the faithful and the unfaithful, the holy and the defiled, is painted in the strongest terms. The saints have been *morally* transformed; this is the hallmark of the church in a pagan culture.

Taken together, these four admonitions, far from advocating passivity, are meant to give vigor to the Christian community as it deals with the cancer of apostasy. They represent tangible means of reaffirming the foundation of faith imparted to them at the outset of their spiritual pilgrimage. A fresh commitment to the "ultimate things" will allow them to deal with those who pose a threat to the life of the Christian community.

The Faithful Dealing with the Unfaithful   Jude 22-23

The text of 22-23 is uncertain and has been the object of several studies (Osburn, 1972:134-144; Kubo: 239-253). A longer as well as shorter text has been proposed by text critics. The longer, consistent with Jude's rampant use of triplets, lists three types of response to apostates. This reading is used in the RSV and the NIV and is defended by B. M. Metzger (727-729): *And convince some, who are in doubt; and save some, snatching them out of the fire; and on some have mercy with fear, hating even the garment spotted by the flesh.*

The primary objection to this longer reading is that it has the same verb, "have mercy" (*eleate*), in both the first and third clauses. This raises questions as to how to translate the whole exhortation. Two factors, however, suggest that the longer reading is to be preferred. First, it has the greater number of manuscript witnesses. Second, it conforms to the pattern of triads that Jude so skillfully employs throughout the letter. One commentator even suggests that the threefold reading is meant to coincide with the three-stage process of church discipline found in Matthew 18 (Bauckham, 1983:111).

A shorter text, having less manuscript evidence, reads: *Snatch some out of the fire, and have mercy on those doubting, with fear, hating even the garment spotted by the flesh.* The strength of this reading is that it allows an easier explanation of the longer reading rather than vice versa (Birdsall: 394-399; Osburn, 1972:139-144).

Adopting a longer reading, as I. H. Marshall has noted, allows us to extrapolate concerning three groups of people (165). The first group consists of waverers, those trapped in a state of doubt and spiritual confusion. The church is to extend compassion to these, that they remain steadfast in the truth. The second group is portrayed as those near the point of being touched by the fire. These, one can assume, have succumbed to the influence of the ungodly and require urgent intervention. The third group appears to have already become tainted by error. Contact with them, as reflected in the "garment" imagery, would result in becoming defiled, since they are badly polluted.

Our acceptance of the longer, triadic reading of 22-23 leaves us, however, with a problem. How shall we appropriately render the same verb used in both verses (*eleate*, "have mercy")? This is not easily done if the first group is to receive pity and is in need of genuine mercy, while the third group is already corrupted. Mayor gets around this by translating the second use of *eleate* in the sense of giving "trembling compassion" (cxci), in light of the modifier "with fear" (*en phobo*).

Some commentators believe *snatch some from the fire* is borrowing from the vision of Zechariah 3:1-5, because of Jude's prior allusion to the Testament of Moses (7:7, 9), itself apparently coming from Zechariah (Kelly: 288; Bauckham, 1983:114-115). Also of note is Amos 4:11, where both "Sodom and Gomorrah" and the phrase "snatched from the fire" appear together. The fire imagery reminds Jude's readers of the relationship between eschatology and ethics. They are to reflect on the reality of future consequences for present moral decisions. Some in the community, in disavowing such consequences, presently stand at considerable risk.

The defilement imagery associated with the third group carries the fear of contamination and is also reminiscent of Zechariah 3. To the Jewish way of thinking, defilement is a picture of one who has passed through ceremonial purification but who, pathetically, has again transgressed the law. Clearly, Jude's opponents have already been corrupted by their lawless spirit. Those risking contact with the apostates are the ones to be rescued, and they are to be rescued in the utter *fear of God*. Believers need to recognize evil for what it is, and hate it. Yet they are to show compassion for its victims. As urged by Jude, sympathy motivated by holy fear will not deteriorate into sympathy for sin.

THE TEXT IN BIBLICAL CONTEXT

The language of Jude 20-21 resembles that found in the Pauline epistles. Being rooted "in the love of God" (cf. Eph. 3:17-19; 5:1-2), "awaiting the mercy of Jesus Christ" (cf. Rom. 8:23-25; 1 Cor. 1:7; Phil. 3:20; 2 Tim. 1:18), "praying in the Spirit" (cf. Rom. 8:26; 1 Cor. 14:15; Eph. 6:18), and being "built up in the faith" (cf. Rom. 14:3-5, 19; 15:2; 1 Cor. 8:1; Eph. 4:12, 16) are a standard part of the apostle's teaching.

We have identified the central theological paradox of Jude's epistle, the tension between divine initiative and human cooperation. Within this paradox, which at times in the history of the church has been mutilated, there is a meeting place, a convergence of both elements. All four of the admonitions contained in verses 20-21 illustrate this very paradox in one form or another.

Although faith is to be understood as a gift, the people of God nevertheless are told, *Build yourselves up*. Although prayer is union and fellowship with God the Holy Spirit, Christians are to cultivate praying with the Spirit. Although believers are *kept* by God, they nonetheless carry the responsibility of Christian discipleship to maintain their walk with God; *keep yourselves* (cf. Phil. 2:12-13). Although the Lord Jesus is the one who extends mercy to believers in the first place, they must measure all moral decisions in light of the coming day of judgment.

Biblical revelation is full of all manner of paradox. While the history of the Christian church is a record of seemingly one theological excess after another, it is also a record of the faithfulness of God in his attempts to counter certain excesses. Balance in perspective is one of the invaluable services rendered by a study of Jude. Theological debate is hereby tempered, helping to inform the people of God of the "whole counsel of God" (Acts 20:27).

Yet the epistle of Jude implies much more than mere theological mystery. It confronts the church in every age with an integral component of Christian community, the need for discipline. The early church was birthed out of a Jewish matrix and thus inherited its structure from Judaism. A prime example of this structure is the Jewish notion of "binding" and "loosing" which appears in Matthew 18 in a discussion of spiritual authority. In Jude, we encounter some outworking of "the keys" of apostolic authority in the community of believers.

In many ways, Matthew 18 anticipates church discipline. Implicit in the text is concern for fellow church members: "If another member of the church sins, go and . . ." Sin left unchecked can lead to a loss of faith. The purpose of the discipline is that the fellow church member be "regained" (18:15). This fits the preceding verses that deal with the return of the lost sheep (18:10-14). However, after due process, if individuals still reject admonition and are impenitent, the community needs to exclude them: "Let such a one be to you as a Gentile and a tax collector."

An intriguing Lukan narrative, Acts 5:1-11, serves as a reminder that sin that is concealed can have catastrophic and indeed fatal consequences. Two members of the community, Ananias and Sapphira, operate under the power of deception and are rebuked for "lying to the Holy Spirit" in the midst of the community. The story, something of an embarrassment to the modern reader, brings us into a thought-world where sin and the fear of God are taken seriously. At first glance, the lack of opportunity for repentance is troubling. Nevertheless, readers should guard against presumption. The early church recognized the possibility of temporal judgment on a lifestyle of sin and grieving the Holy Spirit.

In 1 Corinthians 5:1-13 Paul is explicit and forceful in his command to remove the arrogant, obstinate sinner from Christian fellowship. While God ultimately "judges" those outside the household of faith, those inside are to be "judged" by the believing community itself. At stake is the holy reputation of the Head of the church. First Corinthians 5 makes it clear that the community is to handle matters of spiritual discipline. Believers are strongly exhorted to pay attention to such matters. In Paul's mind, the situation in Corinth constitutes a "crisis of authority" (Fee: 195). It should not strike the reader as unusual that in the fledgling church, sexual ethics had to be addressed on a regular basis. Establishing credibility in a pagan, Gentile world required as much.

The brief portrait by Paul in 2 Corinthians 2:5-11 suggests that someone in the community had created much pain for the apostle. Evidently, censure was brought upon that individual by the majority of the church members, eventually resulting in true repentance. (Perhaps it was the result of a severe reprimand, perhaps exclusion from the Christian community.) Paul's verdict is that the church should now embrace the man and affirm him with love. Forgiveness and restoration are clearly the goal in view.

Elsewhere in the NT, the issues of church discipline and restoration of an individual overtaken by sin are suggested (e.g., Gal. 6:1-2; James 5:20; 1 John 5:16-17). Exhortations to avoid certain types of disobedient persons in the community surface also (2 Thess. 3:6; 14; 2 Tim. 3:2-5; Titus 3:10). The overall tone of discipline in the Christian community, established by loving and firm leadership, finds its expression in 1 Peter 5:1-5. There a true leader in the church, tempered by years of experience and a servant's heart, admonishes "fellow elders" to shepherd God's flock and be examples to those they are leading.

THE TEXT IN THE LIFE OF THE CHURCH

The term *believers church* has historically designated Christian congregations organized as voluntary associations of adults baptized upon confession of faith. Most Protestant Reformers understood discipline to be one of the marks of the church, but such is hardly the case in contemporary American culture. This is tragic. There is mixed appreciation of discipline and little practice of it in the church because of the highly individualistic character of North American society and the devaluation of historic Christian doctrine. Many congregations are content with innocuous conceptions of membership, if they exist at all. Thus a recovery of Christian authority in the household of faith is imperative. The church's authority in broader culture stands or falls with its ability to shepherd its own.

The epistle of Jude takes us past mere theological debate into the realm of divine faithfulness as well as Christian perseverance. To suggest that Jude's exhortations are merely hypothetical in nature will not suffice. The epistle is a call to action. Its message is imperative in a "postmodern" era when much of the Christian church, the believers church included, has become acculturated and seems to reflect the values of broader society more than those of the kingdom of God.

Biblical revelation by its nature is challenging and controversial. Throughout history it has challenged apostasy and heresy (with an assumption that an organic link exists between the two). In most parts of Christendom, the terms "apostasy" and "heresy" have all but fallen by the wayside. Contemporary religion has little use for such outdated categories. They strike us as rather antiquated.

The letter of Jude, nonetheless, is an enduring witness to the ever-present reality of theological and ethical compromise. While the epistle stops short of recommending a specific course of action in dealing with the faithless, the believing community is admonished to *convince* some (from the longer reading; see notes on 22), *save* others, and in the fear of God, *snatch out of the fire* still others. The tone of Jude's exhortation is one of great urgency. Hence, the church of any age needs to reflect on its own cultural situation: Are we contending for Christian truth in a way that reaffirms "the permanent things" of doctrine and morality?

The threat posed to the church's witness is not that it is full of people who sin (Jeschke, 1988:51). Instead, given the cancerous nature of sin, will the church do anything about it? The fear of the Lord is conspicuously absent in most contemporary Protestant churches. The holy fear of God alone will transform the Christian community in a way that will restore its integrity and authenticity.

Church discipline may be defined as the "ministry of discipling a Christian brother or sister whose spiritual health and life are endangered by a particular act or attitude" (Jeschke, 1988:17). Various terms or descriptions have been traditionally used to express this spiritual state: lapse, backsliding, apostasy, or breach of covenant. For the Protestant Reformers, church discipline was central to Christian identity, and one of the constitutive marks of the church.

Calvin, more so than Luther, was successful in incorporating discipline into the life of the Christian community. The modern reader may be startled by the degree of pastoral authority assumed by this Reformer. For him, church discipline constitutes the ligaments that hold the body together. Calvin was acutely aware of its necessity: "Whoever . . . desires either the abolition of all discipline, or the obstruction of its restoration, whether they act from design or inadvertency, they certainly promote the entire dissolution of the Church" (2:1230).

John Knox, in his "Order of Excommunication," compared the exercise of spiritual discipline to the quarantine of disease, decrying the "cruel and uncharitable" idea of putting "people with pestilence or infectious sores" together in one bed with well people (Adams: 140). An inability to separate the unhealthy from the healthy is nothing short of catastrophic.

Discipline was characteristic of the Anabaptist-Mennonite movement from the beginning (Bender: 69ff.). An early Anabaptist rule on the subject was published in 1527: "Discipline of the Believer: How a Christian Is to Live." It stressed the character of admonition, the need for public rebuke where sin was public in nature, the common good of the community, the need for distinctly Christian standards, and the imperative of having a watchful attitude toward sin (Friedmann: 162-168). In contrast to the state churches, the

Anabaptists used verbal warnings and the ban or avoidance rather than physical punishment or death as tools of church discipline.

Menno Simons wrote three treatises on church discipline: "A Kind Admonition on Church Discipline" (1541), "A Clear Account of Excommunication" (1550), and "Instruction on Excommunication" (1558). In addition, the Schleitheim Confession of 1527 reflects the place of church discipline in early Anabaptism. It affirms the practice of the "ban" with

> all those who have given themselves to the Lord, to walk in His commandments, and with all those who are baptized into the one body of Christ and who are called brethren or sisters, and yet who slip sometimes and fall into error and sin. . . . The same shall be admonished twice in secret and the third time openly disciplined or banned according to the command of Christ. . . . But this shall be done according to the regulation of the Spirit before the breaking of bread, so that we may break and eat one bread with one mind and in one love, and may drink from one cup. (Schlabach: 117)

Following the Schleitheim Confession, church discipline is affirmed in practically every formal profession of faith. Among its stalwart defenders were Menno Simons, Dirk Philips, and Leenaert Bouwens, who practiced the ban or avoidance of those who strayed (Smith: 66-69). Indeed, Dirk lists church discipline as one of the characteristic marks or rules of the true church (390ff.).

Generally speaking, the Puritans of the New World carried on the vision of Calvin's Geneva, with a rigorous emphasis on sanctification, the glory of God, and accountability to one another. Holiness to the Puritans, as J. I. Packer (1990) has illustrated, was a foundational motivation. For those in the Methodist-Wesleyan tradition, discipline was certainly no stranger. Both in England and the New England colonies, John Wesley strove to instill a high level of accountability within individual congregations. Early Baptists as well were known to be conscientious in practicing church discipline, especially in frontier congregations, while the Quakers were well-known for their painstaking self-examination.

In short, it is fair to maintain that church discipline has always been integral to the life of God's people, notwithstanding the pioneering free spirit so typical of early American life. Its loss in contemporary society is understandable but to be lamented. Fallen into disuse, discipline is frequently perceived as the antithesis of the love of Christ. It is not uncommon for secular rather than genuinely biblical values to color the church's social and moral agenda. "Relevance" has superseded holiness as the trademark of many contemporary religious communities.

Yet the restoration of a NT church points above all to a disciplined community (Durnbaugh: 220). Discipleship will unquestionably entail discipline. Judging the household of faith (cf. 1 Cor. 5:9-13) will mean bringing God's uncompromising ethical standards to bear on his own people. Discipline, then, is integral to the church's very existence.

When people are brought into a caring community of believers, they are mutually encouraged in their walk with Christ. The church's general failure to discipline its own can be seen as a basic failure in understanding its identity and mission. Placed in the midst of a pagan culture, the church sets sacred boundaries in calling for people's response to the gospel. These boundaries are of saving significance (Jeschke, 1988:163). If the church truly is submitted to the lordship of Christ, then that rule will be felt first and foremost in the community of faith.

Seen positively, church discipline entails how individuals within the body of Christ relate to one another, how the church's ordinances are observed, how the doctrinal essentials of the faith are formulated and upheld, and how believers conduct themselves in a pagan cultural environment (MacGorman: 74). To be consistent with NT teaching, discipline will take on suitable characteristics. "Moral discernment" and a "dialogue of reconciliation" take place in such *Body Politics* (Yoder: 1-13; *Confession of Faith*, art. 14). For example, discipline will not be exercised over trivialities. The church will acknowledge the contagion of sin and evil. Discipline will be redemptive rather than punitive; in some cases, it will even lead to exclusion (MacGorman: 80-82).

A withdrawal of fellowship does not mean a withdrawal of concern for the individual party. Nor does it mean a lack of compassion is present among believers. The fact that discipline has on occasion been misapplied does not negate its necessity or its fundamental purpose, which is corrective and redemptive. Ultimately, believers hope that discipline hastens eventual repentance and restoration through the grace of God.

Jude 24-25

Tribute to the One Who Keeps

PREVIEW

Jude has called forth past examples of divine judgment and exhorted the faithful to realize their part in being a disciplined community. Now he concludes by offering an exalted tribute to the One who preserves them. This is done in the form of a doxology, a "proclaiming of glory." Several basic patterns of speech to God tend to emerge from the OT: petition, praise, and thanksgiving. Hymnic material that offers praise and glorification of God can assume the form of any of these.

This doxology was developed in a distinctly Jewish setting. Although Palestinian Judaism knew certain stages in the development of the doxology, its arrangement did not become liturgically rigid (Werner: 273-276). The early Christian doxology, in style and content, resembled that of the Jewish synagogue and was often accompanied by an eschatological deliverance-call.

Normally framed in the third person, as in Jude 25, the doxology functions to ascribe *glory, majesty, power, and authority* to God: *Now to the One who is able* (*tō dunamenō phulaxai*). The doxology also affirms God's eternal character: *before all time and now and forever. Amen* (Werner: 274).

EXPLANATORY NOTES

The epistle concludes with a benediction praising God for his attributes that express themselves in his power to preserve the saints. This benediction or doxology repeats in the active voice what the author has stated in his salutation through the passive voice: his readers are called, beloved, and kept by God. The introduction and conclusion of the letter thus form a rhetorical inclusio by opening and closing with the same theme: the saints are kept by the power of God.

The conclusion of Jude follows a series of eight exhortations to the faithful that are to serve as antidotes to apostasy in light of the previous condemnations (Marshall: 166). The saints are to remember, build themselves up, pray, keep themselves, anticipate, convince, save, and have mercy (Jude 17-23).

The rhetorical effect of the doxology is deliberate, following the rather brief but rapid-fire hortatory section. After all has been humanly done to safeguard against the cancer of apostasy, it is the power of Almighty God our Savior mediated through Jesus Christ that *is able to keep you from falling* (24).

First, God is able to keep his own from falling. Exploiting a prominent catchword in the epistle, the author uses a strengthened form of "preserve" (*phulassein*) to describe divine action: God is able, literally, to "guard (safely) as does a prison." Moreover, God is able not only to safeguard the saints against falling but even to cause them *to stand without blemish before God's presence with great joy* (24). In the end, then, it is not simply persistence or the great investment of human energies that ultimately is responsible for the saints' salvation; rather, it is the saving and keeping power of God.

To this *God our Savior* alone the following attributes are ascribed: glory, majesty, power, and authority. The cumulative force of these resources is the *surpassing might* of him who called us (25; cf. 1). With precise calculation, Jude employs the language of sovereignty. The saints need not be shaken by the sobering instances of God's judgment in history, if they have a genuine desire to be established in the faith.

Finally, praise is due this Almighty Savior *before all time and now and forever*. Through the rest of the epistle, Jude draws on the language and imagery of Jewish apocalyptic, as known in intertestamental literature. But in his concluding doxology, he aligns himself with a decidedly OT prophetic view of history. The past, the present, and the future are all seen as working toward consummation of the divine purpose.

Structurally, the doxology is normally positioned at the conclusion of kerygmatic or hymnic material and consists of three parts: the person named, an expression of praise often comprised of two or more elements and including the term *doxa*, and finally a formula for time (Deichgräber: 25). Jude 24-25 conforms to this standard pattern.

The Jewish doxology typically concluded with the affirmation *Amēn*. Equally common to the OT and the rabbinic milieu, *amēn* reinforces and makes valid the declarations, confessions, or oaths (Glaue: 184). At times ending a prayer (e.g., Neh. 8:6; 1 Chron. 16:36) and frequently a psalm (e.g., Ps. 41:13; 72:19; 89:52; 106:48), *amēn* can also be doubled in the OT for emphasis (e.g., Num. 5:22; Neh. 8:6; cf. John 1:51, Greek; etc.). In extracanonical apocalyptic literature, *amēn* often appears with eschatological statements. In the synagogue it constituted the most common benediction pronounced by the rabbis (Glaue: 186). It is only natural that the *amēn* found its way into the liturgy of the early church.

THE TEXT IN BIBLICAL CONTEXT

Jewish benedictions clearly inform the NT doxology (e.g., in 1 Chron. 29:10; Ps. 72:19; Dan. 2:20). In the NT the benediction concludes greetings, prayers, as well as letters. Doxologies comparable to Jude 24-25 are found elsewhere in the NT (Rom. 16:25-27; Eph. 3:20-21; 1 Tim. 1:17; cf. 2 Cor. 9:8; 1 Thess. 3:13).

As the Scriptures affirm theological truth, they inevitably assume a doxological character. In both the OT and the NT, they reflect human adoration and passionate worship by the people of God. Believers worship God for his power, majesty, and glory. In the NT, doxology is expressed succinctly in the disciple's declaration, "My Lord and my God!" All that was ascribed to Yahweh under the old covenant is transferred to Jesus Christ.

Doxology in the NT takes on even greater importance where competing loyalties are at stake. It is particularly with this awareness that the NT Apocalypse is framed. John shares with the churches of Asia Minor their persecution and patient endurance on account of the name of Christ (Rev. 1). The saints are confronted with competing claims of lordship. The social and political pressure for people to call Caesar *dominus* (lord), though not always driven by religious assumptions, creates practical tensions for the first-century believers. Their confession "Jesus is *kurios* (Lord)" causes them to be viewed as enemies of the state (1 Cor. 12:3). Jude lays it on the line when he calls Jesus Christ "our only Master and Lord" (Jude 4).

In the throne vision of Revelation 4 and 5, these competing confessions are on display. Christian confession is challenged by the dilemma stemming from claims of ultimacy made for the Roman empire. John borrows the language of imperial sovereignty to acclaim "the one sitting on the throne" and the Lamb. "You are worthy, our Lord and God, to receive glory and honor and power" (4:11; cf. 7:12). "Worthy is the Lamb . . . to receive power and wealth and wisdom and might and honor and glory and blessing!" (5:12-13).

Roman poets did not hesitate to ascribe to the emperor attributes of deity, such as divine power, immortality, light, invincibility, genius, and greatness. According to Martial, for example, Domitian's divine power exerted itself not only over humanity but also over animals and inanimate objects (*Epigr.* 9.61). The populace celebrated the emperor's arrival with a common tribute: "*Vere dignus* ([you are] truly worthy)." In the first century, the emperors began using "blasphemous names" for themselves, claiming to be deity (Rev. 13:1; cf. 2 Thess. 2:4; Elias: 279-280). The eastern provinces, especially the province of Asia, were zealous in developing emperor worship (Rev. 13; Caird, 1966:163).

The imagery used in the NT Apocalypse is intended to encourage the saints. Imperial pretensions are deflated as the language of triumph and sovereignty is transferred to God and to the Lamb (Charles, 1993a:85 97), thereby causing the saints to bow down and worship the Almighty. The myriads in heaven give sevenfold praise to honor the Lamb that was slain, who takes his rightful place beside the one seated on the throne (Rev. 5:5-14; 22:3).

Christian worship and literature acclaim Jesus Christ as divine (cf. 2 Pet. 1:1; Titus 2:13; John 1:1-3; 20:28; Col. 1:15; Phil. 2:6). The splendor of the Caesar pales in the light of the Lamb's infinite and radiant glory and might. The Lamb is "Lord of lords and King of kings" (Rev. 17:14; 19:16).

THE TEXT IN THE LIFE OF THE CHURCH

The function of doxology, literally, "the speaking of [divine] glory," is the transmission of the apostle's vision to the Christian community. In worship, Christian truth comes into sharp focus; it is in worship that Christian vision finds its most concentrated expression. While worship involves and affects the individual, it is not individualistic. Thus doxological expression is always set within the broader context of the Christian community (Wainwright: 3). Worship transforms both individuals and the community from sinfulness to saintliness.

Glorifying God, then, is to be viewed as the transfiguration of human character into the likeness of God's character. In this way doxology, just as all forms of Christian worship, is holy and sacred.

As for the readers of Jude's epistle, it is difficult for Christians today to withstand the seduction of surrounding culture as it presses upon the Christian community. Cultural influences will defile and undermine Christian witness unless believers rely on the power of God. Moreover, the NT acknowledges that the gatherings of the church may be infiltrated by *intruders* who claim to be believers but are not (Jude 4, 12; Matt. 7:21-23; Acts 20:29; 2 Pet. 3:16-17; 1 John 4:1; Rev. 2:2).

One of the marks of the church that will keep it purified and vital in her faith is true worship. In the clash of spiritual kingdoms, Spirit-breathed worship is a key antidote to unbelief, corruption, and ultimately, apostasy. Believers thereby build themselves up in their most holy faith (Jude 20). Through worship and doxology, the church confesses anew the keeping power of God. Accordingly, the end of Jude's epistle stresses the reality of God's activity, closing out what Jude has pronounced to his audience at the start: Christians are called, they are loved, and they are *kept by God in Jesus Christ* (Jude 1).

This doxology waits to be sung, as well as spoken. It has been set to music, as shown on the next two pages.

Now Unto Him

Words and Music by David W. Morris

Now un-to Him who is a - ble to keep you from

fall - ing, And to make you stand in His

pres - ence blame - less and with great joy,

To the on - ly God, our Sav - ior, through

Je - sus Christ, our___ Lord,___ Be the glo - ry___ and the

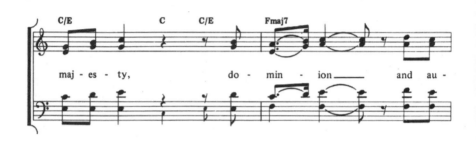

maj - es - ty, do - min - ion___ and au -

thor - i - ty,___ Both now and ev - er, a -

men!_____

Outline of Jude

The Author, His Audience and Purpose for Writing	Jude 1-4
Opening Salutation	1-2
Occasion for Writing	3-4
Profile of the Unfaithful	5-19
Tales of Woe, Part 1: An Intolerable Triad	5-7
Unbelieving Israel	5
The Fallen Angels	6
Sodom and Gomorrah	7
Marks of the Apostate, Part 1	8-10
Tales of Woe, Part 2: An Intractable Triad	11
Cain	11a
Balaam	11b
Korah	11c
Marks of the Apostate, Part 2	12-13
Judgment of the Ungodly	14-15
Marks of the Apostate, Part 3	16-19
Profile of the Faithful	20-23
The Faithful Reaffirming Their Foundation	20-21
The Faithful Dealing with the Unfaithful	22-23
Tribute to the One Who Keeps	24-25

Essay for Jude

APOCALYPTIC LITERATURE The Babylonian exile marked a significant turn in Jewish perspective. Although preexilic OT writings contain bits of an apocalyptic outlook, classical apocalyptic as a literary style is essentially postexilic. From the standpoint of the exile, the burning question that confronted Jews was whether the Lord had forsaken his people. How was one to interpret history, which seemed not to be bringing salvation? A major obstacle confounding the Jewish people was how to interpret the Lord's punitive purposes, using Babylon as an instrument. How were they to make sense of their suffering under prolonged domination by the Gentiles: Assyria, Babylonia, Persia, Greece, Syria, and eventually Rome?

During the second century B.C., a distinct shift in historical perspective was occurring. A younger Israel had written faith-inducing historiography of God saving his people. It was harder to admit in the present that the divine will was being fulfilled while Persian, Greek, and Syrian rule crept by with agonizing slowness. This required an altered vision.

One means of solving this dilemma was by transferring some effective agency to angelic beings. Evil angels, not God, were seen as the principal cause of the present (political) disorder. The result of this is that angelology in intertestamental Jewish literature is pronounced. An example is the role of the "watchers" in 1 Enoch, the Testaments of the Twelve Patriarchs, and Jubilees (cf. Dan. 4:13, 17, 23).

In the apocalyptic outlook, evil on earth was matched or led by celestial models, like the angelic "prince of Persia" or the "prince of Greece" (Dan. 10:13, 20; 11:2ff.). Meanwhile, Israel had its own patron angel, "Michael, the great prince, the protector of your people" (12:1; 10:21). God would not intervene to crush the pagan rule over Israel until things had run their course, based on a heavenly timetable (11:35; etc.).

The rise of this apocalyptic perspective appears to have coincided with several historical developments: the cessation of prophecy, the failure of a restored kingdom of Israel to manifest itself, and the emergence of a "righ-

330

teous remnant." In the light of these factors, apocalyptic writers give literary expression to the sentiments of their day. They did this in response to the perplexing degree of political, cultural, and social upheaval around them.

Attempting to make sense of the future in light of the present, they envisioned eschatological intervention by God in ultimate and cataclysmic terms. Their writing became a crisis literature that mirrored attempts to discern the relationship between events in heaven and earth. Hence, one discovers in Jewish apocalyptic literature a preoccupation with visions of what is to happen in or from the invisible world: angelic warfare, dramatic revelations, theophany, fiery destruction of the godless, and vindication of God's elect. Apocalyptic literature furnishes the necessary imagery with which to depict any situation where affairs seem out of control and sin is rampant.

For the Jewish apocalypticist, the veil which impeded human understanding was the Flood. Those living prior to this catastrophic event, such as Enoch, had greater access to divine secrets. For the prophets, the exodus from Egypt marked a crucial turning point in Israel's history; for the apocalypticist, however, the Flood was pivotal. The apocalyptic view of history differs from that of the prophets in its explanations of present events on earth. The prophets portrayed Yahweh as working *through* the kingdoms of the earth, such as Assyria, Babylon, and Persia (Isa. 7:17-20; 44:28—45:1, 13; Jer. 20:4-6). In contrast, the later intertestamental writers tended to view deliverance and fulfillment of the divine purpose as coming from *beyond* history.

First Enoch 6–11 serves to illustrate the significance of apocalyptic literature for the study of the NT, and Jude, in particular. The material in these chapters is an extrapolation of Genesis 6:1-4 concerning the "sons of God" and the statement in 5:24 that Enoch walked with God. The story of the "watchers" supplies a mythic representation of how evil may abound on earth, while judgment and ultimate vindication have already been prepared in heaven.

There is underlying value in the apocalyptic genre, which early Christian writers inherited from their Jewish forebears. It mirrors the transcendent perspective as people of faith wrestle with the dilemma of theodicy, justifying the ways of God to human beings. Apocalyptic is clearly rooted in the conviction that the present world is passing away.

Nevertheless, an important distinction must be drawn between NT apocalyptic and other apocalyptic writings. Although Jude, for example, uses apocalyptic themes and imagery, the writer's perspective is clarified in the letter's doxology: *God our Savior* is *before all time and now and forever* (Jude 25). That is, Jude aligns himself with the OT prophetic view of history. He sees the past, present, and future as all working toward the consummation of the divine purpose. This is accomplished *through Jesus Christ our Lord.*

In addition to the prominence of angels and the exalted status of mediating antediluvian patriarchs such as Enoch, we also encounter in Jewish apocalyptic literature frequent allusions to the cosmic order and solar phenomena. These features are not fully appreciated by modern readers. Numerous examples from the OT might be cited for the sake of illustration. Isaiah 13 contains an oracle delivered against Babylon, in which the Lord of Hosts, the divine warrior, assembles an army in his wrath (13:4-5). So momentous is this divine response that the very sun, moon, and stars of heaven are shaken

(13:10-13). The glory of Babylon's pride is to be utterly destroyed, to be no more, just as happened to Sodom and Gomorrah (13:19).

Solar imagery is also an important part of the prophetic oracle in Joel 2. The day of the Lord spells gloom and dread (2:2, 11). It is a day of "darkness and gloom," of "clouds and blackness" (2:2). As judgment approaches, the earth shakes, the sky trembles, the sun and moon are darkened, and the stars no longer shine (2:10; 3:15, NIV). On this day, the day of the Lord, the sun will be turned to darkness and the moon to blood before the coming of the great and dreadful day of the Lord (2:31, NIV). At Pentecost, as the Spirit is poured out and the church begins, Peter claims a beginning of fulfillment for such portents (Acts 2:16-21; Faw: 45).

A further feature of apocalyptic literature combines both the angelic motif and cosmic phenomena into a theme of cosmic rebellion. While this motif is found in numerous intertestamental writings, it is magnified in 1 Enoch. Perhaps it serves a strategic literary function in Jude, given the background of the readers. In Jude, the rebel angels who lost their exalted heavenly position are eternally chained in darkness (Jude 6). Simarily, the evil *intruders* and *dreamers* are cast as *wandering stars*, doomed for *deepest darkness, forever* (13).

This allusion would doubtless trigger some association with the fallen stars of 1 Enoch, since Jude (14-15) does cite 1 Enoch (1:9). Within apocalyptic mythology, as already noted, a frequent pattern tends to emerge. War erupts in heaven, often depicted in astral terms. This rebellion spills over to earth and eventually culminates in ultimate vindication of the faithful and punishment of the wicked by the King of Heaven.

The usefulness of adapting apocalyptic motifs by early Christian writers, while it can be overstated, is observed by one student of the intertestamental era:

The penumbrae of the Christian prophetic movement . . . would be almost bound to include certain people (whether originally Essenes, Pharisees, or of some more mixed or obscure allegiance) . . . who could think of no better service to the new faith than to adapt existing apocalypses to make them support Christianity. (Beckwith: 399-400)

However, when we acknowledge the use of apocalyptic motifs by NT writers, we certainly do not suggest that these writers uncritically endorse everything in the apocalyptic perspective. The angels in Jude are illustrative, not causative. Jude's use of moral typology shows that wickedness has both earthly and heavenly antecedents, both of which are morally accountable to God. He does *not* present humans as pawns of heavenly spirit-beings, as 1 Enoch depicts them.

As found in Jude and Revelation, apocalyptic language and imagery extend and reorient an inherited religious worldview so that it fits the Christian faith. The religious and cultural world we witness in the opening pages of the NT is one in which Jewish messianic expectations are unfulfilled. The longing for a restored kingdom of Israel is unsatisfied (Acts 1:6). Nevertheless, this inherited worldview is Jewish to the core.

Effective writers exploit the imagination and sensory dimensions of the engaged reader. *How* a message is expressed is indivisible from its contents.

Form conveys meaning. While form does not *replace* meaning, it is the necessary vehicle by which meaning is communicated.

In Jude, as is true of the prophetic imagination, the burden of the Lord is incarnated in a literary form that may escape the modern reader. Yet Jude speaks forcefully to its intended audience. With some effort, we can listen in and be edified. Part of Jude's literary strategy is to incorporate apocalyptic themes and imagery, which tend to be more appreciated in desperate times.

Bibliography for Jude

Adams, J. C.
    1967   "The Place of Discipline in Christian Ethics." *Crane Review* 9:136-152.
Aulén, Gustaf
    1956   *Christus Victor.* New York: Macmillan.
Bauckham, Richard J.
    1983   *Jude, 2 Peter.* Word Biblical Commentary, 50. Waco: Word.
    1988   "James, 1 and 2 Peter, Jude." In *It Is Written: Scripture Citing Scripture: Essays in Honour of B. Lindars,* 303-317. Ed. D. A. Carson and H. G. M. Williamson. Cambridge: Cambridge Univ. Press.
Beckwith, Roger T.
    1985   *The Old Testament Canon of the New Testament Church and Its Background in Early Judaism.* Grand Rapids: Eerdmans.
Bender, Harold S.
    1956   "Discipline, Concept, Idea, and Practice of." In *The Mennonite Encyclopedia,* 2:69-70. Scottdale, Pa.: Herald Press.
Berger, Peter L.
    1979   *The Heretical Imperative.* Garden City: Doubleday (Anchor).
Birdsall, J. Neville
    1963   "The Text of Jude in p. 72." *Journal of Theological Studies* 14:394-399.
Bonhoeffer, Dietrich
    1961   *The Cost of Discipleship.* Trans. R. H. Fuller. New York: Macmillan.
Boyd, James W.
    1975   *Satan and Māra: Christian and Buddhist Symbols of Evil.* Studies in the History of Religions, 27, Leiden: E. J. Brill.
Caird, George B.
    1965   *Principalities and Powers.* Oxford: Clarendon Press.

1966   *A Commentary on the Revelation of St. John the Divine.*
       Black's New Testament Commentaries. London: Adam &
       Charles Black.
Calvin, John
1960   *Institutes of the Christian Religion.* 2 vols. Philadelphia:
       Westminster.
Charles, J. Daryl
1990   "'Those' and 'These': The Use of the OT in the Epistle of Jude."
       Journal for the Study of the New Testament 37:109-124.
1991a "Literary Artifice in the Epistle of Jude." *Zeitschrift für die
       neutestamentliche Wissenschaft* 82/1:106-124.
1991b "Jude's Use of Pseudepigraphical Source-Material as Part of a
       Literary Strategy." *New Testament Studies* 37:130-145.
1993a "Imperial Pretensions and the Throne-Vision of the Lamb:
       Observations on the Function of Revelation 5." *Criswell
       Theological Review* 7/1:85-97.
1993b *Literary Strategy in the Epistle of Jude.* London and Toronto:
       Associated Univ. Presses; Scranton: Univ. of Scranton Press.
Charles, Robert H., ed.
1913   *The Apocrypha and Pseudepigrapha of the Old Testament.*
       2 vols. Oxford: Clarendon Press.
Charlesworth. *See* Isaac
Chesterton, G. K.
1905   *Heretics.* New York and London: J. Lancaster Co.
1956   *All Things Considered.* New York: Sheed and Ward.
Confession of Faith in a Mennonite Perspective
1995   Scottdale, Pa.: Herald Press.
Deichgräber, Reinhart
1967   *Gotteshymnus und Christushymnus in der frühen Christenheit.*
       Göttingen: Vandenhoeck & Ruprecht.
Dirk Philips
1966   *Enchiridion or Handbook of the Christian Doctrine and
       Religion.* Alymer, Ont.: Pathway Publishing.
1992   *The Writings of Dirk Philips.* Trans and ed. C. J. Dyck, William
       E. Keeney, and Alvin J. Beachy. Classics of the Radical
       Reformation. Scottdale, Pa.: Herald Press.
Dulles, Avery
1989   "Gospel, Church and Politics." In *American Apostasy: The
       Triumph of "Other" Gospels,* 29-55. Ed. R. J. Neuhaus. Grand
       Rapids: Eerdmans.
Durnbaugh, Donald F.
1985   *The Believers' Church: The History and Character of Radical
       Protestantism.* Scottdale, Pa.: Herald Press.
Elias, Jacob W.
1995   *1 and 2 Thessalonians.* Believers Church Bible Commentary.
       Scottdale, Pa.: Herald Press.
Ellis, E. Earle
       "Prophecy and Hermeneutic in Jude." In *Prophecy and
       Hermeneutic in Early Christianity,* 221-236. Tübingen: Mohr.

Exler, Francis Xavier J.
1923   *The Form of the Ancient Greek Letter: A Study in Greek Epistolography.* Washington, D.C.: Catholic Univ. of America Press.
Faw, Chalmer E.
1993   *Acts.* Believers Church Bible Commentary. Scottdale, Pa.: Herald Press.
Fee, Gordon D.
1987   *The First Epistle to the Corinthians.* New International Commentary on the New Testament. Grand Rapids: Eerdmans.
Friedmann, Robert
1955   "The Oldest Church Discipline of the Anabaptists." *Mennonite Quarterly Review* 29:162-168.
Fuchs, Ernst, and P. Reymond
1980   *La Deuxième Épître de Saint Pierre: L'Épître de Saint Jude.* Commentaire du Nouveau Testament, 13b. Neuchâtel: Delachaux & Niestlé.
Glaue, P.
1925   "Amen." *Zeitschrift für Kirchengeschichte* 44:184-198.
Goppelt, Leonhard
1982   *Typos. The Typological Interpretation of the Old Testament in the New.* Trans. D. H. Madvig. Grand Rapids: Eerdmans.
Green, Michael (E. M. B.)
1988   *The Second Epistle General of Peter and the General Epistle of Jude.* Tyndale. Rev. New Testament Commentaries. Leicester: Inter-Varsity; Grand Rapids: Eerdmans.
Guthrie, Donald
1990   *New Testament Introduction.* Leicester: Apollos; Downers Grove: InterVarsity Press.
Hanson, Paul D.
1977   "Rebellion in Heaven, Azazel, and Euhemeristic Heroes in 1 Enoch 6-11." *Journal of Biblical Literature* 96:195-233.
Hengel, Martin
1980   *Judaism and Hellenism: Studies in Their Encounter During the Early Hellenistic Period.* 2 vols. Philadelphia: Fortress.
Hillyer, Norman
1992   *1 and 2 Peter, Jude.* Peabody: Hendrickson Publishers.
Isaac, E.
1983   "1 (Ethiopic Apocalypse of) Enoch." In *The Old Testament Pseudepigrapha,* vol. 1: *Apocalyptic Literature and Testaments,* 5-89. Ed. J. H. Charlesworth. Garden City, N.Y.: Doubleday.
Jackson, S. M., ed.
1911   *Schaff-Herzog Encyclopedia of Religious Knowledge.* Vol. 9. New York and London: Funk and Wagnalls.
Janzen, Waldemar
1972   *Mourning Cry and Woe Oracle.* Beihefte zur Zeitschrift für die alttestamentliche Wissenschaft, 125. Berlin and New York: Walter de Gruyter.
Jeschke, Marlin L.
1988   *Discipling in the Church.* Scottdale, Pa.: Herald Press.

1990   "Church Discipline." In *The Mennonite Encyclopedia,* vol.
        5:138-139. Ed. C. J. Dyck and Dennis D. Martin. Scottdale, Pa.:
        Herald Press.
Käsemann, E.
1952   "Eine Apologia für die urchristliche Eschatologie." *Zeitschrift für*
        Theologie und Kirche 49:272-296. "An Apologia for Primitive
        Christian Eschatology." In *Essays on New Testament Themes,*
        169-195. Trans. W. J. Montague. Philadelphia: Fortress, 1982.
Kelly, J. N. D.
1969   *A Commentary on the Epistles of Peter and Jude.* London:
        Adam & Charles Black.
Klaassen, Walter, ed.
1981   *Anabaptism in Outline.* Scottdale, Pa.: Herald Press.
Kubo, Sakae
1981   "Jude 22-3: Two-division Form or Three?" In *New Testament*
        Textual Criticism: Its Significance for Exegesis: Essays in
        Honor of B. M. Metzger, 139-153. Ed. E. J. Epp and G. D. Fee.
        Oxford: Clarendon Press.
Lampe, G. W. H., and K. J. Woollcombe
1957   *Essays on Typology.* Naperville: Allenson.
Lederach, Paul M.
1994   *Daniel.* Believers Church Bible Commentary. Scottdale, Pa.:
        Herald Press.
MacGorman, J. W.
1991   "The Discipline of the Church." In *The People of God: Essays*
        on the Believers' Church, 74-84. Ed. P. Basden and D. S.
        Dockery. Nashville: Broadman Press.
Malherbe, Abraham
1988   *Ancient Epistolary Theorists.* Society of Biblical Literature
        Series, 19. Atlanta: Scholars Press.
Marshall, I. Howard
1969   *Kept by the Power of God.* Minneapolis: Bethany Fellowship.
Martin, Ernest D.
1993   *Colossians, Philemon.* Believers Church Bible Commentary.
        Scottdale, Pa.: Herald Press.
Mayor, J. B.
1907   *The Epistle of St. Jude and the Second Epistle of St. Peter.*
        New York: Macmillan.
Menno Simons
1956   *The Complete Writings of Menno Simons.* Trans. L. Verduin.
        Ed. J. C. Wenger. Scottdale, Pa.: Herald Press.
Metzger, Bruce M.
1971   *A Textual Commentary on the Greek New Testament.* London
        and New York: United Bible Societies.
Nickelsburg, George W. E., and Michael E. Stone, eds.
1983   *Faith and Piety in Early Judaism: Texts and Documents.*
        Philadelphia: Fortress.
Migne, J. P., ed.
1857-66 *Patrologia Graeca.* Paris: Migne.

Odeberg, H.
1965 "Iannes, Iambres." In *Theological Dictionary of the New Testament*. Vol. 3:192-193. Ed. G. Kittel. Trans. and ed. G. W. Bromiley. Grand Rapids: Eerdmans.
Oleson, John P.
1978/9 "An Echo of Hesiod's Theogony vv. 190-2 in Jude 13." *New Testament Studies* 25:492-503.
Osburn, C. D.
1972 "The Text of Jude 22-23." *Zeitschrift für die neutestamentliche Wissenschaft* 63:139-144.
1985 "1 Enoch 80:2-8 (67:5-7) and Jude 12-13." *Catholic Biblical Quarterly* 47:296-303.
Packer, James I.
1990 *A Quest for Godliness*. Westchester: Crossway Publishers.
Philips. *See* Dirk
Plummer, Alfred
1893 *The General Epistles of St. James and St. Jude*. New York: Armstrong and Son.
Reicke, Bo
1946 *The Disobedient Spirits and Christian Baptism: A Study of 1 Peter III.19 and Its Context*. Copenhagen: Munksgaard.
1964 *The Epistles of James, Peter, and Jude*. Anchor Bible. New York: Doubleday.
Rowston, D. J.
1974/5 "The Most Neglected Book in the New Testament." *New Testament Studies* 21:554-563.
Sattler, Michael
1945 "Brüderliche Vereinigung etlicher Kinder Gottes, sieben Artikel betreffend." *Mennonite Quarterly Review* 29:242ff.
Schlabach, Ervin A.
1977 "The Rule of Christ Among the Early Swiss Anabaptists." Th.D. dissertation, Chicago Theological Seminary.
Sidebottom, E. M.
1967 *James, Jude, and 2 Peter*. New Century Bible Commentary. London: Nelson; Grand Rapids: Eerdmans.
Simons. *See* Menno
Smith, C. Henry
1981 *Smith's Story of the Mennonites*. 5th ed. Newton: Faith & Life.
Swensen, R. B.
1937 *Social Processes in the Rise of Early Christian Heresies*. Chicago: Univ. of Chicago Press.
Turner, H. E. W.
1954 *The Pattern of Christian Truth*. London: A. R. Mowbray.
Wainwright, Geoffrey
1980 *Doxology: The Praise of God in Worship, Doctrine and Life*. New York: Oxford Univ. Press.
Watson, D. F.
1988 *Invention, Arrangement, and Style: Rhetorical Criticism of Jude and 2 Peter*. Society of Biblical Literature Dissertation Series, 104. Atlanta: Scholars Press.

Werner, E.
    1963   *The Sacred Bridge.* New York: Columbia Univ. Press; London:
           Dobson.
Wolthuis, T. R.
    1989   "Jude and the Rhetorician." *Calvin Theological Journal*
           24:126-134.
Yoder, John Howard
    1992   *Body Politics: Five Practices of the Christian Community
           Before the Watching World.* Nashville: Discipleship Resources.

Selected Resources for Jude

Bauckham, Richard J. *Jude, 2 Peter*. Word Biblical Commentary, 50. Waco, Tex.: Word, 1983. See Selected Resources for 2 Peter.

Charles, J. Daryl. *Literary Strategy in the Epistle of Jude*. Scranton/London/Toronto: Univ. of Scranton Press/Associated Univ. Presses, 1993. A scholarly, in-depth examination of the epistle that explores the relationship of form to content. Also contains a survey of Jude scholarship over the last hundred years. Contains an appendix on varieties of pseudonymity theory.

Goppelt, Leonhard. *Typos: The Typological Interpretation of the Old Testament in the New*. Translated by D. H. Madvig. Grand Rapids: Eerdmans, 1982. Perhaps the best treatment available of typology and its use in the New Testament. An important work especially when interpreting Jude.

Green, Michael (E. M. B.). *The Second Epistle General of Peter and the General Epistle of Jude*. Revised. Tyndale New Testament Commentaries. Leicester: Inter-Varsity; Grand Rapids: Eerdmans, 1988. See Selected Resources for 2 Peter.

Hillyer, Norman. *1 and 2 Peter, Jude*. Peabody: Hendrickson, 1992. See Selected Resources for 2 Peter.

Reicke, Bo. *The Epistles of James, Peter, and Jude*. Anchor Bible. Garden City: Doubleday, 1964. See Selected Resources for 2 Peter.

J. Daryl Charles

A native of Lancaster, Pennsylvania, J. Daryl Charles, the writer of the commentary on 2 Peter and Jude, teaches religion, culture, and Christian thought at Taylor University, Upland, Indiana.

Charles earned a bachelor's degree at West Chester State University and a master's degree in religious studies at Southern California College. From 1981 to 1983 he studied German and linguistics at the University of Siegen in Germany.

He completed his doctoral work at Catholic University of America and Westminster Theological Seminary. He studied hermeneutics, exploring how strands of rhetorical and literary artifice, philosophy and theology, and ethics converge in the New Testament writings.

Charles served as lecturer in New Testament at Chesapeake Theological Seminary during 1988-95 and engaged in criminal justice research for Prison Fellowship in 1990-95. He was a fellow of the Center for the Study of American Religion at Princeton University for 1996-97. He has been involved in domestic and international missions under Youth With a Mission.

He has contributed to periodicals such as *First Things, Social Justice Review, Regeneration Quarterly, Journal of the Evangelical Theological Society,* and *Bulletin for Biblical Research*, plus journals of New Testament study. He writes on issues of faith and culture, Christian ethics, ecumenism, and the contemporary relevance of the general epistles for the Christian community.

Charles claims that 2 Peter and Jude, though widely neglected, possess a remarkable ability to address the current confusion in matters of faith and morality. They are books to be heard in our age.

J. Daryl Charles is married to Rosemarie Müller Charles, and they have three children. Daryl and Rosemarie are members of Covenant Community Church, Columbia, Maryland.

Index of Ancient Sources for 1-2 Peter, Jude

OLD TESTAMENT

Genesis
1:26-27 221
2:33....................234
2:34....................234
3 298
4:3-4 299
4:10....................299
5:3 303
5:6 303
5:9 303
5:12....................303
5:15....................303
5:18....................303
5:24.............._......331
6 294
6:1-4 ....294, 331
6:2 298
6:5 233
6:9 233
6:11-12 233
16:5....................254
16:7-11 48
18–19 296

18:12....................97
18:20-21 296
18:25..................254
19 ....235, 296
19:13..................296
27:3....................296
48:15..................166
49 260
49:24..................166

Exodus
12:5 61
12:11..................57
19:5-6 ....74, 77
19:6 ......70, 77, 255
20 132
20:13..................140
20:15..................140
23:22 ....74, 77
24:7-8 29
32:32-33 285
34:6 33

Leviticus
5:6-7 125

11:44-45 ......59, 240
11:45..................59
17–26 59
17:2 59
19:2 ....59, 240
20:26..................240
29:11..................303

Numbers
5:22....................324
11 293
14 293
16:17..................299
16:35..................299
22–24 ....238, 299
22–25 ....230, 238
22:21-35 239
26 293
27:12-13 297
27:17..................166
31:15-16 238
31:16 ....238, 299
32 293
32:13 ....256, 293

Deuteronomy
1:35 ....256, 293
2:14 ....256, 293
6:4-5 40
18 241
21:23..................94
23:4-5 ....238, 299
23:5-6 238
29:23.................296
32–33 260
33:2..................303
34 297
34:5-6 297

Joshua
13:22 ....238, 299
24:9 ....238, 299

Judges
5:4 303
11:27..................254

2 Samuel
5:2 166
7:7 166
24 298

1 Kings
13:30..................300
22:17..................166
22:19..................298

1 Chronicles
11:2..................166
16:36..................324
21 298
21:1 ..161, 168, 298
29:10..................324

2 Chronicles
7:14..................167

Nehemiah
8:6 324
13:2 ....238, 299

Job
1–2 ....161, 168, 298
1:6 298
1:21 45

2:1 298
2:9-10 45

Psalms
2 41
2:7 218
6 253
9:7-8 254
10 253
13 253
13:1-2 249
16:8-11 41
16:10..................41
18:9..................303
18:46..................31
22 253
22:12-13 160
23 166
25:9..................167
25:37..................167
28:6 31
31 253
31:21..................31
33:8a..................37
34 105
34:5b..................76
34:8 66-67
34:12-16 .... 101, 103, 121
38 253
39 53
39:12..................84
40:7..................285
41:13 ....31, 324
42:5 43
42:5-6 45
42:11..................45
45:7 41
46:8-9 303
56:8..................285
68:17..................303
69 253
69:28..................285
71:5 43
72:18-19 31
72:19..................324
73 253
76:9..................303
80 166
88 253

89:52 ....31, 324
90 250
90:2b..................250
90:4..................250
90:10..................250
90:10c..................250
90:12..................250
96:13..................303
103:8..................33
106:48 ....31, 324
110:6..................254
118:22 ....74, 76, 79
139:16..................285

Proverbs
3:34 ....102, 159, 168, 176
10:12b..................135
10:12..................176
11:31..................141
25:14 300-301
26:11..................240

Isaiah
1:9-10 296
1:24..................300
3:9 ....296, 300
3:11..................300
4:3 285
6:10b..................94
7:17-20 331
8:12..................121
8:14 ....74, 76, 79
9-11 41
9:6 41
11:2a..................139
13 331
13:4-5 331
13:9..................254
13:10-13 332
13:19..................332
14 295
14:5-23 295
19:1..................303
28:16 ....74, 76, 79
31:4..................303
40:3-5 41
40:4-6 64
40:10..................303
40:11..................166

40:31.................43
42:1.................218
42:1-4 41
43:20-21 ....74, 77
43:21................78
43:21-22 78
44:28–45:1 331
45:13................331
52–53 61
53 ....41, 92, 105, 125, 185
53:4a................94
53:4-6 ....91, 94, 143
53:5b................94
53:9 91-93
55:1................300
57:15...............167
61:1-3 41
61:10................69
66:2................167
66:15...............303

Jeremiah
6 241
10:21...............166
12:10...............166
13:27...............300
14 241
14:8 43
17:13................43
20:4-6 331
22:18...............300
22:30...............285
23 ....166, 241
23:1-4 166
23:14...............296
25:31...............303
28 241
31:31...............286
46:10...............254
49:18...............296
50:31...............254
50:40...............296

Lamentations
4:6 296

Ezekiel
9:2ff. 294
13 241

14:12-23 233
16:49-59 296
28 295
28:1-19 295
30:2................254
34 ....95, 166
34:1-31 166
34:18-19 170
40:3ff. 294
43:6ff. 294
43:21...............125

Daniel
2:20................324
3:28................294
4:13 ....294, 330
4:17................330
4:23................330
6:22................294
7:10 ....285, 303
7:16................294
8:13................294
9:21.................48
10:4-21 297
10:5ff. 294
10:13 ...48, 298, 330
10:20...............330
10:21 ...48, 298, 330
11:2ff. 330
11:35...............330
12:1 ...48, 285, 297-298, 330
12:1ff. 294

Hosea
1:6 74
1:9 ....74, 78
2:1 ....74, 78
2:23 ....33, 74
7:13................300
11:8................296

Joel
1:15................254
2 332
2:2 332
2:10................332
2:11................332
2:31 ....254, 332
3:2 303

3:15................332

Amos
1–2 254
1:2 303
3:13................254
4:11 ....296, 315
5:20................254
6:1 300

Obadiah
15 254

Micah
1:3 303
2:1 300
6:5 299

Habakkuk
3:3 303

Zephaniah
1:7-9 303
1:12................303
1:14................254
2:3 167
2:9 296

Haggai
2:22................303

Zechariah
1:8ff. 294
2:1ff. 294
2:6 300
2:10................300
3 ....297, 315
3:1 298
3:1ff. 294
3:1-2 161
3:1-5 ....69, 315
3:8 303
4:1ff. 294
5:1ff. 294
6:1ff. 294
9:14................303
11:7-17 166
14:1................254

Malachi
3:2-3 39
3:2-5 251
3:3-5 303
3:16..................285
4:1 251
4:5 254

APOCRYPHA

Apocrypha 275, 278

2 Esdras
7:38ff. 254

4 Ezra (2 Esdras)
6:20 285

Judith
16:17..................254

1 Maccabees
7:13..................302

2 Maccabees
7:14..................133
14:6..................302

3 Maccabees
2:3-7 293
2:5 296

Sirach
16:5-15 293
16:8..................296

Wisdom of Solomon
3:18..................254
8:7 224
10:6-7 296

NEW TESTAMENT

Gospels 48, 211, 286, 305

Matthew
4:1 160
4:1-11 298

5:3-12 45
5:5 167
5:9 103
5:9-16 121
5:10 ....45, 121
5:11..................139
5:12 ....139, 150
5:16 85
5:23..................100
5:38-48 90
5:39..................109
5:43-48 69
5:44..................102
5:45 64
5:48 59
6:9 ....32, 59
6:12..................100
6:14-15 100
6:19-20 35
6:25-34 159
7:6 240
7:12 71
7:15-20 286
7:19..................301
7:21-23 326
7:21-27 286
7:24-27 75
9:36 ....95, 166
10:2..................280
10:3..................280
10:6..................166
10:15..................254
10:17ff. 142
11:22..................254
11:28..................168
11:29 ....102, 168
12:36 ....132, 254
12:41-42 254
13:1-23 241
13:17..................42
13:24-30 241
13:24-43 286
13:35b..................61
13:47-52 241
13:55..................280
15:13..................301
15:24..................166
15:26-27 240
16:13-20 ...221, 247, 252

16:18 ....75, 79, 262, 314
16:18-19 222
16:21-28 222
16:22-23 222
17:1-8 ......221, 247, 252
17:5..................218
18..................316-317
18:3 46
18:4..................167
18:10-14 317
18:15..................317
18:15-19 286
18:15-20 12
19:28..................255
19:29..................47
20:14-16 28
20:21..................255
20:23..................255
20:25-28 167
21:33-46 241
21:42 ....76, 79
21:44..................79
22:2-14 241
22:14..................28
22:23..................49
23:8-12 167
24–25 286
24:22..................28
24:23-24 286
24:24..................28
24:31..................28
24:36-44 ...233, 254
24:37-38 235
24:37-39 254
24:43..................250
25 241
25:31-46 286
25:34..................47
25:34ff. 158
25:41..................169
26:21..................75
26:31..................95
26:69-75 252
27:19..................125
27:52-53 133
28:18..................152
28:18-20 104
28:19-20 28

Mark
1:12-13 298
1:13...................160
1:17....................92
4:1-12 241
6:34 95
8:27–9:8 178
8:32-33 218
8:35-37 85
9:2-8 ....218, 221, 252
9:7 218
9:35...................167
10:15..................46
10:17..................47
10:42-43 157
10:43-45 167
10:45 60-61
12:1-12 241
12:10..................79
12:28-29 40
13:9-10 142
13:11..................139
13:20..................28
13:22..................28
13:27..................28
13:31..................64
14:27..................95
14:36 ....27, 32
14:58..................75
14:66-72 252
15:40..................280
16:7....................104
16:20..................104

Luke
1:19 48
4:1-13 298
4:2 160
5:10 60
6:16...................280
6:22...................139
6:27 ....64, 89
6:27ff. 102
6:27-35 90
6:27-36 69
6:28 93
7:3 156
8:4-10 241
9:28-36 ......221, 252

9:35...................218
10:14..................254
10:18 ....169, 295
10:20..................285
10:25..................47
11:50..................61
12:5 60
12:8f...................158
12:11..................159
12:12..................139
12:32 ....32, 35
12:35..................57
12:35-40 254
12:39..................250
13:1-5 185
13:17..................124
14:11..................167
14:16-24 241
15:3-7 94
15:4ff. 166
15:7 42
15:10..................42
17:22-27 233
17:25-27 235
18:7 28
18:9-14 159
18:14..................167
18:17..................46
18:18..................47
19:10 ....94, 166
20:9-19 241
20:17-18 79
21:12ff. 142
21:34-35 254
22–32 159
22:32..................217
22:54-62 252
23:22..................125
23:34 ...93, 115, 186
23:47..................125
24:12..................34
24:25ff. 41
24:25-27 48
24:44-49 104
24:45-48 48

John
1:1 212-213
1:1-3 325
1:1-4 41

1:40-41 178
1:42 24
1:51...................324
3:2-3 67
3:3 45
3:3-8 46
3:4 45
3:5 33
3:7 33
6:66-69 178
7:5 ....283, 304
9:3 185
10:1-30 166
10:2ff. 95
10:28-29 243
12:31..................295
13:1-20 178
13:2....................160
13:34-35 69
13:36..................217
14–16 142
14–17 260
14:10..................32
15:5....................301
15:13..................221
15:18-25 226
15:20-21 142
16:7-11 243
17:5 61
17:24..................61
20:21..................104
20:28..........212-213, 325
20:30-31 104
21:1-23 178
21:2-23 34
21:15..................170
21:15-17 166
21:15-19 24
21:16..................157
21:17..................170
21:18-19 217

Acts
1:6 332
1:8 104
1:8ff. 104
1:13...................280
2:14ff. 34
2:14...................122

2:16-21 332
2:24 46
2:25-36 41
2:42.................135
2:45 71
3:12.................122
3:14 ....46, 125
4-5 143
4:8ff. 122
4:11 79-80
4:23-31 135
4:32 71
5:1-11 ....286, 317
5:29.................122
5:29-32 143
5:30 94
5:41 ......38, 47, 139,
   143
6:1-6 137
7:52.................125
8:9-25 286
10-15 177
10:39.................94
11:26.................140
11:30.................156
12:12.................165
12:25.................165
14:23.................156
15 211
15:13-21 280
15:14.................211
15:16.................314
16-19 ....143, 164
16:25.................164
16:29.................164
17 306
17:4.................164
17:10.................164
17:14.................164
17:16-34 ...257, 264,
   305
17:30-31 257
17:31.................254
18:5.................164
20:17.................166
20:27.................316
20:28 ....156, 239
20:28-29 166
20:29.................326
22:3.................306

23:8 49
26:18.................78
26:28.................140
27-28 143

Paul's Epistles ...67,
   144, 180, 305

Romans
1:1 222
1:1-6 28
1:8-10 30
1:16.................144
1:18-32 240
2:15 ....221, 289
2:16.................254
2:24.................232
3:2 137
3:6 254
3:23.................221
3:23-24 33
3:24 61
3:24ff. 44
4:23-24 41
5-6 ....143, 146
5:2 126
5:2-5 139
5:3-5 103
6:1-11 152
6:4-9 46
6:5ff. 144
6:11 94
8:11 46
8:15 60
8:17 ....139, 255
8:18 ...51, 139, 179
8:23-25 316
8:24 36
8:26.................316
8:33 28
8:38f.................144
9:33 ....76, 79
11:32.................253
12 152
12:1 ....68, 75
12:1-2 67
12:3 ....123, 181
12:6.................137
12:6-8 ....136, 146
12:9 68

12:14.................102
12:14-17 ....101, 106
12:14-21 147
12:15.................102
12:16 ....101, 181
12:17a.................102
12:17b.................102
12:18.................103
12:18-21 107
12:19-20 116
12:19-21 102
12:20.................109
13 106
13:1-7 181
13:13.................131
14:3-5 316
14:9.................132
14:19.................316
15:4 41
16:7.................304
16:13.................28
16:16.................165
16:22.................263
16:25f.................61
16:25-27 324

1 Corinthians
1:1 ......28, 164, 222
1:4-9 30
1:5 207
1:7 316
1:8 254
1:18.................144
1:19.................164
1:21.................144
1:30 61
2-3 303
2:7 61
2:8 144
2:14-15 40
3 287
3:1-2 69
3:9-15 314
3:10-15 254
3:11 ....76, 262
3:12-14 39
4 222
4:1-2 311
4:7 223
4:15 46

4:19..................223
4:21..................223
5 317
5–7 287
5:1-13 ....207, 317
5:2 223
5:3-5 223
5:6 223
5:9 247
5:9-13 321
5:12-13 223
6:2 254
6:3 255
6:4-10 264
6:11..................145
6:12-20 207
7:1-7 207
7:21-24 207
8:1 316
8:1-2 223
8:1-3 207
8:7-11 207
8:9-13 207
9 222
9:1-23 207
9:9-10 41
10 287
10:1-5 306
10:4 74
10:11.................41
10:29.................207
11 287
11:17-34 207
11:18.................231
11:19.................289
11:22.................141
11:33f................100
12 152
12:3 ....21, 324
12:4-6 28
12:4-10 146
12:8 ....137, 207
12:8-10 136
12:14.................145
12:28.................304
12:28-30 136
12:29.................152
13 225
13:2..................207
13:5-7 135

13:8..................207
13:13 ....43, 216
14:15.................316
14:29..................12
15:3 143-144
15:3-7 ....247, 262
15:4..................148
15:5 ....46, 222
15:7..................280
15:7-9 222
15:9..................304
15:17..................46
15:19..................46
15:23-28 207
15:24-25 144
15:45..................40
15:58..................68
16:20.................165
16:21.................263
18–25 148

2 Corinthians
1:1 ....164, 222
1:3 32
1:3-7 30
1:14..................254
2:5-11 317
2:11..................298
3:18 46
4:6 78
4:16 46
4:16-17 139
5:10..................132
5:17 46
5:19-21 148
5:21..................125
6:6 68
6:7-12 143
6:16..................314
7:14..................124
8:23..................304
9 221
9:4 124
9:7 157
9:8 324
10:17-34 300
11–13 222
11:23-33 143
13:12.................165
13:13..................28

Galatians
1:1 222
1:1-2a 28
1:17..................304
1:19 ....280, 304
2:9 ....280, 314
2:20 ....144, 148
3:1 144
3:13 94
3:28 ....100, 182
3:28-29 180
4:6 60
4:29-31 46
5 287
5:6 216
5:19-23 264
5:22-23 264
5:23..................167
6:1-2 318
6:11..................263
6:15 46

Ephesians
1 289
1:1 222
1:3 32
1:7 61
1:20f.................144
2 ....27, 146
2:1f. 144
2:2 295
2:4 33
2:8 36
2:8-9 33
2:8-10 ....221, 227
2:11 34
2:11-13 103
2:12 ....49, 122
2:13-14 148
2:18..................126
2:19-22 314
2:20...222, 246, 304
2:21-22 75
3:5 ....222, 304
3:5-6 246
3:9 61
3:10..................144
3:12..................126
3:17-19 316
3:20-21 324

4 152
4:2 ....102, 159
4:2-6 264
4:4-6 28
4:11...136, 222, 304
4:11-12 146
4:12.................316
4:16.................316
4:25 69
4:27.................160
4:31 ....65, 69
5:1-2 316
5:8-14 78
5:21 180-182
5:21-33 181
5:22-24 181
5:25-33 181
6:1-3 181
6:4 181
6:5 89
6:5-8 181
6:5-9 181
6:9 181
6:10ff. 104
6:10-18 169
6:11.................160
6:12.................144
6:18.................316
9:1 284

Philippians
1:4 47
1:7 122
1:16.................122
1:18 47
2:2-6 101
2:3 ....102, 159
2:5 101
2:5-11 ....41, 143-
144, 148
2:6 325
2:6-11 168
2:12-13 ......227, 316
2:17 47
2:18 47
3:10.................147
3:10-11 148
3:12.................123
3:17.................157
3:20.................316

4:3 285
4:4 47
4:5 167

Colossians
1:1 ....164, 222
1:3-8 30
1:12 78
1:14 61
1:15.................325
1:15-17 41
1:16.................144
1:19-20 148
1:24 147-148
1:26 61
2:7 314
2:15.................144
2:18 ....49, 218
3:8 69
3:12 ....28, 159, 181
3:12-14 264
3:12-25 181
3:14.................225
3:18.................181
3:19.................181
3:20.................181
3:21.................181
3:22 89
3:22-25 181
4:1 181
4:10.................165
4:18.................263

1 Thessalonians
1:3 43
1:8 251
2:3 289
2:14.................147
3:13.................324
4 287
4:9 68
4:13.................133
4:16 48
4:18.................103
5:1-5 255
5:2 ....245, 250
5:2-4 254
5:4 250
5:4-5 78
5:11.................103

5:15.................106
5:16 47
5:26.................165

2 Thessalonians
2:1-3 261
2:2 254
2:4 325
3 287
3:6 318
3:9 157
3:14.................318
3:17 ....261, 263

1 Timothy
1:1 222
1:5 123
1:9-10 264
1:17.................324
1:19 ....123, 256
2:1-8 181
2:1-11 181
2:4 ....254, 256
2:6 61
2:9-10 97
2:9-11 181
2:12.................255
3:8 157
3:16.................126
4:1-3 241
4:12.................157
5:8 308
5:17-19 156
6:1-2 181
6:3-5 264
6:6-10 157

2 Timothy
1:1 222
1:18 ....254, 316
2:1 104
2:2 109
2:11.................144
2:12.................109
3:1-9 ....241, 306
3:2-5 ....264, 318
3:5 308
3:16-17 223
4:1 ....254, 263
4:1-8 254

4:3-5 241
4:5 241
4:10....................256
4:11....................165

Titus
1 306
1:1 222
1:5 156
1:7 157
1:12....................303
1:16....................308
1:21 61
2:4-5 181
2:4-10 181
2:6 181
2:7 157
2:9-10 181
2:13 ....212-213, 325
2:14 61
3 287
3:1 181
3:1-7 264
3:2 167
3:5 ....33, 46, 50
3:10....................318

Philemon
1 164
19 263
24 165

General Epistles 305

Hebrews
4 287
5:13 69
6 ....287, 289
6:4-6 ....287, 310
6:7-8 287
9:12 61
9:15 61
9:25-28 125
10 287
10:22...................29
10:26-27 287
10:27..................251
10:34...................47
11 ....29, 234-235
11:1–12:4 173

11:4....................173
11:7 234-235
12:1 68-69
12:2-11 185
12:4....................173
12:9....................181
12:14..................103
12:23..................285
13:1 68
13:15-16 75
13:17..................181

James
1:1 ....280, 283
1:1-4 185
1:9f. 168
1:12-15 185
1:18 45
1:21 ....65, 69
1:22 68
3:13-18 264
4:3 100
4:6 ....159, 181
4:6-10 ....168, 181
4:7 181
4:7-10 159
4:10...................181
5:20 ....135, 318

1 Peter (not for commentary on 1 Peter)
1:1 ....211, 222
1:2 212
1:5 313
1:14...................247
1:16...................240
2–4 223
2:5 314
2:8ff. 306
2:9 255
2:11...................247
2:12...................254
2:18ff. 234
2:18-25 222
2:24...................214
3 307
3:8ff. 233
3:8-22 222
3:12...................214
3:13ff. 234

3:14...................214
3:18 ....214, 307
3:18-22 ......234, 306
3:19...................307
3:19-20 ......234, 248
3:20 ....233, 235
3:22 ....234-235, 307
4:5 254
4:10...................311
4:12...................247
4:12-19 222
4:17-18 223
4:18...................214
5:1 ....211, 222
5:1ff. 240
5:1-5 ....247, 318
5:5 212
5:10...................217
5:12 ....260, 263

2 Peter (not for commentary on 2 Peter)
1:1 325
1:2 277
1:2-3 50
1:12...................311
1:20 12
1:21 48
2:1 ....277, 308
2:4 ....277, 294, 307
2:6 277
2:10-11 277
2:11...................277
2:12-13 300
2:13...................277
2:15 ....277, 299
2:17...................277
2:18 ....131, 277
3:2 277
3:3 277
3:16-17 326

1 John
1 John 176
1:1 ....220, 222
1:5-7 78
1:5–2:5 220
1:9 29
2:1 125
2:9-11 78

2:10 68
2:15-17 220
2:22-23 220
2:29 ....45, 125
3:3 256
3:4-10 220
3:7 125
3:9 45
3:10 68
3:11 68
3:14 68
3:22.................220
3:23 68
4:1 326
4:1-6 220
4:4-6 226
4:7 ....45, 68
4:11 68
4:11-12 68
4:15.................220
4:17.................254
4:20-21 68
5:1 45
5:6-8 144
5:16-17 ......220, 318

2 John
1 156

3 John
1 156

Jude (not for com-
mentary on Jude)
4 231-232
5-7 230
6...128, 232-233,254
7 235
11 238
12 237
20-21..................28
24 ....243, 251
25................212-213

Revelation
1:1 165
1:4 26
1:6 255
1:9-11 255
2:2 326

2:9 ....255, 298
2:10.................255
2:16.................107
2:19.................255
2:26-28 255
3:2-3 255
3:3 ....250, 255
3:5 285
3:10.................255
3:14.................216
3:17-18 216
3:21.................255
4 325
4:11.................325
5 325
5:1 285
5:5 160
5:5-14 325
5:7 285
5:8 285
5:10 ....165, 255
5:12-13 325
6:10 ....254, 256
7:12.................325
7:14.................255
9:20-21 256
10:8-11 285
11:18.................254
12:4.................295
12:7.................295
12:9 ....169, 295
12:10 ....295, 298
12:13-17 298
13 ....106, 325
13:1.................325
13:8.................285
13:10.................255
14:8.................165
16:9-11 256
16:15 ....250, 255
17–18 19
17:5.................165
17:9.................165
17:14.................325
17:18.................165
18:2.................165
18:20.................222
19:11.................254
19:15.................107
19:16.................325

20:6...................255
20:12.................285
21:8.................301
21:27 ....254, 285
22:3.................325
22:5.................255
22:15.................240

NT APOCRYPHA

Apocrypha 261

Apocryphal
Legends 278

Acts of Peter 261

Apocalypse of
Peter.................261

Gospel of Peter 261

Letter of Peter ..261

Travels of Peter 261

PSEUDEPIGRAPHA

Pseudepigrapha 275

Apocalyptic
Literature 275

Assumption of
Moses 276, 297

2 Baruch ...139, 295
24:1...................285

1 Enoch....234, 276,
  295, 301-303, 305,
  330, 332

2 Enoch
52:15 285

Joseph and Aseneth
15:4 285

Jubilees 293, 295, 330

10:13-14 234

Odes of Solomon 69

Testaments of the
Twelve Patriarchs
260, 293, 330

Testament of Asher
7:1 296

Testament of Jacob
7:27-28 285

Testament of Moses
7:7 .... 303, 305, 315

Testament of
Naphtali
2:8—4:3 293

DEAD SEA
SCROLLS

Dead Sea Scrolls
58, 64, 69, 75,
277, 286

Community Rule
(1QS)............75, 286

Damascus
Document
(CD)................293

Manual of
Discipline 75

War Rule
(1QM) 286

War Rule
(4QM) 286

MISHNAH

Mishnah 293, 296

Aboth 285
5:10................296

Sanhedrin
4:5 299
5:19................299
10:3................299

BABYLONIAN
TALMUD

Gen. Rabbah 234,
296

Eccles. Rabbah 234

Lev. Rabbah......303

Sanhedrin..........234

OTHER JEWISH
AUTHORS

Josephus ..234, 238,
261, 280, 296-297

Philo....92, 234, 296-
297, 299, 303

APOSTOLIC AND
CHURCH FATHERS

Athanasius 224, 280

Augustine 224,
280, 309

1 Clement 176

Clement of
Alexandria..92, 176,
280, 294, 297, 300

Didache 284, 300

Eusebius 17, 26,
260, 280

Gregory of Nyssa
224

Hegesippus 280

Ignatius 284, 300

Irenaeus 176

Jerome......263, 280

Nestorius 224

Origen 276, 280, 297

Papias................176

Pelagius 224, 309

Polycarp 176

Tertullian ..176, 303

PAGAN AUTHORS

Aristotle 224

Epicureans 278

Hesiod 301

Martial 325

Plutarch 97

Socrates 224

Socratic
philosophers 224

Sophocles..........49

Stoics 180, 208,
251, 264-266, 278